How Real Is Race?

PRAISE FOR THE SECOND EDITION

"An invaluable resource for educators who seek to make sense of the complex issues surrounding race and ethnicity in America today. For those who are afraid to touch the subject but understand that the issue is too important to ignore, this book provides useful insights on how to understand and respond to racial issues as they arise in the classroom and beyond."

—**Pedro A. Noguera**, Peter L. Agnew Professor of Education, New York University

"Race is not a biological reality, but it is a cultural reality, resulting in disparities in residence patterns, wealth distribution, health care, employment, the justice system, education, and many other aspects of our everyday lives. The authors of *How Real Is Race?* explain how this is possible and how it makes a difference in the way we deal with racism in the United States. They offer readers an exceptional way to understand and deal with race-related issues, including racism, not from a reactive stance but rather in a proactive fashion."

—**Robert W. Sussman**, Washington University in St. Louis

PRAISE FOR THE PREVIOUS EDITION

"By clearly laying out the biological fallacies of race and racial classifications, the authors lay the foundation to dismantle historically constituted inequities based on race. This book communicates complex biological material within a framework that is both accessible and compelling."

—**Norma González**, Department of Language, Reading, and Culture, University of Arizona

"One of the most important books written about the illusory idea and enduring salience of race. Why? The authors brilliantly contextualize race with exercises that lead to a deeper appreciation of ideology, power, and human variation. *How Real Is Race? A Sourcebook on Race, Culture, and Biology* ought to be available in all school systems and to all teachers."

—**Alan H. Goodman**, former president, American Anthropological Association (2005–2007); Hampshire College

"This splendid and much-needed resource makes it possible for students (and educators!) to interrogate their own myths and misconceptions about race. Drawing from diverse fields—anthropology, history, biology, genetics, sociology, even literature—the rich readings and exercises help students adroitly manage a counterintuitive two-step: Race is not biological. But that doesn't mean it's not real. Race, or, more precisely, racism, resides not in our bodies but in our history, our social structures, and our cultural beliefs, helping shape life outcomes and opportunities."

—**Larry Adelman**, California Newsreel; executive producer, *Race: The Power of an Illusion*

How Real Is Race?

A Sourcebook on Race, Culture, and Biology

Second Edition

Carol C. Mukhopadhyay, Rosemary Henze, and Yolanda T. Moses

ALTAMIRA
PRESS

A division of
ROWMAN & LITTLEFIELD
Lanham • Boulder • New York • Toronto • Plymouth, UK

Published by AltaMira Press
A division of Rowman & Littlefield
4501 Forbes Boulevard, Suite 200, Lanham, Maryland 20706
www.rowman.com

10 Thornbury Road, Plymouth PL6 7PP, United Kingdom

British Library Cataloguing in Publication Information Available

Library of Congress Cataloging-in-Publication Data

Mukhopadhyay, Carol Chapnick.
How real is race? : a sourcebook on race, culture, and biology / Carol C. Mukhopadhyay, Rosemary
Henze, and Yolanda T. Moses.—Second editon.
pages cm
Includes bibliographical references and index.
ISBN 978-0-7591-2272-7 (cloth : alk. paper)—ISBN 978-0-7591-2273-4 (pbk. : alk. paper)—ISBN
978-0-7591-2274-1 (electronic) 1. Race. 2. Race relations. 3. Culture. 4. Sociobiology. 5. Nature and
nurture. 6. Education. I. Henze, Rosemary C. II. Moses, Yolanda T. III. Title.
HT1521.M785 2014
305.8—dc23
2013044328

∞™ The paper used in this publication meets the minimum requirements of American
National Standard for Information Sciences Permanence of Paper for Printed Library
Materials, ANSI/NISO Z39.48-1992.

Printed in the United States of America

Contents

IV: Resources

List of Tables and Figures

FIGURES

TABLES

Foreword

James A. Banks

The second edition of this significant, informative, and engaging book is being published at a critical time in U.S. history. Racial, cultural, religious, and language diversity in U.S. public schools is greater than at any time since the early 1900s. Students of color in U.S. public schools will equal or exceed the percentage of Euro-American students within one or two decades if current growth rates continue. English-language learners are the fastest-growing population in U.S. public schools (U.S. Department of Education, 2013).The general U.S. population is also becoming more racially, culturally, religiously, and linguistically diverse. The U.S. Census projects that people of color will make up about half of the population by 2050 (U.S. Census Bureau, 2012). Cultural, racial, ethnic, and religious diversity is also increasing in other nations around the world (Banks, 2009).

The nation's rich diversity presents both opportunities and challenges. Future and practicing teachers often say they are color-blind and do not "see" the racial, ethnic, and cultural differences among their students. There continues to be a wide racial, cultural, and language gap between U.S. educators, most of whom are Euro-American and monolingual, and students. This gap may be one factor that makes educators reluctant to openly discuss and teach about race in their classrooms (Schofield, 2012).

The updated version of this incisive, well-conceptualized, and informative book by three perceptive anthropologists who care deeply about and understand learning, contains a plethora of essential concepts and principles about race and diversity that will help educators at all levels to reenvision and transform their curriculum and pedagogy. One of the most salient lessons is that race is a social construction that has no basis in biological science. As the authors insightfully point out, "races are not biologically real but are cultural and social inventions created in specific cultural, historical, and political contexts" (introduction, part I, this volume).

A significant body of social science theory and research supports the authors' keen insights and analyses about race and its meanings. Jacobson (1998) calls races "invented categories" (p. 4). Omi and Winant (1994) state that the "determination of racial categories is an intensely political process" (p. 3). Montagu (1997) calls race "man's most dangerous myth." In his classic book with this title—first published in 1942—Montagu documents extensively and in poignant detail the human tragedies justified and facilitated by race and racism. These painful and unconscionable historical events include chattel slavery in the United States in which people of African descent were treated as nonhumans and many perished in brutal ways. They also include the massive destruction and deaths perpetuated by the Nazis in Europe during the 1930s and 1940s, in which twelve million people were killed—six million Jews and six million other members of stigmatized groups, including people with disabilities and people who were gay. The pain, suffering, and discrimination that are justified by theories of race and by racism continue today.

As the authors of the book explicate, the idea of race as a social construction is an essential component in teaching about race. I have incorporated the idea of race as a social construction into my multicultural teacher education courses through lectures, supplemented by readings and videos that powerfully depict the ways in which various racial and ethnic groups—including White ethnic groups, such as Italians (Guglielmo & Salerno, 2003), the Irish (Ignatiev, 1995), and Jews (Brodkin, 1998)—have been victimized by racism and discrimination.

This rich sourcebook will help teachers and teacher educators implement the kinds of teaching strategies that will enable their students to understand how race is socially constructed. A significant strength of this book is that it combines biological and cultural anthropological approaches to race and helps readers to understand the complex ways that culture shapes the ways in which we construct and interpret the biological aspects of race.

This theoretically strong, useful, and practical book contains well-conceptualized and engaging teaching activities and strategies that educators and learners at all levels will welcome. The publication of the second edition of this book is a significant indication that it has attained the recognition and visibility it deserves. If used wisely and seriously engaged, it will help educators and concerned citizens of all backgrounds to create educational and other societal institutions which are just and democratic and that foster equality for all.

James A. Banks holds the Kerry and Linda Killinger Endowed Chair in Diversity Studies and is founding director of the Center for Multicultural

Education at the University of Washington, Seattle. Professor Banks is a member of the National Academy of Education and is a past president of the American Educational Research Association (AERA) and of the National Council for the Social Studies (NCSS). His most recent books are the Encyclopedia of Diversity in Education *(4 vols., Sage Publications) and the* Routledge International Companion to Multicultural Education. *Professor Banks's work in multicultural education is known and influential throughout the world. His books have been translated into Greek, Japanese, Chinese, Korean, and Turkish.*

REFERENCES

Banks, J. A. (Ed.). (2009). *The Routledge international companion to multicultural education.* New York and London: Routledge.

Brodkin, K. (1998). *How the Jews became white folks and what that says about race in America.* New Brunswick, NJ: Rutgers University Press.

Guglielmo, J., & Salerno, S. (Eds.). (2003). *Are Italians White? How race is made in America.* New York: Routledge.

Ignatiev, N. (1995). *How the Irish became White.* New York: Routledge.

Jacobson, M. F. (1998). *Whiteness of a different color: European immigrants and the alchemy of race.* Cambridge, MA: Harvard University Press.

Montagu, A. (1997). *Man's most dangerous myth: The fallacy of race* (6th ed.). Walnut Creek, CA: Altamira Press.

Omi, M., & Winant, H. (1994). *Racial formation in the United States: From the 1960s to the 1990s* (2nd ed.). New York: Routledge.

Schofield, J. W. (2012). Color-blind perspective. In J. A. Banks (Ed.), *Encyclopedia of diversity in education* (vol. 1, pp. 405–11). Thousand Oaks, CA: Sage Publications.

U.S. Census Bureau. (2012). *2012 National population projections: Press releases.* Retrieved July 29, 2013, from http://www.census.gov/newsroom/releases/archives/population/cb12-243.html.

U.S. Department of Education, National Center for Education Statistics. (2013). *The condition of education 2013.* Retrieved July 29, 2013, from http://nces.ed.gov/pubs2013/2013037.pdf.

Acknowledgments

This book draws upon experiences and ideas we have accumulated throughout our careers as educators. Over the years, we have drawn inspiration and ideas from numerous sources, including colleagues at several institutions, former graduate school advisors, precollege educators with whom we have worked and taught, our own professors, and perhaps most of all, our students, to whom we dedicate this book.

More immediately, we wish to thank the many individuals who have contributed time, energy, ideas, manuscript reviews, editing suggestions, and general enthusiasm and support for the book. They are too many to list. And, this is now a second edition of the book. In addition to people we already acknowledged in the first edition of the book, we'd like to express our appreciation to those who have commented on and in other ways provided suggestions for the revision. Special thanks go to Joseph Jones, Bob Jurmain, and Lynn Kilgore (and their coauthors of a truly magnificent compendium of biological anthropological knowledge), Mica Pollock, Char Ullman, Kristina Wirtz (and her Kalamazoo colleagues), and Elizabeth Weiss.

Tom Koerner, our original editor at Rowman and Littlefield Education, first suggested the book. Without his encouragement, we probably would not have taken on this enormous task. A fine, enthusiastic, and energetic staff at AltaMira, another Rowman and Littlefield imprint, has assisted us with the production of this second edition.

The book has benefited from its connection to the RACE project of the American Anthropological Association (AAA). The RACE project has provided a significant forum for intellectual exchange and collective brainstorming on how to effectively engage with the public on the topic of race. We believe our projects are continuously mutually reinforcing.

Finally, we thank our spouses, families, and friends for putting up with late nights, long conference calls, endless progress reports, and way too many "working" weekends and holidays. Mukhopadhyay, in particular, thanks her chamber music compatriots for helping her maintain her sanity, focus, and sense of well-being during the last two months of the revisions.

Introduction

Welcome to the second edition of *How Real Is Race?* We are very pleased that the first edition generated such interest and we hope this new edition will provide readers with an even more useful resource.

Everyone has heard the statement "There is only one race—the human race." Yet we have also heard and seen contradictory evidence. There are certainly observable physical differences among people, including skin color, eye shape, hair texture, and so on. But is this race? The U.S. Census divides us into groups based on race—but we can select our own race, or races, based on our cultural identity or identities, regardless of how we look. In schools, colleges, and communities, confusing messages proliferate when we are taught that children from diverse ethnicities have "different learning styles" and that students' cultural backgrounds are the cause of the racial achievement gap.

How can we make sense of these contradictory messages? How *real* is race? Or rather, in what sense is race real? What is biological fact and fiction? How well does race describe human biological variation? Where does culture enter and how deeply? And what does it really mean to say that race is a cultural or social "construction"? If race is an invention, who invented it? Through what processes did it emerge? For what ends? And can we eliminate it if we wish to? Are we now living in a postracial "color-blind" society? And if so, is speaking about race unimportant? Does it mean we no longer notice race? What *do* we mean by a "color-blind" society? These are the key questions that frame this book. Our goal is to provide readers with the background, indeed the scientific research, which will allow us to more deeply understand and effectively address these questions. We hope all readers will share new insights with others in their professional and personal circles. But educators, in particular, are crucially positioned to help both young people and adult audiences apply these understandings to their everyday lives and in their schools, colleges, workplaces, and communities.

Anthropologists have long argued that the old 19th-century racial paradigm of four or five races (i.e., Black, White, Asian, Malay, and Native American) is not scientifically valid. In a biological sense, there are no such things as races. Contemporary humans are, and have always been, one species, with roots in Africa. There are no subspecies of humans.

Yet this idea seems to contradict the experiences of many people in the United States and other countries where racial classification is used daily, by individuals and institutions. Race still matters, whether in wealth accumulation, educational achievement, health, the legal system, or in personal safety. How can race not be real when we experience its effects every day?

To make matters more complex, the U.S. cultural system of race *has* had biological consequences. For example, segregating people and restricting intermarriage has tended to preserve visible biological distinctions between racial groups. And racism can negatively impact health status and human development.

The idea that race, races, and racism are cultural inventions—that is, created historically to legitimize social inequality between groups with different ancestries, national origins, and histories—helps explain this contradiction. Race is very much culturally and socially real and has had and continues to have real consequences, both social and biological.

AN ANTHROPOLOGICAL BIOCULTURAL PERSPECTIVE ON RACE?

Race and racism have been the subject of thousands of books written from a multitude of disciplinary perspectives, including books designed for multicultural educational and antiracist purposes (e.g., Banks & Banks, 2012; Grant & Sleeter, 2011; Hernández, 2001; Ball & Tyson (Eds.), 2011; Pollock (Ed.), 2008; Tatum, 1997; Villegas & Lucas, 2002). Readers may wonder why we need yet another book on this topic.

Anthropology offers a unique perspective on race and human variability. It is the only discipline that takes a biocultural approach to human variation—that is, one that includes both biological and cultural perspectives. No other discipline provides a cross-cultural, comparative approach in constructing its theories of race. This book brings together race-related research and scholarship from biological, cultural, linguistic, and archeological subdisciplines of anthropology. The integrated biocultural perspective and the cross-cultural data we offer in this book are simply not found elsewhere in the literature on race and antiracism.

Anthropologists have been writing about the "fallacy of race" as biology since the 1940s. Yet little of this knowledge has reached the wider public, partly because it is difficult to translate into accessible language. However, a wider readership is critical. Why?

First, as citizens of a democracy, we need to learn about the major intellectual and scientific ideas and discoveries that have profoundly shaped the society and world in which we live today. Race plays an enormously important role in contemporary social life. Yet race as biology is reinforced through the continuing use of racial terms (e.g., "Black," "White") which highlight physical differences. At the same time, we often claim to be "color-blind." And the relationship between race, human biological variation, culture, and social inequality remains shrouded in misinformation, fear, and ignorance. The biocultural approach to race not only deserves but requires attention.

Learning about race can increase overall science literacy. In an era of competing doctrines, antiscience rhetoric, and scientific ignorance, exposure to science grounded in the social reality of people's lives may renew interest in science. The biocultural approach encourages critical thinking and interdisciplinary learning. It can help learners of all kinds become scientifically literate, historically and socially informed, and thoughtful citizens in a diverse society and globalized world.

If race and racism are cultural inventions, then we (as individuals and as members of institutions and communities) have the power to alter them. Unraveling the myth of race as biology and discovering the cultural and historical processes through which the "racial worldview" emerged can empower all of us to become agents of change.

Finally, a biocultural approach to race offers the more complex picture of human behavior, biology-environment-culture, nature-nurture interactions, needed to break through the unremitting discourse of biological determinism that pervades our culture. We are not simply our genes; we are not "driven" by our hormones; we humans are far more complex. A deeper understanding of the dynamics and intersection of biology, race, culture, and society will give us a platform to understand other seemingly unchangeable behaviors in our society.

READERSHIP

This book was originally written primarily for educators, at precollege and college levels. However, the response to the first edition made us aware of the broader demand for an accessible book that integrates biological and cultural anthropological approaches to race. The first edition, while heavily used by educators, including in teacher education courses, has also served as a college-level text, a sourcebook for cultural diversity workshops, and a primer on race for a more general readership. It has been used in the American Anthropological Association's museum exhibit RACE: Are We So Different? as a sourcebook for docents and discussion leaders, and as a companion volume, to clarify and further explore concepts and material in (and not in) the exhibit.

The second edition remains appropriate for these audiences as well as members of the general public who wish to gain a better understanding of race. Few books integrate both biological and cultural perspectives on race, in a language that is accessible to nonspecialists, using an activity-oriented approach. For example, public officials, health professionals, counselors, librarians, administrators, parents, religious and community groups, diversity trainers, human resource professionals, book clubs, and other interest groups could use this book as a catalyst for developing dialogues about issues of race in their communities and workplaces.

Finally, although the book is designed primarily for U.S. audiences, several chapters discuss human diversity in a global context. These cross-cultural comparisons may be useful to educators in other countries. Europeans, Canadians, and Australians might find it relevant as they come to terms with a growing racially and ethnically diverse citizenry and school population. People in other countries, especially those heavily impacted by European colonial racial ideas, might find it a useful update and synthesis of contemporary anthropological ideas and approaches to teaching about race. Noneducators, too, might find it a helpful primer for understanding the roots of contemporary United States racial attitudes.

ORGANIZATION

The book has three substantive sections. Parts I and II address the key anthropological themes of the book: the myth of race as biology and the reality of race as a cultural invention. Part III extends the discussion to hot-button issues that arise in educational settings, although they may arise in other organizations as well.

Part I, "The Fallacy of Race as Biology," unravels, chapter by chapter, the myth that races are biologically valid divisions of humanity, explaining why anthropologists have rejected race as a scientifically meaningful description of human biological variation.

Part II, "Culture Creates Race," explores in detail the concept of race as a social construction. It begins with the concept of culture, turns to the role of classification systems in human life, and then describes how a racial worldview emerged in the United States to justify and maintain a system of social inequality. Race is also examined from a cross-cultural perspective. Part II ends by addressing the processes through which visible markers of race have been maintained in the United States, especially through culturally imposed restrictions on interracial mating and marriage. But we also show that racial boundary crossing, while always present to some extent, has been increasing in recent decades.

Part III, "Racial and Hot-Button Issues in Educational Settings," takes the everyday realities of school and college and uses them as a starting point for uncovering the way racial ideologies work in these settings, both from the perspectives of students and educators. Students tend to be naturally curious about race, especially since it is rarely part of the standard curriculum; educators can use the material to develop inquiry-based lessons and units in which participants examine their own campus communities with race, culture, and biology as an analytical lens.

Part IV, "Resources," provides a comprehensive list of references cited, a detailed and annotated list of website resources, those cited as well as websites with additional illustrations, educator-oriented materials, and in-depth information. Part IV also includes a "Comprehensive List of Activities," organized by book chapters.

Each chapter contains a conceptual background section, written in accessible language, with a summary of key points. We have tried to avoid unnecessary educational and scientific jargon. However, the topics covered in this volume are complex and wide ranging, from biology, human evolution, culture, history, and systems of inequality to contemporary school issues. In some cases, specialized terms are required. Part I deals with current scientific understandings of human biological variation and is the most technical. Chapters 2 through 4, especially, utilize recent research on DNA and population genetics to help explain the fallacy of race as biology. Yet we feel this information is essential to the argument we are making about race and is presented in a way that, if not a quick read, is clear and accessible. And it lays the foundation for understanding the intricate, dynamic interplay among race, culture, and biology (the name of our book).

Each chapter also contains a set of related activities. As educators, we emphasize activities that use a constructivist approach. That is, we assume that readers already possess valuable knowledge; the book builds upon this to construct new knowledge and skills relevant to people's lives. We also believe that people acquire concepts more readily and become more engaged when they discover them through their own inquiry; thus, many activities use a hands-on, inquiry-based approach. Some activities also explicitly promote participant empowerment, leadership, and involvement as change agents.

Ideally, the book should be read as a whole since each section builds on and is related to prior sections. However, each part and chapter can also stand on its own. Parts I and II, in particular, provide the core conceptual background material on contemporary anthropological understandings of race.

Part III is more oriented toward educators, college students, or others working in educational settings, and the activities and examples are more student oriented. However, it could be adapted to corporate or other institutional settings. Regardless of how this book is used, we have treated it as a unified whole. Within each chapter, we suggest links to other sections of the book. For those who want a quick sense of the whole, we suggest reading the introductions to each of the three parts.

To keep the book affordable, we have kept graphics to a minimum, referring readers instead to relevant websites. We have shortened the activity descriptions but increased the number of activities, focusing on Activity Ideas, which educators can develop on their own or through website links. Several more detailed Activity Plans, however, remain.

WHAT'S NEW IN THE SECOND EDITION?

The first edition was published in 2007. While this is less than seven years ago, much has changed both historically and scientifically. The United States elected its first African American (and Euro-American), multiracial, Black-identified (at least by the press and most U.S. Americans) president in 2008, and again in 2012. This historic event has certainly had implications for the way we talk about race and racism in this country. We have seen the global financial collapse that hit the world in 2008 and that continues to reverberate, exacerbating inequality; this financial meltdown, along with increasing alarm over climate change, reminds us of the depth and fragility of our interdependence as a global community.

Polarization has never been greater, at least in the lifetime of the authors, on both the cultural and political level. We are experiencing the resurgence of fundamentalisms of all sorts, in our own society and globally, from religious orthodoxies, to rejections of science and evolutionary theories, to the resuscitation of centuries-old commitments (especially for women) to abstinence, virginity, and "modest dress." Biological determinism is again rearing its ugly head, whether disguised as new data on female brains, or as an excuse for male violence, or as an undercurrent in "cultural" explanations for the educational achievement gap.

On the more positive side, we have seen great advances in our understanding of human biology, especially the complex interactions between genes, other DNA, human development, the environment, culture, and health. Old nature-nurture debates are now seen as simplistic. Complexity and contextual influences are the recurring themes in science.

We have also seen cultural advances as more and more U.S. Americans come from and participate comfortably in an array of diverse communities, crossing cultural, racial, ethnic, religious, and gender boundaries. We are becoming a more global, open culture.

In the new edition we place more emphasis on culture as dynamic, negotiated, and mutually constructed; we pay more attention to the fact that people have multiple and fluid identities that cut across race, gender, class, nationalities, religion, immigration status, and other categories of identity. We approach race, especially in parts II and III, not so much as a noun but as a verb, a process. People are not born with race, but in societies where the North American racial worldview prevails, they are "raced" and continue to experience, negotiate, resist, and reinterpret racing throughout their lifetimes. In parts II and III, we consider how this racialization process takes place with newer demographic groups in the United States, including Latino/as, South Asian and Middle Eastern immigrants, as well as religious groups (especially Muslims but also Buddhist and Hindu). We also look more closely at the growing scholarship on "Whiteness" and multiethnic/multiracial identity. All in all, we have tried to move away from old U.S. concepts of race as simply Black/White, of nature versus nurture, of society versus individual, and other binary constructs that do not (and probably never did) capture the dynamic complexity of racial construction in the United States and elsewhere.

We have also updated statistics and demographic information, utilizing recent census data. We have expanded website resources and added a significant number of new learning activities.

Finally, the AAA public education project *RACE: Are We So Different?*, to which two of the coauthors were major contributors,[1] has now debuted. Consisting of a traveling museum exhibit and award-winning website, it has been seen by over two million people in different U.S. venues (http://www.understandingrace.org). Our book, *How Real Is Race?*, continues to both complement and go beyond the content of the museum exhibit and associated materials.

TERMINOLOGY AND KEY CONCEPTS

Given the subject matter of this book and evidence that language shapes people's perceptions of reality, our choice of terminology is a key issue. We feel we should use concepts and labels that are consistent with the ideas about race we are presenting here.

Wherever possible, we prefer to use racial terms that reflect ancestral origins and social groupings or identities, such as African American or European American (Euro-American) rather than terms, like Black or White, that reinforce folk beliefs about race as biology and skin color. The term *White* is particularly problematic, since it is persistent in both popular and institutional usage, although less so than the now-discredited term *Caucasian* (see

Mukhopadhyay, 2012, 2008). Both terms overhomogenize and mask the immigrant origins of European Americans, implying they are somehow more "American" than other groups, like "Asian Americans."

When context seems to require Black or White, we use capitals to indicate these are formal, cultural labels for social groupings and not descriptive adjectives (e.g. "white" or "black"). In general, we avoid the term "people of color" because it implies a false binary distinction (color vs. no color) and overemphasizes biology (skin color). However, we recognize that it is an important term of solidarity among people with common experiences of racial discrimination. And that skin color continues as a social marker that affects how we are treated and treat others.

Overall, we prefer not to refer to large macroracial groupings, such as Asians, Africans, White/Europeans. We feel these are primarily remnants of the old four or five "races" invented by racial science and mask the complexity and diversity of the component populations, whether U.S. ethnic groups, nations, or smaller entities. When possible, we differentiate people residing in the United States from those residing elsewhere (e.g., Asian Americans vs. Asians).

Referring to the United States and its people, we often use U.S. or U.S. Americans rather than the shorter "America" or "Americans" because these latter terms actually include North, Central, and South America.

The term "race" presents special problems. Some authors use "scare quotes" in every instance to hammer home the message that this word is problematic. We decided this would impede the flow of the book and instead generally use quotes only the first time the term appears in a chapter. We have used quotation marks in other ways, to refer to U.S. "folk" concepts, cultural inventions that we normally take for granted, but which we wish to highlight.

A more difficult issue is race versus ethnicity. We recognize the history and contemporary complexities of abandoning this distinction, even though we agree with Kottak that it is both a cultural invention and difficult to apply (2013, p. 133). Both concepts, at heart, really refer to groups based on common ancestry, albeit recognizing that different groups have exceedingly diverse histories and experiences (Mukhopadhyay & Moses, 1997). Like the majority of contemporary U.S. Americans, we find popular uses of the term race often confusing, especially when we talk about racism against Muslims or have census categories which differentiate Hispanics by race. In short, it's a semantic mess and warrants more critical discussion. However, for the present, we use terms that reflect the conception of race we have presented in this book, except when context dictates otherwise.

Finally, pronouns in English are problematic because of their male gender bias. To avoid gender bias, we generally prefer plural pronouns (e.g., they) instead of constantly moving between he and she or the awkward he/she.

FOR EDUCATORS: FINDING A PLACE
FOR TEACHING ABOUT RACE

As noted earlier, the first edition of this book was designed primarily for educators. As educators ourselves, we want the next generation to be equipped with the most recent anthropological knowledge about race. At the same time, we realize that teachers at the precollege level are struggling to keep up with all the legal mandates and "standards" that affect their teaching. How, then, do we expect them to find time to teach about race?

In terms of curricular content areas, the book is appropriate for those who teach science, health education, social studies, language arts, life skills, ethnic studies, anthropology, sociology, psychology, communication studies, or other courses that address human biological or cultural diversity, human relations, and multicultural education. It lends itself particularly well to interdisciplinary teaching, such as a unit on genetics and family history, the environment, wealth and structural poverty, immigration, social inequality, dating and marriage, and of course, race, ethnicity, and culture. It is appropriate for a wide variety of general education courses that look at the U.S. American experience, both historically and in the present. On the biology side, this would be an excellent text for a history of science course.

For precollege educators, the book addresses many of the content standards in social studies and science, as well as the Common Core Standards. The book website provides a more detailed linkage to the Common Core Standards as well as other suggestions for integrating this material into an already crowded curriculum or for dealing with school or community contexts which may not be receptive to discussions of race. Part III also addresses some of the issues precollege teachers sometimes confront when trying to teach about race.

Our decision to write this book comes from our own experience as educators, researchers, and politically engaged, activist *citizens*. We believe in the power of knowledge and the role of education in creating a more equitable society. We hope more people will become engaged in learning about science and the scientific *process*, and then will use this knowledge to consider actions they can take to erase racism and other forms of social injustice.

NOTE

1. Moses chaired and Mukhopadhyay served on the National Advisory project that designed the original exhibit and website. Moses continues to colead the RACE project.

I

The Fallacy of Race as Biology

Carol C. Mukhopadhyay

Anthropologists have for years struggled with how to communicate the idea that races are not biologically real but are cultural inventions created in specific social, historical, and political contexts. Even people with a fairly sophisticated understanding of human biological variation find it difficult to abandon the concept of race as a scientifically valid way of describing and dividing up the human species. Longtime social justice and antiracism activists are often visibly upset when we inform them that "races are biological fiction, not fact." At press conferences, the most jaded journalists still register surprise at our announcement that "there is no such thing as race, biologically speaking."

WHAT IS RACE?

Part of the confusion stems from the term *race* itself. Historically it has referred to everything from one's nationality, religion, ancestry, regional identification, or class status to biological subcategories within a species.

Anthropologists and other scientists have also struggled with the multiple meanings of race. In the biological sciences and in physical[1] anthropology, race was used to describe human biological variation and subdivisions of the human species.

Most scientists now reject the validity of biological races, yet the idea persists in the wider culture. Indeed, it seems obvious to many people that races *are* biologically real. People will say, just look around you, on a school playground or in the local theater or at a sporting event. One can *see, with one's own eyes,* that race is real!

How can race not be biologically real, fellow educators ask, when I can walk into an advanced calculus class and tell at a glance that the students are mainly Euro and Asian American with only a few African Americans and Latinos? Why, some forensic anthropologists ask, can I racially identify murder victims from their physical remains? How can race not be biological, our physician colleagues ask, when African Americans are more prone to hypertension than are "Caucasians,"[2] a term still used to refer to European Americans?

Part of the problem stems from a lack of clarity about what anthropologists mean when they say races aren't biologically real. Anthropologists aren't arguing that there is *no* biological component in U.S. racial categories. Biology *has* played a role in the cultural invention of what we call race, as we shall see in part II. And race, or rather, one's racial designation, socially, can have enormous biological consequences, including on one's health status. But most of what we believe or have been taught about race as biology, as valid subdivisions of the human species, and an important part of human biological variation is a myth.

THE FALLACY OF RACE AS BIOLOGY

Part I focuses on unraveling the myth of race as biology. We explore the reasons scientists have rejected the concept of race as a scientifically valid description of human biological variation. We also look at the reality of human biological variation and its relationship to the concept of race.

We address the question that people constantly ask: if biological race is not real, then what are we seeing? How are we to make sense of the human variation that we normally think of as race? Why are groups of people different from each other in observable ways? And what is the biological significance of skin color? Why do U.S. Americans with ancestors from West Africa or South India or the Philippines tend to have darker skin than those with ancestors from England, Sweden, or Japan? And what does this mean, biologically? Are these traits linked to other biological traits or capacities?

Each chapter in part I is designed to explain one or more key concepts. We first provide conceptual background on the topic and then introduce activities and other resources that illustrate and reinforce these ideas.

Chapter 1, "Why Contemporary Races Are Not Scientifically Valid," addresses the artificiality and arbitrariness of what we call race. Chapter 1 demonstrates that there are no biological traits that allow us to consistently and reliably divide the human species into the same set of racial groupings.

Chapter 2, "Human Biological Variation: What We Don't See," explores relatively invisible biological variation. We show that some of the most interesting and significant areas of human biological diversity consist of traits that are inside the body. Unlike conventional racial markers, these nonvisible traits can have a major biological impact on people's lives.

If there is no such thing as biological race, then how do we explain skin color and other so-called racial traits? We tackle this in chapter 3, "If Not Race, How Do We Explain Biological Differences?" We show how geography and environment influence the genetic structures of human populations through the processes of natural selection. We discuss other evolutionary forces that affect populations. We note that cultural processes also shape human biology and genetics, as well as developmental processes, whether through humans altering the environment, creating systems of nutritional inequality, or spreading their genes through trade, travel, and even warfare. In fact, the statement "it's all in our genes" is a very inaccurate description of contemporary human biological variation.

Finally, chapter 4, "More Alike Than Different, More Different Than Alike," builds upon earlier ideas. We provide further evidence that there is more diversity within than between racial groups. We also show that most biological variability exists at the individual level. Race is rather meaningless when it comes to DNA and genes.

We conclude with the latest evidence on the "Out of Africa" theory. Since the publication of the first edition, even more research demonstrates that modern humans originated in Africa, as one species, and remained a single species, despite a complex history of migrations to different parts of the world. Human history has always been the story of multiple populations of a single species moving, mixing, and settling, again and again.

Human biological variability is a fascinating, ever-changing reality. Ultimately, however, the variability within our species is rather insignificant compared to our shared biological inheritance. It is culture, and the human capacity for creating meaning out of observable biological variability, that has made biology so significant historically and in contemporary social life. Part II will tell that story.

NOTES

Part I primary author, Carol Mukhopadhyay, thanks book coauthor Yolanda Moses for her significant input on the first edition. Mukhopadhyay also thanks UC Riverside, especially Dr. Alan Fix, for providing its cultural anthropology grad students with a substantive foundation in biological anthropology.

1. Physical anthropology, a major subfield of anthropology, is also often referred to as biological anthropology.

2. The use of quotes around the term *Caucasian* signals it is not a scientifically accurate term but a folk or popular term (see chapters 6 and 7). See also the introduction for more discussion of terminology used in this book.

Chapter One

Why Contemporary Races Are Not Scientifically Valid

This chapter challenges the popular myth that American racial categories represent scientifically valid biological divisions of the human species. The race concept has historically been associated with the idea that there are "natural" divisions of the human species, that there are clear-cut, discrete, homogeneous, and easily distinguishable subgroups or "races," and that people can be easily categorized into these racial groups.

This idea partially reflects traditional European and Christian conceptions of the world as "fixed," essentially unchanged since its origins or, in religious terms, its divine creation. This static view applied to the world of plants, animals . . . and humans. Immersed in this framework, early 18th-century European scientists focused on classifying, rather than explaining, variation in the natural world. The resulting systems of classification were called taxonomies, and plants and animals were organized into related divisions, subdivisions, sub-subdivisions, and so forth. Words like "order," "family," and "kingdom" described different levels or subdivisions.

Within this system, the concept of race referred to fundamental divisions or "subspecies" within a species. Among nonhuman species, like gorillas or chimpanzees, subgroups tend to be both physically and geographically distinct, and subspecies or "races" can often be identified. But, as we shall see shortly, this is not the case for humans.

This chapter, along with chapter 2, focuses on the arbitrary, subjective, and artificial nature of any attempt to divide the human species into subspecies, that is, into biological races. We show that races are not scientifically valid because there are no objective, reliable, meaningful criteria scientists can use to construct or identify racial groupings.

CONCEPTUAL BACKGROUND

Despite decades of anthropological evidence to the contrary, many people continue to believe there are three to five basic and natural subcategories of the human species, called races. Until the 1970s, American racial groups were commonly described using terms like "Caucasian," "Negroid," and "Mongoloid." Yet these categories excluded vast populations and regions of the world, such as South Asia, Indonesia, and the Philippines. In recent years, geography-oriented descriptive labels, like Asian or African, have replaced old racial categories. But the notion that these represent natural, scientific, biological divisions persists, reinforced by the continuing use of "Caucasian" for people of European ancestry (Mukhopadhyay, 2012).

What are the scientific grounds for rejecting the idea of biological races? One fundamental basis is that there are no reliable procedures for dividing humans into races.

In the 1950s, scientists typically defined a human race as any population with significant differences in gene frequencies from other human populations. Sounds simple! But this definition does not specify which of our 20,000+ genes are to be used to identify races (Jurmain et al., 2014, p. 57).[1] Perhaps that is why the number of races has fluctuated so widely. Estimates have ranged from three to several hundred or more.

More recently, Relethford has defined a biological race this way: "A group of populations sharing certain biological traits that distinguish them from other groups of populations" (2013, p. 335). This avoids the "single trait defines a race" problem. He goes on, however, to state, "In practice, the biological concept of race has been difficult to apply to human populations" (p. 335). And like other biological anthropologists, he rejects the idea that American racial groups constitute biological races. Why?

WHAT TRAITS SHALL WE USE TO CLASSIFY PEOPLE INTO DIFFERENT RACES?

The first issue is which traits to use in our system of racial classification. Historically, in the United States, racial classification was based on a few visible traits. Skin color was the most widely used, although hair texture, eye, lip, and nose shapes also figured in popular racial descriptions. This is apparent in 18th- and 19th-century American depictions of non-European populations.

Cranial Shape and Body Type

Early scientific attempts at classification drew on similar traits, especially skin color (see chapter 6). But in the 19th century, the emerging ***racial*** *science* began to explore other human biological variations. Scientists developed methods to measure the human face and skull, called craniofacial measures. A Swedish anatomist developed a measure of cranial shape (not size) called the *cephalic index*. The index was derived by dividing the maximum width by the maximum length of the skull and multiplying by 100. Individuals, and then entire populations, were classified and compared by head shape (Relethford, 2013, p. 384). Racial scientists initially argued that "African" skulls had a lower cephalic index than European skulls, ignoring the amount of overlap between the groups or the amount of variation within each group. Subsequent studies, for example, showed that Germans and Koreans had similar average cephalic indices of about 83 percent (Relethford, 2013, p. 385). And they divided Northern and Southern Europeans into different "types": those with "narrow" versus "broader" heads.

Early racial science developed other measures of the body. Entire populations were classified into different body types based on total body size and shape, and on limb lengths (see chapter 3).

It was not until the 1950s, with the rise of modern evolutionary theory, and the rejection of racial science, that scientists began to investigate the geographic distribution of body shape and other visible features that differentiated human populations. Their goals were to understand how evolution works and to reconstruct the past history and the relationships between human populations (see chapter 3).

The primary goal of racial science, however, was quite different. Rather than understanding how human variation arises, racial scientists were seeking additional physical "evidence" for the prevailing system of racial categories, one that envisioned hierarchically ranked subspecies, or "races." We now know these racial groupings are not rooted in nature . . . but in culture, history, and politics, including slavery and colonialism. They were part of a worldview invented and used to legitimize race-based social inequality (Smedley & Smedley, 2012; see also part II).

In essence, then, racial scientists, like most European Americans, were predisposed to notice or motivated to look for *some* visible differences among humans and to *ignore others*. Skin color was significant as a racial marker because it easily distinguished Northwestern Europeans from West Africans, who—along with indigenous Native American peoples—were the major populations in 19th-century America. Other facial features, like lip thickness, hair texture, eye shape, and nose length also served as convenient, visible "markers" of African Americans and other marginalized groups, such as Chinese and Japanese Americans, Eastern European Jews, and Arabs.

The history of so-called racial science illustrates how our preconceptions, and our goals, can shape which visible traits we notice and select to create "races." But that is not how science should proceed. We need a more objective, scientifically meaningful way of selecting a set of traits to use in creating racial categories. And that is the problem. There are a multitude of visible human traits we can use, once we truly start looking at humans in a nonracial way.

WHAT VISIBLE FEATURES COULD WE USE TO CONSTRUCT RACES?

What visible traits could scientists use to classify human groups into races? Let's start with color . . . but not just skin color. Eyes come in a wide array of colors, far more than the categories "blue," "brown," "green," or "black." So does human hair . . . from numerous shades of black, brown, and reddish to nearly colorless. Humans also differ in the number and location of concentrated spots of pigment that we call freckles.

If we extend our analysis of skin beyond color, we find that some groups experience significant skin wrinkling when they age, while others do not. And there are variations in where wrinkles appear or where skin begins to sag.

Hairiness is another trait that varies among human populations. Of course, hair is culturally managed, a significant component of body decoration, and, often, of female gender identity. But variability in hairiness goes far beyond these relatively minor gender differences.

Hair texture, especially the contrast between straight and tightly curled hair, has long been a racial "marker" in the United States. It continues to have enormous cultural and commercial significance, spawning an array of services, products, advice columns, blogs, horror stories, labels ("nappy") . . . and academic treatises. [2]

But hair, even head hair, is more complex. Head hair has design aspects, such as the "widow's peak," or other hairline shapes, or an early-age "receding hairline." Human balding patterns also vary; in some populations, men lose most of their hair as they age; in others, they do not, even at an advanced age.

Humans differ in the amount of body hair they have, from nearly hairless to richly endowed ("bushy" or "bearlike"). As for hair location, some people resemble the Buddha, with very hairy ears; others have hair on toes but not ears. Eyebrows and eyelashes differ in at least shape, amount of hair, curliness, and degree of pigmentation.

Facial Features

The face contains numerous features that could be used to "race" populations, such as dimples. Then there are lips! Lips not only have different degrees of fullness; one lip can be fuller than the other, more or less outturned. Lip lengths vary . . . producing wider or rounder mouth shapes. They can turn down or up, can be "bow-shaped" or "duck-billed." Lips can have poorly or well-defined edges, the latter sometimes called "roller-coaster" lips.[3]

As noted earlier, eye color is quite variable. But so is eye shape. The eyeball, cornea, and lens all come in different shapes, some affecting vision. An elongated eyeball can reduce distance vision (nearsightedness), while a shortened eyeball affects close vision. The iris itself has multiple, variable dimensions. Indeed, it is virtually unique for every individual, allowing it to be used like fingerprints, for personal identification.

There is also the "epicanthic fold," a skinfold of the upper eyelid that covers the inner corner (canthus) of the eye. This is another popular racial "marker," this time for Asians, even though not all Asians, nor even East Asians, have this feature. It is also found among some Central Asians, Scandinavians, and San (so-called Bushmen) of Southern Africa. But why not classify people using other variations in eye shape, sockets, and lids, such as those highlighted by popular labels like "droopy" or "puppy dog eyes," "bulging" or "goldfish" eyes.

Ears, too, come in an enormous array of shapes. Even earlobes vary— some lobes are attached while others are free-standing. And then there is earwax. Scientists have found two basic kinds. One is gray, dry, and crumbly; the other is yellow, wet, and sticky.

Look inside the mouth and you find that some people can make the edges of their tongues curl—that is, the edges roll up and inward, creating a kind of trough. Others find it nearly impossible to do this. Their tongue remains flat. This is not simply a skill or learned behavior. Tongue rolling is another biological difference among humans.[4] For pictures of these types of differences go to http://udel.edu/~mcdonald/myththumb.html.

Teeth

Looking further into the mouth, scientists find that human teeth come in all sizes and shapes. Because teeth tend to preserve well, compared to soft tissue, archeologists and paleontologists are more likely to find teeth than other fossil skeletal remains, even at burial sites. For archeological reconstruction and to identify contemporary human remains, scientists have created a specific type of caliper to measure teeth. Populations can also be classified by tooth size.

Human teeth vary in shape. Some people have teeth with extra cusps or ridges on the inside margins of their front teeth (called "shovel-shaped incisors"). Certain populations—for example, East Asians and Native Americas—are more likely to have the shovel-shape variation than others, although it has also been observed among Europeans and Africans (Relethford, 2013, pp. A2–7). For pictures, see http://johnhawks.net/taxonomy/term/846.

Noses

The nose is another historical racial "marker" of certain populations, such as Jews and Arabs. It consists of two basic parts: the nasal septum, a piece of cartilage which separates the two nostrils; and several bones, including the nasal and ethmoid, at the roof of the nose, extending to the eye orbits, separating the nasal cavity from the brain. Both parts vary and affect the width and length of the nose. Scientists today, as well as plastic surgeons, utilize a ***nasal index*** based on the width and height of the nasal opening, multiplied by 100 (Relethford, 2013, p. 385).[5]

But noses have other interesting genetically based features. One 2011 study of over 1,300 predominantly European or European Israeli noses identified at least fourteen different types, noting variations in fleshiness, pointiness, sloping tips (up or down), bumps, and sharpness of edges. The pictures accompanying the story illustrate how much variability there is even within a small and relatively narrow sample of the world's noses! See link at http://www.dailymail.co.uk/sciencetech/article-2013699/There-14-types-nose--yours.html#ixzz2UdAG63Ag.

Head Size and Body Shape

Scientists continue to study variations in the human skull and face, but using more sophisticated techniques. They can measure the length and width of the face and the skull from different locations. They often use the eyes, the lower jaw, and the cheekbones as base points. One recent study of human populations in six different regions of the world was based on fifty-seven different cranial measures (Relethford, 2013, p. 343).

Other indices have been developed of body shape. The "intermembral index" takes the ratio of arm length to leg length, while the "cosmic index" measures the ratio of arm length to leg length. Many of us are familiar with the body mass index (BMI), which measures weight over squared height, partially to assess body fat (Fuentes, 2012, p. 305).

Hands and Toes

Human hands are a wonderful indicator of how genetics, through slight and often meaningless mutations, can produce variant forms of what are functionally identical parts of the human body. Our fingers vary in shape, size, and nail pattern. Some of us have longer fingers, overall; others have an especially long index finger. Some of us have a *hitchhiker's thumb*—that is, we can bend our thumb so that it is almost at a right angle. Or we have a "fat" thumb or double-jointed fingers. Some of us have flat nails; others more rounded forms. Toes, too, exhibit variations that are linked to biological inheritance and genetics.

Finger and Palm Prints

Some scientists devote their lives to studying variations in finger and palm prints. While each individual has a unique set of fingerprints, certain features and patterns occur more often in some populations than others. For example, there are variations in the number of ridgelines on each finger if you take a count between specified points. And there are different kinds of prints, described as loops, arches, and whorls, for each finger. (For online illustrations, see http://www.pbs.org/race/002_SortingPeople/002_02-traits.htm). Palms, too, show different patterns and designs. This keeps palm readers quite busy!

Height and Other Body Traits

Why not use height as a basis for racial classification? This is certainly a trait that differentiates human groups. Mbuti and Aka forest-dwelling populations in Central Africa average around four feet, seven inches. Scandinavians average around six feet, as do the Tutsi of Rwanda in East Africa. Of course, if we used average heights of populations to form races, it would force us to alter the historical racial groupings. In this case, African Tutsis and European Swedes, females as well as males,[6] would be in the same race. And Mbuti, Filipinos, Vietnamese, Mongolians, and some Italians would end up in the same race. And while Africa contains the tallest and smallest people, there is nearly as much variability in Europe and Asia (see http://www. understandingrace.org/humvar/spectrum.html).

Clearly there are numerous visible traits available for classifying humans into races. Our entire bodies vary—our faces, our limbs, our chest sizes, our necks, our buttocks, our ankles, fingers, toes—one could go on and on. And we're only talking about *visible* human biological traits.

So which should we use for our racial system? Is there any scientific basis for selecting some traits over others? Is there any meaningful reason to choose skin color or hair form or eye shape over other traits? The answer, in one word, is no! We could use any one or any combination of these to create groups that fit the definition of a biological race. But, as we have already seen, one's racial classification depends on which traits you choose. Change the trait, and your racial category may change. And using some traits, members of the same family could end up in different racial groups. This is not a very reliable system for dividing the species into meaningful, biologically distinct subgroups.

FUZZY BOUNDARIES: MOST VISIBLE TRAITS ARE
NOT DISCRETE BUT VARY CONTINUOUSLY

Let's say we wanted to use just a few traits like skin color or height or hairiness to create our racial groups. We'd immediately find it virtually impossible to use these traits to create clear-cut groups. The reason is that few visible traits are what scientists call *discrete traits*—with clear differences between alternative forms, like apples versus oranges. There are some exceptions. Take earwax: it's either sticky or wet. Or shovel-shaped incisors—you pretty much either have them or you don't. Discrete traits make it easy to "race" people. People with the trait would be in one racial category; those without it in the other. So earwax, we'd have two races. If we used a discrete trait with three different forms, we'd have three races.

But most visible genetic traits, like skin, hair, or eye color, or traits with a fairly strong genetic component, like height, are what we call *continuous traits*. There are infinite gradations or forms of the trait. Consider color in the natural world or paint colors in a paint store. There is a continuum of colors. There are no clear breaks between green, blue, purple, brown. They shade imperceptibly into each other.

Skin color is like that. There are just shades . . . infinite variations along a continuum from very light to very dark. So even though we may talk about races as "black" and "white," there are no such clear visual boundaries. All humans, including African Americans and Euro-Americans, come in various shades or degrees of pigmentation, from lighter or paler to darker. To create a reliable racial division based on color, we'd have to figure out a way to divide the spectrum of color. First, we'd need to know the range of skin colors among humans. We could use a device called a "reflectance spectro-photometer" that measures the amount of light reflected back from a given source, like skin, at different wavelengths. Darker skin reflects less light than lighter skin and so produces lower readings; lighter skin has higher readings. One study of twenty-two different populations around the world found enormous variation in the average percentage of light reflected: from a high of over 70 percent (Netherlands) to less than 20 percent (Relethford, 2013, p. 340, figure 14.3).

Once we established this range, we could create a "dividing line." Using the spectrometer, we could "race" individuals, that is, place them into a particular racial category.

Even if we did this, we'd still have to decide how many different categories or races we wanted; and where the dividing line should be for each "race." But there is no scientific, rational basis that we could use. The decision would be totally arbitrary! At least from a biological perspective. Individuals with nearly imperceptible differences in skin color could end up in different racial categories. And because there is so much variability, people from the same population, ethnic group, or even family could end up in different "races."

This problem affects the traits that have served as racial "markers" in the United States and elsewhere. And it applies to virtually all other external physical characteristics we've discussed: height, eye color, lip and eye shape, hairiness, skull shape, face shape, teeth size. None have natural subdivisions. All are just infinite variations on a theme. Any division of the spectrum into separate categories is artificial and unreliable. And folks at the edges of categories would be more similar to each other than to people within their own category. It's the same dilemma as with grades. When percentages on an exam are translated into grades, a B student at the 80 percent cutoff point is as close or closer to many Cs (70–79 percent) than to other Bs (80–89 percent).

The only time traits with continuous gradations work for racial categories is when you don't sample the entire world population but select populations at extreme ends of the continuum. You could create races based on height in a region with two populations—one very tall and one very short. Or you could use skin color in a country like the 18th-century United States, where two of the major populations (Northwestern Europeans and West Africans) represented opposite poles of a continuum—very pale and very dark.

But that is hardly a scientific way to divide the entire human species into races. Any dividing line is purely arbitrary. When we have a continuum, the number of divisions or categories is also arbitrary. We could have 5, 10, 20— indeed, 50—races depending on where we put the dividing line. And that's just using one trait, like skin color.

An additional complication is that many traits like skin color, height, or weight are influenced by environmental factors (see chapter 3). To race people on skin color, for example, we'd have to find a part of the body not exposed to the sun, since tanning is a universal human bodily response to sunlight. Most anthropologists use the inner part of the arm because it is less exposed to the sun.

RACIAL TRAITS DO NOT COVARY; MOST TRAITS VARY INDEPENDENTLY OF OTHER TRAITS

So how are we, as scientists, to divide people into races? We don't know which traits to use. And virtually all traits will be continuous, with no clear racial divisions. How many different races are we going to create, using any single trait? It's easy to see why there has been so much confusion and disagreement regarding the concept of race—and how many races there are!

What, however, if we simply return to our original "racial" traits—skin color, hair form and texture, nose shape, and eye shape. Let's forget that we've arbitrarily selected these visible traits over other ones we could have used. Let's forget that we'll have to arbitrarily create divisions within a spectrum of different forms.

What happens when we examine the distribution of these traits across the populations of the world? Biological anthropologists in the 1960s started mapping so-called racial traits, one at a time, tracing alternative forms of a trait among populations in different geographic regions. They found that many traits exhibit a *gradual* change in the frequency of alternative forms as you move from one population to another across geographic space. There are no abrupt divisions. This type of geographic distribution of a biological trait is called a *cline* (Fuentes, 2012).

More important, they found that each trait they looked at seemed to have a fairly unique and different geographical pattern of distribution. In order to create biologically distinct groups, each racial trait must have approximately the same distribution, that is, be found in the same population. Another way of saying this is that traits used must *covary*. Populations with one form of trait 1 should share the same form of trait 2, trait 3, and so forth. For example, every population with light skin color should also have the same type of hair texture, the same hair and eye color, nose, body, and eye shape. The same goes for every darker-skinned population. In short, the race concept assumes that visible racial characteristics are clustered—that races share multiple, genetically rooted "racial" traits.

C. Loring Brace, a biological anthropologist, created what were called "clinal maps" of skin pigmentation, nasal index, body shape, and tooth size, using data available at that time. The maps showed that no two traits had the same population distribution. The distribution of skin colors was not the same as that of nasal index, body shape, or tooth size.

Although more recent, sophisticated analyses, including DNA-based analyses, have superseded these clinal maps, Brace and his colleagues were the first to illustrate the artificial nature of U.S. and North American and European racial categories. They established that most traditional racial traits are what scientists call *discordant*, that is, they do not covary; they are not *concordant*. Different genetic traits can have different geographic distributions. Each racial trait used produces a different partitioning or racial division of the human species.

Simply put, this means that individuals in one racial group based on skin color would not necessarily be in the same racial group if we used a second trait. Adding more traits just increases the number of different, nonoverlapping, divisions of humanity. We would produce one set of racial categories based on skin color, another using hair form, another using eye shape, another based on nose shape. One's racial identity or category would depend on what trait was used and would constantly shift (cf. http://www.pbs.org/race/002_SortingPeople/002_01-sort.htm).

Perhaps the most important legacy of mapping the geographic distribution of racial traits was that it stimulated scientists to ask new questions about the origins of human biological variation. Why, they began asking, should a particular trait (such as nose size or skin color) have a specific geographical pattern? Why are certain forms closer or farther from the equator? Is it possible that so-called racial traits are linked causally to the environments in which their ancestral populations resided? In short, they began exploring the evolutionary roots of human biological variation, taking an "evolutionary" instead of a "racial" approach to describing and understanding human biological variation.

Chapters 2 and 3 continue to explore geographically patterned human biological variation, at the invisible level as well as visible level. And chapter 3 describes in more detail contemporary evolutionary explanations for why racially marked traits like skin color vary among different populations.

To summarize, races are unstable, unreliable, arbitrary, culturally created divisions of humanity. This is why scientists and anthropology as a discipline have concluded that race, as scientifically valid biological divisions of the human species, is fiction not fact.

KEY CONCEPTUAL POINTS

- There are no scientifically valid biological subdivisions of the human species (i.e., races).
- Contemporary U.S. racial categories arbitrarily utilize only a few of many visible biological traits that differentiate humans.
- Most so-called racial traits are continuous rather than discrete. The number and criteria for racial divisions are therefore arbitrary.
- Racial traits do not covary. They are nonoverlapping and discordant. Using different traits produces different racial classifications or divisions of the human species.
- There are no biological races—that is, there are no visible biological traits that allow us to consistently and reliably subdivide the human species.

KEY TERMS (ITALICIZED AND BOLDED IN TEXT)

racial science
cephalic index
discordant (discontinuous) traits
discrete traits
concordant (or covarying) traits
nasal index
continuous traits

covary

ACTIVITIES

Overall Objectives: Each activity illustrates a major conceptual point in this chapter. Activities can be adapted to illustrate points made in other part I chapters.

Other Information: Appropriate for all ages, with modifications. For all activities, it is useful to have visual illustrations of human variability, especially if your community is relatively homogeneous. For one array of twenty faces, just in the United States, see http://www.pbs.org/race/002_SortingPeople/002_00-home.htm. Participants can also search the Web or other sources for images.

Activity Plan 1: How Many Ways Are There to Create "Races"?

Objective: Participants will realize how many visible human differences could be used to create races.

Procedure:

Step 1. Review the scientific definition of a biological race given in this chapter.

Step 2. See if participants can apply the definition. Compile a list of biological traits they would use to separate people into races. They will likely produce conventional racial traits. Ask them why only those traits and not others? Then proceed to Step 3.

Step 3. Ask participants (in pairs, small groups, or as a whole) to examine closely the people around them (parts of their faces, body shapes, hair, hands and fingers, palms, feet, height, etc.). Then create a list of additional visible human differences. Participants may be surprised at how much biological variability they discover once they go beyond conventional U.S. racial traits.

Step 4. Add traits missed by participants (e.g., tongue curling, hairiness, hitchhiker's thumb, etc.). Save list for later activities in this and other chapters.

Step 5. Emphasize key point: Many visible traits can be used to create biological races. Questions to ponder: With so many traits, which should we use for creating racial groups? Why do U.S. racial categories emphasize some traits and ignore all the rest?

Step 6. Potential follow-up: Look at other people (in family, community, on websites/TV/videos) and identify additional visible human differences. Add to "master" list.

Activity Plan 2: Where Is the Racial Dividing Line? Continuous versus Discrete Traits

Objective: Participants will understand, experientially, the concepts of discrete versus continuous traits as applied to race.

Procedure:

Step 1. Facilitator reviews concept of discrete versus continuous here or at end of activity.

Step 2. Select three to five traits from participants' list of visible physical traits (in Activity Plan 1). Use these traits to create racial groups in the class. Make sure list includes racial markers (e.g., skin color, lip thickness, eye color, hair texture) as well as continuous nonracial traits, like height or hitchhiker's thumb. Participants could also calculate nasal index, cephalic index, body ratios, or teeth size.

Step 3. From the list, try to find one discrete trait to separate the group physically into different racial groups. There are few truly discrete traits: sticky versus nonsticky earwax. Instead, you'll have to use a relatively discrete trait like the ability to curl your tongue. Most people will either have or not have the trait. How many groups are created?

Step 4. Try to find a second discrete trait that will clearly divide the group. It will probably be very difficult. That's because most traits are not discrete, but continuous, which is a key point.

Step 5. Use height next. Have participants align themselves from shortest to tallest (or use a measuring stick). Divide into "races." Discuss how to decide. You may arbitrarily pick a number. Then decide where the divisions should be. Again, there are no objective criteria for deciding. Make the point about the arbitrariness of categories and lack of clear-cut category boundaries for continuous traits.

Step 6. Select a racialized trait, such as skin color. Even in relatively ethnically homogeneous groups, there will be variability. Participants compare skin color on the inside of their arm, the area least altered by exposure to the sun. A continuum should appear. Have participants divide the group into three to five racial "categories."

If participants are predominantly of one racial or ethnic group, slight skin color variations may be dismissed as meaningless given total human variation. To some degree, they are correct. But they still illustrate the arbitrariness of differences. And a quick trip to the Internet will easily produce a broader sample of the human spectrum of skin colors. Avoid geographic "extremes," such as Sweden and Nigeria. Instead sample the "mainstream," densely populated nations like Indonesia, India, the Circum-Mediterranean area (Italy, Greece, Morocco, Egypt), the "Middle East," Iran, and Iraq.

Avoid "exotics," that is people from small-scale societies, in places like New Guinea. Most U.S. major urban areas offer equally diverse samples of human biological diversity. See weblink cited above.

Alternatively, develop a PowerPoint collage of global human variability in body shape, heights, limb lengths, hairiness, and other visible physical traits. After viewing the collage, discuss how difficult or easy would it be to classify these people into "racial" groups using any so-called racial traits.

Activity Plan 3: Racial Traits Do Not Covary

Objective: Participants will understand the concept of covariance and how most racial traits do not covary.

Procedure:

Step 1. Utilize previous list of visible traits. Participants select several traits to create races. Be sure list includes at least skin color, hair form, or nose shape.

Step 2. Select one or two participants to be "racial classifiers" or let participants self-classify. You could link this to material in part II on the census. Identify different parts of the room as "homelands" for each racial group. Select the first racial trait, let's say skin color. Decide how many racial categories to use, say three to five. Then have participants go to their homelands based on their skin color. If they have difficulty "racing" themselves, remind them that boundaries are often arbitrary. Once participants are in racial communities, list members of each racial group (on board, transparency, etc.).

Step 3. Select a second, racially identified trait, such as hair form, eye color, or nose or lip shape. Select what works best for the group. Have members of each racial group classify themselves into one of three races based on this trait. Most traits will require arbitrary divisions. For hair you might suggest three categories: naturally tightly curled, wavy, straight hair.

Ask participants how much variability there is in their group. Is everyone in the same category based on curliness? Generally, the answer will be no, especially if your class is fairly diverse.

Next, reshuffle the participants into new races, designating one area of the room curlies, one straights, and one wavies. Participants will then switch racial locations. Record, for each new racial group, how many members were in the same "race" for the groups based on skin color.

Alternatively, create more races to cover the new combinations this second trait has created. List the new combinations on the board: darker skin-curly hair, darker-wavy, darker-straight, medium-curly, medium-wavy, medium-straight, lighter-curly, lighter-wavy, lighter-straight. You now have nine racial categories.

Step 4. Select a third trait, one that is variable within your own class (e.g., nasal index, eye or hair color, tongue curling). Repeat the "racial shuffle."

Step 5. Summarize results using a table like table 1.1.

Continue with additional traits until participants understand the concept of *discordant* or noncovariance among visible traits.

Activity Plan 4: What Racial Traits Shall We Choose?

This works well with chapter 7.

Objective: Participants will understand that while racial classification is biologically arbitrary, those in power deliberately select racial criteria that are in their own self-interest.

Additional Information: For a brief online version of this, see "Explore Traits" Sorting Activity at http://www.pbs.org/race/002_SortingPeople/002_02-traits.htm.

Procedure:

Step 1. Introduce activity. State that everyone will be placed into a racial group but the races will not have equal power or status. Only one race will have the right to decide on the grades the rest of the class will receive for this activity. Race A will be the top-ranked group. Race B will be the lower-ranked group.

Step 2. Arbitrarily divide into two to five groups, approximately six to ten people each.

Step 3. Each group selects one visible racial trait to categorize people into races A and B (and perhaps C or D). People possessing one version of the trait will be in Race A; people with the other form of the trait will be in Race B.

Step 4. List the traits selected including which form is group A. See if the group can agree on a trait for classifying people.

Step 5. Discussion. Reflect on how participants selected traits. Participants will probably try to select a racial trait that will enable them to end up in Race A. Since the groups were arbitrarily divided initially, it may be

Table 1.1.

Student Name	Trait 1: Color	Trait 2: Hair	Trait 3: Body Shape
JS	Medium	Curly	Round
CM	Lighter	Wavy	Round
SD	Darker	Straight	Linear
AM	Darker	Wavy	Round

difficult to find a common trait. But participants are creative and will probably come up with one that works. This serves to make the point that racial categories are in part social inventions, and those who invent them often are motivated by the desire for power. They select traits that will put their own group at an advantage.

Step 6. Tell participants this will prepare them for part II on the social invention of race in the United States.

ADDITIONAL ACTIVITY IDEAS

Activity Idea 1: The Human Variation Quiz

Take this ten-question quiz that challenges conventional understandings of race and human variation. It is located on the Understanding Race website at http://www.understandingrace.org/humvar/quiz.html. This could also be used at the end of part II.

Activity Idea 2: How Can You Tell Someone's Race? (also for chapter 4)

Ask participants to define what they mean by race. Then ask how you can tell someone's race. Explore these ideas further using the detailed activity plans in the "Empirical Challenges of Racial Classification" teaching module at http://www.pbs.org/race/000_About/002_04-teachers-04.htm.

Activity Idea 3: The Human Spectrum of Height

Explore this short, five-minute video showing how human populations vary in height around the world: http://www.understandingrace.org/humvar/spectrum.html.

Activity Idea 4: Explore Human Diversity Further

Use Human Diversity website modules at http://www.pbs.org/race/004_HumanDiversity/004_00-home.htm.

The module, Sorting People into U.S. Racial Groups, can be used with chapter 7 or chapter 9.

NOTES

1. According to Jurmain et al., 2014, p. 57, 2012 estimates are around 21,000, revised downward from the approximately 25,000 identified after the human genome was sequenced in 2001. Prior to that, estimates were around 30,000.

2. For an interesting video where African American women discuss their experiences with hair, see *A Girl Like Me* at http://www.understandingrace.org/lived/video/index.html.

3. For an array of variations among Europeans see http://www.mmmglawblog.com/top-10-lip-shapes-that-guys-love-the-most/.

4. Some scientists argue that there is a learned component to this trait. See http://udel.edu/~mcdonald/mythintro.html. This website contains visual illustrations and brief discussions of many of the visible traits mentioned here, such as earlobes and hitchhiker's thumb, as well as other traits.

5. A 2009 online article from a scientific research journal concluded that nasal index did not correlate with major races, had no relevance to rhinologists, and there were also no racial variations in physiology. See http://www.ncbi.nlm.nih.gov/pubmed/19531167 (accessed May 15, 2013).

6. Like many other physical traits, gender differences in heights are quite small compared to the amount of variation in the human species.

Chapter Two

Human Biological Variation

What We Don't See

Most long-time residents of the United States have been raised to see race, to notice physical characteristics such as skin color, hair texture, and nose and eye shape. This is not surprising. For nearly 200 years, U.S. religious, legal, political, and educational institutions promoted a belief that physical traits were markers of fundamental biological divisions of humanity (see part II). And U.S. racial ideology, especially racial science, tried unsuccessfully to link visible traits, like skin color, to more profound biological differences in capacities, especially the capacity for civilization and intellectual achievement. This is called ***biological determinism*** (Jurmain et al., 2014, p. 390).

Yet biological race is truly only "skin deep," as over a half century of scientific research has shown. Advances in modern evolutionary theory produced startling new discoveries. We now know that much of human biological variation is invisible to the human eye. Equally important, the most significant genetic variations, with major biological and health consequences, are not visible "racial" traits, but literally lie beneath our skins, inside our bodies.

Perhaps the most significant finding for our purposes is that virtually none of this invisible but biologically significant human variability is racial. That is, knowing one's U.S. racial category—knowing whether one's ancestors are from Africa, Asia, Europe, or the Americas—will tell you little about the kind of biological variability that can save—or cost you—your life!

This chapter reviews human biological variability of the "invisible" type. For science-oriented or other interested readers, we begin with an accessible overview of some basics of human biological variability, genetics, and DNA. Although a bit technical, we feel it is useful background material. However, readers can skip one or more of these initial sections and still understand the remainder of the chapter. The chapter also provides links to Web-based resources for exploring genetics in more depth.

CONCEPTUAL BACKGROUND

Human Biological Variation: Some Basics

Human biological variation is all around us, as we saw in chapter 1. But the new forms of biological variation that scientists are discovering are those less visible to the human eye.

Historically, the study of human biological variation focused on external and visible physical traits. This is not surprising. We are a visually oriented species and, as we shall see in part II, there is some evidence we are predisposed to notice body and facial features.

Some internal traits, like blood or saliva, can also be seen. However, these substances look pretty much the same to the human eye. It took the invention of the microscope, the emergence of modern genetics, and more recent technological advances in understanding DNA, for us to fully comprehend the human biological variability that we cannot see.

We now know that visible traits, such as hair color or lip shape, are manifestations of more complex biological processes and substances. These processes can be studied at multiple levels, from the level of the cell to the individual, to populations, to species. At the cellular level, the field of molecular genetics focuses on *DNA* and the production of biological structures (cells, tissues, etc.). Scientists are beginning to *directly* identify the genes associated with particular traits, whether a visible trait like skin color or something less visible, like the components of our blood.

But we are also discovering how much diversity exists in each individual, to the point that we can use DNA samples for identifying, with a high level of accuracy, a specific person. Not all of this variability has biological significance. It is, however, a marker of our unique developmental histories and of our ancestry, as individuals, populations, and a species. DNA, then, provides a window into the evolution of our species, into the historical relationships among populations, and into the evolutionary processes which produce human biological variation at the population level (see chapter 4).

But let's return to our exploration of invisible human biological variability. Most of us have heard of genes and understand that some variable physical traits, like eye shape, come from genetic variability. Actually, our culture tends to attribute to biology a lot of things that aren't genetically rooted, as in comments like "It's all in our genes."

Biological variability, whether at the individual, population, or species level exists, most fundamentally, at the level of our DNA. However, the relationship between DNA, genes, and human traits is far more complex than we used to think.

WHAT IS DNA?[1]

DNA, short for deoxyribonucleic acid, is a large molecule which provides the genetic information or "code" for biological structures along with the "means" to translate this code (Relethford, 2013, p. 34). It is the fundamental "building block" of living organisms, and, specifically, of cells. In some sense, we are just a gigantic aggregate of cells. We start out at as a cell—a fused egg-sperm cell—which gradually multiplies, forming collections of cells, eventually tissues, organs, and our entire bodies. An adult human body may have as many as one trillion cells (Jurmain et al., 2014, p. 50). We are constantly making new cells, throughout our entire lives, often simply replacing old ones. This is how organisms grow and heal injured tissues, transmit genetic material over time, and produce offspring.

DNA carries the genetic information that cells need to replicate themselves and produce the proteins that are the major constituents of body tissues.[2] DNA is also responsible for the functioning and regulation of cells, tissues, and organs. DNA, then, is the "basis of life" because it directs all cellular activities and provides the information necessary for "building, operating, and repairing organisms" (Relethford, 2013, p. 34).[3]

The structure of DNA is often described as a ladder, or more accurately, a twisted ladder. DNA is made up of two chains or "strands" of smaller units called "nucleotides," creating the so-called double helix structure. Two molecules constitute the "sides" of the ladder. The "rung" of the ladder is made up of a pair of bonded chemicals. Ladder "rungs" can come from four different chemicals (A, T, G, C) but can occur only in specific combinations (A with T, G with C). So AT is one rung; GC is another rung. These are the so-called base pairs.

This ladder is enormously long, with an estimated three billion base pairs or rungs (Jurmain et al., 2014, p. 57). It is the groups or "sequences" of base pairs, of different lengths and arrangements, that is, the segments of the ladder *rather than individual base pairs*, that are genetically significant and the source of human biological traits—and human biological variation. The phrase "sequencing the human genome" refers to the identification of all the ladder segments, or sequences of base pairs found in humans. And an individual's genome consists of their unique version of the entire twisted ladder of DNA.

With so many base pairs, numerous combinations are possible. It's like language. Every language consists of a rather small set of basic sounds. By repeating and combining these sounds into different sequences of varying

length, we can produce a nearly infinite number of words, phrases, conversa-
tional streams. Using writing, we can produce sentences, paragraphs, chapters—indeed, entire books! All out of fewer than twenty-five basic sounds.
DNA works similarly, generating different combinations and permutations,
segments of the ladder called DNA sequences.

Continuing the language analogy, we recognize that not all collections of
sounds are meaningful. Babies and infants can produce fascinating sound
clusters . . . but they are not yet words. To a child growing up in a Tsotsil-
speaking community, English initially appears to be meaningless clusters of
sounds. Similarly, not all our DNA is biologically, functionally significant.

DNA: The Substance of Heredity

The ability of DNA to replicate itself makes it responsible for the transmission of genetic information to the next generation. There are two kinds of
cells: somatic cells and gametes, our reproductive, or "sex" cells. We inherit
our DNA from each of our parents through the DNA contained in the sex
cells (the egg and the sperm).

Every cell contains DNA. Virtually all DNA lies within the nucleus of the
cell. A tiny portion is found in structures called "mitochondria" that lie
within the gel-like cytoplasm that surrounds the cell nucleus.[4] This so-called
mitochondrial DNA (mtDNA) has become famous because of its use in
tracing the ancestry of our species and for investigating relationships between human populations and among individuals (see chapter 4). Females
are the sole transmitters of mtDNA to the next generation.[5] During fertilization, only the nucleus ('head") of the sperm enters and fuses with the egg
cell. So the mitochondrial DNA of the father is not transmitted to the fertilized egg. The female egg cell, however, retains both nuclear and mtDNA, so
all the mtDNA in the fertilized egg comes from the mother (Jurmain et al.,
2014, p. 92).

SO WHAT IS A GENE?

Just as a word is a *meaningful* sequence of sounds, some DNA sequences
constitute biologically meaningful units. These are known as ***genes***. So, at a
basic level, we can think of genes as biologically meaningful sequences of
base pairs. Like language, however, genetic units, that is, genes, and genetic
processes, are far more complicated than originally envisioned.

Recent genetic research has both produced insights and introduced new
complexity into our understanding of genes. For decades, genes were con-
ceptualized as a discrete segment of DNA, each gene "coding for" (containing the information for making) a specific protein. Yet while there are about
21,000 human genes, we are able to make at least 90,000 proteins (Jurmain et

al., 2014, p. 57). So clearly there is no one-to-one relationship between a particular gene and a particular protein, much less between a single gene and a human trait, like skin color, or blood type.[6]

Apparently only some parts of the "gene," that is, the DNA sequence of base pairs, are active. These portions, called "exons," can make more than one protein. Other noncoding pieces of the DNA sequence, called "introns," are often "snipped out" in the process of DNA replication. This allows the "exons" to combine in new ways, generating a new DNA coding sequence. This is one way 21,000 genes can produce so many more proteins!

The other major revision is the old notion that "it's all in our genes." Our genes, that is, protein-coding DNA segments, constitute only about 2 percent of human DNA. Yet until recently, this was considered virtually the only functional, or biologically meaningful, DNA. Indeed, the rest was sometimes called "junk" DNA. Now we know that DNA contains codes for making RNA[7] and other DNA nucleotides (Jurmain et al., 2014, p. 57). And the *crucial* DNA may not be the protein-coding genes. It appears to lie within the so-called noncoding DNA, in segments that control the expression of other genes. These "regulatory" genes can switch DNA segments on or off, can enhance or diminish a gene's expression, and play fundamental roles in cellular function and embryological development (Jurmain et al., 2014, p. 58).[8] There are thousands of such regulatory genes.

Other parts of this "noncoding" DNA may also have biological significance, such as the TEs (transposable elements), sometimes called "jumping genes." These segments can make thousands of copies which can then scatter, inserting themselves ("jumping") at various points in the DNA molecule or genome, including within genes—that is, coding sequences, creating a new sequence. They can be a source of genetic variability . . . and mutations. Some are linked to various forms of cancer (cf. Jurmain et al., 2014, p. 59).[9] They also regulate gene activity, including developmental processes.

Beyond this, almost half of the noncoding DNA is made up of segments that simply repeat themselves over and over and over again. They vary in length and other features but are generically called CNVs for "copy number variants" (see Jurmain et al., 2014, p. 59). They provide an additional source of genetic variation, which is useful, but can also cause disorders. CNVs are also what help to make each of us unique. Some CNVs can be inherited and used to trace family relationships.[10]

Finally, there are millions of SNPs, single nucleotide polymorphisms, or "point mutations," involving a change in one DNA base pair. While some are located in the "genetic" sequences of our DNA, the vast majority are in the remainder of our DNA. They are a wonderful source of information on human populations, and ancestry, as we shall see in chapter 4.

Current research, then, views genes as only a small piece of a larger and more complex process of cellular development and functioning.[11] We are not simply our "genes." The expression of all human traits, visible or invisible, may rest on our nongenes, on the other parts of our DNA, the noncoding DNA. "Thus when we examine any trait, we must look not only at the genes traditionally associated with it but also at the DNA sequences that regulate it. Indeed, it's looking more and more like genes don't really do much by themselves; they just follow orders, and if the orders vary, their effects will also vary" (Jurmain et al., 2014, p. 91).

This "beyond genes" emphasis is reflected in the emergence of a new field, "epigenetics," which focuses on processes and mechanisms underlying gene expression. And just as scientists use the term ***genome*** to describe the totality of genetic material, the *epigenome* refers to the totality of *instructions* that determine gene expression (Jurmain et al., 2014, p. 450). Epigenetics challenges simplistic "nature" versus "nurture" models of how we become who we are. We are not *either* our genes *or* our environment. The two are inextricably intertwined (cf. Schmidt, 2013). Environmental influences, originating both in and outside the organism, can apparently change the way genes are expressed without altering the genes themselves. This is one reason identical twins aren't identical, especially as they age. They may have the same "hardware" (genes) but not the same "software that provides instructions to the unfolding genotype" (Jurmain et al., 2014, p. 450).

Continuing the language analogy, then, we can say that DNA segments, like clusters of sounds, may have different functions. Some sound sequences we call words have conceptual meanings, refer to things or ideas, such as a "gene" codes for a particular trait. Other sound clusters have more subtle, grammatical functions, such as turning a singular into a plural (gene, genes). Still other sounds regulate the meanings of larger clusters of words, such as a change in pitch at the end of a statement that, in English, turns it into a question ("it tastes good?").

Going farther, it seems to be that the biological "meanings" of DNA sequences, like sound sequences, are dependent on the context or "neighborhood" in which they are embedded. Whether a "bank" is a "riverbank" or a "bank" holding our savings (or sperm) depends on the linguistic context. The context helps us to predict the meaning or function of the word.

These same principles apply to how genes work. All somatic (i.e., body) cells, whether nerve cells or bone cells, have the same DNA; yet they behave differently. Clearly the broader "context" is crucial. Noncoding DNA is part of the context, the environment that determines whether potential biological meaning is or is not expressed. The "neighborhood" of the cell, tissue, or organism also influences the "meaning" of our genes. Research on breast cancer, for example, has found that the same breast cancer cell, in a different tissue context, in a different body, behaves differently. It is context that determines the "expression" of the potentially cancerous cell.

At the biological level, then, even for illnesses with a genetic component, the statement "it's all in our genes" is simply inaccurate. The body, down to the cellular level, is part of the environment that interacts with and influences gene expression. And that environment is in constant flux. We are not static creatures, biologically fixed at conception, much less at birth. We are interacting with, being altered by our environment, throughout life. Moreover, environmental factors outside the body, including those associated with race and racism, such as nutritional deprivation, exposure to pollutants, or psychological stress, alter our body environment. Race and racism can not only affect our DNA in our lifetime; the effects can sometimes be transmitted over generations (See Smedley & Smedley, 2012, chapter 15).

GENES, CHROMOSOMES, AND HUMAN VARIATION

Modern genetics (and epigenetics) complicates the story of how both visible and less visible human traits emerge. Yet some basic processes remain unchanged, including those related to heredity and human variation.

Our DNA is still tightly coiled up into structures called ***chromosomes***.[12] And most genes can be identified at a particular location on the chromosomes. The location or site of that gene is called a ***locus***. Some traits are associated with one gene, others with many genes.

Humans have a total of forty-six chromosomes. Chromosomes occur in "pairs": each of the pair carries the DNA and genetic information for the same traits.[13] The first twenty-two pairs are the "autosomes"; the twenty-third pair is called the sex-determining chromosomes. Genetically normal females have a matched pair, the so-called XX pair. Normal males, however, have only one X chromosome plus a Y chromosome.[14] There is virtually no genetic material on the Y chromosome. Instead, the twenty-third chromosome's genetic material lies mainly on the X chromosome.[15]

Most body ("somatic") cells carry all twenty-three pairs of chromosomes—forty-six chromosomes. However, our sex cells (the sperm or egg cells) have only one of each pair of chromosomes, that is, only twenty-three chromosomes. When the sperm and egg cells fuse during conception, the fertilized egg will end up with one set (twenty-three) of chromosomes from each parent's sex cell, hence, all *forty-six* chromosomes. It is the fusion of these two different sex cells, one from the mother and one from the father, that produces the "fertilized egg" or conceptus,[16] that eventually becomes a human baby.

It is important to emphasize that although we inherit two *different* "sets" of the twenty-three chromosomes, one from each parent, we will end up with the full complement of human DNA and genes. There are two exceptions. The first is the genetic material in the mtDNA that comes only from our mother. The second is the bit of genetic material on the Y chromosome that we inherit from our father, and then only if we are a male.

DNA, Genes, and Human Variation

So . . . where does human variation come into all of this? There are different kinds of variation. There is variation at the individual level, at the level of a person's DNA. Because we inherit DNA from both our parents, each somewhat unique, our own DNA will be a new combination. Other processes produce additional variability in both our genes and in the noncoding portions of our DNA.[17] This is why we are all somewhat different (see chapter 4).

But we are primarily concerned here with human genetic variation, that if expressed, produces diverse forms of genetic traits, whether these are visible or not. These varieties can be found among individuals and sometimes, among different populations.

A major source of genetic variability comes from slightly different forms of genes. Most genes (about 75 percent) are exactly the same in all humans, that is, there is only one form (Relethford, 2013). But some come in one, two, or several slightly different versions. These alternative versions of a gene are called *alleles*. In more technical terms, alleles represent very slight differences in the sequence of DNA base pairs that constitute a gene. This is one reason we are not simply genetic clones of our parents.

The Genes We Have versus the Traits Expressed in Our Phenotype

Genes that have alternative versions are called *polymorphisms*, literally many forms.[18] Since we inherit genes from both parents, we could end up with two or more different versions of a trait. An example is hitchhiker's thumb, mentioned in chapter 1. Perhaps only one parent has the gene version for this variation. The other has the "normal" version.

What happens when we inherit two versions of a trait partially depends on other factors. Not all forms of the gene (alleles) have the same impact. They can be *dominant*, *recessive*, or *codominant*. Dominant versions always have an impact on the phenotype, that is are expressed, even if paired with a different form of the gene. Their presence masks or suppresses the alternative form. So if hitchhiker's thumb is a dominant trait, you will have it even if you inherited that form only from your mother.

Recessive alleles usually express themselves only if they are paired with another recessive allele. An exception is the recessive alleles found on the sex chromosomes. Virtually all of these are on the X chromosome. Because males have only one X chromosome, any allele, even a recessive one, will normally be expressed. This is the case for hemophilia, the well-known condition that prevents blood clotting.

If hitchhiker's thumb is recessive, both of your parents must have it for you to have the trait. Some alleles are "codominant" . . . both forms are partially expressed in the trait. If that is the case for hitchhiker's thumb, you could end up with an intermediate form—a thumb that bends slightly.[19]

The existence of dominant and recessive forms of genes means that much of human genetic variability never expresses itself. It exists in the human cells, is part of our DNA, our genetic inheritance, and can be transmitted to our offspring. It constitutes what is called our *genotype*, our total genetic endowment, all the genetic material we have as individuals.

What gets expressed, that is in the form of detectable biological traits, both visible and invisible, represents a smaller portion of our genotype. Scientists call this our *phenotype*. The phenotype also reflects the interaction of biology with environmental and developmental factors. Once again, our genes are only a small part of who we become, physically.

Nevertheless, even if it isn't expressed in our phenotype, all of our genetic material will remain in our cells and can be transmitted to our offspring. A recessive genetic form could be passed on to several generations before it actually expresses itself. Female carriers of the hemophilia allele may eventually transmit it to their sons. Or for non-sex-linked genes, both parents may eventually carry the recessive version. This is why some traits, like albinism, the inability to produce the pigment that colors all human skin, may show up suddenly in the offspring of families whose parents, grandparents, and even great-grandparents were normal.

Some traits, especially those used to illustrate inheritance, like our ABO blood type, are simple traits, referred to as Mendelian traits. That is, they are controlled by one gene and their phenotypic expression, A, B, O, or AB is discrete, rather than continuous (see chapter 1). There is no intermediate form between each of the four blood types. You have A, B, O, or both A and B.

Most traits, especially those that are historically racially marked, like skin color, or other visible traits, like height, are much more complex. They may be "polygenic," that is, linked to several genes, with multiple genotypes and a continuous array of phenotypes. One gene can also affect several characteristics ("pleiotropy"), such as the gene that controls the production of some enzymes related to pigmentation. Skin color is a trait that reflects both types of genes.

Eye color also illustrates these genetic processes. Eye color is more complex than we used to think. It is controlled by at least two or three genes, including some of the ones that influence skin color. As we would expect, eyes, or rather the irises of eyes, come in a wide continuum of shades. One gene, called OCA2, located on chromosome 15, seems to be most important for the development of blue eyes (Jurmain et al., 2014, p. 91). It affects the pigmentation of the iris of the eye, and mutations in this gene produce a form of albinism. One study found that the OCA2 gene accounted for almost three-quarters of the eye color variation among Europeans. In some populations, like in Denmark or Turkey, nearly 100 percent of blue-eyed people had a specific variation of this gene. Apparently other regulatory genes are also involved in the expression of blue eyes (Jurmain et al., 2014, p. 2013, p. 91).[20]

This example may help explain apparent eye color anomalies in some families. If an ancestor, even generations ago, had blue eyes, this OCA2 gene could be transmitted to subsequent generations. If this gene or any of the regulatory genes were *recessive* genes, it might take generations before both parents had the same complement of genes to produce a blue-eyed child. This has, however, happened in African American families whose ancestors, especially during slavery, may have included some Northwestern Europeans (see chapter 9).

Eye color also illustrates the complexity of the pathways through which a phenotypic visible trait might emerge. The disorder phenylketonuria (PKU) is linked to an autosomal chromosome recessive gene. Individuals with two alleles for this gene have the disorder and don't produce an enzyme involved in conversion of an important amino acid. This has several impacts including diminished production of the pigment melanin. As a result, affected people tend to have blue eyes and lighter skin and hair color (Jurmain et al., 2014, p. 93).

MUTATION AND OTHER SOURCES OF GENETIC VARIABILITY

How did different gene forms or alleles come about? Something caused a change in the DNA base pairs at a particular location or locus. This is technically called a **mutation**. Contrary to popular usage, mutations can be positive, negative, or neutral (see chapter 3). In fact, mutations are the only source of totally new variability in the human gene pool. Of course, for a mutation to persist, it must be transmitted to the next generation. Therefore, the only mutations with potential longer-term lives, that affect populations or have evolutionary consequences, are those which occur in the sex cells and can be inherited. Other mutations may produce human variation . . . but it dies when that individual dies.

For the most part, mutation rates that affect functional traits are quite low, partially because of complex regulatory processes that occur during cell replication. As a result, most mutations probably have little genetic impact, and those that do may take thousands of years to show up. But mutation rates for some noncoding DNA segments can be quite high, as we saw earlier, and may have unrecognized functional impacts as well as constitute a future "reservoir" of genetic variation.

Other processes, some during cell development and fertilization, alter or reshuffle the DNA in our genes. Environmental and developmental factors, too, have enormous impacts, especially on the nongenetic, noncoding DNA portions involved in gene expression and regulation. Over time, these and other processes to be discussed in chapter 3 have produced the biological variability we see in the human species.

Genetic Variation at the Population Level

The biological variability we have been describing occurs primarily at the individual level. Nevertheless, human biological variability *can* be examined at the population level. We can ask whether some DNA sequences or, more commonly, whether some forms of a *genetic trait* occur more often in some populations than others. Of course, this is not a new idea. The U.S. concept of race drew upon and manipulated a few visible population differences (see part II). But, as we saw in chapter 1, there are many other visible traits to explore.

But why should we focus on visible, easily observable traits? Some of the most biologically and functionally significant differences between populations occur at the less visible level, literally beneath our skins, in our bodies, in our DNA. Once we go more than "skin deep," we find an enormous number, indeed thousands, of genetically variable traits. They range from some that are virtually neutral to others that can have severe health consequences.

New approaches, especially statistics, allow us to more precisely describe these differences. For example, every population is genetically variable. But we can calculate the frequency of alternative forms of a genetic trait within each population. We can then compare different populations.[21] This produces intriguing results, as we'll see when we look at blood groups. Modern DNA analysis goes even deeper, analyzing actual DNA sequences, rather than phenotypic expressions of underlying genes, in order to make comparisons across individuals and populations.

Invisible but Detectable Genetic Traits: Neutral and Not

Many genetic variations are perfectly viable alternatives of a trait. There is no particular advantage of having one form or another. For example, some genes control our ability to taste certain substances. One chemical, PTC, has a bitter test to tasters; but not all people are able to detect this taste. The taster form is dominant—so if you inherit it from just one parent you will probably be able to taste the bitterness of PTC, although this is to some extent dependent on environmental factors, like your diet. (Relethford, 2013, p. 47) But being a taster or nontaster has virtually no impact on your life.

Lactase: The Gene for Tolerating Cow's Milk

Another relatively neutral variation, at least in some environments, is the gene that affects your ability to tolerate milk. All infant mammals have the ability to digest lactose (a complex sugar in milk). They produce an enzyme, *lactase*, which helps break down lactose into a more digestible form. However, as humans grow older, they stop producing lactase and lose their ability to digest milk. In most populations, this occurs before adolescence and as early as five years of age. People who are lactose intolerant may experience diarrhea and severe intestinal cramps if they drink milk, especially cow's milk, although they may be able to tolerate other milk products, such as cheese. Some people, however, apparently possess an alternative form (one dominant allele), which enables them to produce lactase throughout their life. Even as adults, they can digest milk without experiencing any problems.

Another genetically related trait is gluten intolerance, or difficulty digesting the *gluten* that is found in some cereal grains, like wheat or related grains. Lactose intolerance does not present a problem except if you are in a culture with a heavy emphasis on milk products, such as the United States. Reduced gluten tolerance, likewise, becomes a problem only in a grain-dependent diet. As we shall see shortly, these genetically linked intolerances are more common in populations where cereal grains and milk products are relatively recent parts of the diet. In some cases, these new diets are the result of emergency foreign food assistance from milk-grain-diet-heavy countries (Jurmain et al., 2014, p. 447).

Genetic Defects

At the opposite extreme of relatively neutral variations are genetic defects. As scientists find out more about molecular biology, they are focusing on genetic sources of diseases that have severe consequences. One example is Tay-Sachs, a disease that can cause blindness, mental retardation, and destruction of the central nervous system. Children with it rarely live more than a few years. Huntington disease, involving progressive degeneration of the nervous system, is another example along with hemophilia, a disorder that interferes with the blood's normal ability to clot, cystic fibrosis, and albinism. Some of these diseases may be associated with particular populations, as we will see later.

Even when genetic forms have potentially harmful impacts, they may emerge only in particular environments. Hypertension and diabetes are partially linked to variant forms of several genes. However, both diseases have a significant environmental component.

BLOOD: A MAJOR SITE OF INVISIBLE GENETIC VARIABILITY

Blood is essential to human life. Without blood we simply cannot survive. We can, literally, bleed to death. Although human blood looks, at least at the surface level, pretty much the same across the human landscape, it exemplifies human biological variability.

Our red blood cells are particularly rich sources of human genetic variation. On their surfaces are numerous molecules, each controlled by a different genetic system. Many of the genes involved have alternative forms (or alleles). There are at least ten different blood systems that show significant variations among humans. Interestingly, some of this variability is linked to particular populations and geographic regions. Yet none of these blood group variations correlate with conventional racial groupings. There are no racial blood types. Rather, blood types cross-cut races.

Most of us are familiar with the ABO system, especially if we have ever donated (or received) blood. But in addition, there is the Duffy system, the MN system, the Diego system, the Rh system, the Kell system, and several variant forms of hemoglobin, the proteins in red blood cells. Human blood varies in other ways. G-6-PD is an enzyme in red blood cells, and it has different forms.

Our white blood cells also vary in the substances that are found on their surfaces. The HLA system (human leukocyte antigen) is particularly important because it plays a role in the body's autoimmune response. HLA antigens help the body recognize and respond to potentially dangerous particles or substances. Like most complex biological traits, it involves multiple genes (loci), each with anywhere from a few to more than 100 different alleles (Relethford, 2013, p. 311). The result is an enormous array of possible genetic combinations.

HLA is considered "by far the most polymorphic genetic system known in humans" (Jurmain et al., 2014, p. 397). Different HLA profiles occur within the same population, small community, or even the same family. This variability can complicate organ transplants. An incompatible match between donor and recipient can cause the body to reject the organ. On the other hand, some HLA forms apparently confer resistance to infectious diseases such as malaria, hepatatis B, and perhaps HIV. Other data (on infertile males) suggest links between some HLA gene variations and decreased sperm production and function (Jurmain et al., 2014, pp. 397–8).

The ABO Blood System

The ABO blood system is an excellent example of invisible but significant human genetic variation. ABO blood type is inherited, normally stable throughout life, and is not modified by environmental factors, as is skin color. The ABO system is governed by a single gene that has three forms or alleles—A, B, and O. These forms produce different antigens, substances found on the surface of blood cells. If only antigen A is present, the blood type is A. If only B is present, the blood type is B; if both are present the blood type is AB, and when neither antigen is present, the blood type is O.

Normally, it makes no difference whether one is blood type A, B, O, or AB. Problems only arise when blood types mix, as in a blood transfusion. The most common reaction is the clumping of blood cells. This happens when a "foreign" antigen stimulates the production of antibodies that attack the antigen. For blood type O (no antigen), any blood type containing A or B antigens will cause problems. Those with A antigen will have problems with B antigen and vice versa.

This potential clash of blood types is not a trivial issue. Many of us contribute blood to relatives, friends, or to blood banks. And we may some-day need someone else's blood. Blood type becomes significant in these circumstances. Those with blood type O are universal donors—they carry no antigen. But only type AB can receive all blood types (A, B, O, AB). Other-wise, you must receive blood compatible with your own blood type. This is why many people carry a card showing their blood type. It could save their life!

In this example of human variation, like so many others, one's blood type has, or should have, a greater natural *biological* impact than one's skin color. Finding someone with the same blood type when you need a blood transfu-sion is far more important than finding someone with the same racial classifi-cation . . . except in a racist society. It is ironic that for many years some Euro-Americans refused to accept blood transfusions or organ transplants from (or provide them to) African Americans. Yet race does not predict blood type, whether ABO or HLA or any of the other blood systems. Such old ideas illustrate the power of the racial worldview and ignorance to trump science. [22]

Rh Blood Group

Another potentially problematic variation, especially for pregnant women, is the Rh or Rhesus Blood Group system. This is a system of three linked genes (linked means they are inherited together). One gene has two different forms, one dominant and one recessive. Individuals with at least one dominant form are called Rh positive; those with both recessive forms are called Rh negative.

Problems arise when the alternative forms come into contact. During pregnancy, if the mother has Rh negative blood, the mother's antibodies can harm or even destroy her conceptus if it is Rh positive. If you are thinking of having a child, knowing your partner's Rh status is far more important, healthwise, than knowing your partner's racial classification. And knowing your partner's race will not tell you anything about your partner's Rh type.

CCR5

Another recently discovered but potentially important human biological variation is the CCR5 gene. One unusual mutant version of this gene (CCR5-insert triangle 32), found primarily among some Europeans, is linked to resistance to the HIV (human immunodeficiency virus) that causes AIDS. Individuals with both alleles (homozygous) are nearly completely resistant to HIV-1. Scientists suggest it probably represents an immunity to some set of infectious diseases existing in the past among these populations (see chapter 3).

Harmful Alternative Forms, but Relatively High Frequencies in Some Populations

Some of the biggest puzzles in human biological variation are harmful alleles that occur in high frequency among some populations and in some environmental contexts. One form of the gene is definitely the normal form while the other has harmful effects. The so-called sickle cell gene is one such example.

Hemoglobin is one of the proteins in red blood cells. Its function is to carry oxygen to body tissues. The most famous hemoglobin is hemoglobin B (referring to a *beta* chain), which is controlled by one gene. The normal form of this gene is A. But there are several other forms, including S, C, and E.

The S form (Hb^S) is known as the "sickle cell allele." This form alters the blood cells making them less round and more "sickled," thereby reducing their oxygen-carrying capacity. This can cause severe anemia and death. In the United States, the sickle cell gene is more common among African Americans than other populations—but it is not a "racial" gene. The genetic variation that causes it is also found in parts of South Asia, southern Europe, and the Middle East. And it is found in only some areas of Africa. Anthropologists have puzzled over how such a harmful genetic form survived over time in human populations.

Population-Level Variations

Other variant forms of genetic traits are also distributed differently around
the world. The CCR5 gene, just described, may be linked to particular geographic populations, the result of mutations that arose centuries ago. The
HIV-resistant form has so far been found primarily in Northeastern Europeans.

Years ago, anthropologists and geneticists began tracking the frequency
of ABO blood types in different human populations. At that time, virtually
the only data came from drawing actual blood samples. Getting good data
was both difficult and time consuming, especially from small-scale, remote
populations. And the data was on phenotypes, expressed forms of the trait,
rather than the underlying genes or DNA sequences.

Nevertheless, these early cross-cultural studies showed interesting patterns across human populations. Among all humans, type O was the most
common form (62.5 percent) while type A (22 percent) and Type B (16
percent) were far less frequent (Fuentes, 2012, p. 312). Yet these frequencies
are not the same in all populations. And while most populations have people
with each blood type (A, O, B, AB), there are some exceptions. Native South
and North American populations have very high frequencies of type O blood
and in some native South American Indians, according to Jurmain et al., it
can reach 100 percent (2014, p. 397). You might start to think type O blood
is a racial trait. Yet we find the same high frequencies of O among Native
Australians in the northern and some coastal regions. On the other hand,
some Eastern European and Central Asian populations have higher frequencies of type A or type B blood than the average for all humans. So race and
blood type are not the same thing (cf. http://anthro.palomar.edu/vary/vary_3.
htm).[23]

At this point, with the help of new DNA analyses, scientists are trying to
understand the origins of these patterns. Some suggest infectious diseases,
such as malaria, smallpox, tuberculosis, syphilis, bubonic plague, cholera, or
leprosy, may have played a role in the emergence of particular blood types
(see chapter 3).

What is clear, however, is that this significant area of human biological
variability is not correlated with race. Indeed, there is enormous variability
within continents and even among smaller populations.

Other blood substances have intriguing geographic distributions, such as
the HLA system on the white blood cells, mentioned earlier. Because it is
such a complex genetic system, there is significant variation across populations. Within Europe, some groups like the Lapps, Sardinians, and Basques
have different HLA profiles from other European populations. Other regions,
such as Australia and New Guinea, show high frequencies of many diverse
HLA forms.

The sickle cell form of hemoglobin B, mentioned earlier, is particularly well known and well studied. And it is an example of a potentially very harmful genetic variation that for some reason managed to persist in certain populations. As we shall see in chapter 3, scientists have found that these distributions reflect environmental factors and the workings of natural selection on genetic variability.

Milk and gluten intolerance also varies among populations in different regions of the world, as noted earlier. (For some actual figures, see http://anthro.palomar.edu/adapt/adapt_5.htm.) Tay-Sachs is more frequent among European (Ashkenazi) Jews than among other populations. And the data on CCR5, described earlier, suggests some links to particular populations.

Population differences in these invisible traits interest anthropologists and geneticists. Exploring their roots provides us with insights into the mechanisms through which human variation emerges. We will treat these mechanisms in chapter 3.

Clearly, genetic variability is all around us, affecting our lives, impacting our health, and in some cases, threatening our lives. And human populations do differ genetically, in ways that can have health and other impacts. But these populations are not traditional racial groupings. They are much smaller units, for one thing.

Second, while the frequency of different forms of a trait may vary between populations, there is enormous variability *within* each population. Overgeneralizing about populations can put people at risk, health-wise. For example, the assumption that sickle cell anemia is an African American disease has led to the failure of U.S. doctors to diagnose cases among Southern European Americans. Similarly, the association of cystic fibrosis with only Europeans has resulted in its being virtually ignored in countries like Japan.[24]

Another problem, mentioned in chapter 1, is that the traits do not covary. Populations with trait 1 do not necessarily have trait 2. That is, different populations show different patterns depending on the trait examined. There is no set of traits that would produce the same racial groupings. Most important, there is no evidence that the genetic variability described here is linked to other visible, external racial markers, such as skin color, hair texture, or nose or eye shape.

To summarize, much of human biological diversity is not easily observable and occurs at the cellular or molecular level. For the DNA that does affect human traits, much of that DNA never gets expressed, and simply exists in our genotype. Even those traits that are expressed, and identifiable, such as our ABO blood type, or HLA status, are not visible to the human eye. If we wanted to classify people by genetic traits, it would probably make more sense to form races based on ABO blood type, HLA forms, or lactose intolerance than to base them on skin color or nose shape. Knowing someone's ABO blood type or G-6-PD status, and whether they can tolerate certain antimalarial drugs, even their lactase-enzyme status, is more biologically significant than knowing their skin color. At least in a nonracist world!

KEY CONCEPTUAL POINTS

- U.S. race emphasizes a few external, visible biological traits, whereas much of human genetic variation is invisible and often more significant medically.
- Populations differ genetically, but these populations do not correspond to major racial groupings. And even within such populations, there is enormous variability.
- Most human genetic variability is at the individual level; much of it is not expressed, but is part of one's total genetic makeup and can be transmitted to offspring.
- Additional variability exists at the human *genome* and epigenomic level, that is, all of an individual's DNA. At least some of this DNA plays a crucial directive role in the process of gene expression and regulation, although it is still not clearly understood. Other parts of our DNA are an important source of individual variation, and when inherited, a marker of common ancestry. This DNA also can serve as a reservoir of biological diversity.

KEY TERMS (ITALICIZED AND BOLDED IN TEXT)[25]

allele
lactase
gluten
biological determinism
locus
chromosomes
mitochondrial DNA (mtDNA)
codominant alleles
mutation
DNA, coding and noncoding
phenotype
dominant allele
polymorphism
genes
recessive allele
genome
trait (genetic trait)
genotype

ACTIVITIES

General Overview: These activities link to other chapters in part I. They are appropriate for secondary school or introductory college level courses in the social sciences, biology, and health and for adults of all backgrounds.

Overall Objective: Participants will understand that significant invisible genetic variation, such as in the ABO blood system and intolerance for milk, does not covary with race.

Other Information: Participants will need to find out their ABO blood type and, if possible, their tolerance for milk and their Rh status (from family members, health providers, blood bank, etc.). Milk intolerance may have to be inferred. Similar information about other family members is also useful.

Illustrative ABO blood type maps and lactose tolerance data are available online (see earlier text references).

Activity Plan 1: Sorting by Blood Type and Race

Procedure:

Step 1. Participants find out their own blood type (A, B, AB, O). Class can calculate frequencies of each blood type for the class.

Step 2. Designate sections of the room by blood type: A, B, AB, O. Participants go to the section of the room for their blood type.

Step 3. Each blood type group records the "races" of group members, using self-identification and the 2010 Census categories. Multiracial participants can select more than one racial category. (See table 2.1 for a list of U.S. Census classifications.)

Step 4. Summarize results in matrix or table (see table 2.1). Is there any pattern? Can you predict blood group from knowing race?

Step 5. Optional. Participants compare their geographic ancestry (even if many generations ago) to maps showing geographic distribution of blood types. Discuss findings. Brainstorm what factors (historical, environmental) might be linked to geographic variations in blood types. See chapters 3 and 4 for follow-up discussions.

Activity Plan 2: Lactose Intolerance and Race

Follow the same procedures as for ABO blood groups but have participants divide themselves based on their difficulty digesting milk. Participants can discuss how they might infer whether they are lactose tolerant or intolerant. A third category ("not sure") can be created for participants.

Table 2.1.

Blood Type by Race	Euro-American	African American	Asian American	Native American	Hawaiian or Pacific Islander	Latino or Hispanic	Other
A							
B							
AB							
O							
Total							

Activity Plan 3: Rh Factor

Repeat the same procedures if enough participants can identify their Rh status.

ADDITIONAL ACTIVITY IDEAS

Activity Idea 1. Explore Human Blood

Explore human blood in more depth at http://anthro.palomar.edu/blood/default.htm.

Also play the **Blood Typing Game** at: http://www.nobelprize.org/educational/medicine/bloodtypinggame/index.html. For a chart showing percentages of ABO blood types in the United States, and donor and receiver blood types, see http://www.pbs.org/race/000_About/002_02_b-godeeper.htm. All these sites provide additional weblinks.

Activity Idea 2. Explore Human Genome Research Further

Visit the National Human Genome Research Institute website: http://www.genome.gov/. See the excellent Educators section, including curriculum for teaching about Human variation for ninth- through twelfth-graders. Does not focus on race but illustrates human genetic variation http://www.genome.gov/Educators/. Explore the Human Genome Project website at http://web.ornl.gov/sci/techresources/Human_Genome/home.shtml.

Activity Idea 3. Explore Genetics and Human Heredity

For a brief, three-and-a-half-minute online visual introduction to DNA, see the RACE project link: http://www.understandingrace.org/humvar/molecular/index.html. Or explore the tutorials at the Palomar College website at http://anthro-.palomar.edu/tutorials/physical.htm. Also check out the

"Science Primer" for more in-depth exploration: http://www.ncbi.nlm.nih.
gov/About/primer/genetics_genome.html.

Activity Idea 4. Exploring My Ancestry

Participants collect ABO blood type and milk tolerance data on family members (immediate, more distant) as part of a broader exploration of their ancestral roots (see part II and the Mukhopadhyay website). Be as precise as possible about ancestral roots, for example, India (West Bengal state), Italy (Sicily), China (Shanghai area), West Africa (Northern Nigeria). Do blood type and milk tolerance of relatives match worldwide geographic regional patterns? If not, why not? (e.g., see migration patterns of ancestors, variability within regions and populations, adoption).

Activity Idea 5. Who Should Be Tested for Sickle Cell in the United States?

Discuss the controversy over the NCUAA's decision to test all its athletes for the sickle cell trait. Read the two articles at http://www.cbssports.com/collegefootball/story/11903550 and http://www.npr.org/blogs/health/2012/01/26/145923225/blood-doctors-call-foul-on-ncaas-screening-for-sickle-cell. Should all athletes in all sports be tested? What racial assumptions are being made? Are they valid? Read about a U.S. Euro-American of Italian ancestry whose doctors failed for ten years to diagnose his sickle cell anemia because they assume it was only an "African American" disease. See Goodman et al., 2012, p. 119).

NOTES

1. Readers who wish to omit these more technical parts can go directly to the section heading "Genetic Variation at the Population Level."
2. "Some proteins are structural components of tissues. But enzymes and hormones are also proteins. Other proteins bind to nuclear DNA, regulating its activity. Proteins are made up of smaller molecules, the 20 amino acids. They combine to produce at least 90,000 different proteins" (Jurmain et al., 2014, p. 54–55).
3. Because DNA is a molecule, genetic studies now often occur at the "molecular level" as in "molecular genetics."
4. A fairly penetrable membrane surrounds the entire cell.
5. The entire field of genetics/genomics is in flux, with new research constantly altering prior understandings. This is true for mtDNA being solely transmitted through women. It is impossible for even specialists to "keep up" with the field.
6. New understandings of genes and DNA have put the language associated with genetics in a state of disarray. The term "gene" is in flux, sometimes referring only to protein-coding segments, the traditional "genes"; other times to the noncoding DNA segments, such as the "regulatory genes." Jurmain et al., 2014, admit it is confusing even to specialists.
7. RNA is ribonucleic acid. Recall that DNA produces complementary strands of messenger RNA, which transports genetic instructions to transfer RNA. Introns often get snipped out

of the mDNA; but not always the same ones. For an excellent video that describes some of these processes see http://sciencenetlinks.com/tools/protein-synthesis/.

8. Within one regulatory group, called "homeobox genes," are Hox genes. These are responsible for the early segmenting of embryonic tissues; they also direct the development of individual segments into different parts, such as the head or limbs (Jurmain et al., 2014, p. 59).

9. These include ALUs, mentioned later, a class of transposable elements (TEs) apparently found only in primates.

10. They can be used to trace paternity, including among nonhuman primates, like chimpanzees. This is useful in research on primate mating patterns.

11. See the ENCODE Project Consortium, 2012. According to Jurmain et al., 2014, p. 74, this project found that "as much as 80 percent of the human genome is involved in some form of biochemical function," although not all may be important. Results also suggest that at least 9 percent of the human genome has "regulatory functions." Ibid.

12. Actually, it only coils up as the cell begins to replicate/divide.

13. They are not "identical" if only because they may have different alleles for the same traits. For example, the ninth chromosome has a locus that determines which ABO blood type one will have. Jurmain et al., 2014, p. 65.

14. The reference to "normal" females and males recognizes there are many exceptions, such as an XXY type, which occur in fairly high frequencies. Abnormal numbers of nonsex chromosomes (autosomes) usually are fatal. A rare exception is three copies of chromosome 21, linked to what is commonly called Down syndrome (also trisomy 21) with rates of 1/1000 births. But other XY-related anomalies are also remarkably high. See Jurmain et al., 2014, p. 65–71.

15. The complexity of male sex chromosome function is fascinating, given that females have two Xs and males only one. The X chromosome influences several nonsex, traits and apparently one is enough. Essentially, the "basic plan" is female. Much of the genetic material on the second X chromosome in females is normally suppressed. The Y chromosome carries little genetic material but is primarily sex-determining. It is only the presence of one gene on the Y chromosome that initiates the differentiation of the embryo along male lines. This may be why it's quite possible to live without a Y chromosome. Jurmain et al., 2014, note, of course, that "roughly half of all people do" (p. 71).

16. "Conceptus" is the human organism from fertilized egg to birth (Hyde & DeLamater, 2014).

17. There is "crossover" of alleles during meiosis plus all the deletions, insertions, repetitions, and SNP alterations previously described. Even identical twins are not identical given the processes of change that occur through every cell duplication from the time of fertilization as well as other environmental influences on cells.

18. Technically, a gene is defined as polymorphic only when the alternative form (allele) reaches a certain frequency in some population. Polymorphic genes, then, are always relative to a population.

19. Previously undetected impacts of recessive alleles are now being identified through more advanced biochemical techniques. Some traits, like hitchhiker's thumbs, and perhaps tongue-rolling, are examples.

20. Northern European populations and their descendants are apparently the only ones with significant numbers of blue-eyed people and show more variability in eye color than any other human population. See Jurmain et al., 2014.

21. Although the term "phenotype" is sometimes defined as "observable" traits, a better definition is "expressed" or "detectable" traits, particularly since many cannot be easily observed, such as blood components. The phenotype is not just influenced by genes but also by developmental and environmental factors, such as nutrition and chemicals. So the phenotype is a complex product of biology-environmental interactions.

22. Another variant is G-6-PD, glucose-6-phosphate deficiency. The lack of this enzyme (G=6=PD) in red blood cells can produce severe anemia, especially in the presence of some foods like fava beans; or some drugs, like the antimalarial drug primaquin. (Jurmain et al., 2014, p. 88).

23. While these Palomar College maps have probably been superseded by more recent DNA data, they still illustrate the varied but complex and nonracial distribution of blood types in the world.

24. For a compelling account, see Twin Triumph Productions, 2011, *The Power of Two* (video).

25. For a more detailed glossary, see the Palomar College website tutorials on physical anthropology previously cited.

Chapter Three

If Not Race, How Do We Explain Biological Differences?

Scientists may have abandoned the concept of biological races, but human biological variation is real and can have both beneficial and life-threatening impacts. Differences in skin color, facial traits, and body form—which our culture has taught us to notice—are also real even though biological race isn't. So . . . how are we to explain group differences, especially ones that we have historically associated with race?

CONCEPTUAL BACKGROUND

This chapter introduces new and more useful scientific approaches to human biological variation. In the past, the scientific emphasis was on classification, on trying to divide the human species into subgroups, into static, homogeneous types or categories, usually called races. And the focus was on a few visible traits. Today, scientists are trying to understand human biological variation, using modern genetic and evolutionary theory. The Human Genome Project and other advances in technology now allow us to go far beyond the previous study of detectable, phenotypic traits. Current research is focusing on the molecular level, on the variation in our DNA (see chapter 2).

But current evolutionary approaches also offer a framework for understanding more traditional, visible, racialized traits like skin color, as well less visible blood traits, like the *sickle cell trait,* once thought to be racial.

GENETICS, EVOLUTIONARY THEORY, AND HUMAN BIOLOGICAL VARIATION

We can talk about human biological variation at the level of the individual, at the population level, and at the species level. We saw in chapter 2 that there is enormous individual biological variation—we are all somewhat unique, even identical twins—although much of our individuality may lie in the noncoding portions of our DNA and not all of it is biologically significant.

At the species level, compared to other species, we are relatively genetically homogeneous. Only a small percentage of human genes have variant forms, and these are fairly insignificant. *Macroevolution*, that is, major genetic changes in our species, occurred thousands of years ago, and we have long been one species, with one basic gene pool. On the other hand, *microevolution*, smaller changes within our species, at the level of populations, is an ongoing process and may have even accelerated over time.

It is population-level differences that have historically preoccupied North Americans, particularly for a few visible traits, like skin color. This chapter focuses on populations, especially on new ways of understanding differences between traditional U.S. "racial" groups whose ancestral populations inhabited different geographic regions of the world.

EVOLUTIONARY FORCES IN THE EMERGENCE OF VISIBLE HUMAN VARIATION[1]

Today's modern evolutionary approach to human population variability combines Charles Darwin's idea of *evolution* as change in species forms over time through natural selection with current understandings of genetics and molecular biology From this perspective, microevolution is about the transformation in the genetic structures of populations over time, over multiple generations. Population genetics focuses not just on individual genotypes or phenotypes (expressed genetic traits) but on patterns within an entire population. This is why microevolution is generally defined as changes in *allele frequencies* in a *population*, such as in the proportions of A, B, AB, or O blood types.

The concept of a "population" can be difficult to define. At core, we are tracking genetic changes over generations. So the crucial population is the mating population, that is, a group of people who mate and reproduce. Some definitions add sharing a common geographic area. People are usually more likely to mate and reproduce with those nearby. But that is not always the case, as both the history of African slavery and 20th-century U.S. laws prohibiting racial "miscegenation" (intermating) prove. And sometimes the "mating" population may not be the "breeding population," that is, the group of people who reproduce and transmit their genes to the next generation.[2]

Another problem is setting the "cutoff" level for a "breeding population." Few human populations, even in the past, mated totally or even 90 percent within their own community. Those that did were exceptionally isolated and perhaps atypical in other ways. In most cases, defining "the community of individuals where mates are *usually* found" (Jurmain et al., 2014, p. 503) is somewhat arbitrary, and is often guided by the goals of researchers. This can make it difficult to interpret the results of scientific studies.

Despite these complexities, population genetics research has virtually revolutionized our understanding of race and human biological variation. The modern evolutionary synthesis explains evolutionary change, whether macro or micro, in terms of four basic processes: mutation, gene flow, genetic drift, and natural selection. These are sometimes called the *four forces of evolution*. Mutation is the only source of new genetic variability in a species. But at the population level, genetic variation can occur through two other processes: gene flow or genetic drift.

Briefly stated, *gene flow* involves the exchange of genes between populations through intermating. As noted above, this has been a constant feature of human life and is the reason we are still one species. *Genetic drift*, another evolutionary force, alters the genetics of small populations through random factors—that is, not through natural selection.

Natural selection is the fourth evolutionary force and one of the most powerful sources of human variation. Natural selection, acting on mutations, can help explain some visible traits that have figured prominently in U.S. racial theories.

Mutation

In chapter 2, we introduced the concept of a genetic *mutation*. In popular culture, mutation evokes an image of a monster or a freak of nature. But mutation is the only way that *new* genetic forms are introduced into the human gene pool, and mutations can be transmitted to the next generation through our sex cells. Mutations in nongenetic portions of our DNA may accumulate and provide a "reservoir" of genetic variation in populations that can be available for future "selection." Genetic variability within a species, and the ability of populations to respond to environmental changes, therefore depends heavily on mutations.

Mutations are introduced into a population at the individual level, but evolution occurs at the population level. Every individual mutation transmitted to the next generation will cause a minor shift in the gene pool or genetic structure of that population. Mutation rates, however, are usually quite low and by themselves, normally take many generations to have a discernible genetic impact on a population.[3]

Scientists do not even define a trait as ***polymorphic***, that is, having alternative forms, unless the occurrence is fairly high, usually greater than .01 or 1:100 people in the population (Relethford, 2013, p. 68). But when levels are this high, scientists assume that something other than mutation is occurring, that other evolutionary forces are at work.

Mutations by themselves, then, do not cause most evolutionary change. Contemporary population genetic variability, whether in skin color, body size, or ABO blood type, cannot simply be explained by mutation. We must look at other processes that affect mutations. One of the most important is natural selection.

What Is Natural Selection?

Natural selection works on existing genetic variation, selecting for genetic forms that contribute to the reproductive success of individuals with that particular version of a trait. What do we mean by "selecting for"? Mutations, or variable forms (alleles) of a trait, aren't really selected for in any conscious way. Rather, some mutations enable carriers to survive or reproduce at higher rates than others. As a result, some individuals are more likely to transmit their genetic version of a trait to the next generation. These genetic forms will be passed on to the next generation at higher rates than other forms. Over time, these changes will alter the population. So natural selection describes this process of differential reproduction.

For example, if a new mutation of the ABO blood system causes an individual to die before the age of eight, then that mutation will be quickly eliminated (or "selected against"). If another form enables its carriers to resist major killer diseases, they will be more likely to have descendants who carry the same version (allele) of the gene. Over time, these transmission differences accumulate and alter the genetic structure of the population. In short, the frequencies of alternative forms of the trait change over time—and the population becomes somewhat genetically distinct from other populations.

What causes some genetic mutations, some alternative forms of a trait, to do "better" than others? More technically, what makes some versions of a trait more adaptive than others? And some individuals more reproductively fit than others? The concepts of ***adaptation*** and ***fitness*** are always relative to a particular ***environment***. What makes a skin color, nose shape, or blood type adaptive depends on the context. As we shall see, some blood traits, like the sickle cell gene, might confer a selective advantage in some environments.

Natural selection, then, is a mechanism through which, over time, genetic forms better adapted to a particular environment predominate over less-adaptive alternatives. More technically, natural selection changes the frequencies of alleles in a population over time through variations in the survival and reproductive success of individuals with different genotypes. This is what we mean when we say that evolution has resulted from natural selection. Adaptation, ***reproductive fitness***, different survival rates of alternative forms, natural selection, and evolution are linked concepts and processes.

Individuals with reproductively advantageous genetically transmitted traits are by definition more reproductively fit. But survival of the fittest, contrary to popular usage, says nothing about what kinds of genetic traits will be more or less fit. "Fit" at one point in time or in one environment may become "unfit" in another time and place. Fitness simply measures the reproductive impact of a specific trait or, put simply, the relative number of viable offspring different genetic forms produce.

NATURAL SELECTION AND HUMAN VARIATION: SKIN COLOR, NOSE SHAPE, AND BODY TYPE

Natural selection provides a framework for understanding some human biological population differences that we have historically called racial. In the 1960s, biological anthropologists and geneticists started using the ***clinal approach*** to describe and explain human biological variation. As you will recall from chapter 1, this approach looks at single traits, one at a time, and maps their distribution across geographic space.

Frank Livingstone, C. Loring Brace, and others discovered some intriguing relationships between genetic traits and climatic and other environmental factors. Their work stimulated investigation into the role of natural selection in the evolution of many visible human differences. One of the most significant is skin color.

Human Skin Color

> Throughout the world, human skin color has evolved to be dark enough to prevent sunlight from destroying the nutrient folate but light enough to foster the production of vitamin D. (Jablonski & Chaplin, 2005, p. 169)

Human skin color is a very complex trait, controlled by several genes. Skin color comes mainly from a pigment called ***melanin*** produced by cells in the skin (called melanocytes). Variations in melanin produce different shades of skin, from deeper to more lightly pigmented skin. Hemoglobin, which gives blood cells their red color, also affects skin color, particularly in people without much melanin (Relethford, 2013). The red in their blood tends to show through the surface of the skin, giving their skin a pinkish color.[4] Just as black, brown, yellow, or red doesn't really describe the skin color of the major races, neither does white. We all produce melanin, we are all to some degree "colored."

Skin color illustrates the short-term ability of the body to adjust to local conditions without genetic change. Tanning, like sweating and shivering, is an adaptive, physiological capacity. All melanin-producing humans can tan, and tanning is the body's short-term physical response to stressful environmental conditions.

But the population differences we see in skin color today are mainly the result of evolutionary processes that took place over time, thousands of years ago. Skin color represents a striking example of how natural selection produces human variability in response to different geographic and climatic conditions.

Mapping the Distribution of Skin Color

Human skin color, as C. Loring Brace and others showed, is distributed in a clinal fashion. To illustrate, if we could go back in time, perhaps 1,000 years ago, or at least before slavery and other major population movements, and walk from the tip of Africa to Northern Europe, we would see people with differing amounts of melanin in their skin. Travel from the tip of Southern India to the farthest northern state of Kashmir, and you would find a similar gradient of skin colors from heavy production to relatively little melanin. The reverse spectrum would appear going from Northern Korea through China, to Vietnam, to Indonesia. Even if you were to simply walk from Equatorial Africa to the southern tip of Africa, looking at the indigenous populations, you would see skin shades going from darker to lighter.[5]

Why is this the case? All humans produce melanin because it is adaptive for them to do so, whether short term or as an evolutionary adaptation. Human skin is a "built-in sunscreen" (Jablonski & Chaplin, 2005, p. 169). It reduces our exposure to ultraviolet (UV) radiation. We synthesize melanin in response to UV radiation. Physiologically, too much UV can destroy skin cells, but humans produce different amounts of melanin.

Anthropologists today attribute the differences we see in skin color primarily to past adaptations of populations to varying levels of ultraviolet radiation in different microclimates. Scientists believe it would take thousands of years for related mutations to accumulate through natural selection. So these adaptations occurred long ago, as populations inhabited different geographic regions of the world.

Maps of the geographic distribution of skin color show the close relationship between skin color and latitude or distance from the equator. Populations with more melanin tend to be closer to the equator. Those with less melanin tend to be farther from the equator, closer to the North and South Poles. For maps, see http://anthro.palomar.edu/adapt/adapt_4.htm or select

Physical Appearance at http://www.pbs.org/race/004_HumanDiversity/004_ 01-explore.htm. Also see range of groups at http://www.understandingrace. org/humvar/race_humvar.html.

Scientists have long known that ultraviolet radiation is strongest at the equator and diminishes as one moves away from the equator. Because too much UV destroys the skin cells and can cause skin cancer, the first theory was that darker skin evolved to protect against UV rays. And as human populations settled areas farther from the equator, selection pressures relaxed. Lighter skin allowed for sufficient vitamin D production where UV rays were less strong.

Current explanations are a bit more complex and go back farther in time (Jablonski & Chaplin, 2005; Jablonski, 2012). They start with humans, some one to two million years ago, living in Africa near the equator. And they begin with hair loss. Anthropologists point out that only humans are relatively hairless and have varied skin colors. In contrast, our closest primate ancestors, the chimpanzees, are covered with hair and have pale skin, although it is darker in hairless areas exposed to the sun.

Anthropologists believe we humans lost our hair as we became upright, gained larger brains, and traveled longer distances. Humans had to stay cool and protect the brain from overheating. The evolution of sweat glands on the surface of our body, along with the loss of most hair, was our adaptive solution to the heat and cooling problem.

Once we lost our hair, we faced the new problem of protecting our skin from the damaging effects of sunlight, particularly UV rays. This is where melanin, the natural sunscreen, comes into play. Melanin filters the harmful effects of UV in two ways: through absorbing UV rays and through neutralizing harmful chemicals that form in the skin after UV radiation damage (Jablonski & Chaplin, 2005).[6] Scientists reasoned that through natural selection, humans with higher concentrations of melanin came to predominate.

Melanin apparently does more than protect us against skin cancer. Jablonski and her colleagues pointed out that skin cancer tends to occur in older people, after they have stopped reproducing. Hence, skin cancer would have little evolutionary impact. That is, skin cancer wouldn't affect reproductive rates of differently shaded individuals. Instead, new evidence suggests that darker skin color evolved to protect against the effects of UV on the essential B vitamin called folate.

The Role of Folate

Folate (from folic acid, a necessary nutrient) plays an important role in reproduction. Folate is essential for the synthesis of DNA in dividing cells. Folate deficiency in pregnant women can cause severe birth defects in offspring. It also can severely depress sperm production in males.

Exposure to UV radiation apparently breaks down folate, causing folate deficiencies. Current explanations for the evolution of darker skin, then, focus on the adaptive benefits of melanin for preventing the breakdown of folate. In short, scientists believe that individuals with darker skin, in UV-intense environments, located close to the equator, were protected against folate deficiency and hence had higher reproductive rates than paler-skinned folks.

Anthropologists know that modern humans evolved in Africa around 150,000 to 200,000 years ago. So they assume modern humans, through natural selection, evolved dark skin as an adaptation to the high levels of UV radiation near the equator (see chapter 4).

But how did variation in human skin color shades arise? Modern humans migrated to other parts of Africa and then out of Africa. As humans moved away from the equator, their exposure to UV radiation decreased. This reduced selective pressures for darker skin and allowed individuals with less melanin to survive and reproduce. But that was not the only factor. UV rays have some positive benefit.

The Significance of Vitamin D

Scientists have long recognized the importance of vitamin D for human well-being, especially the ability of our intestines to absorb calcium. This allows for normal development of the skeleton as well as the immune system. Vitamin D deficiency can produce rickets and other skeletal diseases. Among these are deformed pelvises, which can interfere with successful childbirth. Thus vitamin D deficiency can affect both the fertility of women and the survival of their offspring. Vitamin D has other significant functions, including in regulating more than 1,000 different genes, may provide some protection against cancer, and can help produce natural antibiotics in the body (Jurmain et al., 2014, p. 418).

UV rays do have some positive effect. They initiate the formation of vitamin D in the skin. Indeed, the sun has been the major source of vitamin D throughout human history, although some foods (such as cod liver oil) provide significant amounts of vitamin D.[7] In tropical areas, while darker skin blocks UV, the amount and intensity of sunlight guarantees that enough UV will penetrate the skin to provide sufficient amounts of vitamin D.

But what happens when humans start migrating to areas farther from the equator, where the sunlight is less intense and even virtually absent during some seasons? As humans moved away from the equator, the risks of UV decreased and the risks of vitamin D deficiency increased. By the time one reaches Finland or Siberia, the UV problem is far outstripped by the vitamin D factor (at least thousands of years ago).[8]

Scientific evidence now suggests selection for lighter skin (reduced melanin production) allowed sufficient UV to penetrate the skin to stimulate vitamin D production. In short, lighter skin was more adaptive in latitudes farther from the equator. As we go farther from the equator, ancestral populations exhibit lower levels of melanin.

Natural selection, environmental factors (specifically, UV exposure), and the need for both folate and vitamin D have combined to produce the variations in skin color we see today. But as Jablonski and others point out, these selective forces operated long ago, and over thousands of years.

Meanwhile, for the past several hundred—even thousands—of years, people have been migrating (or have been forcibly taken) to geographical regions that are quite different climatically from their ancestral homes. Africans from equatorial regions like Nigeria or Kenya sometimes ended up in areas like Boston, Hawaii, or Canada, and the British ended up in India, West Africa, and the Caribbean. As a result, humans increasingly relied on cultural rather than biological adaptations, such as clothing, shelter, and dietary changes or dietary supplements to handle the UV and vitamin D issues.

The people of the West Bank of the Red Sea, in East Africa, have inhabited the region for approximately 6,000 years. They have darkly pigmented skin and long, thin bodies with long limbs. Both are excellent adaptations for high-intensity UV and heat/cooling issues (see the next section). In contrast, more recent migrant populations on the Eastern Bank of the Red Sea, the Arabian Peninsula, have been in the region for scarcely 2,000 years. They have primarily adapted through cultural means—clothing that fully protects the body and tents that provide portable shade (Jablonski & Chaplin, 2005).

More recent population shifts, partially due to colonialism and globalization, have affected some disease rates. Skin cancer is more common among lighter-skinned people of European ancestry living in areas of prolonged sunlight than among other native populations. And diseases associated with vitamin D deficiency (e.g., rickets, pelvic deformities) are found among darker-skinned people residing in northerly-latitude nations such as England, Sweden, and the northern United States.

Skin color, then, is an example of human genetic adaptation. But cultural adaptation can trump biology. We can add vitamin D to food to augment natural sources. And we can wear clothing, visors, hats, or apply sunscreen to protect against harmful UV rays.[9]

The evolution of skin color provides further ammunition for the argument that race is biological fiction. Skin color is an example of real human biological variation. But contemporary variations in skin color are a continuum, reflect ancestral geographic roots, and do not necessarily correlate with conventional racial categories. Skin color and race are two different phenomena! Skin color, like many other physical variations, can be explained as an adaptation to the environment through natural selection. Race is a cultural invention and a misreading of biology.

BODY SIZE AND SHAPE AS PARTIAL
RESPONSES TO CLIMATIC CONDITIONS

Other visible human differences, like body shape, may in part reflect natural selection. Humans, like other animals, have evolved biological mechanisms for dealing with climate-related stresses, including heat stress and heat loss. Humans evolved in East Africa, in hot climates, traveled widely, and needed cooling mechanisms for survival. The capacity to reduce excess heat through sweating is a major biological capacity all humans possess.

This capacity was enhanced, in the evolution of modern humans, through the loss of virtually all body hair and an increase in the number of sweat glands throughout our skin. This distribution of sweat glands provides our evaporative cooling system, essential for human survival.

Can sweating and other heat-related needs help explain variations in human body types? Scientists seem to think so. All human populations have about the same average number of sweat glands, approximately 1.6 million (Jurmain et al., 2014, p. 420). However, human groups vary in size and body shape. Body heat is mainly lost at the surface. Thus the more surface, the more heat loss.

Smaller bodies (of similar shape) have more surface area relative to volume than do larger bodies. Hence smaller bodies lose heat more rapidly; larger bodies conserve heat longer.

But body shape, including limbs, also affects surface area and heat loss or retention. The more linear the body, the greater the surface area. The rounder the body, the less surface area. Applied to humans, this means that people with relatively longer torsos, heads, arms, legs, fingers, and thus more surface area, relative to overall body size, lose heat rapidly. And those with rounder bodies are better at conserving heat.

When scientists examine the distribution of human body size and shape by climatic zones, they find a general correspondence. Populations in hot and more humid tropical and subtropical areas tend, on average, to be smaller and/or have more elongated body shapes and the longer limbs (including fingers and toes) that tend to be adaptive in these climates. This applies to taller groups like the Maasai of Kenya as well as to the shorter populations of Sri Lanka or South India.

Populations living in colder, drier climates tend, on average, to have a greater body mass, with a larger trunk relative to arms and legs, and rounder shapes. Once again, these overall body shapes can be found among taller populations, like Swedes, as well as shorter populations, like native Alaskans. For illustrations, see http://www.pbs.org/race/004_HumanDiversity/004_01-explore.htm.

These relationships are far from perfect. There is a lot of variability within the native populations of each region. And some human populations don't conform to these generalizations. There is increasing evidence that both genetic and non-climate-related environmental factors, like nutrition and health care, influence body size and shape. This may help explain why some Central African forest-dwelling populations, such as Aka and Efe (so-called pygmies) are short-limbed (cf. Relethford, 2013, p. 383).

Head size and shape also show similar adaptations to climatic conditions. Cranial measurements were one basis for racial classifications in 19th- and 20th-century racial science. More recent research shows that head shape corresponds to climate. Groups living in colder climates tend to have wider skulls (relative to length) than populations residing in hotter climates (Relethford, 2013, p. 384).

Nose size and shape may also reflect historical adaptations to local climate. Human noses are quite variable, including within Africa, despite racial stereotypes. But studies have found a relationship between the average nasal index (see chapter 1) and both average temperature and average humidity. Populations in colder and drier climates tend to have narrower noses (lower nasal index) than those in hotter and more humid climates. Apparently, high, narrow noses are better at warming air than lower, wider noses and are adaptive in cold climates. But humidity also affects nasal index. High, narrower noses are adaptive in drier climates because they have more internal surface area that can be used to moisten air (Relethford, 2013, pp. 385–6). Populations in drier or colder climates, whether in East Africa or the Caucasus, tend to have longer, narrow noses.

Population differences in human body size and shape, then, may partially reflect past adaptations, through natural selection, to different climatic zones. For maps of nose shape and head size, see Physical Appearance at http://www.pbs.org/race/004_HumanDiversity/004_01-explore.htm.

On the other hand, there is a lot of variability within and between populations living in the same climatic zones. Environmental factors, including diet and nutrition, as well as cultural factors, like social status and ideal body types, can have a major impact on body size and perhaps even shape. The human adult body is quite plastic. An individual's weight can go from 140 to 210 pounds by moving from one country to another or switching from a physically active to sedentary job.

Most important, none of these differences produce population groupings that correspond to traditional North American macroracial groups. Looking at head shape, Germans, Koreans, Central African forest dwellers, and Greenland Eskimos have very similar head shapes (average cephalic index of

77 to 83 percent; Relethford, 2013, p. 384). Yet they are from different races, using conventional U.S. racial categories.

As for body shape, we find relatively long-limbed individuals in Kenya, Afghanistan, South India, and Greece. We find large and small bodies, and wide and narrow noses in Europe, Asia, and Africa. Of course these are huge, diverse continental regions. But even smaller regions, such as South Asia, are quite variable.

OTHER ENVIRONMENTAL ADAPTATIONS: HIGH ALTITUDES

Human populations not only live in a variety of climates. They also live at different elevations. An estimated twenty-five million people may currently reside at altitudes above 10,000 feet (Jurmain et al., 2014, p. 425). High altitudes pose multiple stresses, including cold, dryness due to low humidity and high wind, more intense solar radiation, and a limited nutritional base. Most important is the problem of oxygen "starvation" or "hypoxia," due to less concentrated oxygen at high altitudes. (See Relethford, 2013, p. 389; Jurmain et al., 2014, p. 391, 425–27). Scientists have conducted research to understand how these populations survive. Studies, not surprisingly, have focused on the native inhabitants of the Andes in South America (Quechua) and of the Himalayas, especially Tibetans.

Comparisons of these populations with low-altitude natives reveal several mechanisms at work. Some are species-wide short-term adaptations, such as increases in metabolism, heart rates, and production of red blood cells, that we all experience at high altitudes. Others are nongenetic developmental responses, such as increases in lung capacity and chest dimensions found among long-term migrants to high-altitude areas, especially those who came as children. Like the tanning response to sun, this reflects, within certain genetic limits, our biological plasticity, the capacity of our bodies to respond to environmental changes.

High-altitude native populations also acclimate during growth and development in ways that have longer-term impacts. They grow and mature at somewhat slower rates, develop greater heart and lung capacity, and may have more efficient ways for getting oxygen from the blood to body tissues and organs. Some of these adaptations may have a genetic basis and result from natural selection over time.

For example, glucose (blood sugar) is crucial in producing energy for the heart and brain. Scientists have found that both highland Tibetans and the Quechua natives of high-altitude regions of the Peruvian Andes "burn glucose in a way that permits more efficient oxygen use" (Jurmain et al., 2014, p. 426). This suggests natural selection over time for certain mutations that occurred in the mtDNA, the DNA that directs how cells process glucose.

The best evidence comes from Tibetan populations who have lived in permanent settlements above 12,000 feet for at least 10,000 years, perhaps up to 25,000 years. In addition to the adaptations already described, Tibetan women do not seem to experience the negative reproductive effects seen in some other groups living at high altitudes, such as reported for Colorado in the United States. Instead, infant birth weights are similar to lowland Tibetans and higher than recent Chinese migrants to Tibet. "This fact may be the result of alterations in maternal blood flow to the uterus during pregnancy" (Jurmain et al., 2014, p. 426).

Recent DNA analyses provide more direct evidence of natural selection for genetic forms that are adaptive in high altitudes. According to Jurmain et al., 90 percent of highland Tibetans have a mutant form of the gene EPASI, which is involved in the production of red blood cells. This mutation apparently prevents the normal body's increased production of red blood cells in high altitudes. Without this mutation, Tibetans' "thick blood" would put them at risk for blood clots, heart attacks, and stroke (Jurmain et al., 2014, p. 426–27).

This is only one of many potential genetic adaptations among high-altitude populations. Quechua Andes groups apparently do not have this mutation and have developed other mechanisms for survival. These remain to be identified. But high-altitude adaptations further illustrate the complexity of the processes through which human biological variation emerges. And how little of it is "racial" as that term is conventionally used in North America.

NATURAL SELECTION, HUMAN BIOLOGICAL DIVERSITY, AND CULTURE: THE SICKLE CELL VARIATION

Modern evolutionary approaches to human variation also help us understand genetic forms that have been associated with race in the past and that appear to have negative impacts. Earlier we described the hemoglobin sickle cell found throughout West Africa, the Mediterranean, and South Africa. Anthropologists, like Frank Livingston, wanted to understand how such a harmful trait, causing severe blood anemia, could become common in so many populations. He hypothesized that it had some selective advantage.

Livingston examined the geographic distribution of the sickle cell trait around the world. He noticed that the sickle cell gene tended to be found in areas known to have malaria. Was there perhaps a relationship? Looking next at the geographic distribution of malaria, he found a striking correspondence between higher frequencies of the sickle cell (S allele) and higher incidence of a particular form of malaria.

Subsequent research has established that having only one (vs. two) copies of the mutant sickle cell conveys an adaptive advantage. That is, individuals who inherit the sickle cell version from both parents are at a distinct health disadvantage and often die from anemia. But those with one normal and one sickle cell allele have increased resistance to malaria without being anemic. Their survival rates are highest. They die neither of malaria nor sickle cell anemia.

In malarial environments, then, the evidence suggests strong selective pressure for this particular mutation. This has produced the high frequencies of the mutant sickle cell that we see in certain populations. Maps showing the *malaria–sickle-cell relationship* can be found at http://anthro.palomar.edu/synthetic/synth_4.htm and at http://www.understandingrace.org/humvar/sickle_01.html. See also the Mukherji lab website, http://www.sicklecellinfo.net/who_suffers.htm. Scientists continue to explore selective advantages in malarial environments of other blood type variants.

Infectious diseases, in general, such as tuberculosis (TB), smallpox, influenza, cholera, and bubonic plague, have been extremely important in human history, and until the 20th century were probably the major cause of human deaths. Even in the 20th century, the influenza pandemic of 1918 killed an estimated twenty million people (Jurmain et al., 2014, p. 432). And today, in developing countries, infectious diseases may account for as many as half of all deaths. In the 1990s, an estimated thirty million people died from TB; and malaria causes one million deaths a year (ibid.).

As in the case of the sickle cell gene and malaria, described earlier, culture plays a major role in the rise and spread of infectious disease. Cultural inventions and changes, especially the rise of domesticated agriculture and plants, higher population densities, housing and sanitation practices, and urban life seem to have produced new environmental stresses, conditions that allowed such diseases to thrive and spread.

Infectious disease is now recognized as a major agent of natural selection in human populations, affecting the frequencies of genes that influence the response of the immune system. But with the exception of malaria, research is just beginning to document the ways in which human populations have responded, both genetically and culturally, to these diseases.

The HIV virus, leading to AIDS, is a relatively recent infectious disease but with major consequences. As of 2010, nearly thirty-five million people were infected worldwide and more than twenty-five million had died, mainly in developing countries (Jurmain et al., 2014, p. 428). Recent research has identified a genetic mutation, a form of the CCR5 gene, mentioned in chapter 2, that affects the functioning of receptor cites on certain immune cells (e.g., T4 cells). As a result, the virus has difficulty entering the cell. Individuals with both mutant alleles may be completely resistant to several types of HIV infections; those with just one allele may suffer milder forms of the disease (Jurmain et al., 2014, p. 429).[10]

This gene variation appears mainly in people of European descent (as high as 10 percent), and not among Japanese or West African populations, at least in the research reported by Jurmain et al. (2014, p. 429). One study found a 2 percent frequency of the allele among African Americans, perhaps the result of gene flow from contact with European Americans.

Scientists do not believe the selective agent is HIV; rather, they think the presence of the mutant allele reflects past selection for some pathogen or disease agent that required the same receptor site. Bubonic plague in the 14th century was considered a possibility until the same allele was found in German skeletal remains dating back nearly 3,000 years (Relethford, 2013, p. 368).

Smallpox, a major killer disease in 18th-century Europe, is another possible candidate. Smallpox may also have selected against Europeans with type A blood during that same period, affecting the current ABO genetic structure of this population.[11] Regardless, the CCR5 case illustrates how a trait selected for in one disease can be adaptive in another context at some other point in time.

NATURAL SELECTION, POPULATION VARIATIONS, AND CULTURE: OTHER EXAMPLES

Even relatively mild genetic-linked health problems that vary across populations may have partial roots in natural selection and culture-related environmental changes. One example, introduced in chapter 2, is the persistence of the enzyme *lactase*, allowing *milk digestion* into adulthood.[12] Once again, we have an example of biocultural evolution, of the interaction of cultural and biological change. Recent DNA analyses support older hypotheses that the ability to tolerate milk into adulthood is linked to the emergence of agricultural systems heavily dependent on dairy farming. These systems probably first arose in the "Near East," in the regions of present-day Iraq, Iran, Northern Pakistan, Central Asia, earliest sites of cattle-sheep-goats-dependent economies. This cattle-dairy complex spread to Central and Northern Europe, especially Scandinavia. In such a cultural environment, there was probably strong selective pressure for the mutant gene allowing continued lactase production (and thus milk tolerance) through adulthood.

Data on the frequencies of lactase persistence in populations around the world support this theory, according to Tishkoff et al., 2007 (cited by Jurmain, 2014, p. 409). Swedes and Danes have the highest lactase frequencies, followed closely by Swiss, all at least 88 percent. Thais, Chinese, Ibos (of Nigeria), Baganda (Uganda), and Asian Americans are at the opposite end of the spectrum. Native Americans are in between.

At first glance, lactase persistence looks suspiciously like a "racial" trait. Yet if we look at populations and cultural context, rather than massive "macroracial" continental groups, we get a different picture. Among the African populations studied, there are two groups that *do* have high frequencies of lactase persistence: the Fulani, of West Africa, and the Tutsi, of East Africa. Both are pastoralists, with a long tradition of cattle herding and milk use in their diets.

Recent DNA evidence also finds a slightly different DNA mutation in East Africa than in Europe, suggesting lactase persistence evolved independently in the two regions. And it may have evolved several times just in East Africa as different populations shifted to this new dietary complex (Jurmain et al., 2014, pp. 409–11).

Not all dairy-reliant populations have evolved in this way. Some may have adapted culturally, by developing milk products, like yogurt and cheese, which contain bacteria that breaks down the lactose.[13] Others perhaps adjusted to experiencing flatulence, as do garlic and onion eaters.

These and other studies clearly demonstrate the lack of correspondence between what we have conventionally called races and biological variation at the population level. Even within the same region of Africa, different populations exhibit different patterns of biological variation.

Equally important, contemporary studies of natural selection on human populations illustrate how profoundly culturally introduced environmental changes have affected current human biological variation and human microevolution. Indeed, most biological anthropologists today talk about human biological variation as a *biocultural* phenomenon. That is, they recognize the powerful interaction between biology and culture in human biological evolution.[14]

The idea of races as stable, biologically distinct human groupings is a fiction, a cultural invention. We have seen several examples of how so-called racial diseases, like sickle cell anemia, lactose intolerance, or even cystic fibrosis, are found in only some populations and that those populations can be in more than one "racial" group. A striking illustration is the case of sickle cell anemia, long considered an African American racial disease. The maps of sickle cell populations show that within Africa, it is found in only some populations. And it is found outside of Africa, in parts of Europe, the Mediterranean area, and South Asia. Once again, there is no correspondence between North American racial groupings and this very significant biological variation.

HUMAN BIOLOGICAL VARIATIONS DUE
TO OTHER EVOLUTIONARY FORCES

How do we explain other biological differences historically associated with race? Scientists are exploring possible selective advantages of different eye shape, hair form, and other variable human population traits. But not everything is due to natural selection. Other evolutionary forces affect the frequencies of traits in populations. And recent DNA analysis suggests these may be extremely important sources of contemporary human population variability.

One is called *genetic drift*. Some genetic forms become more or less frequent in future generations for reasons having nothing to do with their selective or reproductive advantage. Often it is simply statistical "chance." A small group breaks off from a larger group to start a new community. By chance, one version of a genetic trait in the larger population (e.g., type A blood) doesn't appear in the subgroup. This phenomenon may partially explain the virtual absence of type A or B blood among some South American populations (Fuentes, 2012, p. 314).

Genetic drift also describes how a rare form of a trait, even if detrimental, can become relatively common in a small population. One classic example is Tristan da Cunha, an island settled in 1816 by a small group of British settlers. By chance, a member carried a single, rare recessive allele for an eye disease called retinitis pigmentosa. After 100 years of virtual isolation, no gene flow, and inbreeding, the trait had become frequent in the population[15] (Fuentes, 2012, p. 101).

Tay-Sachs disease, mentioned in chapter 2, also illustrates genetic drift. The underlying gene mutation (or one form of it) is commonly found among Jews of Eastern European (Ashkenazi) ancestry. But Cajun populations living in Southern Louisiana also have unusually high frequencies of the same mutation, traceable to a single "founder," an 18th-century French couple. And a third population, French Canadians, apparently acquired a slightly different version of the mutation as descendants of a small-founder, intermarrying population. All these cases illustrate how evolutionary processes, like genetic drift, also interact with cultural factors, human migration patterns, and intragroup mating practices[16] (Jurmain et al., 2014, p. 104).

In the case of genetic drift, then, any changes in population gene frequencies over time are random. Populations may acquire distinctive characteristics, such as red hair, purely by statistical chance. But that doesn't mean that everyone in the population has the trait or that the trait couldn't appear in other populations. Genetic drift may, in combination with other factors, help explain the relatively high frequency of the "epicanthic fold" eyelid form among some, but not all, East Asians and among some other groups, like the San ("Bushmen") of Southern Africa (see chapter 1).

GENE FLOW AND POPULATION VARIATION

Gene flow refers to the exchange of genes between groups. Humans have been on the move for most of our existence as a species. True, we settled down long enough to produce some traits that reflect adaptations to local geographic and environmental conditions. But individually, in small groups, for both brief and longer periods of time, we have been interacting sexually with our close and more distant neighbors. It is this intermating that has produced extensive gene flow between populations.

Our interactions have taken many forms—migration, trade, and, in recent human history, warfare, conquest, slavery, and colonialism. Genghis Khan and his armies conquered the people living in China and in Eastern Europe in the 14th century, spreading their genes along the way, often through force. The Spanish conquistadors mated with native peoples of Latin America and Mexico during the 15th and 16th centuries. Bantu-speaking Africans migrated from West to Southern Africa, undoubtedly mating along the way. Zanzibar, off the coast of Tanzania, was visited by an array of Indian Ocean traders from East Africa, the Southern Arabian Peninsula, and Oman, to the west coast of the Indian subcontinent. Persians, and later, Mughals, invaded and eventually ruled virtually all parts of South Asia. All of these were cultural phenomena . . . but they inevitably left a genetic mark, in some cases, a substantial one.

Slavery in the Americas produced extensive and primarily involuntary mating between African female slaves and their European male masters. The genetic impact can now be traced. Using data on blood groups, as well as DNA markers (mitochondrial DNA and Y-chromosome polymorphisms), scientists have estimated ranges from around 10 to 25 percent European ancestry in African American populations in the United States (cf. Jurmain et al., 2014, p. 97).[17] Most important, these DNA-based studies reveal significant differences in the contributions from paternal and maternal lineages: the European DNA contribution is much higher from paternal lineages and the African contribution much higher from maternal lineages (Relethford, 2013, p. 361; Jackson & Borgelin, 2010, p. 95). This is what we would have expected.

Warfare and conflict in general, especially prior to women's access to contraception and pharmaceutical or other forms of abortion, has been a major source of gene flow, probably more than has generally been acknowledged. And in the 20th century, two world wars, the Korean War, and the war in Vietnam brought U.S. genes into contact with other gene pools. While some of these matings were consensual and even produced GI marriages, others were not, at least not fully. Prostitution by women, widespread around military bases, was often economically driven and marginally "voluntary."

Recent 21st-century examples of women being forced to serve as "sexual slaves" for males, whether through the institution of sex tourism, the international trafficking of young women for prostitution, or as captives taken in warfare zones (Bosnia, Rwanda, Congo), are not a new phenomenon. Japan only recently acknowledged and finally apologized for the "comfort women" (mainly Malaysian and Korean women) who were forced into providing sex for Japanese soldiers in World War II.

The pervasiveness of massive rape in 20th-century military conflicts is only now being fully explored. Clearly, individuals do not have to remain physically in a population for their genes to remain in its gene pool. Once introduced, genes stay even if individual contributors depart.

Despite these examples of coercive mating, human sexual contact has probably been mainly amicable and voluntary, at least for the families involved and most males. This is especially true in small-scale societies, before the rise of so-called civilization, the expansionist state, massive warfare, and significant social-political-economic inequality (see chapter 7). Throughout most of human history, and in most societies, even today, mating between populations has always been a significant strategy for human survival (see chapter 9). Many cultures have traditionally required young people to marry outside their own group. Sometimes the "group" is simply one's own extended family or kinship group, as in the U.S. prohibition against marrying first cousins. But it can also be a larger kinship unit like a clan, a village, a larger community, or even a different linguistic group. Such marriage practices often have social, economic, and political benefits. But "marrying out" also produces gene flow across populations, increasing variability within the local gene pool.

GEOGRAPHY AND GENE FLOW

Recent studies of "genetic distances" between native populations around the world have found an overall correspondence between genetic similarity and geographic location. These studies do not rely on just one trait but utilize multiple physical and genetic traits, including DNA markers, for each population. When possible, researchers try to select traits not strongly affected by natural selection since they are essentially trying to measure common ancestry and gene flow. One study used data on 120 variant traits for forty-two human populations, mainly ones found in the blood. Another used multiple cranial measures and DNA markers.

Results document the multiple influences of history, migration patterns, and proximity on intermating and, eventually, on population genetics. The closer two populations are to each other geographically, the closer they are genetically; the farther apart geographically, the farther their genetic distance (Relethford, 2013, pp. 350–53).

Gene flow, then, is an important force in human population genetics. While it doesn't introduce new genetic material into the species, it does alter the gene pools of specific populations. It produces new combinations and permutations of genetic traits. We can see this today in multiracial and multi-ethnic offspring.

The sickle cell allele, mentioned earlier, may not have been present in the United States prior to the African slave trade. And gene flow, through inter-mating between African Americans and European Americans, is partially responsible for lower sickle cell frequencies among African Americans today compared to contemporary Africans in malarial regions.

Gene flow between populations, in the long run, reduces difference be-tween groups, making them less distinctive, more similar. Indeed, gene flow and intergroup mating have been essential to our species. No human groups were reproductively isolated long enough to develop a genetically distinct path, a unique and distinct species. Gene flow, over time, creates one large gene pool.

CULTURAL FACTORS IN HUMAN EVOLUTION AND HUMAN BIOLOGICAL VARIATION AND RACE

The evolutionary forces we have described in this chapter offer a set of scientific guidelines for understanding human biological variation. Yet these forces do not operate in a cultural vacuum. Indeed, contemporary anthropolo-gists talk about human biological variation as a "biocultural" phenomenon, highlighting the inextricably intertwined relationship between human biolo-gy and culture. Culture has been the primary mode of adaptation for humans, and it has altered us in the process. We have seen how cultural inventions, such as agriculture, dairy farming, cities, and modern war machines, have altered the "environment" within which natural selection and gene flow oper-ate. And . . . altered our bodies, as individuals and in populations. We live in a culturally modified environment; this is the context in which evolutionary processes operate. Culture shapes biological processes.

Evolutionary processes are embedded in a social context. We also live in a social environment that shapes our sexual interactions in "nonrandom" ways, affecting gene flow and genetic drift. Human mating has probably never been truly "random," and nonrandom mating due to cultural and social factors affects the genetic structures of populations. Some individuals con-tribute disproportionately to the gene pool because of their status or their power. Some societies restrict mating between higher and lower ranked groups. High-status or powerful, dominant individuals, usually males, often have access to many women. Economics can have a more powerful impact on infant survival rates or disease mortality rates than genetics. We will be discussing these cultural and social forces in more detail in part II.

How does all this relate to race? Once again, we've shown how much human biological variation exists at the individual and population level. But this genetic diversity can often be explained by modern evolutionary theory. Natural selection, working in particular environmental contexts, seems to explain some variations, including the most racialized of all human traits, skin color. Similar processes, along with other evolutionary forces like gene flow and genetic drift, may explain other so-called racial traits. [18]

But we've also seen that the genetically distinct populations we've identified bear little resemblance to traditional racial groups. These populations are much, much smaller, for one thing, than the huge, macroracial groupings that we call "races." There are hundreds if not thousands of populations. And these populations are themselves diverse; any differences refer to "average" frequencies of traits rather than typological, uniform group characteristics.

Most important, our species, and its populations, are constantly undergoing change, as we alter our physical and cultural environment and ourselves. Microevolution is a continuous, never-ending process. Populations are dynamic, changing, diverse configurations of human biological diversity immersed in a cultural context. Races, in contrast, are fixed, typological, discrete, historically rooted, culturally created biological fictions.

Knowing one's racial identity or how one is racially categorized in the United States, then, tells us very little about most areas of human biology. The rise of so-called racial medicine confuses "populations" with much larger, incredibly biologically heterogeneous groups called "races." Racial medicine also assumes that everyone in a population is the same. This can lead to failure to diagnose traits, like sickle cell anemia or cystic fibrosis or osteoporosis or lactose intolerance, on the assumption that these traits only occur in certain contemporary racial groupings.

KEY CONCEPTUAL POINTS

- Old approaches to human biological variation focused on static, fixed classification, human subdivisions, or types, called races.
- Modern approaches to human biological variation use genetic and evolutionary theory to explain human variation at the individual and population levels.
- There are some genetic differences between populations, but these populations are much smaller groups than what are popularly termed races.
- Both geography and the environment work with natural selection to influence the genetic structure of human populations. This helps to explain

some so-called racial markers, such as skin color, body shape, and the sickle cell gene as well as milk tolerance.

- Other population differences may reflect more random processes, like genetic drift, especially *founder's effect*, when small populations split from larger ones.
- Gene flow has been an important evolutionary force. Gene flow between populations produces new permutations, increases local population variability, decreases variability across populations, and has kept us one species.
- Only a dynamic, biology-culture interactive, *biocultural perspective* can explain human biological variation; cultural changes have had major impacts on human biology. And culture continues to interact with and influence human biology.

KEY TERMS (ITALICIZED AND BOLDED IN TEXT)

allele frequencies
polymorphic
environment
malaria–sickle-cell relationship
adaptation
macroevolution
clinal approach
melanin
evolution
microevolution
fitness
milk digestion
founder's effect
mutation
four evolutionary forces
natural selection
gene flow
population
genetic drift
reproductive fitness
lactase
sickle cell trait
biocultural perspective

ACTIVITIES

Overall Objectives: Understand the relationships between geography, environment, and human biological variation for several traits. Explore hypothesis testing.

Other Information: Mainly high school and older, though some are adaptable to younger audiences. Interactive. Participants will need some way to measure skin color, body type, head form, nose shape, and should have blank maps (see also earlier chapters).

Several activities ask for geographic origins of participants' ancestors. Ancestry can be a sensitive issue. One alternative is to interview other people with known ancestors (adults or other participants) or for participants to work in groups using only one "volunteer" from the group.

Activity Plan 1: Body Type, Climate, and Ancestry

Step 1. Participants measure their body types and explore the relationship of body type to climate described in this chapter. See also the Palomar College website (http://anthro.palomar.edu/adapt/). See also http://www.pbs.org/race/004_HumanDiversity/004_01-explore.htm/. Or participants can develop their own measures of the relationship between body size, body proportions, and ancestral climate: compute the ratio of finger length to hand width; arms to their total height; measure noses, using the nasal index or develop some other measure.

Step 2. Using a world map that shows climatic zones and body types, participants compare their body type or other body feature and see where they "fit" geographically. Is this where their ancestors came from?

Step 3. Discussion. Are results consistent with the "climate" hypothesis of body types? If not, why not? Could your ancestors have come from a different region, earlier in time? Could culture be more important in survival these days than natural adaptations to climate? How does your body type (or body parts) compare to those of family members, especially older family members? Have any changes occurred?

Activity Plan 2: Facial Size, Shape, and Geographic Ancestral Location—Does Natural Selection Hypothesis Apply?

Follow the same procedures as above, except measure head shape using calipers, if available. Otherwise, use "cephalic index" or other participant-developed measures.

ADDITIONAL ACTIVITY IDEAS

Activity Idea 1: Ancestry and Skin Color

Participants analyze skin color on their inner arm (see activitites in chapter 1). If a spectrometer is available, actual measurements can be taken. Otherwise, compare visually, lining up by shades, for example. If the group is too homogeneous, add pictures from other sources. Participants discuss if there is a relationship between family ancestry (geographic roots) and skin color. What other evolutionary factors (e.g., gene flow or migration) could be at work?

Activity Idea 2: Milk: Lactose Intolerance and Lactase Persistence

Participants assess their and their family and friends' tolerance for milk (see chapter 2). Then look at Web-based information on the global distribution of lactose tolerance and intolerance. In what regions and what types of agricultural practices is lactose tolerance most common? Finally, explore the relationship between one's own milk tolerance and geographic ancestry. For website sources see http://anthro.palomar.edu/adapt/adapt_5.htm, and read the article at http://geocurrents.info/cultural-geography/culinary-geography/global-geography-of-milk-consumption-and-lactose-intolerance. See also the overview and interesting population and ethnic group data at Ohio State University Medical Center website: http://medicalcenter.osu.edu/patientcare/healthcare_services/digestive_disorders/lactose_intolerance/Pages/index.aspx.

Activity Idea 3: Gluten Intolerance

Adapt the above procedures to explore gluten intolerance, and its relationship to ancestry, geography, and agricultural practices. Use information at the following website: http://www.mcdonald.cam.ac.uk/projects/genetics/projects/cereals/index.html.

Activity Idea 4: Gene Flow Illustration

To illustrate the rapidity with which mating can spread a new gene throughout a population, use the short five- to ten-minute Gene Flow activity in the RACE project downloadable High School Teacher's Guide available at http://www.understandingrace.org/resources/for_teachers.html.

Activity Idea 5: Sickle Cell Anemia

Explore sickle cell anemia in more depth at the Mukherji lab, http://www.sicklecellinfo.net/info_links/links.htm. And see information at http://www.cdc.gov/ncbddd/sicklecell/index.html.

Activity Idea 6: Environmental Adaptations

Explore more fully a range of population-level biological adaptations to environments using tutorials at http://anthro.palomar.edu/adapt/.

Activity Idea 7: Modern Evolutionary Theory

Explore these ideas further, including the concept of genetic drift, using the tutorials at http://anthro.palomar.edu/synthetic/default.htm.

NOTES

1. Science Primer, also mentioned in chapter 2, is an excellent, accessible resource on genetics: http://www.ncbi.nlm.nih.gov/About/primer/genetics_genome.html.

2. The mating population has always included prepuberty and postmenopausal women as well as those people using some form of contraception other than abstinence.

3. Mutation rates in noncoding CNVs (copy number variants) can be extremely high, with uncertain impacts (cf. Jurmain et al., 2014).

4. All humans have approximately the same number of melanocytes. But the amount of melanin produced varies. Melanin production is affected by several different genes interacting in complex ways, also influenced by regulatory genes. Skin color is also influenced by the protein carotene (Jurmain et al., 2014, pp. 91, 415).

5. For online geographic distribution see http://www.pbs.org/race/004_HumanDiversity/004_01-explore.htm.

6. For a useful discussion of skin cancer and UV radiation, including the effects of overexposure to the sun, such as from sunbathing, see Jurmain et al., 2014, pp. 422–23.

7. The Inuit are darker than many populations living in northerly latitudes. Jablonski and Chaplin attribute this to their relatively recent migration to the Americas (about 5,000 years ago) but also to a diet rich in vitamin D from fish and cod liver oil.

8. Jablonski and Chaplin divide the Earth's surface into three vitamin D zones: tropics, subtropics and temperate zones, and circumpolar areas 45 degrees north and south latitude. The latter zone normally does not have enough UVB to initiate vitamin D synthesis, and people tend to be very pale and burn easily. Those in the midregion have insufficient UVB only about one month a year and hence tend to "tan." Those in high UVB synthesize vitamin D all year (Jablonski & Chaplin, 2005, p. 171).

9. For a discussion of skin color from Nina Jablonski and others see the following website: http://www.understandingrace.org/humvar/skin_01.html. See also Jablonski's more recent work, such as *Living Color: The Biological and Social Meaning of Skin Color* (2012).

10. Receptor cites are protein molecules that enable HIV and other viruses to invade cells (Jurmain et al., 2014, p. 429).

11. Jurmain et al. (2014, p. 40) report data that the immune systems of type A folks, exposed to smallpox, failed to recognize the virus as foreign and didn't have an adequate immune response.

12. Relethford (2013), citing 2011 research, says lactase production is related to a gene on chromosome 2 with two alleles. The LCT*R allele causes lactase to stop being produced. The

LCT*P allele is dominant and allows lactase throughout life, or lactase persistence. It is the homozygote recessive form that causes severe problems. Heterozygotes are apparently fine. He says several different mutations were associated with lactase persistence among dairy farmers, going back as far as 7,000 years (pp. 375–76).

13. Both Jurmain and Relethford report an apparently recent mutation, around 9,000 YA, in Middle East areas of cow domestication, like North India/Kashmir/Afghan. Both lactose tolerance and gluten tolerance reflect adaptations to agriculture and heavy reliance on grains and milk/cattle. Populations lacking these agricultural complexes, or where they have only recently introduced, tend to lack the digestion enzymes (e.g., San of southern Africa).

14. Some cultural anthropologists have long called for a more "biocultural" approach to race on the part of *both* biological *and* cultural anthropologists (cf. Mukhopadhyay & Moses, 1997; for a more recent example, see Gravlee, 2009).

15. This is called founder's effect. These concepts are based on probability theory. We know small samples can be quite different from the population as a whole. Over time, nonrandom traits can accumulate in a population, especially if they are neutral. Some harmful traits may also accumulate over time.

16. Jurmain et al. (2014, p. 104) say there are at least three different forms of Tay-Sachs and more than 100 mutations in the gene. All impact enzyme functioning and produce different expressions of the disease. The disorder is caused by the lack of an enzyme produced by the HEXA gene.

17. Estimates vary, partially depending on the population sampled. See more detail in chapter 9.

18. Scientists currently have no adequate explanation, especially based on natural selection, for variations in hair texture, particularly the range from straight to tightly curled whorls. Genetic drift may be partially at work, as populations repeatedly split off and migrated out of Africa. See chapter 4.

Chapter Four

More Alike Than Different, More Different Than Alike

CONCEPTUAL BACKGROUND

This chapter brings together ideas from earlier chapters. We have shown that scientific reality often contrasts with what our culture has taught us about human biological variation. Many people, including some racial scientists, once thought that biological differences between races were so great that interracial mating would not produce viable offspring. And not long ago, donors and recipients of organ transplants or blood transfusions had to be the same race. The racial biological gap was supposedly enormous, and racial differences trumped all other human biological differences.

Science has come a long way. We now know that conventional "racial" traits, biologically speaking, represent a small and not very significant segment of human genetic variation. And while genetic differences between populations can be identified, neither the populations nor the traits resemble the large, continent-wide, macrogroups we call "races." Compared to other species, we are not very genetically variable. This may be due to our recent common origins in Africa. Of the variability that exists, far more lies *within* than *between* racial groups. Most human biological variation is at the individual level.

Finally, we are far more than the genes we inherited from our parents. Our biological "selves" are not fixed at conception. Our genes are themselves controlled by other parts of our DNA. We are constantly changing, being altered, whether by the environment within our bodies (cells, tissues, chemicals) or by the environment outside of it. And human culture plays a major role in human biological variation, shaping human biology and human evolution. Race and racism have biological consequences. But the concept of "race" is an outmoded, inaccurate, meaningless way of describing or understanding human biological variation.

THERE IS MORE VARIATION WITHIN
THAN BETWEEN SO-CALLED RACES

We have seen in earlier chapters that racial traits represent a small sample of visible human variability. We've also discovered that much of human genetic variability, indeed some of the most significant, is inside the body, such as our blood.

Given the 21,000 or so genes in the human genome, then, so-called racial markers constitute a small fraction of total human genetic variation. Moreover, as we saw in chapter 1, virtually none of these, such as skin color or hair form, covary. For most of humanity, one's racial group is unstable and depends on which racial trait you use.

It should not surprise us that when scientists began to systematically examine genetic variability within the so-called races, they found more variability *within* each racial group than *between* racial groups. Once we start *noticing*, it does not take a sophisticated statistical analysis to discover how much visible diversity exists within each major racial group.

Traditional racial categories tend to correspond to major continental land masses. But these are huge, geographically diverse regions, incorporating highly variable ecological and environmental features, such as climate, altitude, and food-getting systems. They contain millions of people, with myriad languages, political systems, cultures, mating and migration patterns, and disease histories. Given how microevolution works (see chapter 3), we would expect considerable biological variability within each of these regions or so-called races.

Take, for example, the so-called White race, mainly Europeans and people of European ancestry. Euros come in myriad sizes, shapes, colors, facial features, heights, body builds, and blood types. Indeed, what we call "Europe" includes countries as far north as Sweden and as far south as Spain, Greece, Southern Italy, and even Turkey. Geographically, Europe is really an artificial division of the Eurasian continent, with a line between Europe and Asia that shifts over time.[1] The term Caucasian, inaccurately used for "White" or "European or European Americans," comes from the 18th-century racial classification system developed by German anatomist J. Blumenbach (see chapter 6 and Mukhopadhyay, 2012), and originally included people from the Ukraine, Georgia, Saudi Arabia, Afghanistan, and North India.

The "Asian" racial category is equally huge, heterogeneous, and artificial. South Asia alone incorporates at least India, Bangladesh, Nepal, Sri Lanka, and Pakistan. East Asia ranges from Korea, Japan, and China to Vietnam and

Thailand. India and China, each with over one billion people, represent myriad geographic regions and physically variable ethnic groups, nationalities, and languages. It is difficult to discern the boundaries of Asia and the Asian race. Should we include Indonesia, Malaysia, and the Philippines? And then there is the diversity of "Native American" populations within North America much less the entire Americas.

When we turn to the racial category "Black," we again find enormous geographic and human variability. Africa has desert, mountains, oceans, tropical areas, and spans a range of latitudes, some distant from the equator. It has hundreds, if not thousands, of linguistically, culturally, politically, and historically distinct populations. Africa is home to the shortest and the tallest people of the world. Other traits vary significantly, including skin color, facial traits (nose, eye shape), overall body shapes, even the frequency of the sickle cell and lactose (milk) tolerance, as we saw in chapter 3.

Our quick review of the major geographic regions associated with conventional U.S. racial categories only hints at how much genetic diversity there might be within each "race." What do more recent analyses, especially the wealth of studies using human DNA, tell us? And how does variation within races compare to the variability between races?

HUMAN BIOLOGICAL DIVERSITY: MORE DIFFERENT THAN ALIKE, AT LEAST WITHIN RACES

Population geneticist Richard Lewontin's now-classic study (1972) was virtually the first to compare the amount of variation *between* different "racial groups" to how much variation existed *within* each group. At that time, there were no methods to study genetic or DNA segments directly. Lewontin instead analyzed seventeen different biochemical markers found in the blood, using blood samples on diverse populations around the world. For his "races," he created seven macroracial groups roughly corresponding to distinct geographical regions and sampled populations from each region.

Lewontin's data showed more variability *within* than *between* races, whether one looks at continental races or more localized subregional populations, at least for his sample of blood traits and populations. Most of human genetic variability, he argued, exists within nationalities, within ethnic groups, within villages, within kinship groups, and even within families.

The concept of race, he concluded, was biologically virtually meaningless. Using racial classifications hindered rather than advanced our understanding of human genetic variation, and he advocated abandoning them in biological studies.

The past decades have produced a wealth of increasingly sophisticated scientific studies of human biological variation, made possible through advances in genomics research, including the sequencing of the human genome, and new methods for detecting and analyzing DNA directly. DNA research is providing insights at the individual, population, and species levels. Individuals can now explore their ancestry through several online sites.

Perhaps more important, it is giving us information about our history as a species, how evolutionary processes have worked on and altered populations, the impact of cultural change and human diseases, and how unique we are as individual humans. It is also allowing us to compare populations and evaluate the validity of the race concept.

Chapter 2 provided some background on genetics and the new DNA research. New technology allows scientists to essentially cut the DNA into small pieces so that they can look directly at the exact sequence of chemical base pairs at particular points or locations. These same sequences can then be compared among different individuals and among populations. And it is now easy to collect DNA samples, using hair samples or cheek swabs. So we can truly do global analyses of human DNA. We can even do DNA analyses of fossils.

One major finding is how much variability exists among humans at the DNA level. Some variations are genetic, that is, they are in the portions of our DNA that "code" for alternative forms of traits, such as skin color, blood type, lactose tolerance, or susceptibility to various diseases. Most are not, strictly speaking, "genetic." Rather, they occur in the remaining 98 to 99 percent of our DNA that used to, wrongly, be called "junk" DNA.

We now know that some of this DNA plays a crucial role in directing and regulating gene expression. Some variations in these "regulatory" segments, like some genetic forms, may reflect past evolutionary forces, like natural selection. Other portions of DNA may reflect random variations that have no discernible current impact on our bodies, although they may provide a "reservoir" of future biological variation. Other segments may simply be markers of our unique developmental histories which may or may not be transmitted to future generations. Many DNA sequences are transmitted and become part of our family inheritance, enabling us to construct family and "ancestral" trees.

We know now that our bodies, our genes, our DNA patterns are not static, fixed at birth, but constantly being altered in complex ways. These alterations start at the time of conception, as the fertilized egg multiplies and grows, developing tissues and organs. It continues throughout our lifetime, as our cells constantly reproduce, replace, and repair themselves. Scientists have identified several processes through which our DNA is altered, many involving seemingly random insertions, deletions, and repetitions that occur in the normal processes of cell replication.

One category of segments, collectively called CNVs (copy number variants), includes small sequences of DNA bases that copy and repeat themselves over and over again, sometimes hundreds of times. One type of analysis simply counts the number of repeats. For example, the DNA sequence CACACACACA contains five repeats of the CA sequence, and the DNA sequence CACACA contains three repeats. The number of repeats can be used to compare individuals (Relethford, 2013). These *microsatellites* are extraordinarily variable, differing significantly from one person to another. In fact, every individual apparently has a distinctive pattern or arrangement of these repetitions, providing each of us with a unique DNA fingerprint (Jurmain et al., 2014). This enables forensic scientists to accurately identify individual human remains, whether at the scene of crimes or at major disasters, such as the 2005 hurricane that flooded New Orleans.

Other types of CNVs, sometimes called "jumping genes," move around, inserting themselves or deleting themselves, sometimes seemingly randomly, into other DNA locations. For example, *Alu* are short pieces of DNA that have a similar sequence or order of base pairs. These pieces, or rather copies of them, have a tendency to "travel." Sometimes a piece will copy and insert itself, at random, into a new position on the same or on another chromosome. Usually this produces no biological impact even if there are genes nearby, although there are exceptions.

But each insertion is a unique event and the particular sequence (and its location) remains in place and is transmitted from one generation to another. So this tiny piece of DNA, with its special location, provides a marker of common ancestry. If two people have the same *Alu* sequence at the same spot in their genome, we can infer that they share a common ancestor from whom they inherited that piece of DNA (Bamshad & Olson, 2003).

Some DNA segments within a gene simply drop out or are deleted during cell replication processes. They mainly occur in the nongenetic or "noncoding" segments of our DNA.

One of the most significant and analyzed sources of alterations in our DNA are the SNPs or *single nucleotide polymorphisms*, also known as "point mutations," in which only one DNA base pair is altered. Given an estimated three billion bases (or base pairs) in the human DNA, it's perhaps not surprising that at least fifteen million SNPs have already been identified (Jurmain et al., 2014).

Current research, called "whole-genome" analysis, utilizes very large portions of DNA, for analyzing SNPs in human populations worldwide. Some studies have looked at the entire genome for more than 1,000 individuals. One study identified the patterns of over 500,000 SNPs that were expressed in only a few dozen populations worldwide (Jurmain et al., 2014, p. 399).

Perhaps the most ambitious is the 1000 Genomes Project, a worldwide collaboration among over 400 scientists (see http://www.1000genomes.org/). Among other things, the project has already "reported on" nearly fifteen million SNPs as well as other types of DNA insertions, deletions, and repeats (see above section). They were able to reconstruct the entire genome for nearly 200 individuals. This enabled them to identify somewhere between 50 and 100 alleles (variations of genes) that are associated with different diseases. According to some reports, they may have found "the molecular basis for 95 percent of all fairly common patterns of human variation" (see Jurmain et al., 2014, p. 399).

Some researchers have tried to identify clusters of DNA markers, called "haplotypes," which are inherited together, as a single unit. These are particularly useful indicators of common ancestry. This type of analysis was used to investigate whether Thomas Jefferson could have fathered a child with Sally Hemings, an enslaved African American woman. The analysis utilized nineteen ***DNA markers***: seven SNPs, and twelve CNVs (eleven microsatellites, one minisatellite). This combination of markers was apparently unique to the Jefferson family and also appeared in one of Hemings's sons. So this established that some male in the Jefferson line, although not necessarily Jefferson, was the father (Relethford, 2013, pp. 348–49).

The research of the past decade has produced an enormous biological "library" (Jurmain et al., 2014, p. 398) of information at the molecular level, now available to scholars around the world, including those interested in human biological variation, population genetics, and human population history. What are they finding?

"RACES" ARE MORE DIFFERENT THAN ALIKE

Recent DNA-based research has superseded, in some ways, Lewontin's work along with older research approaches we cited in the first edition of this book. Yet Lewontin's basic conclusion, that there is more variation within than between races, remains valid. Multiple studies, whether using traditional traits like blood groups or nuclear or mitochondrial DNA, whether using "gene" or noncoding DNA sequences, have demonstrated how little genetic variation there is between large, geographic, "racial" groups.

New estimates of the amount of within-vs.-between group variation have emerged. One statistical measure used is called "Fst," for the fraction of variation in a gene with multiple "versions" that is found between population samples. Using multiple DNA genes, one estimate is that within our genome, an average of 83 to 97 percent of human genetic variation occurs within populations. Only 3 to 17 percent is found between populations (Fuentes, 2012, p. 314). Equally significant is the distribution of genetic diversity in the African continent compared to other non-African, macrogeographical, "racial"-type populations. Africa contains more human genetic diversity than any other geographic area in the world! Using the Fst measure, Kittle and Weiss (2003) estimate there is nearly twice as much genetic diversity among

African populations as among non-African populations. Results from **whole genome analyses** also show that human populations outside Africa, in Europe and Asia, are much less genetically diverse than African populations. Other studies of DNA markers have led some to conclude that genetic diversity outside of Africa is simply *part* of the diversity found within Africa. They argue that Europeans and Asians are genetically subsets of Africans (cf. http://www.understandingrace.org/humvar/africa.html).

Some of these findings provide further evidence of our common African origins, as we shall see shortly. The longer a population has been in a region, that is, the more ancient the population, the more genetic variability exists (see chapters 2, 3). This is partially because mutations accumulate over time and because it takes time for natural selection to produce variability. Africa, as the oldest site of modern humans, should be the most genetically variable of all regions. Moreover, we would expect that as segments of this ancestral human population dispersed to other parts of the world, some of the original diversity would be lost (see "genetic drift" and "founder's effect" in chapter 3).

Recent data support this interpretation. Not only is genetic diversity in non-African populations less than in Africa; but, overall, the farther the population is from Africa, the less the level of genetic diversity (Relethford, 2013, p. 349).

Other recent "whole genome" analyses of African small, indigenous populations of gatherer-hunters reveal even more diversity within Africa, and within populations and even individuals. One 2012 study (Lachance et al., 2012, cited in Jurmain et al., 2014, p. 400) sampled gatherer-hunter preagricultural populations from South Africa (San or so-called Bushmen), two populations from Tanzania in East Africa, and one from Cameroon in Central Africa (a so-called pygmy forest-dwelling group). Genetic variation found within these indigenous foraging groups apparently is not only far greater than that in other African groups but is greater than that found anywhere else in the world (ibid.).

But individual genetic diversity is also huge. Jurmain reports that the "whole genome analysis" of the two San individuals in the sample found them as distinct, genetically, from each other as a European from an Asian. And the small sample of five South African men, which included Archbishop Desmond Tutu, produced 1.3 million *new* DNA differences that had never been reported in other populations. Diversity, on the individual level, was even greater than previously documented. No wonder contemporary scientists have concluded that "Genetically, humans differ individually within populations far more than large geographical groups ('races') differ from each other" (Jurmain et al., 2014, pp. 400–411).

WE ARE ALL ALIKE BECAUSE WE HAVE
A COMMON ANCESTOR—IN AFRICA

Despite what we've said about human biological variation, we are really "remarkably uniform, genetically" (Jurmain et al., 2014, p. 389), a rather homogeneous species, especially relative to other species. That is, despite the variability we've talked about at the DNA level, and even for some genetic traits, most human genes come in only one form. Two chimpanzees from two different populations in East Africa are far more genetically different from each other (four times, according to some estimates) than two humans from the most geographically distinct or remote areas of our planet (Fuentes, 2012, p. 314).

When we think more about it and examine the most recent evidence on our origins and history, this is not surprising. The story of our species, as we have said, has been primarily one of intermating between groups, of migration, of constant contact rather than isolation, of continuing gene flow. This is why we have remained a single species with much of our genetic variability found within rather than between populations, and much of it in the noncoding portions of our DNA.

The unity of the human species goes back to Africa. Scientific evidence has conclusively established that modern humans (*Homo sapien sapiens*) evolved in Africa, around 150,000 to 200,000 years ago (YA), and began expanding out of Africa within the last 100,000 years (see Kidd, 2012, p. 135, and http://www.understandingrace.org/humvar/africa.html). Timing estimates vary, depending on the type of data and analytical methods used. But scientists agree that we, as modern humans, come from a common ancestor in Africa. Subsequently, segments of that original population dispersed to other parts of the world, eventually replacing, with some minor interbreeding, the premodern human populations, like Neanderthals and Denisovans, of the regions to which they migrated. This is called the ***Out of Africa or African replacement***, or, more recently, the partial replacement[2] model of the evolution of our modern human species, *Homo sapiens*.

Until the last few years, there was a rival theory, the so-called ***multiregional hypothesis***. According to this theory, modern humans evolved separately and independently, in many different regions of the world, *after* leaving Africa. These regional populations were largely isolated from each other but evolved into modern humans at about the same time. As a result, they developed distinctive biological features which we today think of as racial differences.

The most recent research, based on both nuclear and mitochondrial DNA, using data from both contemporary populations and fossil remains, and utilizing a multiplicity of DNA markers to establish the approximate age of lineages, does not support the multiregional hypothesis. Instead, the data clearly establish a common African ancestry of all modern humans, followed by subsequent migrations of modern humans to different parts of the world (cf. Jurmain et al., 2014; Kidd, 2012; Relethford, 2013; http://www. understandingrace.org/humvar/africa.html).

Current evidence suggests major dispersals of human populations out of Africa somewhere between 50,000 and 75,000 years ago. While there is some difference of opinion, recent nuclear DNA data suggests one major dispersal of modern humans out of Africa along a single southern route beginning in East Africa, with some groups traveling north and a larger migration following the "southern tier," that is, across the Red Sea through the Arabian Peninsula (Jurmain et al., 2014, p. 400).[3]

After leaving Africa, some populations spread fairly quickly into the Middle East/Central Asia. Recent nuclear DNA from Neanderthal fossils suggests this may have been the major site of interbreeding with local Neanderthal populations, as early as 70,000 years ago (Relethford, 2013, p. 325). Archaic Neanderthal human populations had a wide range, including the Middle East (e.g., Israel, Iraq), Central Asia (e.g., Uzbekistan), along with Europe. If interbreeding had occurred later, after the migration of early humans to Europe, Neanderthal DNA should be higher in contemporary Europeans than in Asians (Relethford, 2013, p. 324). But both European and Asian living populations show the same amount of Neanderthal DNA, approximately 1 to 4 percent (Relethford, 2013, pp. 324–25; Jurmain et al., 2014).

Another migration route traveled through Southeast Asia, perhaps in two waves. The first wave populated Australia, New Guinea, and other nearby islands (of Melanesia), and, judging by fossil and contemporary population DNA, shows evidence of archaic Denisovan ancestry (4 to 6 percent). Another wave populated Southeast Asia and Indonesia but without evidence of interbreeding (Lewton, 2012).[4] A second Asia migration path, perhaps 40,000 years ago, produced the first modern populations of East Asia, including the ancestors of contemporary Han Chinese. (Jurmain et al., 2014, p.401). Modern Europeans can be traced back to at least five periods of migration, beginning around 45,000 YA and continuing to as recently as 5,000 years ago.

Multiple sources of data, including genetic data, also document the origins of Native American populations in Asia. There were probably at least three distinct migrations to the Americas, judging by results of a recent comparison of some 350,000 SNPs from Siberian and American populations (Jurmain et al., 2014, p. 401, citing Reich et al., 2012). Most present-day Native Americans and Native Alaskans trace their ancestry to the first migration. The two later streams of migration from Asia mixed with these first Americans once they encountered them in the Americas. The second and third migrations included ancestors of Inuit, Aleut, and Na-Dene populations, the latter a language group in Canada and North America.[5]

In the process of migrating and settling new regions, our African ancestral populations experienced microevolutionary changes, partly due to "selective" pressures, stemming from natural and culturally induced environmental challenges. Genetic drift, as a result of small populations splitting off from large populations, also shaped these populations genetically. Gene flow through intermating, including with archaic local populations, and later, with neighboring groups, played a bigger role in producing contemporary genetic patterns than previously thought. Geographic proximity does, other things being equal, lead to greater genetic similarity between populations. The genetic patterns of contemporary indigenous populations in large, contiguous geographic regions do, to some extent, reflect ancestral migration histories, genetic "drift" and "founder's effect," along with gene flow and other evolutionary pressures (e.g., natural selection).

Ancestry alone also produces commonalities, especially in noncoding portions of our DNA. But these are not "races"; they are much smaller groups. And there is still enormous variability within these populations. But it is not just large-scale populations that show more variability within than between groups. Relethford (2013) found significant genetic variability among Irish populations living in different counties in the same general region. At virtually every level of analysis, whether the unit of study is an entire continent, a region, a linguistic or ethnic group within a region, small town, or village, or a large multigenerational family with long-standing ancestral ties, we find more variability within than between groups.

When geneticists examined 100 *Alu* in a sample of South Indians, they could not find enough similarities among individuals to characterize them as a distinct ancestral cluster (Bamshad & Olson, 2003, p. 82). Instead, the results reflected what anthropologists and historians have long known: that South India consists of a myriad of populations who have been mating with a myriad of other populations for a long time.

Some analyses using multiple DNA markers (haplotypes, haplogroups) can produce regional clusters of populations that are in some ways biologically similar. However, these are not biological races in the traditional sense.[6] They bear little resemblance to the macroracial groupings we have historically used or use today in the United States. These "ancestral trees" are often not even genetically significant subdivisions of national or regional populations.

Of course, we can identify some resemblances between populations that are geographically contiguous or that have historically interacted, or represent historical migration patterns. This is what we would expect, given the propensity of humans to intermate, producing "gene flow." But these are not races. And most human variability still occurs within smaller populations.

These are local geographic populations or local ethnic groups, and there are hundreds, if not thousands, of them.

What we are seeing is the impact of ancestral history, common ancestry, generations of mating and marrying, and sometimes the impact of natural selection in common environments. In all these cases, culture plays an important role, whether in altering the natural environment through cultural inventions, like agricultural, or in shaping mating patterns, whether through arranged marriages, religiously mandated celibacy, or warfare (see chapter 9).

CONCLUSION: WE ARE MORE DIFFERENT THAN ALIKE, EVEN WITH COMMON ANCESTORS

New understandings and sophisticated analyses of human DNA are providing extraordinary insights into how our bodies work as well as into human biological variation. It is showing us exactly how similar—and how variable—we are as a species, as groups with common ancestry embedded in culture, and as individuals. Most important, it is providing more evidence that race is a cultural rather than biologically meaningful classification of human groups.

We are one species that emerged in Africa and radiated across the globe, mating with each other along the way. There have never been any biological races, any distinct subdivisions of our species, and there are none now. All modern human populations have the same fundamental biological structure and the same capacities. All modern human populations have the same reproductive capacities, the same intellectual capacities, the same emotional, behavioral, and moral capacities.[7]

Race, then, is not biologically real or meaningful. It neither accurately describes nor provides many insights into human biological variation. But if race is biological fiction, then what have we been experiencing that we call race? How are we to understand race? We turn to these questions in part II.

KEY CONCEPTUAL POINTS

- There is only one modern human species, and it evolved in Africa. All modern human populations are subsets of this single African lineage. And there are hundreds and thousands of such populations. There are no distinct races, which evolved separately, in different regions of the world.
- Racial traits represent a fraction of total human genetic variation. Knowing someone's race tells us virtually nothing about that person's biology, DNA, or behavioral or intellectual capacities.
- There is far more variation *within* than *between* racial groups.

- Human biological variation exists, but mainly at the individual level and in our DNA.
- Common ancestry produces DNA similarities, but mainly outside the portion of our DNA that we call our "genes." Most of it lies in the noncoding sections of our DNA, and in those areas that seem to have little genetic impact.
- Most human biological variation exists at the individual level, *within* families, kin groups, and communities. There are more differences within than between small populations.

KEY TERMS (ITALICIZED AND BOLDED IN TEXT)

DNA markers
CNVs (copy number variants)
whole genome analysis
Out of Africa or African replacement model
microsatellite DNA
multiregional hypothesis
SNPs (single nucleotide polymorphisms)

ACTIVITIES

Overall Objectives: These activities all provide a summarizing experience and build on material in earlier chapters.

Activity Plan 1: Human Biological Variation: More Alike Than Different?

Objective: Participants will discover there is more variability within than between racial groups.

Additional Information: Utilize the module "The Empirical Challenges of Racial Classification" at http://www.pbs.org/race/000_ About/002_04-teachers-04.htm.

Procedure:

Step 1. Participants create a list of visible and invisible genetic traits, drawing on earlier chapters and websites.

Step 2. Reduce list to about ten traits (including some invisible traits) that participants can describe in themselves and other people. This is harder for invisible traits, like ABO blood group. Create a matrix of these traits (see the above website for samples).

Step 3. Divide participants into racial groups. You can use the 2010 census categories. Do not force multiracials to select one category. They can create a separate "multiracial" category if they wish. If you have virtually no racial diversity, use religion or gender as the basis for groupings. Using gender groups can illustrate how much variability lies *within* each gender.

Step 4. Participants assess themselves on each item on the chart of traits.

Step 5. Each group summarizes the data for their racial group (counts or frequencies/percentages). Compare groups' results. Participants should discover that there is more variability within than between the groups.

Step 6. Explore the possibility of collecting DNA samples to further explore the amount of variability within U.S. racial groups.

ADDITIONAL ACTIVITY IDEAS

Activity Idea 1: Exploring One's Own Ancestry

Explore websites available for examining one's own ancestry, including using DNA analysis (cf.). Visit the Dolan DNA Learning Center, Cold Spring Harbor Laboratory, Cold Spring Harbor, New York, at http://www.dnalc.org. Or visit "Tracing Ancestry with mtDNA," from NOVA Online at http://www.pbs.org/wgbh/nova/neanderthals/mtdna.html. Discuss limitations and problems with interpreting ancestry analyses. Read the comments of scholars in "Perspectives on Genetic Genealogy" (Goodman, Moses, & Jones, 2012, pp. 141–143).

Activity Idea 2: Sorting People into Races Using Online Modules

This brief online, interactive activity illustrates the difficulty of "racing" people by visual appearance, partially because we use social criteria. It also illustrates the distinction between self-identification and external imposition of categories. In the "Sorting People Interactivity" (http://www.pbs.org/race/002_SortingPeople/002_01-sort.htm), participants sort twenty pictures of people into racial categories using U.S. Census categories.

Discuss any surprises and reflect on the meaning of race and racial markers. Identify nonphysical markers used in "racing" other people, like speech, clothing, social context, situational features, hairstyle, material items, or body movements. This connects to other material in parts II and III.

Activity Idea 3: The Story of Desiree's Baby

This activity was developed in 2003 and is available at http://www.pbs.org/race/000_About/002_04-teachers-06.htm. The detailed lesson plan can be used to introduce the social meaning of race (parts II and III) and to explore the genetics of skin color. The activity begins with a short story by Kate Chopin published in 1893 entitled *Desiree's Baby*. The story makes a poignant statement about racism. In doing so, it illustrates how skin color is not mainly about biology but about the meanings individuals, society, and culture give to skin color. The second part goes into greater depth on the genetics of skin color (see chapter 3).

Discussion can explore *culturally rooted* environmental factors that influence skin color. These include occupation (farming or other outdoors versus indoor work), recreational activities, cosmetic products that lighten, darken, or in other ways affect skin color, and the recent popularity, among some U.S. Americans, of the tanning salon.

Activity Idea 4: Exploring Our African Ancestor—Eve

This activity reviews the origins of modern humans at http://anthro.palomar. edu/hom02/mod_homo_4.htm. The regional continuity model on the website is similar to the multiregional evolution model in this chapter. For more about the mitochondrial Eve theory and the inheritance of mitochondrial DNA through the maternal line on "Tracing Ancestry with mtDNA" from NOVA Online, see .

Activity Idea 5: Exploring My Ancestry

Participants explore the home countries or regions of their biological ancestors, prior to coming to the United States (unless Native Americans, the only true "natives"). Most participants will have multiple ancestral origins. If ancestry cannot be traced, they can work with or interview other participants.

In conjunction with part II activities, map family geographic ancestry more carefully, using information from family history interviews and family kinship chart. Focus initially on immediate family members, then move farther out. If used with "The Ethnic Me" in part II, participants could also trace marriage patterns to see to what extent their ancestors married "out" with regard to region, ethnicity, religion, education, or other local marriage criteria.

Once participants have some idea of a family tree, regardless of how crude or small, they can apply several activities in part I to their relatives. For example, they could literally map ABO blood types, body shapes, skin color, or nose form onto geographic origins of relatives. They could also look at environmental influences, such as the effect of diet on height, by comparing heights of different generations of their relatives. For more details, see http://www.sjsu.edu/people/carol.mukhopadhyay.

Activity Idea 6: Endless Human Variability

Explore human genetic variation further at National Human Genome Research Institute website: http://www.genome.gov/. Don't miss the excellent Educators section at http://www.genome.gov/Educators/. Focus on variability in Mendelian traits using the OMIM "Online mendelian inheritance in man [*sic*]" website. Search the home page at http://www.omim.org or http://www.ncbi.nlm.nih.gov/omim/.

Activity Idea 7: Explore the 1000 Genomes Project

http://www.1000genomes.org/

Activity Idea 8: Explore the HapMap project

http://hapmap.ncbi.nlm.nih.gov/thehapmap.html.en

NOTES

1. In some ways this is as much a division between Christian and Islamic dominated areas.

2. The "partial" replacement refers to evidence of some interbreeding with archaic human Neanderthal and Denisovan populations. Thus, modern human populations did not totally replace existing populations, as evidenced by the DNA of living human populations. Some scholars use slightly different labels for these theories (cf. Fuentes, 2012).

3. New DNA evidence, especially Neanderthal and Denisovan fossil remains, are fueling, in a positive way, debates about the number and timing and location of migration routes and the extent of interbreeding between Neanderthal and Denisovan archaic species. But there is current agreement that Neanderthal and Denisovan genes occur in Eurasian populations (i.e., European Asian) and *not* in African populations. This is one basis for arguing for *one* major migration out of Africa with subsequent dispersals. Another is the same percentage of Neanderthal genes found in *all* Eurasian populations along with DNA evidence showing Neanderthal and Denisovans share common ancestry, with later divergence into the two lines (e.g., Reich, 2010, cited by Lewton, 2012). As new evidence emerges, there will probably be additional shifts and refinements in these theories.

4. As noted above, there are multiple and shifting interpretations. The one cited here comes from a 2012 *American Anthropologist* review article of the latest research. The results suggest that Southeast Asia was settled in at least two waves. The first wave included the ancestors of modern New Guineans and Australians ("Melanesians"), the second those of East Asians and Indonesians. (Lewton, 2012, p. 197). Relethford (2013) suggests that living Melanesian populations have ancestry from both Neanderthals and Denisovans (p. 326).

5. Once the populations began to settle in geographically distant areas, according to Ruiz-Linares (2012), there was relatively little further mixing.

6. This is a controversial area of research because some geneticists persist in generalizing to macroracial groups, such as Europeans, Asians, and Africans, even when their data come from much smaller regional populations (e.g., Northern Italians, Scottish, Northern Greeks, Mbuti Pygmies, Nigerian Ibos, South Indian Tamils).

7. Individuals, within populations, of course, vary.

II

Culture Creates Race

Carol C. Mukhopadhyay

Race may be a biological fiction, as we have shown in part I. But that doesn't mean race doesn't exist. Race is a social and cultural reality and profoundly impacts our lives. [1]

Most people recognize that race in the United States is real. And most U.S. Americans probably *experience* race as a social (rather than biological) reality. We may have been introduced to the concept of race as a social or cultural *construct* or race as socially or culturally *constructed.*

But the idea that race is a human invention, a social construction, a cultural creation, is complex and difficult to communicate. There is particular resistance to the idea that race is *only* a cultural construct. Race seems so real! How can race be pure invention?

In part II we identify and address some key barriers to understanding race as a cultural construct and social invention. Each chapter provides both conceptual background materials and illustrative learning-oriented activities.

CULTURE IS REAL

What does it mean to say that race is a cultural creation? To understand this, we must first explore the concept of culture itself and how profoundly culture can shape our view of reality. Culture shapes, to some extent, virtually every aspect of human experience—our senses, our perceptions, our behavior, our interpretations, what we hear, smell, taste, feel, and see. It structures our social world and social interactions. It provides us with sets of beliefs, values, explanations, with a "worldview." The human world is largely a cultural and social invention—but one that is very real. Race, too, is a cultural invention—but it is experientially, emotionally, cognitively real, deeply internalized in our psyche. Chapter 5 addresses the concept of culture.

Race is also a system of classification, a culturally and historically specific way of categorizing, of thinking about and treating, groups of human beings. Like other human creations, classifications shape how we experience reality. Chapter 6 first traces the role of classification in human life and then focuses on the U.S. system of racial classification.

RACE IS ABOUT POWER AND INEQUALITY

Race is not simply a cultural or psychological phenomenon. It emerged in a context of unequal power relations, as an ideology to legitimize the dominance of certain groups. Race, then, is fundamentally part of a system of stratification and inequality.

People who have grown up immersed in the U.S. ideology of individualism often have difficulty understanding abstract notions of a social system, social stratification, and how one's social position impacts individual experience and opportunities. Chapter 7 addresses these issues and suggests activities to help us understand how systems of social (and racial) inequality function.

RACE SHIFTS OVER TIME

U.S. racial categories, even if not universal and natural, are often seen as permanent fixtures of our history and culture. But culture is not static, fixed, immutable. It is dynamic, contested, negotiated, fluid. Long-standing and deeply embedded cultural inventions can be reinvented, altered, dismantled, or reconfigured to accommodate changing circumstances. We show, in chapter 7, how American racial categories have shifted over time, in different political contexts, and are continuing to do so today. We want people to realize that the future of race in the U.S. is at least partially in our own hands.

RACE IS NOT UNIVERSAL OR INEVITABLE

A long-standing U.S. assumption is that race, racial discrimination, race-based hierarchy, or something similar is a universal, pan-human phenomenon, indeed "built into our genes" as humans. Chapter 8 surveys the anthropological evidence and concludes this is one more long-standing and convenient myth.

RACE AND BIOLOGY

In addressing race as a cultural or social invention, we must ask, where does biology fit? There is a mistaken notion that because races are not biologically real, there is no biology associated with U.S. racial categories. But race is a cultural phenomenon, and biological markers of race are embedded in, shaped by, and experienced in a cultural context. Chapter 9 deals with the cultural creation of biological markers of race, and how biological processes (mating, reproduction) have been manipulated to maintain the social reality we call race. In addition, we show how race, in a culture of racism, can have major biological impacts, can actually shape biology.

NOTES

Part II, especially chapters 5, 6, and 9, synthesizes ideas its author, Carol Mukhopadhyay, has been developing throughout her career.

1. Social scientists sometimes use the terms *cultural* and *social* interchangeably. To anthropologists, "cultural" (*culture*) encompasses the social world but also shared belief systems, cultural meanings, values, and other forms of cultural knowledge. The term *social* focuses more on society, social identities, and social institutions such as the family and the law, but can also include economics, politics, religion, the entire social world.

Chapter Five

Culture Shapes How We Experience Reality

Most of us think we know what *culture* is. The word and its offshoots, like "cultural" or "multicultural," have become part of public discourse. Through films, videos, television, the Internet, and increasingly, our own experiences, we have been introduced to a myriad of different cultures, in which people live, dress, eat, and behave in ways quite different than our own. Travel and the growing diversity of our own regional communities have allowed us to sample other cultures' food, music and dances, celebrations, and even acquire their clothing, jewelry, or other cultural art forms. Some of us have attended workshops on cultural diversity, through schools, workplaces, or other groups we participate in. From an anthropological perspective, however, most of these experiences only tap the surface of the phenomenon we call "culture."

A deeper understanding of culture is necessary if we are to grasp the meaning—and power—of race as a cultural construction. This chapter starts with examples of culture that are deliberately socially neutral, like greeting behaviors, food, and language. Our primary goal is to convey to readers a vivid, deep sense of the power of culture, the extent to which culture shapes all aspects of human life, including our biological capacities. We want to produce a minor *culture shock* at the realization that we do not experience the world directly but through a cultural lens. We have found this a useful prelude to discussions about the idea that "race" and racial categories do not exist in "nature" but are cultural inventions. It also lays the ground for understanding how racial categories, like other cultural preconceptions, can profoundly shape our perceptions of and behavior toward other people. What we notice (e.g., skin color), how we interpret what we see, how we are seen and treated by others, are all powerfully influenced by culture.

CONCEPTUAL BACKGROUND

The Concept of Culture

There have been numerous attempts to define culture precisely (whole volumes), yet no single definition adequately expresses the complexity of the concept. The one thing all definitions have in common is that culture is *learned.* We are not born with a particular culture. We acquire culture as an integral part of our development within one or more human communities. This is true for all humans. All human groups have a culture. And all humans have the same capacity to learn any culture. We may learn different cultures but we all *learn* some culture.

For many people, their primary exposure to anthropology has been through archeology and the "material" remains of past cultures that often end up in museums. But if we think about most items in our own culture, such as a "notebook,"[1] "dishwasher," "garage," "smart" phone, even a toilet, much less a wall clock, Barbie doll, or a Valentine's Day card, there is clearly more to what makes these "cultural" than what is physical and tangible. An archeologist from Mars would have difficulty identifying that circular, metal band some people wear on the "ring finger" of the left hand as a "wedding ring." Indeed, the concepts "wedding ring," "wedding dress," and "wedding" would require much explanation. The meaning and purpose of large, seemingly obvious physical structures, like a house, library, campus dormitory, prison, or the White House, or more complex structures such as a shopping mall, Disneyland, or the Vietnam War Memorial, would hardly appear obvious to a Martian.

Anthropologists have always understood that culture goes far beyond the concrete, beyond tangible, material things. The classic definition over 130 years ago by British anthropologist Edward Tylor describes culture as "that complex whole which includes knowledge, belief, arts, morals, law, custom, and any other capabilities and habits acquired by man [*sic*] as a member of society" (cited in Kottak & Kozaitis, 2012, p. 12). Tylor, like contemporary anthropologists, recognized that much of culture is intangible, consists of behaviors and practices, but even more important, of ideas, values, beliefs, of *shared knowledge*, whether about expressive forms like "hip-hop music," behaviors like "handshakes," or elaborate belief systems associated with such material objects as "wedding rings," "crosses," "clocks," and the Bible or Koran.

In order to really understand culture, we have to move beyond the concrete to focus on what Mukhopadhyay calls the ***mental products of culture***—the collective, shared understandings in our heads; the culturally rooted concepts, beliefs, theories, worldviews, and values; the *meanings*, including the emotions and feelings, that we have learned to associate with material objects and other human inventions. This culturally shared knowledge is actually stored in our brains—as what psychological anthropologists sometimes call *schema* (pl. *schemata*) or in more complex, broader interpretive frameworks, called **cultural models** (see Strauss & Quinn, 1997). These mental models provide a set of guidelines for behaving and responding that we can apply in our daily lives.

But culture is more than mental products, more than ideas in our heads. Culture includes behavior, culturally patterned ways of interacting with each other and the world around us. We can easily observe these **behavioral products of culture**. For example, we can notice similarities in how people greet each other in our culture. We even have labels for common greetings: hugs, handshakes, kisses, high-fives, backslaps, and fist-bumps. And there are the less friendly culturally available gestures for "greeting" other people.

We can also observe culturally conventional ways of decorating our bodies: shaping, coloring, or in other ways dealing with our hair; covering (or not covering) certain body parts; piercing or coloring some facial features but not others (e.g., lips, fingers, ears). Of course, we have several "styles" available to select from, but, as we'll see shortly, these are often limited by our social category or social identity (e.g., gender). We also learn to walk, sit, cross our legs, eat food, and perform bodily functions in ways that are visibly culturally patterned and not the same around the world.

But culture also consists of more elaborate observable behavioral patterns, from "dancing," "graduation," or "Thanksgiving dinner," to complex behavioral events such as a "basketball game," a "marriage," or a "funeral." The quotation marks again signal that these are cultural inventions, ways of moving, learning, dealing with hunger, life, or death. Our language contains thousands of labels for culturally patterned, observable behavioral events. Most of our actions—whether minute or elaborate sequences of events—are guided, without thinking, by these culturally shared mental models.

Our behavior is also constantly shaped by social considerations, the social context we are in, our various social identities, to what social categories and social groups we and others belong. Culture is more than behavior—humans live in **society**, defined broadly as "organized life in groups" (Kottak, 2013, p. 5; Kottak & Kozaitis, 2012, p. G8). But cultures organize human society in different ways, create different types of social organizations, social structures, social institutions, social divisions, social groups, and social roles or identities. They use different criteria (e.g., gender, ancestry, occupation, age) to organize people into groups that perform economic, political, religious, educational, or artistic functions.

These are fairly abstract concepts . . . except when you think about the "natural" world. Even animals with complex social interactions, such as chimpanzees, do not create cultural inventions such as "governments," "nations" with "armies," "Courts," and "Parliament" or "ruling monarchs." Our society, like other large-scale societies, has thousands of groups: religious (churches, temples); educational (schools, universities); economic (corporations, factories, labor unions, banks); and a slew of other voluntary associations, from Girl Scouts to "country clubs."

Less obvious, but universal, are culturally invented social groups based on common ancestry, or kinship, such as "families," whether small household-based units or larger networks of relatives. Indeed, families are a good example of how biological processes, like sexuality and reproduction, have become culturally defined, regulated, and in other ways shaped—and constantly reshaped and redefined—by culture.

Associated with most groups are a set of social roles, or social identities, often involving behavioral expectations, rights, and responsibilities, as well as a sense of belonging or identification. Examples from U.S. culture include social roles associated with educational institutions (professors, students) or with courts of law (judges, jurors).

Social groups can range from long-standing, formal, fundamental societal institutions, governed by explicit rules or laws, such as "corporations" or "families," to more informal communities, based on common interests, identifications, or broader societal divisions, like gender, age, or ethnicity. With the growth of mass culture, the Internet, and other globalizing processes, new social forms are arising. Social media, like Facebook, LinkedIn, and YouTube, create more diffuse but broader social networks, connections, and identities. Popular cultural inventions, like "hip-hop" or other elements of "youth culture," have become global. Nevertheless, we all remain immersed in a culturally invented, if fluid and dynamic, social world that guides our daily behavior.

To understand most observable behaviors, then, especially a complex event, like a "wedding," we'd have to understand the ***social products*** of culture. If this was a traditional, heterosexual, Judeo-Christian U.S. wedding, a Martian would have to learn about U.S. social organization, especially "families" and perhaps religion. To understand why the "father" and not the "mother" gives away the "bride" to the "groom," the Martian would have to be familiar with the (non-biology-related) roles of "father" and "mother," "husband" and "wife." It would also help explain why the bride's family, and not the groom's, paid most of the wedding expenses. Our Martian might encounter other social inventions, like "city hall," "rabbi," "best man," "caterers." Families, marriages, weddings are very complex, elaborate social-behavioral inventions. Like other cultural inventions, they change over time, have microcultural variants, and reflect and are embedded in a larger cultural system.

Our lives, especially as preadults, and for many of us as adults, are spent immersed in another social creation—schools—with their associated social groupings, roles, and identities—teachers, students, administrators, reading coach, sports coach. U.S. educational institutions are the site of numerous culturally invented observable behavioral events. Many are widespread, like assemblies, proms, "recess," "exams," sports, and other recreational events. Others are more local, related to both the socioeconomic conditions and the microcultural characteristics of particular communities.

While we are able to observe culturally shared social and behavioral products, such as weddings or the enactment of social roles by "brides" versus "grooms," our observations are dependent on and interpreted using cultural knowledge that cannot be seen. This is the "mental" level of culture mentioned earlier, the scripts, concepts, understandings, associations, values, meanings, stored in our brains, along with other acquired understandings that enable us to function appropriately in our culture. The concept of "marriage" is exactly that—an intangible, mental product of culture, a complex set of ideas and beliefs and values, with associated social, behavioral, and material products. But concepts, like "marriage," have enormous consequences, as recent U.S. debates over same-sex marriage demonstrate.[2] These debates also illustrate how cultural inventions are subject to change, interpretation, reinterpretation, and reformulation.

We are immersed, then, in a world of ***cultural products*** of all types—most which are intangible, many which cannot be observed, and all profoundly shaping how we experience reality. For this reason, Mukhopadhyay prefers to define culture simply as what human groups collectively create, recognizing that these cultural productions and processes, though sometimes material, are more often social, behavioral, and most of all, mental, that is, they consist of ideas, concepts, beliefs, meanings, entire worldviews.

CULTURE AS A SYMBOLIC SYSTEM

To many anthropologists, one crucial aspect of culture is that it is a ***symbolic system*** (cf. Kottak 2013). Humans possess the ability to bestow meanings on things in the world, to take an object that has no intrinsic meaning—like a band of metal or a set of sounds ("dawg")—and arbitrarily imbue it with meaning. Individuals can create their own private and unique symbols—small children often do that, inventing new combinations of sounds to label objects or people. But culture consists of more widely shared symbols—collectively shared meanings that entire groups of people associate with things in their world.

In the United States, a circle of gold on the third finger of the left hand ("the ring finger") means that one is "married"; a green light at a street means "go ahead"; a red light means "stop." Most religions use material objects to convey religious meanings or identities: a six-pointed star, a cross, a turban, a thread across the chest. Ethnic, adolescent, occupational, or other social groups often use clothing, body decoration, or other objects as markers of group identity.

As with all symbols, the relationship between the object and its meaning is *arbitrary* rather than a property of the object. That is, there is no intrinsic, inherent, natural, or logical link between the object or sign and its meaning. A gold band does not intrinsically mean marriage. Low-slung baggy pants have no inherent meanings. The links—the meanings—are cultural and historical creations. The object has become a symbol of something else. A different object could symbolize marital status or peer group identity, such as a ring in the right earlobe, or two red dots on each cheek.

It is not just material objects that function as symbols. Cultures also bestow meanings on gestures and bodily movements. Think for a second about how you greet a friend. You might wave your right hand, you might clasp hands, you might give the friend a "hug" or a "kiss." Once again, there's nothing about the movement that inherently conveys any particular meaning. All are culturally shared and learned appropriate greeting devices that also carry more complex information about you and your relationship to this person.

They are also intrinsically meaningless gestures. A Martian could not interpret their meaning! Nor could someone from a culture that used other greeting gestures (e.g., stroking ears, tilting heads). Our culture uses, in court, a bent vertical arm with palm facing away from the body to symbolize that one is "swearing to tell the truth." A totally arbitrary meaning has been linked to a body movement enacted in a specific social setting.

Normally, we are unaware that most behaviors (or other symbols) have two parts: the "sign" (whether an object, behavior, sound, design, body part) and the meaning culture has attached to it. Once we've learned the linkages, we internalize them and forget they are arbitrary. The symbol becomes unified, and we experience it as natural and normal. In a new culture, however, the arbitrariness of the linkages is striking! We neither know nor can easily guess the meaning of a slap on the back, the color purple on a door, or unfamiliar sounds or designs.

Virtually all aspects of human sensory experience can function as *meaning-carrying vehicles.* Cultures have bestowed meanings on sounds, smells, tastes, touch, colors, shapes, and designs and on visible human physical characteristics. The links are not intrinsic but cultural. Whether the smell of a steak cooking on a barbecue evokes tasty images or the burning flesh of a slaughtered, innocent cow depends on culturally created linkages. Smell and taste have been filtered through culture. Sight too has been filtered. The meanings of skin color, a fleshy belly, a sharp nose, or other physical features are not intrinsic but cultural and historical creations.

Culture then can be thought of as a complex symbolic system. Language, as part of culture, exemplifies the symbolic complexity of culture. Sounds and combinations of sounds acquire, in a rather unpredictable fashion, meanings that are agreed upon and shared by users. Most words refer to concepts or things in the world. Whether the sounds "dawg" or the sounds "perro" or "koota" are used to represent a particular type of four-legged animal is arbitrary and a historical cultural-linguistic phenomenon.[3] But once linkages are learned, hearing the sounds evokes the visual image almost automatically. These clusters of sounds we call words also evoke more complex connotations and associations. In the United States, dogs are often seen as pets, companions, "man's best friend," lovable, even "sleepable." There are multiple varieties, each with its own set of associations. What a different set of meanings the word "rat" evokes!

By the time most children are five years old and ready to enter school, they can speak at least one language. They have learned not only the relevant sounds of their language but a set of arbitrary links between sounds and meanings (words), and a rich and complex set of conceptual associations and meanings.

Writing is another set of arbitrary designs cultures have created to represent sounds and numbers. That's why there are so many different scripts or writing systems, virtually all mutually unintelligible—"scribbles." Just think about English compared to Greek, Arabic, Hindi, Chinese. Yet by the time students have left the first grade, they have acquired the relevant culturally shared meanings for the written form of their language, such as "a," "b," "c," and so forth, in English (roman) script.

Early in school, children encounter one more complex cultural symbol—a "clock." In the classic analog clock, we see the concept of time represented in arbitrary objects and designs, with "hands" and "numbers" representing the units of time. But the clock also reflects a rather arbitrary division of "time." A day, which has some basis in the natural world, is arbitrarily divided into twenty-four "hours." Why should there be twenty-four rather than twenty divisions of the day? Actually, in the United States, in contrast to many parts of the world, we divide the day into two twelve-hour segments, one a.m. and the second p.m.

Not only do we divide time by hours, but each hour consists, arbitrarily, of sixty "minutes" and each minute sixty "seconds." Learning to "tell time" is not a trivial accomplishment in such an arbitrary system. Moreover, children have to learn the concept of a week—that is, that there is a larger seven-day unit, consisting of five workdays and a "weekend." Not all cultures have a seven-day week, although small cultures with four-day weeks are disappearing.

And then there are calendars. As of this writing, we are in the year 2013. But the earth is far older than 2,013 years. Our species goes back at least 100,000 years, and urban centers go back at least 4,000 years. So . . . why are we in 2013 and not 5774, or 2572, or 100,000 YA (years ago)? Not surprisingly, when different cultures invented calendrical systems, they used their own interpretation of the origins of human life, or, more often, significant events in their own culture or religion. So 2013 reflects, at least originally, the Christian calendar, which begins with the death of Jesus, as in "AD" and "BC." The Jewish, Hindu, Persian, Chinese, or Buddhist calendars will have us in different years. And . . . their New Year celebrations will usually not fall on December 31.

Culture, then, is filled with culturally shared symbols that differ from one culture to another, and which we must learn if we are to function in our culture. Amazingly, we manage to learn them, beginning at birth and throughout childhood and adolescence, and, at a less intense pace, throughout the rest of our lives. And we learn primarily informally, rather than through formal education, through cultural immersion, observing and listening to and imitating others around us, through our families, from other social interactions, though language, increasingly through commercial and mass media sources.

Because cultural symbols and meanings are generally learned early, informally, subtly, and are widely shared by other people in one's culture, they come to be taken for granted. This is especially true for those of us who grow up in a fairly homogeneous society or microworld. We assume everyone shares our cultural meanings. This is a mild, widespread, perhaps universal form of what anthropologists call ***ethnocentrism***. Ethnocentrism is the tendency to assume that one's own cultural ways are normal, universal, and natural, and to judge others by one's own cultural standards. In its more extreme forms, especially in situations of unequal power, ethnocentrism can lead to cultural arrogance and to cultural domination.

Culture, because it is a symbolic system, can also lead to misunderstanding and misinterpretation in culture-contact situations. We automatically assume others share our symbolic systems, that behaviors have the same meanings everywhere. In short, ethnocentric reactions are common, normal, and predictable. To interpret other cultures correctly, one must understand their cultural symbols, the meanings they attach to objects, behaviors, sounds, designs, and other meaning-carrying vehicles.

Ethnocentric reactions can also occur within our own culture. Like any complex, large-scale society, the United States is not and has never been culturally homogeneous. (See chapter 7). There are many ***microcultures***, smaller cultures that reflect our diverse ancestries, national origins, religions, ethnicities, geographic regions, occupations, educational levels, incomes, ages, genders, sexual preferences, and other aspects of our lifestyles. This cultural diversity has intensified in recent decades, partially due to immigration and globalization.

But our society has also opened up, allowing new opportunities for individual and collective expression and for the creation of new social identities and social groups. We can see this in the multiplicity of sexual identities emerging among some gay youth ("fluid," "bi," "questioning," "trans"), in hip-hop and other music-cultural forms, in new hybrid ethnic groups, like "Hindish" or "Nuyoricans", in the growth of "multis," in new forms of blended families.

Microcultures within a culture present both opportunities and challenges. As cultures, they too are symbolic systems, often very complex ones. When encountering individuals from another microculture, it is easy to interpret their behavior (or other cultural symbols) through our own cultural system, leading to misinterpretation and ethnocentric reactions, including denigration of other cultural ways. This can happen when members of different racial, ethnic, and religious groups interact, especially if they live in socially isolated worlds with little opportunity for broader contact. We will see examples of this in part III. If the two cultures are of equal status, then the damage from such miscues may be limited to negative feelings and stereotypes about individuals of the other culture. But when one culture has more societal power, then damages to the less powerful culture can be significant, cumulative, and long lasting (see chapter 7).

THE PSYCHOLOGICAL REALITY OF CULTURE: CULTURE FILTERS REALITY

Many years ago, the famous linguist Edward Sapir wrote an article titled "The Psychological Reality of the Phoneme." Sapir was making the point that we do not hear sound objectively. Instead, our language (or rather, the system of sounds used in the hearer's language) shapes our perception of sound. In short, we do not experience reality directly. Reality (in this case, sound) is filtered through a cultural-linguistic lens.

Building on Sapir's work, others have shown how profoundly culture can alter our perception of reality. The notion of ***psychological reality***—that culture affects how we experience reality—can be extended to all aspects of culture, not just to what we hear.

Our basic senses—our sight, taste, smell, touch, and hearing—are experienced through a cultural filter. Our bodily processes—what we eat, how and where we sleep, how we handle and experience reproduction and excretion—these are not natural but culturally shaped and experienced. The impact of culture is even greater in other realms of life, in the world of ideas, values, and beliefs, and most importantly, for this book, in the social world, in the culturally created social world of race.

Illustration: How Culture Shapes the Sounds We Hear

All languages select a small set of sounds to use from the vast range of possible sounds the human voice can make. One part of learning a language is figuring out which sounds are significant and which can be ignored. For example, English speakers learn to hear the distinction between "w" and "v," as in "wail" and "veil," as clearly as a bell.

Speakers of some other languages learn to ignore this difference. In Hindi, the national language of India, you could say either Di*w*ali or Di*v*ali—both would have the same meaning—namely, the Hindu "festival of lights" for the goddess Lakshmi.

Just as Hindi speakers learn to "not hear" sounds that are irrelevant to their language, English speakers ignore—do not hear—sounds that would be relevant in Hindi and many other languages. For example, all humans are capable of making what linguists call *aspirated* and nonaspirated sounds. *Aspiration* refers to the puff of air that comes out of your mouth when most of us born in the United States say a word such as "pet" or "keg." Try holding your finger or a tissue in front of your lips and see if a slight puff of air comes out or moves the tissue when you say the "p" and the "k." It probably will, because native English speakers tend to automatically produce this airy form.

But there is another (nonaspirated) form of these (and other) consonants. If you are a native English speaker, it may be difficult to produce. But it's not genetic! Simply suppress the air when you say the "p," "t," or "k" in "pet" or "keg." You may have to press your lips together and swallow to keep the air from emerging. But you can do it and you will hear how it slightly alters the sound.

However, U.S. English doesn't employ this sound difference to alter the meaning of words. The meaning of table (or pet or kitchen) remains the same whether or not we suppress the air from coming out.

In every language, speakers unconsciously learn to hear or ignore certain sounds. Our perception of physical sound is altered by the language we speak. Even though we are presented with the same physical reality—that is, sound—we do not perceive it similarly. Rather, what we perceive is structured by what our language has taught us to notice.

If this is true for sound perceptions, it is equally true for our other senses. We do not experience the world directly. We do not see everything that is out there. Our observations are filtered through our brain—through our culturally shared as well as more individualized experience.

CULTURE TRANSFORMS NATURE

Our perception of taste, our sense of smell, our response to touch, what we visually notice, and how we interpret what we see—all our senses are subject to cultural influences. Indeed, culture takes "nature," that is, our bodies and our natural biological capacities, and transforms "nature" into "culture." (Mukhopadhyay, 2006, p. 162). Let us take the example of food. The human stomach is very generalized, that is, we have the biological capacity to consume a large variety of different types of animals and plants. Yet the fact that something is edible does not make it "food," culturally speaking. Cultures define what "food" is, and grasshoppers, rats, mice, horses, termites, cats, and dogs are not part of the conventional "American" cuisine. Our concept of food is a matter of culture not biology.

Another example is touch. All humans are naturally responsive to and crave touch, as infant studies long ago demonstrated. Our relative hairlessness, compared to other primates like chimpanzees, makes our bodies particularly sensitive to touch. Humans use touch for a variety of purposes, especially to establish or express social relationships, even to diffuse tension. Our culture has a myriad of ways through which this natural capacity is culturally expressed. We even talk about "keeping in touch," though this may not involve actual physical contact.

But like any other natural capacity, culture shapes and restricts how, when, and with whom, in what situations, we can touch. Take the simple example of a "hug." There are many types and versions of the conventional U.S. "hug." But there are also commonalities. A hug is about touch . . . but only certain parts of the body touch or are touched: the upper torso, not legs, buttocks, noses. It usually involves gentle squeezing or stroking, rather than punching; and the body is positioned in certain ways (face-to-face, though the head may be slightly averted to the side). There's also a time element. Touching generally last seconds rather than minutes, although it depends on the relationship.

This leads to another significant way culture shapes our capacity to touch. We cannot just hug anyone! Hugs are a "greeting behavior" appropriate for certain social categories of people and not others, in certain contexts, and not others. One wouldn't greet a prospective employer, one's physician, or a professor you just met with a hug. One doesn't generally hug strangers. Or even all nonstrangers and family members. Or all genders.

Some U.S. American men are uncomfortable engaging in a stroking (vs. punching) hug with another male. It wasn't long ago that U.S. culture implicitly restricted postpuberty males from mutual "hugging" and other intimate forms of touch, even among male family members. Ironically, males often felt culturally comfortable greeting a female colleague, or even a virtual stranger with a hug or even a kiss.[4] Of course there's enormous variability among U.S. microcultures. Some, such as immigrant communities that traditionally restrict male-female contact, are quite comfortable with male-male hugging and intimate same-sex touch, overall.

Hugs, then, are actually quite complex cultural products, reflecting the many different ways in which our culture has shaped touch.

CULTURE IMPACTS OUR AFFECTIVE AND EMOTIONAL RESPONSES TO REALITY

Culture not only shapes our biological capacities, our senses, our behaviors, perceptions, and interpretations. Culture shapes our affective responses to reality, our feelings and emotions, desires, our values, and our beliefs about what is good and bad, pleasant and unpleasant, attractive and unattractive, desirable or disgusting. Internalizing a culture creates emotional as well as cognitive patterns in the brain. Culture is emotionally real—the thought of eating a rat does produce a visceral negative emotional response in most native U.S. residents. And many South Asians would find a "rare" steak, in a pool of "blood," equally repulsive. Breast-feeding a child in public still produces discomfort, even value judgments, among some U.S. Americans who are quite comfortable with shirtless males and nude females on calendars. Being asked to "hug" a stranger of the same sex or of the other sex can produce embarrassment and discomfort, depending on what your culture has taught you. Male-male, and perhaps interracial male-female, kissing and other intimate touching may still evoke varied emotional responses in the United States.

Given our deep emotional commitment to our own culture, it is not surprising that attempts to alter cultural patterns can produce resistance and psychological discomfort. Ethnocentrism is in part a positive emotional response to one's own culture and a negative emotional response to cultural difference. Regardless, it is not surprising that situations of cross-culture contact can produce anything from mild dismay at the "weird" behavior of "foreigners" or people from other microcultures to extreme disorientation— bewilderment, anxiety, anger, despair, hostility, and paranoia.

More extreme responses, commonly termed ***culture shock***, occur when individuals are immersed in an alien culture. In the United States, many children, especially language minority and non-Anglo children, experience culture shock when they first enter public school, especially if the staff is predominantly middle class and Euro-American.

Awareness of the ***psychological reality of culture***, including its emotional dimension, its tendency to produce ethnocentrism, and the phenomenon of culture shock can be very useful in all culture contact situations, whether at home or in cross-national encounters. But it is particularly valuable in educational settings. First, it sensitizes us to likely initial reactions when encountering faculty, staff, and students from different cultural backgrounds. Cultural differences and cultural misinterpretation are a possible, though not inevitable source of at least some student conflicts and disciplinary problems, as we will see in part III, especially chapter 10.

Second, it makes us aware that the school is a complex microculture that includes material, social, behavioral, and mental products. People from other cultures, or even microcultures within our own society, may experience culture shock when first encountering the U.S. school or college culture. Cultural awareness can help members of dominant cultural groups develop empathy toward those from culturally different backgrounds.

Introducing the concept of **cultural relativism** offers one useful antidote to ethnocentrism, especially when it is primarily the result of internalized cultural values rather than the type of structured inequality described in chapter 7. Cultural relativism does not exclude the possibility of moral judgments. It recognizes and teaches a basic respect for cultural diversity as part of the human experience. Second, it emphasizes *understanding* other cultures rather than simply making value judgments about them. It argues that cultures are best understood by viewing them in their own cultural context and from the native perspective.

The goal of this approach is cultural understanding—but that is not the same as cultural acceptance. In fact, one can understand a cultural practice (e.g., warfare, female infanticide, slavery) while recognizing its dysfunctional or negative consequences. And one can understand the processes underlying cultural practices, like polygamy, sexual segregation, or lavish, expensive, themed birthday parties for two-year-olds, even though they might be in opposition to your own values.

CULTURE IS DYNAMIC, FLUID, CHANGEABLE

Culture is an incredibly powerful shaper of all aspects of human life and experience. And cultures are systems, that is, a set of interrelated, linked, and reinforcing parts. Weddings, even marriage, are parts of a much more complex cultural system. But that does not mean we, individually or collectively, are prisoners of culture, past or present. Culture and **cultural systems** are human inventions. They are fixed neither in time, nor place, nor in any one group of individuals. Cultures are dynamic, fluid, rich, negotiated, contested, performed, enacted, resisted complexes of material, social, behavioral, emotional, and mental products. They are constantly being produced, reproduced, transformed, internalized (partially), renegotiated, discarded, expressed through a myriad of complex processes that we are only beginning to fully understand.

We have experienced enormous cultural changes in our own lifetimes, just in the area of race, ethnicity, and gender. All three authors of this book were born during an era when states could still outlaw interracial marriage, when housing was legally segregated by race, ethnicity, and religion, when medical and engineering schools could refuse or limit entry based on gender, race, ethnicity, and religion, when there was no birth control pill or access to a legal abortion, even to save the life of the mother. All three of us grew up in microcultures quite different from the ones we now participate in.

These changes did not occur by accident. Cultures are powerful . . . so is society. But we are not cultural robots, blindly internalizing and reproducing culture. We are individuals, we do have agency, we can think about, challenge, reject, reform, reinvent aspects of culture. We have multiple, intersecting identities. None of us are simply our race, ethnicity, gender, nationality, class. We are a combination of and participate in complex, social identities, which can shift with circumstances and time. As the world around us changes, as it always has, we individually and collectively respond, transforming ourselves and our culture. Indeed, culture is the human mode of "adaptation" to our environment, both our physical and our social environment. Cultures have always been transforming their environments (see chapter 3) and then transforming ourselves in response, sometimes consciously, sometimes through more subtle cultural processes. This is how we have survived as a species.

KEY CONCEPTUAL POINTS

- Culture is what humans collectively create over time and includes mental, behavioral, social, and material products.
- Culture primarily consists of cultural knowledge and shared meanings that are intangible and often cannot be observed.
- Culture is a symbolic system—cultures bestow meanings on the world of experience.
- Cultural meanings are not intrinsic or natural; they are arbitrary and vary across cultures.
- Culture profoundly affects how we experience reality: our perceptions, interpretations, actions, emotions. Culture is a human invention but profoundly "real."
- Culture is primarily learned through informal processes, rather than formal education.
- No culture is totally homogeneous; there are always some microcultures, and there are many in modern, complex societies. And individuals have multiple, intersecting social and cultural identities.

- Individuals, though shaped by culture, are not prisoners of culture. Cultures arise through complex processes, are negotiated, resisted, manipulated, and altered, through individuals acting alone and collectively.
- Cultures are systems of interrelated parts; a change in one part can affect other parts. This can also make them resistant to change.
- Cultures are dynamic, not static, and are in constant flux, changing over time through complex processes.
- Ethnocentrism is a common result of the deep internalization of one's culture.
- Culture contact can lead to misinterpretation and even culture shock.

KEY TERMS (ITALICIZED AND BOLDED IN TEXT)

cultural models
society
cultural systems
cultural products: material, social, behavioral, mental
culture shock
cultural relativism
culture
culture as a symbolic system
ethnocentrism
culture as psychologically real
microcultures

ACTIVITIES

Activity Plan 1: The Hug: Transforming Nature into Culture

Objectives: Participants will experience and reflect on the power of culture to shape natural capacities, like our desire for touch, into complex, cultural behavioral inventions like "hugs."

Additional Information: This requires a facilitator (familiar with the concepts in chapter 5) to lead the discussion that follows the brief activity. It is participant centered, interactive, and appropriate for all ages and all size groups, from 2 to 140 people. The activity takes only a few minutes. Allow ten to forty minutes for discussion. No materials required. It may be particularly useful at the beginning of a class or workshop on culture and cultural diversity.

Procedure:

Step 1. Facilitator asks participants to stand up. Pause for a few seconds until they are all standing.

Step 2. Ask participants to hug the person next to them (or nearby). You may have to repeat it a second time, or even a third, for those reluctant.

Step 3. Ask them to sit down and then begin discussion.

Step 4: Discussion. Reflect on what has occurred and what it illustrates, especially key points in chapter 5. A hug is a culturally shaped way of greeting through touch. It requires complex, detailed cultural knowledge. See if you can identify the cultural knowledge a Martian might have to know in order to "hug" in a culturally appropriate manner. Explore the where, what, how, and how long, and by and to whom cultural "rules" that underlie a simple "hug." This creates an opening to discuss hugging rules that reflect one's social identity (including gender, religion, relative status), social relationship (nonstrangers), and also social context.

Explore the extent to which cultural knowledge of hugging is taken for granted, stored as a cognitive pattern, a cultural schema, at an unconscious level. Note that an intrinsically meaningless set of sounds uttered by the facilitator immediately evoked a rather complex behavioral image, the "hug," and then a set of actions. Ask, naively, if participants had to consciously think of "how" to perform a hug, what to do, whether to use their feet or their upper torso, what to do with their eyes, and so on. Explore the processes through which they might have "learned" the "hug."

You can also explore variations in participant responses to this activity. Mild discomfort ("embarrassment") may come from violating implicit social norms, such as that one doesn't hug strangers in a workshop or class. This illustrates the internalized nature of culture as well as how informal sanctions, such as embarrassment, and other forms of social pressure, work.

Some participants may experience more distress because of their own microcultural background, gender, religion, ethnicity, or race. These variations and their meanings can be examined, including cultural attitudes about touch, sexuality, and same-sex or male-female physical interactions.

Cultural rules on touching, including hugging, often are linked to broader themes in a cultural system. As a prelude to discussions of race, explore cultural "rules" for hugging across racial lines, historically and today. These can be linked to other features of the broader U.S. racial system, especially historical sanctions on interracial mating and marriage (see chapter 9).

Activity Plan 2: The Albatross: Culture as a Symbolic System That Shapes How We See the World

Objectives: Participants will be able to describe how cultural knowledge can lead us to misinterpret the behavior we observe. Participants will provide examples of what it means to say that culture shapes reality. Participants will understand how greetings are part of a culture's system of symbols.

Additional Information: All ages, including adults. Time required: ten to fifteen minutes for ritual; thirty to sixty minutes for discussion.

There are two ways to use the Albatross: a "live" version or using a CD/DVD version Mukhopadhyay recorded many years ago. The "live" version requires preparation, mainly by two people who will play the role of the Albatross couple. Those participating in the greeting ritual are drawn from members of the class or workshop. Both males and females are required, ideally in equal numbers, usually from one to four pairs.

The Procedure section below briefly summarizes the major steps. A detailed lesson plan and explicit instructions for a live performance are available through the RACE exhibit Teacher's Guides at http://www.understandingrace.org/resources/for_teachers.html. For access to the CD or DVD version of the activity, see http://www.understandingrace.org/resources/.

Procedure: Brief Version

Step 1. Participants view a live or videotaped greeting behavior sequence in a hypothetical culture called Albatross.[5] In the live version, one to four male-female pairs are selected to participate in the greeting ritual.

Step 2. After the ritual, participants describe (orally, written form) the Albatrossian culture, especially gender (male-female) relations and female status, as illustrated in specific features of the ritual. Participants uniformly perceive it as a male-dominated culture and provide evidence from the ritual. For example, unlike men, women take off their shoes, sit on the floor, are served after the men, and the Albatrossian woman seems to be dominated by the Albatrossian man, as indicated by her frequent "bows" to him.

Step 3. The discussion facilitator (or the Albatrossian couple) reveals this is a female-dominant culture. Women are regarded as superior to men, as reflected in numerous parts of the ritual. For example, only women are pure enough to sit on the ground, the sacred earth.

Step 4. Discussion. Compare participant interpretations of the ritual to their meaning in the Albatrossian culture. Facilitator notes that misinterpretation occurs because participants, predictably, have interpreted the ritual through a U.S. cultural lens. This illustrates how culture is internalized, inside our heads, as cultural models that shape our perceptions and interpretations of what we see and believe about other people, especially from other cultures. Facilitator can also point out how verbal descriptions of behavior can encode interpretation, such as "the woman *bowed* her head to the man" or "the women *had* to sit on the floor."

Step 5. Prepare participants for how other cultural inventions, like race, shape our perceptions and interpretations. How might misunderstandings occur in cross-racial and cross-ethnic encounters? How might the lessons of the Albatross simulation help us to understand tensions between members of different ethnoracial, religious, or other cultural backgrounds or lifestyles? Have participants discuss instances of cultural misinterpretation they've encountered.

Step 6: Extension of discussion to school settings.

This activity also links to part III and discussions of cultural misunderstandings that can occur in school contexts. Ask participants to apply the lessons of Albatross to an encounter with someone from another racial, ethnic, or religious group in their school (e.g., in a classroom, the cafeteria, other settings). What types of misinterpretation could occur?

How might this lesson have a bearing on which students seem to be "smart" or "good students" or "bad students"? What specific behaviors do students or faculty use to form impressions of each other? Could "speaking out" in class be considered disrespectful in some cultures? Antisocial and competitive? What alternative interpretations are possible?

How might people from different cultural backgrounds differently interpret student-related behavior (e.g., student clothing, kissing in public, playground activities, disagreeing with the teacher in class, etc.). Can behavior of school personnel, such as teachers, also be misinterpreted?

ADDITIONAL ACTIVITY IDEAS

Activity Idea 1: The Pervasiveness of Culture

Objectives: Participants will discover how much of their daily life, at the most basic levels, is shaped to some extent by their culture.

Additional Information: Participant-centered, appropriate for all ages, takes five to twenty minutes, depending on how facilitator handles the discussion.

Procedure: Ask participants to think about or make a list of everything in their life, everything they did, from the time they awoke, that was to some extent "cultural," whether it involved material, social, behavioral, or mental products of culture.

Discuss, being sure to include how culture shaped how they handled basic bodily needs, like sleeping (where, in what, when), bodily waste, and nutrition, how and with what products they cleansed and in other ways modified and decorated their bodies.

Activity Idea 2: Exploring the Concept of Culture Using School Culture

Objectives: Participants will be able to apply the concept of culture and cultural products to their own school, college, or university, or other institutional culture.

Additional Information: Participant centered, interactive, appropriate for all ages; takes ten to thirty minutes. No materials required.

Procedure: Participants explore the concept of culture pretending they are Martians trying to understand their own school (or other cultural setting). Participants provide examples of material, social, behavioral, and mental products of culture. They can explore a particular school site (e.g., library, playground, cafeteria), a single event (a dance, assembly, lunch), or school greeting behaviors (handshakes, hugs, etc.). For examples of school-related cultural products, see http://www.sjsu.edu/people/carol.mukhopadhyay.

Activity Idea 3: Teaching about Race

Explore additional activities in the Teaching about Race module at http://www.sjsu.edu/people/carol.mukhopadhyay and at http://www.understandingrace.org/resources/.

NOTES

1. Quotes in these contexts refer to folk terms or concepts that are cultural inventions and not universal.

2. It is interesting to think about parallels with historical debates over interracial marriage. See chapter 9.

3. A few words are not totally arbitrary, such as "buzz," which resembles the sound of a bee.

4. Recall the infamous touchy shoulder rub former President George W. Bush once gave the seated German Chancellor Angela Merkel at a major conference, to the consternation of Merkel and many other observers.

5. This is an adaptation of a simulation called "The Albatross," which was circulating among multicultural education people in the 1970s (Gochenour, 1977). Although the basic ritual is similar, the pedagogical context, principles illustrated, and discussion aspects are different.

Chapter Six

Culture and Classification

Race Is Culturally Real

Chapter 5 explored the concept of culture and the power of culture to shape how we experience both the natural and social world. A key point is that while cultural productions include material objects and observable, culturally patterned ways of behaving, much of culture is invisible, and consists of complex meanings, concepts, and associations. It is this cultural knowledge which allows us to "read" the meanings of what we can see and touch.

Language is an important part of culture and illustrates how culture works. Languages have a physical reality: we can hear sound. But what turns sounds into language is the shared meanings we have learned to associate with these sounds. Words can be thought of as clusters of sounds linked to particular concepts. But concepts and the way we classify them are also cultural inventions. Classification is basic to human thinking and central to human language. Words, in part, reflect cultural classifications of things in the world, whether animals, foods, time, greetings, or groupings of human beings.

Chapter 6 explores culture's role in the systems of classification we use in daily life. We then examine the idea of race as a cultural and historically specific system for classifying the human world. We show that racial categories, like other cultural inventions, become deeply internalized and unconscious, and profoundly shape our perceptions and experiences of the social world.

CONCEPTUAL OVERVIEW

The Role of Classification in Human Life

Reality is enormously complex. Even the smallest thing, like a flower, has many elements. And each flower differs from every other flower, if only in minute ways.

This is true for the natural world of plants, leaves, flowers, soils, rocks. It also applies to the human world. Color is a continuum of an infinite number of shades, as a trip to a paint store will tell you. So is sound. Just ask anyone who has tried to play a stringed instrument, like a violin, or even a flute or French horn. We encounter thousands of different objects in our daily life. Despite mass production of goods, two items are hardly ever exactly alike. And then there are gestures. A simple greeting like a "wave," or a "hug," will vary somewhat when performed by different people, or on different occasions. And human bodies, as we saw in part I, are quite variable, in minute but potentially noticeable ways, even before we add body decoration.

Humans probably could not survive without the ability to classify. Classifying is partially a device for reducing the complexity of reality, for eliminating "noise" that would otherwise make life chaotic. It helps us focus on and notice what is relevant. It enables us to create generalizations about the physical or social world and formulate general rules that we can apply to people, things, and situations. Can you imagine having to treat every human being, every classroom, object, and situation as totally unique? We would go mad!

So *classification* is an essential, functional part of human thought and language. It rests on categorizing and labeling some things as different and some things as alike, of separating apples from oranges, fruits from vegetables, blue from green, breakfast from dinner, Sunday from Monday. It often involves levels, or a hierarchy, of classification; things that are different at one level (Sunday and Monday) are often similar at a higher level, part of a more comprehensive category (e.g., different kinds of days in a "week").

CULTURES CREATE PARTICULAR CLASSIFICATIONS OF REALITY

Because most of reality is a continuum, without clear boundaries, there are many alternative ways to subdivide and organize reality into a smaller set of categories, to create a system of classification. As individuals, we could devise numerous ways to classify any set of objects, but most of us rely on our culture to provide us with categories. Cultures have come up with diverse ways of classifying things in the natural and social world and in the world of ideas. Indeed, some anthropologists consider this a crucial aspect of a culture's conceptual system and worldview.

Language, as a part of culture, reflects the culture in which the language is spoken. For anthropologists, studying language, especially words and the relationships among words, is one way of finding out how people in a culture conceptualize their world. Cultural knowledge is encoded, at least partially, in language.

Not surprisingly, language is one of the primary ways through which children learn about their culture, including major categories and underlying cultural concepts. This is true for racial as well as other categories. By learning a language, anthropologists argue, children learn a particular system of classification, a conceptual framework, and a cultural way of noticing the world around them (see chapter 5). Racial categories subtly teach children what is important about people in their social world. Racial labels also carry complex meanings and associations which children learn. Like most learning, we acquire our knowledge of *racial classifications* informally, through observation, participation, both directly and indirectly, in our own culture and microcultures.

Research has established that our systems of classification, embedded in language, shape our perceptions, thinking, and ways of acting in the world. Anthropologists once argued that language categories *determine* thought and perception. For example, some believed that people whose language did not contain verbs in the past tense could not think about the past. Such extreme views have been rejected. On the other hand, there is no doubt that cultures classify reality in different ways and that through immersion in a culture and a language, we acquire that culture's slant on reality.

Cultural Classifications: An Array of Alternatives

Cultural classifications provide us with at least two types of information. Systems of classifications consist of categories, and categories are groups of items, considered similar, at least for some purposes. So culture, partially through language, tells us what kinds of things "go together." Take, for example, the U.S. English word "food." The concept of "food" includes a lot of disparate items, from broccoli, to apples, to salmon, to ice cream. It does *not* normally include grasshoppers, or nasturtiums. Or take one subcategory of food, "sandwiches." Again, there are many different items in this category, but they all fit our cultural concept of a "sandwich" and are different than "salads" or "casseroles." Other food items, "desserts," "entrees," "appetizers" also share some common features.

Second, culture, through language, provides us with a set of *classifying devices*. These are principles or criteria for lumping together some things and for separating others. The category "food" implicitly contrasts items in the category with items that are not food. So the classifying principle which allows us to lump together lettuce, salmon, and French fries (but not caterpillars) in the category of "food" is that our culture considers them appropriate to eat. In contrast, cats are not considered food in the United States—they are "pets."

Similarly, sandwiches have certain properties which make them fall into the category "sandwich"—something like two pieces of bread with a filling in between. Or at least, that's the "core" or prototypic image of a sandwich. We have other sandwiches that don't quite fit, such as an "open-faced" sandwich, with only one piece of bread. Or a hamburger sandwich that uses a "bun" rather than bread. The point is that sandwich is a categorizing device (both a concept and a category), with a set of core meanings, represented by the "typical" (prototypical) sandwich. But the category "sandwich" also includes a range of less typical sandwiches.

These general principles of classification are not just relevant to sandwiches. They also apply to social classifications, such as racial categories. Racial categories, like "Black" or "White" or "Asian," are classifying concepts, ways of grouping humans, using particular classifying devices. As with other concepts, we tend to learn and think about them in terms of *prototypes*, that is, a "typical" member of a racial category. And when someone doesn't fit our prototype, we may signal that by using words like "but"— "she is African American but can't dance at all"; "he is Asian but is terrible at math." In a sense, stereotypes partially reflect a broader human tendency to classify, to use prototypes, to overgeneralize, to ignore the diversity within any category, including social categories. And while some stereotypes are negative, there can also be positive stereotypes (e.g., U.S. Asians as the "model minority"). The point is that stereotypes are overgeneralizations, derived from culturally created prototypes and culturally relevant classifying devices.

Classifying devices can provide insights into what a culture considers important, what distinctions are relevant to make, its beliefs and theories, its values, its prejudices, which social groups have power. Again, this is particularly relevant to the area of racial classification.

Our culture, like all other cultures, is replete with systems for organizing and classifying reality. The educational system is filled with such categories and classifications. For example, schools are organized into "elementary," "middle," and "high schools," using student age and level of learning as the primary classifying devices.

Classification may be basic to human culture, but the particular classifications are human, culturally and historically specific inventions. Anthropologists have discovered enormous cultural variability in how cultures divide up the same reality, in what they group together, what they separate, and in the classifying devices they use. This applies to the natural world but is even more striking in the social world.

Classifying Drinking Vessels: "Cups"

Let us take a simple example from U.S. culture, the concept of a cup.[1] The word *cup* labels a set of objects that differ dramatically in size, shape, material, design, and so on.

There are subcategories (e.g., coffee cups, tea cups, soup cups). And cup is part of a larger classification that includes "glasses," "mugs," "bottles," and other drinking vessels. Each of these, like "glasses," also has subcategories (water glasses, wine glasses).

Native U.S. English speakers tend to have similar criteria for classifying drinking vessels. How is a cup different from a glass? Many of us would answer "handles"—are they present or not? Other features we'd notice are the use of the vessel—for hot versus cold liquids—and the construction material (glass versus nonglass).

But not all potential differences are utilized in the U.S. classification system. We don't care about the color of the vessel, its cost, the type of people who use it, or even its shape, apart from handles. Should we go to another culture, even an English-speaking one, we would find a different system. In rural India, for example, tea is often served in a "tea cup," a disposable small clay vessel that lacks a handle, or in a glass tumbler that resembles what we would call a "glass."

The "cup" example is only a small, rather trivial illustration of classification. But the crucial point is the potential for variability cross-culturally. This is because our labels, our classifications and categories, are cultural creations. They are not found in nature, even when they refer to natural objects (color, plants).

Color Terminology

Let us take an example from the natural world, color. Color is a physical reality, like sound or smell. We are very visually oriented as a species, with both stereoscopic and color vision.

But not all languages have the same number of *basic color terms*. Some languages take the entire color spectrum and divide it into two basic types of colors (dark versus light); others have only three or four categories. Still others, like English, have as many as eleven basic color terms (black, brown, gray, blue, green, purple, orange, yellow, red, pink, white). There is no evidence that people in cultures with fewer color categories lack the capacity to *see* color distinctions. They just break up the color spectrum into different numbers of groups. And they divide the continuum of color at different places in the spectrum. This should not be surprising, when we think about it. Color is continuous and there are no natural divisions. (See also chapter 1.)

Not only do languages have different numbers of color terms, but they also use different criteria to differentiate colors. In English, for example, hue (shade), brightness, and intensity are used (e.g., blue versus green). The Hanunoo, in the Philippines, however, have developed specialized color terms based on additional features, such as whether or not a plant is succulent and whether it is wet or dry. Both affect the visual appearance of plants and are thus important in Hanunoo culture.

The point is that while color has a physical reality, it can be divided in many ways, and different languages divide and label the same reality differently. Humans organize nature into culturally specific categories that reflect what is relevant in their culture.

Culture—through language—categorizes all aspects of reality. We have classification systems for animals ("reptiles," "mammals"), plants ("roses," "pansies," "vegetables"), landscapes, bodies of water, body parts, furniture, types of entertainment. We classify activities ("housework," "studying," "working," "going out," "exercising") and, as we saw in chapter 5, time ("weeks," "minutes," "centuries").

CLASSIFICATIONS OF THE SOCIAL WORLD: KINDS OF PEOPLE

Kinship: What Kinds of Relatives Are There?

Besides classifying the natural world, humans classify the social world. Classification of relatives is preeminent, particularly in small-scale societies. Indeed, the concept of "relative" or "family" is itself a way of classifying the human world. Many cultures traditionally divided the social world into two basic categories: relatives and nonrelatives.

If we speak only one language and have lived in only one country, we probably think of our labels for relatives as natural. That is, as native U.S. English speakers, we may assume that everyone around the world uses kinship terms equivalent to our "aunts," "uncles," "grandparents," and "cousins." We think of these as natural divisions of relatives rather than as culturally specific ways of classifying a broad range of relatives into a few different categories. Yet studies of *kinship terms* in other societies illustrate the many different ways cultures can classify relatives.

Kinship is partially about biology—but not all biological differences are recognized in a culture's kinship terms. Only some classifying attributes are used to categorize relatives. Some of the most common are gender (e.g., brother versus sister) and generation (above, below, same as you). U.S. kinship terminology tends to differentiate relatives to whom we are directly related (parent-child-grandparents) from those who are siblings of a parent (e.g., father's brother).

Many cultures utilize more distinctions than we do and so have more labels for relatives. It is quite common to have different kinship terms for mothers' and fathers' relatives; or to differentiate relatives with common ancestry ("blood') from in-laws.

Standard U.S. English kinship terms, however, are few in number. Let us take the term "uncle." Think about how many biologically different kinds of relatives are lumped into this one category! We include mother's brother as well as father's brother even though they are from totally different "sides" of the family and are usually unrelated. We also throw in people who are not even genealogically connected but simply relatives through marriage. So in addition to father's brother, our concept of "uncle" includes "in-laws" like father's sister's husband and mother's sister's husband. The term "cousin" is even broader and does not differentiate males and females.

Such a classification would be inconceivable and incomprehensible in many cultures. Gender distinctions between maternal versus paternal sides of the family and between "blood" relatives and "in-laws" are often crucial to social life. They can affect inheritance, marriage, household responsibilities, and political representation. Not surprisingly, these significant features are highlighted by having separate labels for mother's versus father's brother and for relatives through marriage. Relative age ("elder" brother) may also be recognized.

On the other hand, U.S. Americans recognize distinctions that some cultures ignore. Most of us find it natural to separate "mother" from mother's sister, with the label "aunt." Or, as mentioned earlier, "father" from father's brother ("uncle"). Yet some cultures use the *same* kinship term for both types of relatives. The Tiv of Nigeria traditionally lumped father and father's brother together, with only one kinship term. But they have separate terms for mother's brother and father's brother (Bohannon, 2000).[2]

The point, once again, is that there are innumerable ways to classify and label relatives. All cultures ignore some potential distinctions and highlight others. The different choices they make produce the cross-cultural variability we see in kinship terms.

Why Do Cultures Classify Kin Differently?

But how do we explain these variations? Anthropologists have long asked this question. Is it just random? Chance? Hardly. Relatives are very important in most cultures, socially, economically, politically, religiously, emotionally. Indeed, family and kinship have traditionally been the core of social organization in human societies.

Categorizing people in certain ways tends to reflect the local system of social organization, the kinds of rights and obligations allocated to different kinds of people, the system of values and beliefs. Labels have real meaning and refer to concepts that are deeply internalized. The 1950s U.S. conservative political slogan "He's your uncle, not your dad" embodies Anglo-American concepts of family obligations, that your father and not your uncle is responsible for your welfare. In the above phrase, "He" refers to the government and is an argument for limiting the "welfare state."

Whether one is labeled a sister, a mother, an aunt, a grandmother, a first or second cousin, signals a particular type of relationship, and in some cases, marital rights and legal obligations. Authority, power, economics, marriage and sexuality, living arrangements, emotions—all are to various degrees encoded in our culture's system for categorizing and labeling relatives. We are supposed to and generally feel and behave differently toward mothers versus aunts, cousins versus siblings, parents versus great-uncles, relatives versus nonrelatives. Culture is cognitively, socially, economically, and emotionally real, and how we classify relatives shapes how we experience the social world of family.

Race: A Cultural Classification of the Social World

Large, complex cultures often use criteria besides kinship to divide up and categorize the social world. North American racial categories, as we have shown in part I, do not exist in nature. They are a cultural creation, a system of classifying people, first invented by Europeans and subsequently elaborated in the United States.

The North American racial system relies on a few physical traits, such as skin color and hair form, as visible markers of one's racial classification and racial ancestry. Other societies may select *different* biological traits to create races (e.g., height, nose or ear shape) or ignore biology altogether and utilize other visible markers of identity (see chapter 8).

Humans apparently have a propensity to classify other human beings, and to recognize and often classify others based on observable features. Indeed, some psychologists have argued that we are hardwired to recognize physical differences in humans. That is, they suggest our brains are predisposed to recognize and then classify people using visual markers (see Hirschfeld, 1997).[3]

Certainly this ability would have been adaptive in early human societies. Recognizing age or gender variations, for example, would be advantageous for infant care, child rearing, and organizing social relationships and responsibilities on the basis of age and gender. The cognitive propensity to remember detailed physical features would help people differentiate among their own relatives, between relatives and strangers, and to develop a system of social roles based on kinship.

Some psychologists, like Hirschfeld, go further and suggest there is a human cognitive propensity to attach invisible meanings to visible traits, to see what is visible as evidence of a more fundamental, innate set of characteristics, to link surface appearances with a deeper or inner essence. In this view, *essentialist thought* is innate in human thinking, and racial thinking builds on this.

Yet not all cultures create social categories based on visible physical traits. Nor do all complex, stratified societies rank groups from inferior to superior based on biological traits. European and North American racial ideology, especially during periods of colonialism and slavery, influenced other cultures' ways of classifying people. In some cases, racial categories were superimposed on existing indigenous social systems. Nevertheless, even in places like Latin America and the Caribbean, local cultures neither attach the same meanings to "color" nor define race as in the United States (see chapter 8).

Race, like any other system of social classification, is a culturally specific device for categorizing people that emphasizes certain distinctions and ignores others. Its roots lie in historical and social conditions, in relations of power and subordination—not in nature.

THE EMERGENCE OF THE NORTH AMERICAN RACIAL WORLDVIEW

There is a wealth of scholarship that explores the origins and development of the American racial classification system, what Smedley calls the American *racial worldview* (Smedley & Smedley, 2012). Scholars recognize at least two separate strands of thinking about race in the United States (Haney-Lopez, 1996). One might be called "folk beliefs," the ideas of ordinary people about race and other social divisions. Historians find race as a folk concept in the English language as far back as the 16th century. Between the 16th and 18th centuries, race was used interchangeably with other terms such as *type, kind, sort, breed,* and even *species* (Smedley & Smedley, 2012).

Another prominent strand came from the world of science, especially 17th-, 18th-, and 19th-century European natural science. Building on European Enlightenment themes, the belief in "reason" and human perfectibility, philosophers and intellectuals preoccupied themselves with systematically describing and classifying the natural world. They created a science of classification called *taxonomy*.

In the 18th century, these principles of natural science were extended to humans, and the search for biological subdivisions of the human species began in earnest. The first formal definition of human races in taxonomic terms—that is, using modern principles of biological classification—was by the Swedish naturalist Carolus Linnaeus, in *Systema Naturae* (Systems of Nature), first published in 1735. Linnaeus classified humans into four sub-species, corresponding to the four major continents (Europe, America, Asia, Africa). Each was described by skin color (white, red, yellow, and dark or black). Linnaeus, like others during this time, linked character traits to physical traits and anatomy. *Homo sapiens Europaeus* had white skin color, blue eyes, was "muscular," inventive and ruled by law. *Homo Asiaticus* was, among other things, sallow, melancholy, and avaricious. *Homo sapiens Americanus* was reddish, obstinate, and regulated by customs. The most negative description was of *Homo sapiens Africanus*, "women without shame, they lactate profusely," "indolent," and "governed by caprice" (Smedley & Smedley, 2012, p. 219).

U.S. racial categories were most heavily influenced by German anatomist **Johann Blumenbach** (1752–1784), sometimes called the father of physical anthropology. After carefully studying Linnaeus's system, Blumenbach proposed five instead of four fundamental subdivisions of the human species. He separated out dark-skinned Africans from the African category and labeled them "Ethiopian." He split non-Caucasus Asians into two separate races. The first was the category "Mongoloid" and included inhabitants of Asia, including China and Japan. The second race was the "Malay" race and incorporated native Australians, Pacific Islanders, and other island people in the region. Indigenous Americans remained a separate race.

Blumenbach also coined the term **Caucasian**. Apparently, he was impressed by the beauty of a woman's skull from the Caucasus Mountains region, located between Russia and Turkey. He admired it because it was more symmetrical than other skulls in his collection. To him, the skull reflected nature's ideal form, the circle, and he reasoned it must have resembled "God's original creation" (Haviland, Prins, Walrath, & McBride, 2005, p. 81).

Blumenbach eventually visited the area, declaring its people the most beautiful in the world. From their beauty he inferred that the Caucasus Mountains area must be near where humans originated. He decided all light-skinned peoples from this region, plus Europeans, belonged to the same race, which he labeled Caucasians.

Blumenbach went farther. Based on the Judeo-Christian belief that humans were created in God's image, he believed Caucasians most closely resembled the original ideal humans. Other races, he argued, had degenerated physically and morally as a result of moving away from their place of origins and adapting to new environments (Haviland, Prins, Walrath, & McBride, 2005, p. 81).

These so-called scientific categories were actually social inventions that drew upon long-standing European folk and religious beliefs in hierarchy, in "superior" and "inferior" religions, "stock," peoples, languages, and cultures. But combining popular ideas and religious authority with scientific authority created a powerful ideology that quickly spread to the U.S. scientific community.

As U.S. *racial science* emerged, racial classification drew upon the 19th-century preoccupation with identifying evolutionary stages in everything from human language, technology, and religion to forms of marriage and kinship. Nineteenth-century scientists created grand evolutionary ladders, categorized diverse forms from "primitive" to more "advanced," and ranked the world's cultures accordingly. Cultural "advance," in these theories, primarily resulted from human biological—indeed, intellectual—development. Culture and biology were intertwined.

In *Ancient Society* (1877), the American anthropologist Lewis Henry Morgan identified three major stages of human evolution (cultural and biological). The earliest stages were Savagery and Barbarism (each with lower, middle, and upper stages). The most advanced form was Civilization. Not surprisingly, the British (and Caucasians) topped the evolutionary pyramid, representing "Civilization" and "civilized" family forms, including monogamy (one husband–one wife).

European scientists occupied themselves with identifying the evolutionary position of societies under their colonial control. Morgan, in the United States, concentrated on Native Americans. Physical anthropologists focused on identifying "primitive" and more "advanced" physical forms, measuring skulls and other presumed indicators of intellect (see chapter 1).

Blumenbach's racial categories dovetailed with 19th-century evolutionary theories, and different races were assigned different evolutionary ranks. Although the theories were long ago discredited, labels and categories from this period persist: "savages," "barbarians," "civilized," "primitive," "advanced." And the race–evolutionary stage association remains alive in the minds of some U.S. Americans in assertions that some races are more evolved, primitive, advanced, or closer (or farther) from the apes.

Blumenbach's and Linnaeus's racial categories found their way into U.S. American law. The categories White and Black appear in legal documents during the colonial period. Racial science was appropriated to justify slavery and, later, to counter legal and other perceived threats to the dominance of elite Euro-American males. Legal debates in the 20th century over the meaning of White and Caucasian explicitly cite Blumenbach and employ other racial categories like Mongoloid (see chapter 7). This framework, including the label Caucasian, persists today in popular discourse and in some scientific writing (Mukhopadhyay, 2012).

Chapter 7 discusses some dilemmas posed by Blumenbach's racial categories. U.S. naturalization laws, beginning in 1790, restricted citizenship to Whites. How was White to be defined? What about new immigrants such as Syrians or Armenians or Bengali Muslims or Jews? And was White equivalent to Caucasian, as Blumenbach implied? If so, naturalization would be open to people from India who had, partially on the basis of their Indo-Aryan languages, been defined as Caucasian.

The late 19th century also witnessed a surge of European immigrants quite different from the predominant U.S. "Yankee" stock. Was this hodgepodge of Jews, Catholics, Irish, Greeks, Italians, and other "refuse" from the shores of Southern and Eastern Europe going to be accorded the same "White privilege" given to immigrants from England, France, and Germany?

As early as the mid-19th century, perhaps in response to the wave of Irish Catholic immigration, U.S. racial science began to make distinctions within the White race. Samuel Morton, a wealthy Philadelphian physician, divided the "Modern Caucasian Group" into six "families." He purported to show, using now discredited data on skull size, that the "Teutonic Family"(Germans, English, Anglo-Americans) was superior in intelligence to other "families": the Semitic group, the Celtic family, and the Indostanic family (Gould, 1981).

By the 1920s, eugenicists,[4] building on the work of scientists like Morton and on other popular writings, had divided European Whites into three or four ranked subraces: Nordic, Alpine, Mediterranean, and Jews (Semitics). The rankings not only asserted the inherent intellectual superiority of Nordics (and inferiority of groups such as Russian Jews), but also argued for fundamental differences in "character" and the capacity for civilization.

Arguments about the superiority and inferiority of White subdivisions played a prominent role in popular and legal arguments for restricting immigration in the 1920s. Supporters argued that the influx of inferior "Mediterraneans" would dilute the purity of the White population already in the United States.

One popular book by Kenneth Roberts, *Why Europe Leaves Home*, was typically blunt:

> The American nation was founded and developed by the Nordic race, but if a
> few more million members of the Alpine, Mediterranean and Semitic races are
> poured among us, the result must inevitably be a hybrid race of people as
> worthless and futile as the good-for-nothing mongrels of Central America and
> Southeastern Europe. (cited by Brodkin, 1998, p. 25)

Arguments for restricting immigration prevailed. Some Whites were deemed more White, or more accurately, superior Whites. Immigration laws (and other practices) were designed to preserve the ethnic dominance of Nordics—the earliest North-Western Anglo-Saxon Protestant ethnic groups to arrive in the United States. It wasn't until after World War II that ethnic, religious, and racial barriers among European Americans began to dissolve and the White racial category became more homogenized.

The U.S. system of racial classification has shifted over time, partly in response to changing demographics and historical circumstances (see chapter 7). But some things have remained stable. One has been the Linnaeus/Blumenbach framework of major color-coded racial categories: White, Caucasian; Black, African; Red, American Indian; and Yellow, Mongoloid or Asians.

These categories remained enshrined in U.S. institutions until the 1960s, when they began to be challenged, especially in the context of immigration and naturalization law. Yet they continue as a conceptual foundation for categories used in census, educational, and health statistics, although these too are under scrutiny. The outmoded, archaic term "Caucasian" seems particularly impervious to change, especially as a formal, seemingly scientific, substitute for the term "White," that is, for the category European Americans (Mukhopadhyay, 2012).[5]

Race is fundamentally a social category, rooted in history and culture, rather than in nature. Sadly, remnants of these discredited beliefs about race as biology, about superior and inferior races, about race and intellect, and about links between biology and culture can still be found in contemporary popular U.S. American culture. Cultural categories—and their associations—are very deeply rooted.

Racial Classifications Are Learned: Race Is Culturally Real

Racial categories, like other labels, are classifying devices we use to negotiate the everyday world we live in, yet they are not natural. They have to be *learned.*

We said earlier that learning a culture involves learning the conceptual framework and classification system of that culture. Part of the job of culture is to transmit to children the culturally specific versions of what things—and kinds of people—are similar and different and in which culturally significant ways they differ. The North American system of *racial classification* is transmitted in a myriad of subtle (and not so subtle) ways. Children, through language, learn racial categories at an early age, just like they learn other cultural systems of classification, whether of drinking vessels, colors, or relatives.

This knowledge is reinforced by schools (see part III). Part of the school's job is to transmit to children the dominant cultural categories, with their associated concepts, values, attitudes, and connotations. Children have a substantial vocabulary by age five, so they enter school with a social classification system already shaped by their home culture and language. If this matches the racial classification system taught at school, children's existing knowledge will be reinforced.

But some children who have not learned the U.S. system of racial categories, such as immigrant children, may experience difficulty, a kind of culture shock. This is an example of what anthropologists call ***cultural discontinuity***, contrasts between the home culture and school culture. Part III discusses other forms of discontinuity and how this, along with power differences and other social and material racially linked disadvantages, can affect school achievement.

Race Is Culturally Real

We experience the world in part through the categories and concepts our language and culture give us, without thinking about them. Once learned, racial categories, like other cultural categories, become deeply internalized, often at an unconscious level, especially for members of dominant racial groups. Racial classification becomes automatic, seems natural, as do races. For people who have grown up in a U.S. racialized world, race feels natural and normal, like a seven-day week or a sixty-minute hour.

Racial categories, like other cultural categories, profoundly shape how we experience the world. We unconsciously focus on race and racial markers and ignore other characteristics of individuals. We literally perceive people racially. Racial attributes, such as skin color, become perceptually salient; they "stick out." Other racially irrelevant physical features, like earlobes; hair color; or hand, tooth, or body shape, recede into the background (see chapter 1).

When we encounter new people, we try to categorize them racially, fit them into our existing set of categories. Is this person Black? White? Latino? Asian? Native American? If they don't fit, we may feel confused, even disoriented. The categories have become internalized, "natural," culturally real.

In short, we have learned to view people through a racial lens. Race is psychologically real (see chapter 5). We notice (and interpret) racially marked traits in ways different from other aspects of human biological variation. Racial traits become symbols—and we are often unaware of the elaborate cultural meanings, associations, emotions, beliefs, assumptions about behaviors, capacities, or even diseases propensities—they invoke. Without necessarily intending to, we may racially stereotype people, that is, draw upon and apply to individuals the "cultural knowledge," the "prototype," "typical" image we associate with members of this racial category. Others do the same to us.

Racial categories, the concept of race, the racial worldview, is so deeply embedded conceptually (and institutionally) in our culture that it is hard to imagine it is a cultural creation. And race *is* real as a social phenomenon. Race—along with our other social identities like gender, class, and religion—impacts our lives, how we experience and act in the world, how others experience and act toward us. Race impacts our pocketbooks, our access to opportunities, residential patterns, educational achievement. Race has strikingly real health consequences, as recent studies have shown (Smedley & Smedley, 2012; see also website list).

The cultural and social reality of race, the deep yet subtle processes through which people learn to experience the world through a racial lens—these continue, despite claims that we are living in a "postracial" world. Race remains meaningful today because of its continuing social and economic significance in the United States and in the world affected by European and European American culture.

This makes it hard for many U.S. Americans to really *hear* that races aren't real *biologically*. They think, instead, that the message is that races don't exist as a social invention, as a cultural reality. But cultural reality is enormously powerful, with real consequences, as seen in cultural inventions like slavery, warfare, and child marriage.

KEY CONCEPTUAL POINTS

- Classification is basic to human life, thinking, and language.
- Classifications categorize some things as similar and others as different using one or more classifying attributes.
- Classifications consist of conceptual categories defined in terms of prototypes or "typical" members even though not all category members fit.
- Classification reduces complexity and allows us to generalize about the world.
- Classification can also lead to stereotyping, including racial stereotyping.
- Classifications are cultural inventions, vary cross-culturally and over time, and reflect cultural and historical contexts, including the power relations within the societies in which they are invented.
- Color and kinship (relatives) are two examples of cultural variations in classifying "reality" that reflect cultural context. Racial classification in the United States is another.
- Classifications, as human inventions are dynamic, unstable, can be challenged, manipulated, transformed. This has been the case with U.S. racial classifications.
- Classifications, while cultural inventions, are deeply internalized, feel real and natural, and shape how we experience the world.

KEY TERMS (ITALICIZED AND BOLDED IN TEXT)

cultural classification
prototype
Caucasian
racial science
basic color terms
essentialist thought
Blumenbach
kinship terms
classification
racial classifications
classifying devices
racial worldview
cultural discontinuity
taxonomy

ACTIVITIES

The activities below utilize and build on illustrations in the conceptual background section. They also dovetail with chapters in part III, especially chapters 10 and 12.

Activity Plan 1: Color Terms

Objectives: Participants will be able to provide examples of the arbitrariness of color classifications.

Additional Information: All ages. Interactive. Materials: Numbered paint chips in a wide continuum of colors representing basic color categories: brown, blue, green, red, yellow, and so on (at least four or five sets).

Procedure:

Step 1. List basic color terms on board.
Step 2. Participants divide paint chips into basic color categories (whole group, led by facilitator; or in small groups)
Step 3. Chart paint chip numbers, listing under basic color terms. Participants are most likely to disagree on boundaries of color terms. Participants from different cultural or linguistic backgrounds, nationalities, or genders may group same colors differently.[6]
Step 4. Discuss results and significance. Point out that reality is a continuum but language arbitrarily divides reality into distinct categories. This reinforces the concept of "continuous distribution" in chapter 1.

Step 5. Find some participants fluent in another language, preferably a non-European language, and have them list the basic color terms in their language. They may have a different number. Or there may be the same number, but the boundaries between colors may differ (i.e., a chip called "blue" in English may be labeled "green" in Spanish or Tagalog).

Activity Plan 2: Classifying Relatives

Objective: Participants will understand that labels for relatives, like for color, are somewhat arbitrary divisions of reality.

Additional Information: All levels, with appropriate modifications. This activity can be linked to other chapter activities where participants explore family background (see chapter 5).

Procedure: Overview. Participants explore *kinship terms* or labels for relatives in English and in another language and culture. Kinship terms are labels used to *refer to* relatives, such as "uncle" or "sister." We may use different terms when *addressing* relatives. For example, we talk about someone being our "sister." But if we see her, we generally address her by her name ("Hi, Shana!"). We are not concerned here with the way relatives are addressed. Participants should focus on the labels used when we formally *refer* to relatives, such as the label "sister" or "cousin."

For further information, including cross-cultural examples and sample kinship charts, consult the excellent Palomar College Cultural Anthropology tutorials, especially the two modules on Kin Naming Systems, Part I and Part II (see http://anthro.palomar.edu/kinship/).

Step 1. Describe the concept of kinship terms—ways of classifying and categorizing relatives (see conceptual background material).

Step 2. Show participants how to construct a "kinship chart," a chart that uses symbols to represent different types of relatives. See the Palomar website listed above or any standard cultural anthropology text (cf. Kottak, 2013).

Step 3. Participants construct kinship chart of their family (including beyond their household).

Step 4. Participants identify U.S. American English *kin terms* for each relative on their chart (in small groups or individually).

Step 5. Discuss which kinship-biological distinctions are ignored and which are recognized. Discuss possible reasons, such as roles of various relatives, living arrangements, economic sharing.

Step 6. Discusses changes in kinship terms reflecting contemporary family patterns, including multiple marriages, blended families, and same-sex marriages.

Step 7. Compare American English kinship terms to those from another language, using either bilingual participants in class or other multilingual people that participants can interview.

Step 8. Summarize the key point: Cultures, through language, classify the same biological reality in different ways, reflecting cultural and historical context.

Activity Plan 3: Classifying in Other Cultures—A Cultural IQ Test

Objective: Participants will be able to recognize and cite examples of different ways and criteria for classifying the same set of items. Participants will recognize that most IQ tests are at least partially based on cultural knowledge and classification systems that are learned and culturally specific.

Procedure: Give participants a hypothetical "test" of their aptitude and intelligence using examples that partially come from ethnographic data gathered by anthropologists (see, for example, Lee, 1974). For each example, participants select the *most different* of the set of items. These activities also could be used with chapter 11.

Additional Information: No materials except to record responses. Time: Five to ten minutes. Age: All.

Set 1. Turtle, Basket, Bird

Discussion: Participants from the United States often select basket, utilizing a familiar cultural distinction: animals versus nonanimals (animate versus inanimate). But there are other possible classifying devices, like self-propelling versus can't move (basket). Some non-Western cultures emphasize size and shape and would select birds as most different because they are relatively angular versus rounded compared to turtles or their baskets. Thus correctness on this "test" would be culturally dependent.

Set 2. Laundry, Beer, Clothing

Discussion: Participants often, with great assurance, select beer as most different. For U.S. culture, functionality is major classifying device and so this would link clothing and washing machines. Yet, at least one culture views visual appearance as most salient. From this perspective, clothing is most different because laundry and beer are both "foamy." U.S. slang for beer ("suds") also recognizes the attribute of foaminess.

Set 3. Chair, Spear, Couch

Discussion: Participants in the United States again tend to select the "wrong" answer—at least according to some Ashanti in Ghana (Lee, 1974). U.S.

Americans tend to emphasize *use,* thus placing couch and chair together as types of sitting devices (i.e., furniture). In Ashanti culture, both a chair and a spear can symbolize authority, making the couch the most different.

Set 4. Pig, Cow, Horse, Goat, Snake or try different combinations of three (e.g., Cow, Pig, Snake) or add other animals

Discussion: This hypothetical example can generate discussion of alternative classifying devices, both in theory, and classifications that reflect cultural or religious beliefs. One can use scientific taxonomy, mammals versus non-mammals. An alternative classifying device could be edible versus inedible animals, or culturally defined "food" versus "not food." But the category placement of a cow, pig, or horse as "food" would depend on the culture and the religion; for example, whether Hindu, Muslim, Jewish, Christian, Buddhist. Some Bengali Hindus make an "edibility" distinction, on religious grounds, between fish which feed only on plants (vegetarian fish, which are edible) and those which feed on animals (nonvegetarian fish; not allowed).

Discussion: Participants explore other alternative responses and what they might reflect.

ADDITIONAL ACTIVITY IDEAS

Activity Idea 1: Classifying People on Social Media Sites[7]

Use Facebook or Google Plus or equivalent as an example of social classification. In Facebook, you can place people you know into the default categories family, close friends, and friends. In Google Plus, you can place people into the default categories family, friends, and acquaintances. Explore how you and other people decide how to categorize people, what criteria are used, and what that says about our culture or the microculture of the classifier. What do concepts like "family relationship" or "friends" mean? How does one classification affect behavior toward them, such as what message they receive, and so on?

Activity Idea 2: Examine Old and Nonmainstream U.S. IQ Tests

Use old Army IQ tests or old school IQ tests to illustrate how much "cultural" information is contained in what purport to be tests of "intelligence." One useful example is *The Psychological Examination in the United States Army, Group Examination Alpha, Form 5, Test.* Ask participants which items measure "intelligence," which measure "achievement," and which measure "personality." This test strikingly illustrates how cultural knowledge is being tested in most so-called intelligence tests.

Alternatively, use IQ tests created by members of nonmainstream U.S. cultures. One example is the Central West Virginia Cultural Awareness Quiz (Morgan & Beeler, 1981). Ask participants to discuss what it would take to do well on this test. For samples of these and other IQ tests see http://www. understandingrace.org/resources/.

Activity Idea 3: Create an IQ Test for Peer Group

Participants can construct (in groups or individually) an IQ test that reflects knowledge specific to their peer group and generation or other microculture. It can be "culturally biased" in favor of their culture. Once they have constructed the test, let participants and teachers, staff, or other adults take it and have participants score the exam. Discuss results. Participants will probably do far better than adults.

Activity Idea 4: Analyze a Current IQ Test for Cultural Bias

Use a current or relatively recent test of achievement, aptitude, or intelligence and analyze it for cultural bias. Include regional, religious, class, rural-urban, and gender biases as well as ethnic and racial biases.

NOTES

1. This example and much of the material in this section, as well as many of the ideas in chapter 5, has benefited from the work of David Kronenfeld (cf. Kronenfeld, 2008, and Kronenfeld et al., 2011).

2. For more material on kinship terminology cross-culturally, see the tutorials, Kin Naming Systems, at the Palomar College Anthropology website, http://anthro.palomar-edu/kinship/kinship_5.htm.

3. *Ethos* (vol. 25, no. 1, 1997), the journal of the Society for Psychological Anthropology, extensively reviews Hirschfeld's work.

4. Francis Galton, a wealthy Englishman, invented the term in the 1880s to describe efforts by some to "improve" the human species through selective breeding. Galton felt the "superior" races, namely the British, were declining in numbers and wished to halt this. See chapter 9.

5. See Mukhopadhyay website for this article and a related one designed for educators (Mukhopadhyay, 2008).

6. To read more about how color terms were investigated, and for more ideas for student projects, see the classic study by Brent Berlin and Paul Kay (1969), *Basic Color Terms*. The book also includes a color chart based on Munsel color chips.

7. Rosemary Henze first suggested this idea. See also applications to part III.

Chapter Seven

Race and Inequality

Race as a Social Invention to Achieve Certain Goals

> There is indeed a meaning to the term race, but it is not to be found in the physical features of differing human populations. . . . We must peel away the intricate layers of Western cultural history and look at the material conditions, cultural and naturalistic knowledge, motivations and objectives, and levels of consciousness and comprehension of those who first imposed the classifications of race on the human community.
>
> —Audrey Smedley & Brian Smedley (2012, p. 11)

Classification, as we have seen, is pervasive in human culture, and there are numerous ways we can classify the same set of things in the natural or social world. So how does a particular cultural system of classification—whether of colors, time, food, or human beings—arise?

Classifications do not emerge in a vacuum but in a cultural context. The U.S. system of racial classification developed in the context of what anthropologists call *social stratification*, that is, a system of structured social inequality.

CONCEPTUAL BACKGROUND

Stratification: Systems of Inequality

Contrary to popular stereotypes, most human cultures have been fairly egalitarian. Only with the rise of civilizations in the past 6,000 to 8,000 years do we find societies with significant differences in wealth, political power, social rights, and status. These are what anthropologists call *stratified societies*.

Yet stratified societies have had a disproportionate influence on the world, gradually incorporating smaller-scale, less-powerful societies into their powerful empires, often as subordinate, lower-status groups.

Stratified systems of inequality have common features. First, they constitute what social scientists call a *social system*. A system is a set of interrelated social institutions (kinship, educational, occupational, legal, political, religious) that functions at a societal level. That is, although systems have consequences for individuals, they exist beyond the individual. While small-scale societies have social systems, they are more elaborate and formalized within large-scale societies, especially stratified societies.

Within any social system there is a range of *social positions* or *social statuses*, or what we today sometimes call *social identities*. They are cultural inventions, as we saw in chapter 5, and are often linked to social institutions, such as the social position of "principal," "journalist," "colonel," "slave," and "U.S. citizen." Families also generate social positions such as husband, wife, grandmother, and great-aunt. We all have multiple social positions and identities, each linked to roles, rights, and obligations as well as more diffuse and complex associations.

Society and individuals treat us according to their perceptions of our social position. Others may categorize us racially or ethnically in ways that do not agree with our own perceptions or choice of identities. The U.S. Census, for example, uses large ethnoracial[1] categories, such as Asian, White, and Black, that may not reflect how people identify themselves.

The point here is that structural or institutional forms of privilege and discrimination affect individuals as members of a social group, rather than on the basis of their personal characteristics. In the colonial period, for example, only "free white males" who were citizens could serve on juries. All persons classified as "female" or "not white" were automatically excluded as a group, regardless of their individual qualifications. Legal, educational, governmental, political, medical, and religious institutions treat people differently, depending on their social group or social identity, including their racial classification.

Ascribed versus Achieved Statuses and Systems

Anthropologists sometimes use the terms *ascribed* and *achieved* (cf. Kottak, 2013, p. 125) to refer to alternative ways individuals acquire a social position or membership in a social group. Often your social status is ascribed (determined solely by birth) through your ancestry or kinship group, your gender, or on the basis of unalterable physical features, like skin color.

In contrast, some social statuses can be achieved. That is, the status or social position is the result of accomplishments, behaviors, talents, choices, or valuables that are available to anyone, regardless of their birth.

Stratified societies can be based on ascription, achievement, or some combination of both. The traditional Hindu caste system is often used to illustrate an ascribed system of social stratification. In theory, caste (*jati* or *varna*) is determined by birth, cannot be changed in your lifetime, and is a prime determinant of your social rank. European "royalty" is another example of a stratified system historically based on ascription. Access to political power and other upper-strata privileges was based on birth within the royal lineage. And gender. Until recently, "royal" daughters could inherit the "throne" only when there were no sons.

Stratified systems are not necessarily based on ascription but can also be based on achievement, at least in theory. There can be different strata (classes) with significant inequality, but there is social mobility between classes. Individuals born into one class can move upward or downward, again, in theory. There are no institutional, legal, or other explicit, formal restrictions. Your social position is not determined at birth but can fluctuate during your lifetime.

The United States is frequently described (and describes itself) as a stratified *society* based on achievement, a ***meritocracy***, despite its history of ascribed structural barriers to mobility. "All men are created equal," so the Bill of Rights states, although the Founding Fathers excluded women, non-Europeans, and many poor European Americans from their conception of equality. Recent research on the United States continues to document the role that race, gender, and class play in advantaging or disadvantaging individuals. The past several decades have seen a dramatic increase in economic inequality within the United States, along with a corresponding importance of "family background" to what one actually can achieve. In reality, most stratified societies contain elements of ascription and achievement. Britain is a class society with some mobility, but Prince Charles acquired his "royal" (vs. "commoner") status simply by birth.

Justifying Inequality: Legitimizing Ideologies

Stratified systems of inequality are not just about wealth or control of political institutions. Dominant groups influence belief systems and often devise elaborate and complex ideologies to explain and justify their dominance.

Creation stories, one common mechanism, trace the social system to human origins or to the beginning of human social groups. The creator tends to be a deity-like figure with the creation story embedded in sacred text. In Hinduism, some sacred texts attribute the creation of the universe, humans, and the major social divisions to a primeval giant cosmic being, Purusha. In the United States, Christian biblical sources were used to justify African slavery (see Smedley & Smedley, 2012).

Creation accounts often articulate the reasons for each group's rank and why some are inferior or superior. In the Hinduism example, each group's social rank (from higher to lower), according to one version, originated in the part of Purusha's body from which it was created, from head (highest rank) to feet (lowest). But in Hinduism and most other social systems, the fundamental basis for one's social or "caste" position is common ancestry, the group into which you are born.

Stratified systems are not always based on biological characteristics (see chapter 8). There are many potential visible symbols of group membership and relative social status. Groups may have to wear different clothing, eat different foods, perform different work, or use (or not use) specific linguistic forms. Nazi Germany forced Jews to wear a visible cloth symbol that marked them as Jewish and distinguished them from non-Jews.

Occupational segregation, residential segregation ("ghettoes"), and other forms of social separation (distinct public spaces, burial grounds, educational, religious, medical and recreational facilities, restrictions on intermarriage) have been used to differentiate and mark higher- and lower-ranked groups. Surnames also transmit information about one's social standing.

But physical differences are one easy basis to use for identifying members of ranked social groups. The U.S. American system of stratification drew upon visible markers of ancestry to create an ideology of race, a racial worldview (Smedley & Smedley, 2012) based on distinct, immutable, ranked categories of humans, created by God or nature. Racial categorization assigned individuals, at birth, to permanent, different, and unequal social strata and used racial status to regulate access to opportunities. In a society already inegalitarian, race became the dominant *legitimizing social ideology.*

THEMES IN THE AMERICAN RACE-BASED SYSTEM OF SOCIAL STRATIFICATION

The U.S. racial system developed in the context of at least three competing pressures: a long-term policy of population expansion, fueled by a demand for cheap labor; the desire of dominant groups to maintain their economic, political, and cultural dominance; and the need to reconcile the reality of persistent and deep stratification with an equally persistent political rhetoric of individualism, freedom, democracy, and meritocracy.

These competing pressures generated ambivalence about an increasingly diverse American population, particularly in the postcolonial and post–Civil War era. Both helped shape attitudes, policies, and laws about labor, immigration, naturalization, social interaction, education, marriage, and definitions of Whiteness.

Race became a central organizing principle of social relations, superseding even religion. A binary, bipolar system of White and non-White emerged in which White social status was linked to an array of political, legal, social, and economic privileges. Over time, lower-ranked European ethnic groups gradually achieved White status, if somewhat marginally. Racializing the labor force helped to mask the pervasive class stratification that has always characterized American society.

The following sections explore these themes in greater detail.

Race as a Device to Organize and Exploit Labor

A major theme in U.S. history is the demand for labor, first in the labor-intensive Southern plantation system and then in the growing industrial centers of the Northern states. Scholars tracing the evolution of the racial classification system argue that race functioned as a device for organizing labor in ways that benefited the dominant property-owning classes (see Omi & Winant, 1994).

This process can be seen during the colonial period as the planter class began to view African labor as more desirable than other "indentured" servants of European ancestry. Slavery was extremely profitable for planters, and profits from slave labor vastly surpassed those produced by free labor, that is, nonslave labor. According to some estimates, on the eve of the Civil War, enslaved workers (bonded persons) received annual clothing and food equivalent to twenty dollars a year, one-fifth of what free workers required (Brodkin, 1998, p. 69).

Joel M. Sipress describes the *racialization* of slavery in colonial Virginia. Racialization is a process through which people, both individuals and groups, come to be viewed through a racial lens and incorporated into a culturally created racial framework (Goodman, Moses, & Jones, 2012, p. 251). Sipress argues that racial categories of Black and White can be traced to plantation management and labor control. He notes that Virginia colonial law at first made no distinction between African slaves and European servants.

> Both could own property and could enter into contracts. Servants and slaves ate together, worked together, slept together, and sometimes escaped together. In matters of crime and punishment, the law treated both alike. A slave was, in effect, a servant who served for life. . . . As Virginia's tobacco planters became increasingly dependent upon African labor, they began to elaborate a distinct legal status of "slave," as well as a racial ideology to justify it. Beginning in the 1660s, the Virginia colonial legislature passed a series of laws that stripped slaves of the rights, such as freedom of assembly, to which they had previously been entitled. Other laws enacted distinct forms of punishment for disobedient slaves. . . . As the legal status of slaves sank, the Virginia legislature began to

write racial categories, such as "black" and "white," into law. (Sipress, 1997, p. 181)

Throughout American history, racial classifications were creatively and consciously manipulated to pit segments of the labor force against each other and to give dominant Euro-American Anglo groups a competitive advantage. The westward expansion led to the recruitment of immigrants for the newly acquired territories of the Southwest and the Hawaiian Islands.

The Treaty of Guadalupe Hidalgo, signed after the Mexican American War, initially promised full rights and federal government protection to Mexicans living in the Southwest. However, economics trumped treaty arrangements when gold was discovered in California. Fortune-seeking Anglos came in massive numbers, soon outnumbering Mexican Americans and dominating politically. Anglos passed discriminatory laws to make it more difficult for Mexican Americans to compete in mining gold. The 1855 antivagrancy act, the so-called Greaser act, and a foreign miner's tax of twenty dollars per month applied to all who spoke Spanish, even if they were U.S. citizens (Bigler, 2003).

Despite experience in mining, Mexican Americans were segregated in lower-skilled mining jobs, paid less than their Anglo counterparts for the same jobs, and given fewer food rations. This discrimination was increasingly rationalized in racial terms, using naturalistic, essentialist arguments, that is, citing permanent, intrinsic, immutable group traits. For example, one mine owner said that Mexicans "have been 'peons' for generations. They will always remain so, as it is their natural condition" (Bigler, 2003, p. 212).

Here, and elsewhere, workers from different ethnic groups and nationalities were pitted against each other. Building the U.S. intercontinental railroad required an enormous labor force, and workers from China were actively recruited to the West Coast. Anglos accused the Chinese of competing unfairly because they were willing to work for lower wages. Instead of organizing the Chinese, U.S. labor organizations fought to exclude them from economic sectors where they competed with native-born Euro-Americans. But they were allowed to work in high-demand areas, such as the laundry business, where there was no competition from Anglo labor. The Chinese Exclusion Act of 1882, however, banned Chinese from entering the United States and from becoming citizens.

Planters in the Hawaiian Islands recruited labor from all over the world. The Japanese first came to the United States to work on Hawaiian plantations. When Japanese plantation workers organized a major strike in the early 20th century (1909), Filipino workers were recruited by the Hawaiian Sugar Planters' Association to help break the strike, becoming 70 percent of Hawaiian plantation workers by the 1930s (Benson, 2003, p. 245).

With Japanese migration to California, competition heated up between Japanese and Anglo farmers. Anglo political elites passed a series of restrictive land laws that barred aliens ineligible for citizenship from owning or leasing agricultural land. Under the 1790 naturalization laws, only free Whites could apply for citizenship. As non-Whites, Japanese immigrants could therefore neither own nor lease land. The same applied to the Sikhs from India that settled in the Northwestern United States and then migrated to Central California.

Social and occupational segregation along racial and ethnic lines maintained class divisions. When there was a labor shortage, immigration from Europe, South Asia, the Philippines, Chile,[2] and other countries was promoted. Restrictions on immigration, such as in the 1920s, often coincided with lower demands for labor. Immigrant labor was segregated in particular industries and jobs, hindering native-born, usually Anglo, workers from bargaining effectively for better wages and working conditions. African Americans were either still sharecropping on farms in the South or were relegated to the lowest-paying, least-desirable jobs in the nonagricultural sectors. Immigrants, and sometimes African Americans, were used to undercut labor rates and union organizing, including being hired during labor strikes.

The primary issues underlying strife were economic and economic stratification. But both the propertied upper classes and U.S. born, Euro-American workers tended to frame the labor conflict in racial terms. Progressive leftist groups, including socialists and communists, tried to promote unity and worker solidarity. While the Socialist Party, under Eugene Debs, did gain support, socialism in general, and the Communist Party in particular, were portrayed by powerful business interests and mainstream political parties as both anticapitalist and anti-American. Scarce jobs and exploitative labor conditions, then, were repeatedly masked by racial and ethnic competition. Native-born U.S. workers responded by supporting discriminatory practices and laws such as exclusionary immigration laws, or laws prohibiting interracial marriage. This further weakened worker unity movements and reinforced the power of upper-status, propertied groups. These same processes continue today, despite occasional successful efforts, like that of the Farmworkers Union in the 1970s, to organize across ethnic and racial boundaries.

Cultural Dominance: Preserving the White Nation

The demand for labor in U.S. history produced a large culturally and religiously diverse population. This diversity has always represented a challenge to dominant cultural groups.

Scholars point out that the United States was founded as a self-consciously White nation. The Founding Fathers agreed upon the need for a racially and culturally homogeneous nation if the "republic" was to thrive.

John Jay, coauthor of the *Federalist Papers*, writes in 1787, "Providence has been pleased to give this one connected country to one united people—a people descended from the same ancestors, speaking the same language, professing the same religion"(Stokes & Meléndez, 2001, p. xx).

Social characteristics besides race, especially wealth and being "indentured," as well as gender, initially affected a person's social status. Nevertheless, the first U.S. Naturalization Act, adopted in 1790, applied only to "free white persons," suggesting, as future court cases would argue, that only Whites could bridge the status of alien and become true Americans.

White . . . and Christian . . . Preferably Protestant

The dominant cultural group in 1790, however, was not simply White. It was also Christian, Protestant, English speaking, and predominantly of English or Anglo-Saxon origins. These were the "united people" to whom Jay was referring—and the predominant population of "free whites" coming to the United States.

There were, of course, two other significant U.S. populations: Native Americans and Africans. References to both groups as "heathens" suggests their non-Christian status was more significant than their ancestry. According to Sipress, "the original justification for perpetual servitude was not the 'blackness' of Africans, but rather their 'heathenism.' In the early years of the Virginia colony, a number of African slaves sued successfully for their freedom on the grounds that they had been baptized and had accepted Christianity" (1997, p. 181).

As race, rather than religion, became the ideological justification for slavery, conversion to Christianity was not sufficient to change a slave's legal status. As early as 1667, Black and White racial categories appear in Virginia legislative records, reflecting the declining legal status of African slaves relative to Europeans in similar positions of servitude. Simultaneously, racial ancestry (an *ascribed* status) trumped religion (*achieved*) as a determinant of social status. And in 1667,

> legislators shifted the justification for slavery from religion to ancestry by declaring that all children born into slavery would remain slaves regardless of baptism. (Sipress, 1997, p. 181)

Tolerance . . . among Christians

Christianity remained a significant, if not sufficient, implicit requirement for being U.S. American. The famous Maryland Toleration Act (1649) was not about tolerance for non-Christians. It required all persons in the colony to believe in Jesus Christ under penalty of death.

> That whatsoever person or persons within this Province and the Islands there-unto helonging [*sic*] shall from henceforth blaspheme God, that is Curse him, or deny our Saviour Jesus Christ to bee the sonne of God, or shall deny the holy Trinity the father sonne and holy Ghost, or the Godhead of any of the said Three persons of the Trinity or the Unity of the Godhead, or shall use or utter any reproachfull Speeches, words or language concerning the said Holy Trin-ity, or any of the said three persons thereof, shalbe [*sic*] punished with death and confiscation or forfeiture of all his or her lands and goods to the Lord Proprietary and his heires.[3]

Colonial Maryland is often praised for its religious tolerance, as a place where Catholics could freely practice their religion. However, the Maryland legislation addressed tolerance for Catholics at a time when Protestants were beginning to dominate numerically. The need for legislation reflects the prevalence of anti-Catholic feeling in other predominantly Protestant colonies!

Relations between Protestant denominations were apparently also rancorous, prompting additional laws mandating tolerance among Protestants. The language of the law is explicit:

> Whatsoever person or persons shall from henceforth upon any occasion of offence otherwise in a reproachfull manner or way declare care call or denomi-nate any person or persons whatsoever inhabiting, residing, traficking, trading or comercing within this province or within any ports, harbours, creeks or havens to the same belonging, an Heretick, Schismat-ick, Idolator, Puritan, Independent Presbyterian, Antenomian, Barrowist, Roundhead, Seperatist, Popish Priest, Jesuit, Jesuited Papist, Lutheran, Calvenist, Anabaptist, Brown-ist or any other name or term in a reproachful manner relating to matters of Religion shall for every such offence foreit and lose the sum of ten shillings Sterling or the value thereof to be levied on the goods and chattels of every such offender and offenders. (Maryland Toleration Act, 1649)

Fines for acts of intolerance were not to be treated lightly. Individuals who could not pay fines were to be "publickly whipt and imprisoned without bail" until "he, she, or they shall satisfy the party so offended or grieved by such reproachful language."[4]

IMMIGRANT CHALLENGES TO THE WHITE, CHRISTIAN, ANGLO-SAXON NATION

Concerns over White (WASP[5]) dominance probably existed in the early colonial period, especially in Southern plantation regions with large African populations. Later population waves in the Southwest and in Eastern and Midwestern industrial centers threatened to "swallow" the native White population, especially politically, should the voting franchise be extended to all citizens.

Growing populations of Mexican Americans challenged old definitions of White culture. Within the Spanish territories, intermating and intermarriage with indigenous Indians had been common. Most Mexicans were "mestizos" ("mixed"), that is, of multiple ancestries. Were they to receive the privileges accorded Whites? Even "pure" 100 percent Spanish were considered by some upper-strata WASPs to be relatively lower-status Whites, "mongrelized" during the period when the Moors, North African Muslims, ruled Spain.

Naturalization Law as a Barrier

As immigration increased, the 1790 "White only" naturalization law was employed to prevent "alien" groups, such as the Chinese, Japanese, and later, East Indians and Mexicans, from challenging the cultural and political dominance of native WASP elites. Court cases forced judges to wrestle with the definition of Whiteness.

Haney-Lopez (1996) argues that judges tended to rely on either "scientific" criteria, that is, on Blumenbach's classification of races (see chapter 6) or on popular "common sense" notions of Whiteness. There was no particular consistency to the rulings—except that they almost inevitably reinforced the existing system of class and racial stratification.

Earlier we mentioned competition between the Japanese and Anglos in California. The *Ozawa v. United States* case (1922) involved a Japan-born applicant for naturalization who had lived most of his life in the United States. He argued he was White using his own skin color, which he said was similar to most Anglos. The court circumvented the question of color by arguing that White legally meant Caucasian and that Japanese were Mongoloid according to scientific classifications. Ozawa lost the case and could not become a citizen (nor own land, nor sponsor relatives or spouses for immigration).

East Indians started migrating to the United States in the late 19th and early 20th century. Most were not Hindus, but of the Sikh religion, and settled first in the northwest coast of the United States and then moved to California. Some were Bengalis, mainly Muslims, from Calcutta and contemporary Bangladesh, residing in the East Coast and Louisiana (Bald, 2013). East Indians presented particular problems because of their racial ambiguity within the prevailing U.S. racial framework. Their applications for citizenship produced a legal dilemma. Scientific classifications clearly designated East Indians as "Caucasian." The U.S. Court, in the Ozawa case cited above, had ruled that White legally meant Caucasian. On these grounds, East Indians should be eligible for citizenship.[6] This was the argument for naturalization used by Bhagat Singh Thind, an immigrant from India, who had attended the University of California at Berkeley and served in the U.S. military in World War I.

The court was in a quandary. This time, however, it reversed itself, rejected prevailing science, and earlier legal precedent, in order to find some grounds on which to deny Thind's application. Justice George Sutherland, writing the majority opinion, noted the original naturalization law did not use the word Caucasian "but only 'white persons.'" Erroneously equating all East Indians with Hindus, although Thind was actually of the Sikh religion, Sutherland essentially excluded all people from the Indian subcontinent from the category "White" and therefore, from eligibility for naturalization.

> What we now hold is that the words "free white persons" are . . . to be interpreted in accordance with the understanding of the common man, synonymous with the word "Caucasian" only as that word is popularly understood. As so understood and used, whatever may be the speculations of the ethnologist, it does not include the body of people to whom the appellee belongs. It is a matter of familiar observation and knowledge that the physical group characteristics of the Hindus render them easily distinguishable from the various groups of persons in this country commonly recognized as white. (*United States v. Bhagat Singh Thind*, 261 U.S. 204 [1923]. Source: http://www.pbs.org/rootsinthesand/i_bhagat2.html, accessed July 15, 2013.)

Significantly, the court also implied East Indians were too culturally alien (as non-Christians, linguistically, culturally) to become White, that is, to assimilate to the dominant "American" (WASP) culture.

"It may be true that the blond Scandinavian and the brown Hindu have a common ancestor in the dim reaches of antiquity, but the average man knows perfectly well that there are unmistakable and profound differences between them today" (ibid. re: citation).

Both cases coincided with a period of economic recession, extreme labor competition between U.S. and foreign-born workers, and political upheaval as organized labor grew and the Socialist Party gained support, partially from recent European immigrants. The Bolshevik (Communist) Revolution in Russia also exacerbated fears by propertied classes of the spread of a socialist revolution to the United States. The rise of anticolonialist, nationalist movements around the world presented additional threats.

Mongrelizing the "White" Race

> The population of the United States will, on account of the great influx of blood from South-eastern Europe, rapidly become darker in pigmentation,

smaller in stature . . . more given to crimes of larceny, kidnapping, assault, murder, rape and sex-immorality . . . (and) the ratio of insanity in the population will rapidly increase. (Charles Davenport, 1911, *Heredity in Relation to Eugenics*. Cited in Goodman, Moses, & Jones, 2012, p. 50, taken from RACE exhibit, *Inventing Whiteness*.)

Japanese, Chinese, East Indians, Mexicans, and Filipinos were not the only challenges to U.S. American Whiteness. New waves of European immigrants threatened the "cultural" purity and political dominance of the prototypic White (WASP) nation originally envisioned by the Founding Fathers.

By the 1880s, European immigrants and their children were numerically dominant in major urban areas of the United States (Brodkin, 1998, p. 27). These new European immigrants were not Anglo-Saxon. They included Italians, Greeks, Bulgarians, Russians, and other Southern and Eastern Europeans. Nor were they Protestant. Many were Roman and Eastern Orthodox Catholics or Jews. A few may have been Muslim. Many were uneducated. Some were politically radical.

What was the United States to do with these new and different immigrants from, according to some, the inferior stock of Europeans (see chapter 6)? Would they be treated like earlier European immigrants from England, Germany, Scandinavia, and France? Were they really White? Would they be accorded the legal and social position of other Whites?

To the courts, at least, South and Eastern Europeans had the "potential" for assimilation. With proper education (formal and informal), they could aspire to "cultural citizenship," that is, becoming true Americans. And their labor was essential in the industrial centers of the East and West Coasts. They made up the bulk of the industrial working class.

Restricting "Those" Immigrants: The 1920s

By the 1920s, however, economic recession had dampened the demand for foreign labor. Fears of foreign political radicalism coupled with pseudoscientific racial theories fueled native Anglo demands to restrict immigration. Laws were designed to preserve the dominance of the high-ranking "Nordic" populations (English, Germans, French, Scandinavians) while restricting lower-ranked European groups (Alpine, Mediterranean, Semites/Jews).

Immigration restrictions on those not designated White were even more severe and also employed arguments about their racial inferiority. The 1917 Immigration Act had already created a "barred zone," which denied entry to people from South Asia through Southeast Asia, and islands in the Indian and Pacific Oceans. The Oriental Exclusion Act of 1924 declared all Asians ineligible for citizenship except people from the U.S. possessions of the Philippines and Guam. Citizenship ineligibility often affected property ownership, such as in the California Alien Land Law of 1913, which prohibited "aliens ineligible for citizenship" from owning property in the state.

Clearly, the intent was to bar East Indians and other Asians from becoming a permanent economic, political, and cultural force in the United States. Citizenship did not simply imply voting and property ownership rights. Citizens could sponsor relatives, marry or bring wives from the home country, and produce "native-born" U.S. children (see chapter 9).

Fears of "Race Suicide"

As early as the mid-19th century, school textbooks echoed the theme that Americans were "God's Chosen People" with a Manifest Destiny to prevail over other cultures. However, these were the "old" Americans, the Anglo-Saxon Protestants, and among these, the "refined" propertied classes or upper strata.

As the 20th century got under way, upper-class Euro-American males increasingly voiced concerns about race suicide. For one thing, immigrant women had higher fertility rates than native-born U.S. women, especially upper-middle-class women. The late 19th–early 20th century witnessed a decline in the White birth rate relative to others—"down" to an average of four children per woman (Davis, 1981).

This partially reflected an emerging progressive vision of womanhood that envisioned fuller engagement in public life, education, careers, voting rights, and control over fertility and the number of offspring. Of course, this vision was available to only a small fraction of women, regardless of race.

Theodore Roosevelt, in his 1906 State of the Union message, criticized upper-class, privileged White women who engaged in "willful sterility—the one sin for which the penalty is national death, race suicide" (Davis, 1981, p. 209). Such beliefs fueled the eugenics movement, which was directed toward controlling, even eliminating, the fertility of the less "fit" while encouraging the "fittest" to reproduce. Even Margaret Sanger, despite her progressive politics, adopted eugenics language as a pragmatic way to convince male politicians to support family planning and birth control, arguing that "the chief issue of birth control" was "more children from the fit, less from the unfit" (Davis, 1981, pp. 213–214).

The goal of maintaining European American racial dominance had the effect of racializing reproductive policies. One result was a racist strategy of population control that included sterilization of African American women and girls, often without their knowledge. Another was through essentially restricting elite, literate women's access to family planning information by classifying these written materials as "obscenity," therefore making it illegal to send them through the mail.

A third strategy was to prevent the predominantly male immigrant population of non-Whites from marrying, having families, and producing offspring. This was accomplished through restrictions on naturalization, on immigration of non-Whites, and through antimiscegenation laws that prevented non-White males from marrying White women (see chapters 9 and 13).

RECONCILING DEMOCRACY AND MERITOCRACY WITH INEQUALITY AND STRATIFICATION

Contradictions between political rhetoric and social reality have existed since the founding of the republic, when "all men are created equal," as noted earlier, excluded women and those of African or Native American ancestry along with the vast majority of nonpropertied European Americans.

But U.S. American political rhetoric was forged in the context of creating a unique national identity, one that contrasted with "old Europe." America was "destined" to be a democracy, a society based on achievement, unfettered by European notions of class, royalty, and rights based on one's birth. The language of the Constitution and Declaration of Independence reflects this theme, with an emphasis on individualism, freedom (from government constraint, from state-imposed religion, from aristocratic-ascribed privilege), and the pursuit of happiness.

As the United States matured and expanded, native-born U.S. Americans felt an "obligation" to spread their "superior" democracy to other parts of the world. The rhetoric of Manifest Destiny (today called American "exceptionalism") and an expansionist foreign policy brought the Philippines, the Hawaiian Islands, and Puerto Rico under the U.S. flag.

At home, it produced a policy of assimilating (into WASP culture) European populations deemed capable of assimilation. Other groups were excluded, through immigration and naturalization laws and through Jim Crow racial segregation laws and practices.

But stratification and inequality in the United States have always been pervasive, regardless of the rhetoric of freedom, opportunity, and equality. Elites, whether the plantation class of the South or the industrial barons of the North, have controlled enormous power and wealth, as have their descendants. In short, a *class system* existed, not primarily based on merit, but on ascription, on birth, inherited wealth and connections, and on ethnicity, religion gender, and especially race. The political rhetoric of democracy had to be reconciled with a class and racially stratified social system. So a rather unique ideological justification emerged—the notion of a meritocracy.

The United States as a Meritocracy

A meritocracy can exist simultaneously with enormous inequality because it assumes everyone has the opportunity make it to the "top." Success, according to this ideology, is dependent only on natural abilities and how hard people work. Using this logic, the failure of some groups to achieve economically or educationally can be attributed to their own deficiencies rather than to any structural features of the prevailing social and cultural system. In short, in a meritocracy, the system is "fair," but some folks—indeed, entire groups—simply lack "what it takes" to succeed (see Mukhopadhyay, 2004b).

The essentialist, naturalistic racial ideology of biologically based, intrinsic, immutable racial differences, the core of the U.S. American racial worldview, was creatively reinterpreted to reinforce this ideology of meritocracy. Supporters of racial stratification argued that not all races or cultures possessed the same natural abilities or the kinds of character traits and capacities of the Anglo-Saxon, Protestant Founding Fathers who had "built the nation." Some races were simply more capable of being Americans than others. Remnants of this ideology appear in current discussions of minority student educational achievement (see chapter 11).

Racializing Inequality

Race, although invented partially to justify a very profitable economic system based on slave labor, became a primary way of organizing labor in the United States (Brodkin, 1998, p. 75). Ideologically, the racial worldview provided an ideal justification for inequality, especially in the context of the U.S. claims of "exceptionalism" as a democracy. Since races were naturally "unequal," then a race-based system of inequality could arguably be consistent with notions of merit and justice.

Using race to legitimize inequality under the guise of meritocracy appears early in the colonial era, but it becomes more elaborate as race emerges as a fundamental social division of American society. The strategy of racializing Africans, of rationalizing legal discrimination, of justifying African American slavery on the basis of immutable race-based traits, was extended to other ethnic and racial groups. Racial categories, intrinsically malleable and always shifting, expanded, contracted, or in other ways were altered to accommodate the changing conditions and needs of dominant Euro-American groups. Racial ideology, which employed linking visible traits to undesirable character traits or capacities, was also extended beyond African Americans, justifying the permanent lower social position of other groups.

We see this process in depictions of immigrant groups, especially working-class immigrants. Mexicans in the 19th century were characterized as "superstitious, cowardly, treacherous, idle, avaricious, and inveterate gamblers." In the famous Los Angeles "Sleepy Lagoon" case, the Sheriff's Department described Mexicans as inherently criminal and violent because they were Indians and Indians were "Orientals," and Orientals have "no regard for life" (Bigler, 2003, pp. 211–13).

The Asiatic Exclusion League argued that Asian Indians were not White but an "effeminate, caste-ridden, and degraded" race who did not deserve citizenship (Haney-Lopez, 1996, p. 4). Filipinos, Chinese, and Mexicans were all stereotyped as violent and immoral, using as evidence their desire to date White women. Ironically, race-based immigration and naturalization laws exacerbated an already dramatic shortage of women among male immigrants.

Increasingly, issues of economic and political stratification in the United States became framed in racial terms, with negative stereotyping directed toward immigrants and non-White workers. However, it was not just the powerful and dominant ethnic groups that used race as a strategy to further their own interests.

Jobs held by immigrants were often defined as inappropriate for native workers, using racial justifications. This is seen in one worker's description of a blast-furnace job: "Only Hunkies (i.e., Hungarians) work on those jobs, they're too damn dirty and too damn hot for a 'white' man" (Brodkin, 1998, p. 57).

Native White workers applied negative racelike stereotypes to immigrant workers forced into lower-status jobs. The stereotypes embodied the very traits of the menial jobs themselves. In essence, workers acquired the low-status characteristics of their low-status jobs.

> There is a . . . crowd of Negroes and Syrians working there. Many of them are filthy in their personal habits, and the idea of working with them is repugnant to any man who wants to retain his self-respect. It is no place for a man with a white man's heart to be. The Negroes and foreigners are coarse, vulgar and brutal in their acts and conversation. (Cited in Brodkin, 1998, p. 57)

Marginal White groups, like the Irish, also employed these stereotypes. They manipulated their White status to obtain political and economic advantages, to keep African Americans from voting, to keep non-Whites out of labor unions, and to discriminate against and physically attack African Americans in the East and Chinese on the West Coast.

> The "whitening" of Irish-Americans provides an example of a marginal social group that embraced a racial identity to advance its own interests. The Irish, who began arriving in the United States in large numbers in the 1840s, found themselves in a society whose culture and politics were already characterized by a strict racial hierarchy. To native-born Americans, the racial status of the Irish, like that of the Poles and Italians who followed, was unclear. Antebellum

ethnologists spoke derisively of the "Celtic" race. To political cartoonists, "Paddy" bore an uncanny resemblance to an ape.

"Whiteness," according to historian David Roediger, served as a powerful weapon in the Irish struggle to carve out a place in a hostile American society. By asserting their whiteness, the Irish were able to claim the status of full-fledged Americans. The Irish wielded whiteness to assert control over jobs. White supremacist doctrine cemented the relationship between the Democratic Party, the party of slavery and Indian removal, and an Irish community desperately in need of political patrons. Although anti-Irish and anti-Catholic attitudes persisted, Irish-Americans were successful in their struggle to establish their identity as full-fledged white men and women. (Sipress, 1997, pp. 181–182)

Significantly, recurring negative stereotypes of lower-status ethnic and racial groups as lazy, stupid, dirty, unable to control themselves, untrustworthy, and less intelligent are the opposite pole of the idealized attributes of the dominant Anglo cultural group. The "free white American," the prototypic WASP of the Founding Fathers and their descendants, the Horatio Alger heroes in the 19th-century best-selling novels, are all smart, energetic, self-disciplined, go-getters, able to defer gratification in pursuit of their goals.

Implicitly, then, race and racial stereotypes served to justify, within the rhetoric of meritocracy, the relative social positions of racial and ethnic groups. Racial stratification, the argument goes, is merit based even though one's race is determined at birth. Races are just naturally different.

The rhetoric of race and race-based capacities and characteristics not only justifies but also masks a class-based stratified society. The initial use of race to justify economic exploitation becomes an explanation of why social inequality is consistent with a meritocracy, with democracy, freedom, and a society based on individual merit. Success and wealth reflects merit. Lack of success and poverty simply reflects one's personal failings, a lack of ability. The "system" is fair!

CONCLUSION

The American system of racial classification is a historically and culturally specific, a complex and unique way for explaining, justifying, and perpetuating a system of social, economic, and political inequality.

Racial ancestry, bolstered by racial science and religion, became the rationale for stratification and inequality. A race-based system of social classification became a way of maintaining the dominance of elite Northwestern European American, mainly Protestant "White" groups, politically and socially, while simultaneously recruiting new populations to fulfill labor demands.

Race became a central basis for organizing labor and maintaining an economically stratified system, first in the agricultural sector and then in the growing industrial sectors. And racializing the labor force helped to mask the pervasive class stratification and structural inequality that has always characterized American life.

While this chapter has focused on the historical evolution of race, these same processes continue today, although sometimes on a more subtle level. New immigrant groups often experience racializing stereotypes, are recruited for the least desirable occupations, such as agricultural labor or the poultry processing industry, and may end up competing with other native-born populations or immigrant groups for scarce housing, jobs, and public services. The consequences of centuries of racial inequality persist and can be cumulative over time, as in housing and education (see chapter 11).[7] At the same time, we are witnessing unprecedented levels of inequality in the United States, economically, politically, educationally, and in access to health services (Smedley & Smedley, 2012). The middle class is shrinking while more and more wealth is accumulating in fewer and fewer hands, both privately and in the corporate sector. Our political system is arguably being distorted by this unprecedented accumulation of wealth. Yet inequality continues to be masked by racial and meritocracy discourses, whether directed at "foreigners" taking away "American jobs" (at both ends of the educational spectrum) or at those who must rely on food stamps or unemployment benefits to survive. Part III examines some of the ongoing impacts of racialization processes on schools and communities.

KEY CONCEPTUAL POINTS

- Cultural classifications emerge in a cultural and historical context, serving certain purposes.
- Race in the United States emerged in a context of a stratified society, as an ideology to justify, maintain, and mask a system of structural inequalities based on class, national origins, gender, and religion.
- Social stratification, while not universal, is a widespread social system of ranked social groups.
- Stratified systems can be based on ascription, achievement, or both. The U.S. racial system contains elements of both despite a rhetoric of achievement (meritocracy).
- The U.S. racial system, definitions of Whiteness, and immigration and naturalization laws, have fluctuated in response to population changes, fueled by the demand for labor and the desire of the dominant social strata to preserve the White, Christian nation.

- Race and racialization processes have been used to exploit, divide, and weaken labor and to mask class inequality. This continues today, although in more muted ways.

KEY TERMS (ITALICIZED AND BOLDED IN TEXT)

ascribed versus achieved status
class system
legitimizing ideology
meritocracy
racialization
social identities
social stratification
social system
society
stratified societies

ACTIVITIES

Activity Plan 1: Census Activity

Objective: Participants discover that racial classifications (as reflected in the census) shift over time and reflect cultural and historical context and debates. (This exercise is also appropriate with chapter 5 and with part III chapters.)

Additional Information: For census materials, see websites below.

Procedure:

Step 1. Introduce participants to the U.S. Census. Tell them they are going to analyze census categories over time. Examine the United States Census home page at http://www.census.gov/. Examples of census categories at other time periods are available, such as: "Measuring America: The Decanal Census: From 1790 to 2000" at http://www.census.gov/prod/2002pubs/pol02marv.pdf; see also the Historical Census Browser, http://fisher.lib.virginia.edu/collections/stats/histcensus/. For a fee, there is also http://www.ancestry.com. See also websites listed in part IV, Website Resources.

Step 2. Present participants with 1790 census categories (see table 7.1). Participants first identify relevant social distinctions. For example, one census category is "free white male ages 16 and older." This indicates four relevant social distinctions: "free" versus "slave"; "white" versus "nonwhite; "male" versus "female"; and age, "over 16" versus "under 16."

Step 3. Participants explore reasons why these distinctions might be relevant in 1790 to the government.

- Take the distinction between "slave" and "free," which could affect representation in the House of Representatives, based on population. But how were slaves to be counted? Were they property or legal persons? Plantation slave owners wanted all slaves to be counted to increase their states' (and their own) political power in Congress. Non-slave owners and states objected, probably for similar reasons—political power. The "compromise" was to count "free persons" as 1.0 and slaves as .6 of a person for purposes of political representation.
- Another reason to count slaves separately was probably for taxation purposes, since they were legally property.
- Apparently slaves were not listed by name on the census, unlike free persons. This may reflect slaves' status as property rather than persons. And since they couldn't vote or serve on juries, there may have been no need for their formal names.
- Gender (male or female) information may reflect significant legal rights not available to females, such as the right to vote or serve on juries or be drafted. And married women couldn't sign legal contracts or own property in their own names.
- Age was probably useful for the draft, voting, serving on juries, except for slaves or free White females, who both lacked the full legal rights of adult White males.
- Point out that the only racial reference is to White (for males and females). Other free persons existed, but their race was not specified. Nor was a racial distinction made for slaves. Why might that have been the case? See chapter 9 for some possibilities.

Step 4. Participants discuss how they would have been classified in the census. Point out that until 1970, the census maker made that decision, using visual criteria. Discuss old and new self-identification methods. This is particularly relevant to chapter 9 and part III.

Step 5. View other historical census categories. For example, select a postslavery census, such as 1870 (see below) and discuss how the end of slavery is reflected in the census. For example, the category "slave" disappears and more races are listed (in addition to White, Black, mulatto, Chinese, and Indian). This activity could also work with chapter 9 or chapter 6.

Immigration patterns and politics are reflected in questions about foreign birth and whether males (but only males) are citizens (and eligible to vote). Indicators of marital and socioeconomic status, like property ownership, value of real estate, occupation or trade, and literacy also appear.

Other interesting census years, for racial categories, are 1920 and 1930.

Step 6. Examine and discuss the 2010 U.S. Census categories (see U.S. Census website for forms and data). Note changes, as well as stability in the major racial categories used, and in the labels or descriptive terms. Note the proliferation of new ethnic categories, and how "Hispanics" are handled. Does this make sense? Note new information, items that have disappeared. Point out that people can select their own racial and ethnic classification and, starting in 2000, can select more than one race or ethnicity. Category labels and numbers of categories have changed. This activity could also be used in part III.

Step 7. Discuss racial and ethnic classifications, participant opinions on and reasons for their views, the larger societal impacts of who (and how many people) end up in each census category, or the impacts of redefining and creating new categories. Reinforce the key points that categories are shifting, unstable constructions motivated by self-interest and have significant impacts. They are under human control. This would be very useful as part of one of the change-oriented activities in part III.

Step 8. Connect to contemporary educational and societal issues, such as the controversy over whether racial and ethnic data should be collected at all, and if so, what categories should be used, for what purposes. This dovetails nicely with part III.

ADDITIONAL ACTIVITY IDEAS

Activity Idea 1: Starpower: Experiencing a Stratified Society

Objective: Participants will understand the concept of a meritocracy as a legitimizing ideology in a class-stratified society. Participants will experience the impact of ascribed class on achievement. This activity simulates a U.S.-type system of stratification, based on the idea of a meritocracy, with some mobility, but prior group membership is the primary determinant of social, economic, and political status. It is highly interactive, intense, and emotional, takes one to three hours, and requires one to two hours of preparation the first time, unless you have access to a Starpower "kit." However, it is well worth the effort and provides participants with a visceral, direct experience of how the U.S. system of stratification works and feels.

An anthropologically oriented adaptation of the original Starpower simulation, with detailed step-by-step instructions and postgame discussion, is available in the RACE Project Teacher's Guide, downloadable as a PDF file at http://www.understandingrace.org/resources/for_teachers.html. It is also available at http://www.sjsu.edu/people/carol.mukhopadhyay.

Table 7.1.   1790 U.S. Census Data

Sample Census Data [1]
1790 Census (12 States). August 2, 1790
Total Population: 3,929,214[2]
head of household
number of free white males ages 16 and older
number of free white males under the age of 16
number of free white females
number of all other free persons
number of slaves

[1] *Source*: compiled from U.S. Census information
[2] *Note*: 1790 census records exist for Connecticut, Maine, Maryland, Massachusetts, New Hampshire, New York, North Carolina, Pennsylvania, Rhode Island, South Carolina, Vermont, and Virginia (Virginia schedules were reconstructed from state enumerations).

Activity Idea 2: Ethnic Diversity in the United States

Use Web or library sources to find data that reflect the presence of multiple, diverse ethnic groups within each major racial category (White or European; Asian; African; Native American; Hispanic). For example, names of towns (Little Italy), neighborhoods (and street names, school names) within major urban areas, civic and religious organizations, and local newspapers and magazines and restaurants reveal the multiplicity of ethnic groups and their distinct identities. Census data is also revealing, such as birth country, languages spoken at home, or in schools. English has not always been the only language spoken at home or even in U.S. schools, as early census data will show. Even as English-only schools arose as part of the 20th-century attempts to assimilate Southern and Eastern European immigrants, immigrants sent their children to after-school programs to learn their parents' native language. This is continuing today.

Activity Idea 3: Relevant Social Categories on Public Documents

Participants explore (using library, family documents, Web sources) the kinds of social categories previously used on key documents such as birth certificates, marriage certificates, hospital admission forms, police reports, school forms, real estate loan application forms, health statistics, and employment applications. Note any references to race, ethnicity, or religion, and the terms or labels used. What changes, if any, have occurred?

Activity Idea 4: Exploring My Ancestry: The Ethnic Me

Incorporate student investigations of their ancestry from earlier chapters into this chapter. Explore what happened, over time, to distinct European nationalities and ethnic identities among U.S. "Whites." Examine media and popular culture representations, intermarriage patterns, rituals, holidays, food traditions that remain alive. Ask, do "Whites" have and express ethnic identities? See http://www.sjsu.edu/people/carol.mukhopadhyay for a more detailed description of this activity.

Activity Idea 5: Mating Choice Activity

See Mating Choice Activity in chapters 9 or 13 and relate the activity to class stratification.

Activity Idea 6: Race, Class, Gender Intersections

Explore relevant videos that address various dimensions of race, race-class, and race-gender intersections, especially in popular culture. Video topics include sports, hip-hop, the culture of masculinity (Tough Guise), Latino stereotypes, music video images (Dreamworlds III). See website, http://www.mediaed.org/.

Activity Idea 7: Explore Educator Resources at *RACE: Are We So Different?* Project Website

See part IV and also downloadable teaching guides at http://www.understandingrace.org/resources/for_teachers.html.

Activity Idea 8: Explore Activities Developed for *Race: Power of an Illusion* Video Series

See http://www.pbs.org/race. Explore links between U.S. racial ideology and stratification:

1. Jamestown: Planting the Seeds of Tobacco and the Ideology of Race, http://www.pbs.org/race/000_About/002_04-teachers-01.htm.
2. Just an Environment or a Just Environment? Racial Segregation and Its Impacts, http://www.pbs.org/race/000_About/002_04-teachers-02.htm.
3. The Growth of the Suburbs and the Racial Wealth Gap. Explores structural racism and how, through housing discrimination, the accumulation of wealth has been racialized, at http://www.pbs.org/race/000_About/002_04-teachers-07.htm.

Activity Idea 9: Racial Inequality and Human Biology

Explore the impact of racial inequality on human biology through information at the African Burial Ground Project website at http://www.nypl.org/research/sc/afb/shell.html.

NOTES

1. Cultural anthropologists are struggling to develop conceptually appropriate terms for race, ethnic, religious, nationality-based groups. Some like Kottak conceptualize race as a kind of ethnic group, which Mukhopadhyay and Moses also suggested in 1997. Others, like Brodkin, use the term ethnoracial to signify the intertwining of what some used to think of as distinct (see Mukhopadhyay & Moses, 1997). We find this merging useful.

2. For a highly readable, complex picture of Gold Rush immigrants, see Isabel Allende's novel *Daughter of Fortune* (1999).

3. All quotes from the Maryland Toleration Act are found at http://msa.maryland.gov/msa/speccol/sc2200/sc2221/000025/html/preface.html. Accessed July 15, 2013.

4. The Maryland State Archives website offers excellent related materials for the public and educators at http://msa.maryland.gov/. Accessed July 15, 2013.

5. Scupin (2003) and some others use the term WASP for the Northwestern European, predominantly Anglo-Saxon Protestant Christians that dominated the White U.S. population until the 20th century and, politically and culturally, thereafter, even today. Inclusion of other European groups in this White category is recent and, we would argue, contingent and incomplete.

6. One basis for including East Indians as Caucasian was because North Indian languages were part of the Indo-European (or Aryan) language family. That argument was explicitly discounted by the Court in the Thind case as being, basically, ancient history.

7. See excellent modules on Race and Wealth Disparities at the *Race: The Power of an Illusion* website: http://www.pbs.org/race/000_About/002_04-teachers-07.htm.

Chapter Eight

Cross-Cultural Overview of Race

How widespread is the U.S. system of racial classification? Is race a common, even universal, way for humans to classify people? And how often is it used to justify stratification and inequality?

Anthropologists love to ask these types of questions. Anthropology is fundamentally a comparative discipline. At heart, our goal is to explore and understand similarities and differences in human cultures. In order to do this, we must include all types of societies, not just Western societies, not just major, complex societies ("civilizations"), even though they have had a powerful impact on human history and dominate today. Large-scale, stratified, politically centralized "states" with urban centers are relatively new cultural inventions (4,000 to 6,000 years ago), and industrialized nation-states have emerged only within the past century or two. Our ***cross-cultural comparisons*** must take into account small-scale, politically decentralized, nonurban, preliterate cultures, including preagricultural (foraging-gathering-fishing-hunting) societies, and those based on herding and on simple horticulture. These are part of the human spectrum of possibilities and, until recently, the predominant forms.

This chapter examines how different cultures classify humans and finds, once again, that there is significant variability and that our U.S. racial system is far from universal.

CONCEPTUAL BACKGROUND

So . . . are racial classifications a universal feature of human societies? The answer partially depends on what we are asking about. The U.S. racial worldview is specific to North America, although certain features can be found in other racially stratified societies (Smedley & Smedley, 2012).

In chapter 6, we discussed the human propensity for classification as a way to simplify the complexity of everyday stimuli. But anthropologists reject the idea that racial classifications are automatic, universal, widespread, or even very easy to learn. In the words of Sue Estroff, "the way that race is thought and seen and experienced depends very much on who is thinking, about whom, and why" (Estroff, 1997, p. 115). Adults, as well as children, have tremendous difficulty learning new social classification systems, especially when they emigrate to new cultures. Their own cultural systems, as we pointed out in chapters 5 and 6, have become deeply internalized and culturally "real."

HOW IMPORTANT ARE VISIBLE FEATURES
AS A BASIS FOR CLASSIFICATION?

The U.S. racial system utilizes easily observable, human physical features as a basis for classification. But visible differences, whether natural or culturally created (e.g., clothing), may not even be a common basis for human social classification, at least prior to European colonialism. Some argue that the notion of race goes back to ancient Greece, to the concept of *genos*. But apparently its prime meaning is a community linked over generations through common ancestry—families, clans, and tribes (Lieberman, 2003, p. 38). Those not part of one's *genos* were designated as *barbaros* or barbarians. The word *Xenos*, in modern Greek, means foreigner, and a *Xenodoheion* is a hotel (literally, a container for foreigners!). So the crucial classifying device is common origins, cultural or group identity, and belonging rather than visible, physical traits.

Language and culture play an extremely significant role in social classification cross-culturally. There are thousands of linguistically identified cultural groups in the world, even today, despite the homogenizing impact of colonialism and globalization. Many countries, like Nigeria, Kenya, South Africa, and Indonesia, consist of hundreds of language-cultural groups, often sharing common ancestry. In such contexts, the primary social and political divisions, and social identities, may fall along "ethnic" (aka "tribal") lines. Indeed, this can be a barrier to creating a national identity and pursuing goals that transcend ethnic groups. But language is also a basis for social divisions and social identities in Europe, Canada, and countries in South and Southeast Asia . . . and increasingly, in the United States.

In Latin America and the Caribbean, most indigenous (native) groups continue to use linguistic and cultural features for social classification rather than visible biological traits. The Yanomama, a small-scale farming-foraging (horticulturalist) group living in Northwestern Brazil and Southern Venezuela, divide people according to those who know their language and culture (*Yanomama*) and those who don't (*nabuh*).

For indigenous groups living around Tupi, Peru, collective identity is closely linked to their language, which they call *Jaqaru,* from the words *jqi* "human being" and *aru* "speech." They refer to themselves as "Jaqaru" people. And despite European imposition of a common racial term, *indios,* or "Indians," on the diverse cultures in the region, most Native American people today still identify with and prefer to be called by their original names, such as Maya, Kumeyaay, and so on (Kephart, 2003).

Most of us seem aware that Indian Hindu traditions classify people based on so-called caste (*varna, jati*). But language and language-related cultural forms (e.g., Bengali songs, Tamil poetry) are the basis for significant social divisions and social identities, along with religion. When people ask about one's "community," they could easily be referring to one's linguistic community, such as Bengali, Tamil, Gujrati, Punjabi, or Telugu. Indeed, names of major Indian states (Tamil Nadu, Gujarat, Punjab) reflect the main language spoken. The nation of Bangladesh, named for "Bangla," the Bengali language and people ("land of Bengalis"), was the eastern part of British-ruled Bengal until partition, when it became East Pakistan. Even now, Bengalis, whether Hindu or Muslim, in India, Bangladesh or the United States, feel a common cultural identity. Hindi may be India's official national language, but many Indians, especially in South, prefer their "own" languages (Tamil, Telugu, etc.). India's Hindi films are known throughout the world, but films in other Indian languages are a thriving industry as well.

Music, poetry, and other art forms are often language specific. And when it comes to marriage, language compatibility can be crucial, even if the bride and groom speak multiple languages. Language is one means through which social identity is collectively expressed and transmitted to the next generation.

Even among Europeans, steeped in racial ideology, anthropologist Ann Stoler discovered that nonracial characteristics, personality traits, psychological and moral dispositions, and various cultural competencies were central to British, Dutch, and French colonial policies and definitions of who was European or White (Stoler, 1997, p. 101). In addition to appearance, specific attitudes and behaviors were associated with people from certain ethnic, caste, or class groups.

When visible features are socially significant, they may be attributes other than skin color. In pre-20th-century China, the basis of racial classification was body hair. Extensive body hair signified a lack of "civilization." Chinese writers described European male missionaries, with their beards, as "hairy barbarians." Some 20th-century Chinese social scientists continued to divide humans into evolutionary stages based on body hair. One survey of humanity provided a detailed classification using types of "beards, whiskers, and moustaches" (Miller, 2002, p. 17).

Even when skin color is culturally noticed—that is, used as a basis for creating named social categories—the meanings associated with racial categories differ. Brazil and other Latin American cultures, with their varied notions of *mestizaje* (Gledhill & Wade, 2012), illustrate this, as we shall see shortly.

IS DIFFERENCE UNIVERSALLY DEVALUED?

What anthropologists call **ethnocentrism** is widespread and normal (see chapter 5). Most people internalize and value their own cultural systems, their own ways of classifying humans, their own aesthetic and behavioral standards. Indeed, one's culture becomes part of one's personal identity and sense of normalcy. From this perspective, it is not surprising that individuals often find people from other cultures quite "strange" and may make value judgments about their behavior or appearance.

Mukhopadhyay recalls her first visit to India, in 1970. At that time, few Indians had personally encountered young females of European descent, especially traveling alone with an Indian male. She recalls several occasions when a small crowd of people, including children, would simply gather and stare. Once on a local bus in rural northern India, a fellow passenger kept looking over at her, particularly at her arms. Finally he leaned over and sympathetically asked her Indian husband what kind of disease his wife had. He said he had noticed all the dark spots on her arms. Her husband smiled and politely tried to translate the concept of "freckles" into Hindi.

The human ability, indeed propensity, to notice and even classify people by visible traits does not inevitably lead to a hierarchical system of races. Sometimes groups exaggerate minor physical or cultural differences simply to assert their collective group ethnic or cultural identity. The region anthropologists call Melanesia (located in the South Pacific) is very diverse culturally and linguistically. Papua New Guinea alone, with a population of over six million, has at least seven hundred distinct linguistic groups. Most New Guineans live in small rural villages that traditionally were egalitarian and politically autonomous.

To an outsider, their cultures and languages are far less distinct than to natives. One anthropologist (Brison, 2003) found that neighboring villages described each other's language as mutually unintelligible and impossibly difficult to learn. Yet the languages are virtually identical except for slight differences in pronunciation. Moreover, the two groups intermarry, are culturally indistinguishable, and once were one village. Nearly everyone has relatives in both villages.

Apparently villages deliberately accentuate minor linguistic differences as "emblems of ethnic dissimilarity," part of a broader claim to local ethnic distinctiveness (Brison, 2003, p. 377). Brison traces this to colonial and postcolonial conditions. She argues that whether groups emphasize or deem-phasize potential differences, cultural or physical, depends on circumstances, relations among ethnic groups, and political consequences.

Not All Differences Are Perceived as Negative or as a Basis for Social Stratification

It does not seem to be basic human nature to fear and denigrate difference. Indeed, anthropological evidence suggests quite the opposite. The appeal of the exotic—or at least, variety—is not a recent phenomenon. Difference can delight and generate desire. Human cultural inventions of all types, whether things, behaviors, or ideas, have traveled huge distances and are partially in response to demand. Trading routes have existed throughout the world for thousands of years, creating complex, hybrid cultural regions, such as those lying along major bodies of water like the Mediterranean Sea or the Indian Ocean. The lure of cultural difference, the demand for "foreign" cultural products, has propelled people to cross mountains, oceans, and vast deserts. Some of the earliest East Indians to come to the United States were peddlers from Bengal, bringing local handicraft items to satisfy the late-19th-century European and American desire for "exotic Oriental" goods (Bald, 2013).

But it is not just things that cross cultural boundaries. *Homo sapiens* have remained one species partially because of the human urge to mate across social boundaries, with people from different groups and cultures. Traders have left their genetic mark throughout the world. And some, like those Bengali peddlers, settled down, in this case in New Orleans, marrying African American and Creole women (Bald, 2013).

But entire cultures may seek out mates from different groups. According to linguistic anthropologist Dr. Claire Insel, groups of people living in the Vaupés region of the Amazon Basin (in Brazil and Colombia) are known for seeking marriage partners specifically outside their language group. A member of one kinship group will not only marry someone from a different descent or kinship group, but from a group that speaks a mutually unintelligible language. In this way the twenty or so descent groups of the region constantly are creating and renewing social ties with each other.

Humans clearly have the capacity to be attracted to difference and variety. However, the appeal of difference is not random. Or rather, culture can shape the associations we attach to difference. Desirable traits, especially in stratified societies, tend to be those associated with or defined as superior by high-status or powerful groups. Undesirable traits are often linked to lower-status groups. The traditional U.S. cultural value placed on lighter skin color, blue eyes, blond hair, narrow noses, and straighter hair reflects physical features of historically dominant groups and our system of racial stratification. What constitutes attractive difference, then, is heavily shaped by history and power relations among groups, both locally and globally.

The appeal of Bengali peddlers' Oriental goods to U.S. Americans was partially due to their having been first adopted by Europeans, especially people in Britain, and then by upper-status U.S. Americans. More recently, cultural objects from Japan, like animation characters as well as Japanese food and language, have acquired great popularity. Japanese cultural crossover into mainstream U.S. norms is not just a coincidence; it partially reflects Japan's role as a global power. Part of the global appeal of contemporary popular cultural forms of music, dancing, and clothing (e.g., hip-hop culture) may have originally come from their association with the United States and other wealthy countries, although other influential non-Western forms have now arisen (e.g., Bollywood). Rising stars of the East, such as South Korea, are flexing their own cultural muscles, in a sense, reinterpreting Western culture. For example, when K-pop musician PSY released his "Gangnam Style" music video in June 2012, part of its enormous appeal (reportedly 1.7 billion views on YouTube) may have been that it was a South Korean version of hip-hop, not simply a U.S. import (see http://www.youtube.com/user/officialpsy).

STRATIFIED SOCIAL GROUPS CAN EXIST WITHOUT AN IDEOLOGY OF RACE

The anthropological record shows that humans can have stratification and slavery without an ideology of race (chapter 7). The Romans and Greeks had slaves who were also Roman and Greek! Cultural groups that share the same ancestral roots but differ in local ethnic identity or political orientation can oppress, even slaughter, each other, as happened in countless European wars as well as in China, Algeria, Vietnam, El Salvador, Rwanda, and the U.S. Civil War.

Religion has been an enormous, although downplayed, source of group divisions, identity, and differential treatment and conflict. Just think about Ireland, the Crusades, the South Asian continent (Pakistan and India), the former Yugoslavia, especially Bosnia-Serbia, Lebanon, the Sudan, Nigeria, and numerous other contemporary sites of conflict along religious lines, including the Islamophobia sweeping Europe. In most wars, arguably, and certainly in virtually all major 20th-century wars, participants have not aligned along racial lines. World War II, despite Hitler's racist-religious ideology, saw German "Aryans" aligned with Japanese and Italians. In contrast, in Latin America conflicts have been primarily political, perhaps because it is so overwhelmingly Christian, indeed Catholic.

Societies Can Have a Racelike Ideology Not Based on Actual Biological Differences

Japan offers another permutation on the race theme. Japan is stratified by class but portrays itself proudly as culturally homogeneous. Former Prime Minister Nakasone once suggested that Japan's success in international business was due to its being *"tan'itsu minzoku,"* a term that connotes ethnic homogeneity. Yet scholars estimate that approximately 10 percent of Japan's population is from minorities. This includes aboriginal Ainu, annexed Okinawans, Burukumin, immigrants, especially more than 700,000 Koreans, and children of multiethnic parentage (Kottak, 2013, p. 137).

The Burakumin are one significant minority, anthropologically speaking. Burakumin were the lowest group in the system of social stratification that emerged during the Tokugawa period (1603–1868). They have been compared to India's "untouchable" lower strata because they are forced to do "unclean" jobs, like killing animals, disposing of dead bodies, and working with leather, and then are stigmatized for doing these jobs!

Burakumin were traditionally viewed as innately biologically and morally different and inferior to mainstream Japanese. Yet Burakumin are physically and genetically indistinguishable from other Japanese. They can and sometimes do "pass" as non-Burakumin. The markers of their low status are not visible or physical. Their social status is identifiable only through their family names, the segregated residential areas they traditionally have been forced to live in, and their occupations. Legal forms of discrimination no longer exist, but old attitudes and stigma persist (Kottak, 2013; Takezawa, 2011).

Another example is related to the Japanese colonization of Korea in the early 20th century. Japanese colonial discourses focused on visible differences between Koreans and Japanese despite their shared physical features. Indeed, in an October 1913 Japanese Ministry of Home Affairs secret document, officials expressed concern over their inability to identify Koreans, especially those in Japan. So they compiled a list of distinctive Korean features, often combining physical and cultural traits: "less hair, which is also softer . . . most of them have flat faces . . . skull alterations; feet thin and small . . . better posture and rarely have a bent back . . . the back of their head is usually flat because they use wooden pillows . . . they use salt to brush their teeth, so the teeth are white and well aligned" (Lee, 2011, p. 54). A Japanese racial science also developed and purportedly discovered "racial" differences between the two groups, such as Korean skeletons being larger and heavier but with "inferior" muscles and "smaller brain size" than Japanese. In this case, there was an attempt to create visible markers of Korean-ness, partially by transforming cultural and linguistic traits into physical forms of difference.

The Greek philosopher Aristotle justified slavery on the grounds that humans were unequal even though many slaves came from other Greek city-states and looked physically similar. But dominant groups have the power to define the subordinate group as inferior as well as to force them to dress and behave in ways that reinforce their supposed inferiority.

Ancient Greece linked social status to a type of inner essence, one's "soul." The idea that different groups are created to perform different societal functions apparently existed in Greek thought. Socrates, in the so-called tale of the metals, purportedly argued that a stable society required three classes. Souls corresponding with gold were designated rulers, those corresponding to silver were administrators and officials, and those to brass and iron were farmers and craftsmen (Lieberman, 2003).

Early justifications for North American slavery rested primarily on religious beliefs about ancestral relationships and past deeds rather than on race as biology. Within the European Christian tradition, St. Thomas Aquinas and others justified social stratification as part of the "divine plan" of God. Using biblical stories, slavery apologists in Europe and the United States attributed the enslavement of Africans (and in some versions, Native Americans) to their relationship to Ham, one of Noah's sons (Smedley & Smedley, 2012).

MEANINGS: SKIN COLOR AND OTHER PHYSICAL TRAITS AS THE BASIS FOR SOCIAL RANKING

The proximity and interaction of two cultures that look physically different does not inevitably lead to those differences becoming culturally and socially significant, nor is it a basis for inferior or superior social rank. Ancient Egyptian wall paintings depicted humans of various shades of skin colors, but this apparently simply reflected variability in the Egyptian and surrounding populations.

In India, the term *varna* or "strata" is partially associated with skin color—higher *varna* are supposedly lighter. In this case, it is likely related to the political dominance of Aryan-Indo-Europeans from more northerly latitudes over Southern Dravidian, darker-skinned populations, living closer to the equator (see chapter 3). But skin color is only one superficial and often inaccurate indicator of ancestry and social status.

In stratified societies, skin color can be a marker of class status, even when the biological potential for melanin production is identical. "Tanning" is a universal human response to sun exposure, as we know from chapter 3. In predominantly agricultural societies, like India, lower-status groups were more apt to toil in the sun, as farmers or laborers, than their upper-status counterparts. Lower-status groups, then, were often visibly darker than elite groups.

For women in societies with strict sexual segregation, linkages between class status and color were even more intense. Elite women remained in family compounds, inside the home, or were fully covered, from head to foot, when they ventured into the public sphere. These cultural practices not only minimized exposure to the male gaze—but also to the sun. Lighter skin symbolized high status and, thus, became a particularly desirable trait in women.

The status symbolism of "tanned" or "untanned" skins, or muscularity, for that matter, can shift over time and place. In the late 19th and early 20th century, as the United States moved from an agricultural to an industrial society, "pale" skin among Euro-American women started to be associated with poor "factory girls." In contrast, wealthier Euro-American women began to engage in outdoor recreational activities, such as bicycling, badminton, tennis, and even swimming. Today, the image of fitness and, for Euro-Americans, a "tanned" look, tends to imply higher rather than lower status.

Cross-cultural evidence, then, indicates that while visible traits are sometimes used for social classification, racial thinking and racial stratification is neither inevitable nor particularly common prior to European colonial expansion. Other contextual factors, motivations, historical circumstances, and especially power relations play a crucial role in the emergence of race as a central basis for social differentiation and social stratification.

VARIABLE CONTEXTS ALTER THE MEANINGS OF RACIAL SYSTEMS

Even in areas dominated by Europeans, local racial ideologies were shaped by local circumstances. Europeans generally shared similar popular beliefs about human variability and types of humans. But the term *race* as a way of classifying human groups did not appear in the English language until the 17th century; then it referred to characteristics of certain types of persons, such as dispositions or temperaments, or to a class of persons, as the race of womankind (Smedley & Smedley, 2012, p. 14). From the 16th to 20th centuries, the concept of race and its social manifestations evolved along distinct paths, in different colonial regions, reflecting local contexts and goals.

This is perhaps most striking in the Americas. Scholars have long contrasted the racial system that emerged in North America with the forms it has taken in Central America, the Caribbean, and South America.[1] The North American system, historically, has been characterized as binary and bipolar, organized into two fundamental categories, White-Black or White–non-

White. It is an "ascribed" system, at least in theory. One's race is established at birth and is not changeable during one's life again, at least in theory.

U.S. American racial categories have tended to be, until recently, mutually exclusive, that is, you are monoracial even if your parents are of different races. A brief exception occurred in the late 19th century and early 20th century census (1850–1890, 1910–1920), when "mulatto" appeared for persons of mixed "Black" and "White" ancestry. The 1890 census went farther, creating separate categories and precise definitions for "quadroons" and "octoroons," previously simply included in a generic "mulatto" group.

> The word "black" should be used to describe those persons who have three-fourths or more black blood; "mulatto," those persons who have from three-eighths to five-eighths black blood; "quadroon," those persons who have one-fourth black blood; and "octoroon," those persons who have one-eighth or any trace of black blood. (U.S. Census Bureau, 2002, p. 27)

The census definitions, however, suggest these "mixed races" were not a reformulation of the basic White-Black paradigm but simply finer versions of blackness. By 1910, octoroon and quadroon again merged with mulatto. And in 1930, mulatto disappeared completely. From that time on, anyone with "mixed White and Negro blood" was counted as "Negro, no matter how small the percentage of Negro blood." The same applied to other offspring where one parent was "Negro," such as Black-Indian offspring (U.S. Census Bureau, 2002, p. 59). Offspring of White-Indian parents were categorized as Indian. This is consistent with the historic tendency for offspring of "mixed" parentage to be placed in the racial category of the lower racial status parent, what Kottak calls *hypodescent* (2013).

Periodically, the U.S. system has been forced to create additional racial categories beyond Black-White. In addition to Indians, the 1890 Census included separate categories for Chinese and Japanese. "Other" appeared in 1910, Mexicans in 1930, Filipinos in 1950, Hawaiians and Koreans in 1970, and several others since then. Yet these all fall into the "not White" pole of the binary White–non-White U.S. racial paradigm. And it is only with the 2000 census that multiracial ancestry was once again recognized and, more important, that individuals could formally identify themselves with more than one racial or ethnic category.

Color and other physical characteristics carry an enormous ideological load in the U.S. racial worldview, linked historically to racially differentiated capacities, especially intelligence. The U.S. racial system established rigid social boundaries and barriers to social interaction through laws and other forms of coercion (see chapter 9). One's race was considered a fixed, permanent condition.

Latin American and Caribbean racial systems are more flexible, less exclusionary, more situation and context dependent, more under the control of individuals. They also have far more racial categories and a different concept of race. One's racial classification can change over time. There have been virtually no explicit race-based bars to social interaction, mating, and marriage. We can see the effects in Latin American and Caribbean populations. Most people aren't easily categorized using the U.S. system. In many Latin American/Caribbean nations, class stratification (and gender) is a more powerful and pervasive basis for social status than race. Thus an individual's racial designation can change as the result of an alteration in one's economic and social status (Kottak, 2013).

Brazil exemplifies these contrasts. Like the United States, it is a large, complex society historically derived from a plantation slave economy that lasted until the last half of the 19th century. It continues to be racially stratified, part of the legacy of slavery. Yet, unlike the United States, Brazil never legally encoded its racial system; interracial sexual relations and marriage were widespread among Africans, Europeans, and Native Americans. This is reflected in population figures for Brazil. Using macroracial categories, one study found that 54 percent of the population was classified as White, 40 percent Mulatto, 5 percent Black, and 1 percent Other (Kephart, 2003, p. 297).[2]

In ordinary life, however, Brazilians use far more racial labels, and some anthropologists have identified over 500 terms. The Portuguese word *tipo*, meaning "type," is used to classify people using a complex set of visible physical characteristics including skin color, nose shape, eye color and shape, hair color and type, and lip shape. One family can have many *tipos*. There are regional differences in *tipo*s reflecting variations in the historic mix of populations.

The classification system is complex, as seen in Jefferson Fish's description of one city in the northeastern state of Bahia. Terms ranged from the "whitest" to the "blackest" *tipos*. For example, a *loura* is whiter-than-white, with straight blond hair, blue or green eyes, light skin color, narrow nose, and thin lips. A *branca* has light skin color, eyes of any color, hair of any color or form except tight curly, a nose that is not broad, and lips that are not thick. A *morena* has brown or black hair that is wavy or curly but not tight curly, tan skin, a nose that is not narrow, and lips that are not thin. A person with tight curly blond (or red) hair, light skin, blue (or green) eyes, a broad nose, and thick lips is a *sarará*. The opposite features—straight black hair, dark skin, brown eyes, narrow nose, and thin lips—are those of a *cabo verde. Sarará* and *cabo verde* are both *tipos* that are considered by Brazilians in Salvador, Bahia, to be neither black nor white (Fish, 2003, p. 277).

In another small Brazilian community, about half of the villagers considered themselves *mulatto*, but within that category there were ten to fifteen different terms. Kottak (2013) found that one's racial description could alter, depending on who was talking, when, or even the time of day. Besides *branco* (white), he could be *claro* (light), *louro* (blond), *sarará* (light-skinned redhead), *mulato claro* (light mulatto), or *mulato* (mulatto). One of his informants constantly changed the term he used for himself—from *escuro* (dark) to *moreno escuro* (dark brunette) to *preto* (black).

The above example illustrates that racial descriptors are always relational; that is, they depend on who is talking to whom.[3] Apparently people also take into account features like clothing, language, location (urban or rural), and attitude, along with wealth when calculating one's "race." For example, a person wearing old clothes and standing in front of a rather ramshackle dwelling might be described as *preto* (black). Dressed up and standing in front of a middle- or upper-class house, the same person would be classified as *moreno* (brown) or even *branco* (white).

This allows Brazilians to "change" their race, to shift from one category to another, from one descriptive label to another, through their own behavior, at least to some degree. Kottak suggests this reflects how relatively insignificant race is in Brazilian social life, at least compared to the United States. He notes that people are not always consistent in the racial terms they apply to others or even to themselves (Kottak, 2013, p. 139).

Brazil's racial classification system today is influenced by larger global and international movements, including international minority rights and African diaspora and pan-African movements. There is more self-conscious assertion of "blackness" by some African-Brazilians and more attention to racial discrimination and racial disparities among Brazilians (Kottak, 2013). Nevertheless, it is still significantly different from the U.S. system.

The Brazilian case illustrates how deeply racial classifications are embedded, albeit to differing degrees, in the prevailing system of social stratification. In some Caribbean societies, like Dominica, the society is primarily stratified by economic class rather than by color. The social class structure is almost totally based on wealth, and there is no substantial White elite as there is in other Caribbean nations like Trinidad, Jamaica, and Barbados.

Variability within Latin America and the Caribbean is enormous due to the different colonial histories and local circumstances (cf. Wade, 2010). Areas where plantation culture dominated tended to have large African populations and relatively few Europeans, affecting mating, marriage, and future demographic patterns. In Brazil, for example, most Portuguese colonizers were males, often traders or adventure seekers. Many married local women and their offspring were treated as their legal heirs. As in the United States, male plantation owners often had sexual relations with their female slaves. But they tended to free the children that resulted, and these offspring, in turn, had economic and social mobility, sometimes rising to high social positions.

Today, as a result of different histories, some countries, like Barbados, have less than 5 percent of their population categorized as "Mulatto/Mixed," while other countries, like the Dominican Republican, have over 70 percent who are so categorized (Kephart, 2003, pp. 300–301).

In some countries, like Dominica, "Carib" is an important ethnic group. In others, like Barbados, a group called *redlegs* was originally laborers recruited from the British Isles. Although they were the poorest group on Barbados, they took pride in being "white" and identified, by color at least, with the European planter class. Later on, they began to mix and mate with the African populations but still retained their identity—and prejudices (Kephart, 2003).

There are also so-called maroon communities (from the Spanish word *cimarron*, meaning "wild"), African slaves who escaped from their plantation and founded communities in Jamaica, Colombia, and, most significantly, in what is today Suriname. These groups have retained much of their African ethnic cultural and linguistic backgrounds, as reflected in their social categories and labels. They speak Creole languages, which combine West African sentence structure with mainly European vocabulary.

In the postslavery period, the planter class in colonies like Trinidad actively recruited Indian (and some Chinese) immigrants for agricultural work, partially to prevent Afro-Trinidadians from becoming economically and politically powerful. This common strategy of pitting racial-ethnic groups against each other, as in Hawaii (see chapter 7), significantly altered the ethnic composition of the island. Today, Trinidad has approximately equal populations of African and Indian descent, along with some Chinese, Spanish, British, French, other Latin Americans, and a significant number of multiethnics. It also has Muslims, Christians, Hindus (multiple varieties and languages), Sikhs, Jews, Buddhists, and secular humanists enriching its cultural complexity.

One study of racial categories produced seven basic terms: *negro, Indian, dogla* (a mixture of East Indian and African), *mestizo, panyol* (Venezuelan), *Spanish* (i.e., European), and *white*. There were also nine compound terms: *madrasi-Indian, kuli-Indian, Tobago-negro, chinee-negro, French-creole* (local, white), *clearskin-dogla, koko-panyol, half-white* (mulatto), and *local white* (Kephart, 2003, p. 301).

Some Caribbean islands, like Carriacou and Cuba, have been able to preserve early census information on the African ethnolinguistic groups present among the island's slave populations. Those born in the Americas were designated *creole* but retained an ethnic identification with their mother's line (what anthropologists call matrilineal descent). Apparently, African ethnic groups were not only ranked, but there were beliefs about the mental and physical attributes of different groups. Marriage was exogamous—that is, marriage partners had to be outside of one's own ethnic group.

On Carriacou, according to Kephart, writing in 2003, no one born and raised there is thought of as White. Nor do they think in Black-White terms. They apparently use some racial terms found in other parts of the Caribbean, such as red/redskin, brown/brown-skin, white, and pink (i.e., albino) but as simple descriptive adjectives. For example, someone might be referred to as "the *brown-skin* one." Their significant social identities are as *Carriacou people,* aware of their African ancestry and of belonging to different African *nations* or *bloods.* They contrast African behaviors and beliefs with White behaviors and beliefs. Sharing food, for example, is what *negro people* do, in contrast with *white people* (Kephart, 2003).

WHAT HAPPENS WHEN IMMIGRANTS COME TO THE UNITED STATES?

Given that the U.S. system of racial classification is not universal, people from other cultures are often confused by our categories. At the simplest level, they find that the labels they use in their home countries don't work here. Brazilians are surprised to find that the American term "blond" refers to hair color only. Many Brazilians of the *branca* ("white") *tipo* are not considered White, often to their dismay. Ironically, they are frequently categorized as Hispanic even though they speak Portuguese and not Spanish. Jefferson Fish, married to a Brazilian woman, describes how their daughter, who is brown-skinned, can change her race from Black to *morena* (brunette) by taking a plane from the United States to Brazil.

Haiti, for historical reasons, is (with respect to ancestry) one of the most African of the Caribbean islands. But Haitians use both physical appearance and ancestry in their classifications. And one drop of White blood is sufficient to make one racially "white." Haiti's folk taxonomy includes a term for foreigners of African appearance that literally means "a black white" (*un blanc noir*; Fish, 2003).

More significantly, U.S. institutions demand that all groups fit within our system of racial and ethnic classification. As race and ethnicity have re-emerged as significant dimensions of identity, with political consequences, immigrants (and their children especially) struggle to find their own identity within the available categories.

Immigrants from India and the Indian subcontinent have never fit American or European racial categories. In the Thind case (see chapter 7), East Indians were viewed by scientists and some legal scholars as Caucasian but not White. The Bengalis Indians who came to the United States in the late 19th and early 20th centuries tended to be treated like, reside in, and sometimes marry into non-European communities, mainly African American, Puerto Rican, and other Caribbean groups. But official government records reveal how little they fit into the dominant racial system. Take, for example, the racial designations for a list of eighteen Indian males in "Mixed Marriages" in Harlem and the Lower East Side, from 1922 to 1937, recorded by the City of New York, Certificates and Record of Marriage, 1899–1937. Nine Bengalis were categorized as "white," 1 as "negro," 6 as "colored," 1 as "Indian," and 1 as "East Indian" (Bald, 2013, pp. 168–69).

With the emergence of the pan-Asian category in the 1970s, Indians have been recruited for the Asian category, albeit as "South Asians," despite the diversity of "Asian" histories, cultures, languages, and political entities. Even more comprehensive is the "people of color" category—all non-Europeans (ancestrally). To many Indian and other non-European immigrants, this classification as "colored" (vs. White) is quite foreign. Not surprisingly, U.S. Americans from the Indian subcontinent, as well as from other regions of the world, have lobbied for distinct categories that reflect their background and sense of identity. The 2010 U.S. Census, for example, allows individuals to select such categories as Indian, Bangladesi, Bhutanese, Burmese, Chamorro, Vietnamese, and an array of other identities.[4]

When Puerto Ricans first came to the mainland United States, they encountered a world of bipolar, bounded racial categories that profoundly shaped their lives. After the Spanish American War and the U.S. occupation of Puerto Rico, immigration increased to the mainland. As the immigrant population grew, working-class Puerto Rican and Cuban women tried to organize along lines of shared interest. Perceived as an "interracial group," most meeting halls refused to allow them to meet (Bigler, 2003). Puerto Ricans inducted into the military after 1917 served in racially segregated units. American racial attitudes shaped how business and political leaders saw the potential of Puerto Rico, including as a potential state, an issue that remains unresolved today.

Immigrants from the Dominican Republic, now a major group in New York City, often find themselves categorized as African American—whereas in the Dominican Republican, anyone partly "white" is considered nonblack, usually mulatto. In the 2010 U.S. Census, however, when Dominicans were forced to select between Black, White, or Other, 13 percent identified as Black, 29 percent as White, and a majority, 57 percent, identified as "Other" (http://www.law.cornell.edu/supct/html/02-241.ZO.html). The "Other" category is thought to primarily represent individuals who identify as having multiracial ancestry. Dominicans, like many other ethnic groups, find negotiating their identity in the Unites States complex. They are shades of brown, speak Spanish, dance to a Latin/Caribbean beat, and are used to color being a physical feature not a social identity.

In essence, immigrants such as Puerto Ricans, Dominicans, and East Indians, along with Filipinos, Samoans, Guatemalans, Brazilians, Iranians, Indonesians, Arabs, and a myriad of other immigrant groups, are being forced into a North American racial system—they have been racialized according to the criteria of the predominantly Anglo, Protestant culture. And skin color is acquiring a new meaning for many of these immigrants.

Piri Thomas's 1967 autobiography *Down These Mean Streets* describes his painful realization of what it means to be dark-skinned in the United States when he applies for a sales job. Unlike his light-skinned Puerto Rican friend who was hired on the spot, when he goes in, he is told that they will contact him when a job opening comes up. "I didn't feel so much angry as I did sick, like throwing-up sick. Later, when I told this story to my buddy, a colored cat, he said, 'Hell, Piri, Ah know stuff like that can sure burn a cat up, but a Negro faces that all the time.' 'I know that,' I said, 'but I wasn't a Negro then. I was still only a Puerto Rican'" (Bigler, 2003, p. 220).

Puerto Ricans, along with other ethnic groups, especially the generation born in the United States, are beginning to rebel against the binary racial (and language) system operating in the United States. They are adopting new labels that are expressive of their own identities: Nuyoricans (Puerto Ricans in New York), Dominican Yorks, Chicanos, Mexicanos, Desi (South Asians, East Indians), Afro-Caribbeans. They are rejecting rigid, fixed identities and instead embracing hybrid, fluid, multiple, shifting, context-dependent, strategically relevant identities. And they are crossing ethnic, religious, racial, even gender boundaries. They are confusing and confounding the prevailing racial system.

Immigration presents an enormous challenge to the U.S. system of racial classification. So does the growth of intermarriage between individuals of diverse ethno-racial-linguistic-religious backgrounds (see chapter 9). It is not surprising, then, that the most rapidly growing census category in the United States is "Other."

KEY CONCEPTUAL POINTS

- Race is not a universal system of social classification.
- Not all cultures use visible differences, including skin color, for social classification, nor do they rank or stratify groups on this basis.
- Skin color, when a basis for classification, has variable cross-cultural meanings.
- Language and culture are probably as important for social classification and identity as physical features.
- Cultural groups can either minimize or exaggerate differences, physical or cultural.
- Contextual, historical factors, and especially power relations, are crucial in the emergence and maintenance of systems of racial classification. Ra-

cial systems developed along different paths in North America, Latin America, and the Caribbean.

- The cultural specificity of the U.S. system makes it difficult for people who immigrate from other cultures.
- U.S. racial categories have shifted and continue to shift in response to changing circumstances.
- Immigration and interethnic and interracial marriage is challenging the current U.S. system of racial classification.

KEY TERMS (ITALICIZED AND BOLDED IN TEXT)

cross-cultural comparison
ethnocentrism
hypodescent

ACTIVITIES

Overall Objectives: Participants will be able to describe cross-cultural variations in racial and other systems of social classification as well as difficulties people from other cultures might have adapting to the U.S. system.

Other Information: Some of these activities can be used with other chapters in part II and part III, particularly chapter 12.

Activity Plan 1: Census Categories in Other Nations

Procedure

Step 1. Explore the census categories in a selection of countries around the world, such as Australia, Mexico, Brazil, Bulgaria, Canada, and the United States. Begin by using the Global Census module available on the RACE project website. Go to http://www.understandingrace.org/lived/global_census.html.

Step 2: Go further by looking on the Web for census or statistical abstract population summary categories for countries, especially with different population characteristics than the United States, such as India, South Africa, Indonesia, Nigeria, Brazil, Bolivia, Cuba, Trinidad, and so on. Notice what categories are used and what social characteristics of people seem to be most important.

ADDITIONAL ACTIVITY IDEAS

Activity Idea 1: Fitting the World into the U.S. White–non-White Binary Model of Race

Participants take the "Who Is White?" quiz and explore other aspects of the module available on the RACE project website at http://www.understandingrace.org/lived/who_is/index.html.

Activity Idea 2: How Immigrants Experience the U.S. Racial System

Interview (individually or in a group) someone born outside the United States, preferably at least one person who does not easily fit traditional U.S. categories. Develop interview questions (alone, in groups, or as a class). Questions should explore the kind of social categories used in that person's home country as well as their experiences and reactions to the U.S. racial classifications. How do others see them, how do they see themselves, how do they respond to categories on official forms (school, census, birth certificates, and other documents that request ethnic-racial data)?

Activity Idea 3: How History and Local Circumstances Shape Racial Classification and Class Stratification

Use a more sustained research project as a way to understand how history and local circumstances shape systems of racial classification. Sample research topics include the following:

- European Plantation Slavery System and Regional Diversity in Latin America and the Caribbean. Participants (individually or in groups) study different countries. Use census data or other sources to identify racial and other relevant social categories. Compare plantation and nonplantation economies. Then look at diversity within plantation economies. Participants explore historical and other conditions with diversity.
- European Colonial Impact. Look at places where there was no slavery, like Kenya, India, Indonesia, and Nigeria. How have racial categories evolved there?

NOTES

1. For a recent review of such comparisons, see Gledhill & Wade, 2012. They also suggest adding a continental perspective, that is, exploring parallel ideas and processes in the Americas.
2. See Brazilian categories in the Global Census module at http://www.understandingrace.org/lived/global_census.html.

3. The Brazil example also suggests microcultural variations in racial classification. U.S. African Americans, or other ethnic groups, do not necessarily share the same system as European Americans. And there may be variability among EuroAmericans.

4. See http://www.census.gov/prod/cen2010/briefs/c2010br-11.pdf.

Chapter Nine

If Race Doesn't Exist, What Are We Seeing?

Sex, Mating, and Race

Part I focused on why scientists have rejected the notion that race is "biologically real." But if that is the case, one might ask, why am I able to racially identify so many U.S. Americans? Recognizing that races are culturally constructed doesn't mean there are no observable physical differences between U.S. racial groups. There *is* a biological component to the cultural invention we call race. But cultural processes, not nature, are responsible for the continuing visibility and social significance of race in the United States.

CONCEPTUAL BACKGROUND

So where does biology fit into all of this? Human biological variation is a fact, and some of that diversity is visible. U.S. American racial groups share common ancestry, and common ancestry can produce common DNA markers as well as, occasionally, shared, visible features. So some of what we see, when we "see race," is the result of biology. However, physical markers of common ancestry can either be exploited or rendered meaningless. They can persist or disappear over time. In the United States, *cultural* processes— politically and economically motivated controls over mating, marriage, and kinship—are responsible for preserving biological markers of race. Culture shaped and continues to shape biology in order to maintain a racial hierarchy and race-based system of social stratification.

CULTURAL PROCESSES THAT AFFECT BIOLOGY

Part I described how microevolutionary forces operating thousands of years ago produced human biological variation. Some visible physical traits, such as skin color or body shape, reflect these past biological adaptations of human populations to different environmental conditions.

Major racial groups in the United States, historically, came from geographically widely separated and distinct places—West Africa, Northwestern Europe, and the North American continent. And skin color, as we now know, took different evolutionary paths in these regions (see chapter 3).

But it was cultural processes—first European colonization and then the African slave trade—that brought these populations together in North America. Skin color was available as a convenient *marker* of ancestral background, social group identity, and, eventually, racial status.

Subsequent immigrant populations (e.g., East Indians, Italians, Chinese, Jews) also possessed visible, equally superficial remnants of common geographic origins and ancestral past. Sometimes it was skin tone, but often it was facial features, such as eyes, nose shape, or hair. Markers, often with negative connotations, emerged in Anglo descriptions of these groups: the "shifty" eyes of Chinese, the "beaked" noses of Semites, the "greasy" hair of Mexicans, the "swarthy" faces of southern Italians, versus the blue-eyed blond "clean," "Nordic" look.

But there was a second and more significant cultural process responsible for the continuing visible biological component of U.S. race. That was the creation of legal and social barriers to mating and marriage between "Whites" and non-Whites, especially between Euro-Americans and African Americans.

Humans have remained one species, without subspecies, because of *gene flow*, that is, constant intermating between populations (chapter 3). Prehistoric humans didn't restrict their mates to local folks but ventured outside their own groups. Gene flow occurred through migration, temporary unions, and marriage exchanges between neighboring or even distant groups. In-group mating (*endogamy*) tends to preserve local population traits, while out-group mating (*exogamy*) tends to increase the diversity of the gene pool and the variability of subsequent generations. From an evolutionary perspective, finding mates outside of one's own population is a biological plus.

But human cultural processes are not simply driven by biology. Marriage, as opposed to mating, is an enormously complex cultural invention which can take many different forms. And one common feature is that it connects the families of the newlyweds. Another is that it controls the social status and identity of the offspring of women, it specifies to what family or social group ("caste" or "race") children will "belong." Marriage, traditionally then, is at least partially about social alliances and social descent.

Throughout most of human history, the social advantages of "marrying out" have arguably been at least equal to the biological ones. Marriage establishes and reinforces ties between groups, through "in-law" kinship relationships and, most important, through new descendants. It facilitates other exchanges, material, social, and political. It also helps reduce conflict between groups. "Marry out or die out," so the classic saying goes.

HOW CULTURES REGULATE MATING AND MARRIAGE

Romantic love notions aside, all cultures regulate marriage and mating to some extent. The parent-child incest taboo is universal, and restrictions on sibling sex and marriage are nearly universal. Beyond this, societies can either encourage or discourage mating and marriage outside one's own group.

In small-scale, nonstratified, egalitarian societies, people tend to marry outside their own circle. Children's marriages are arranged, sometimes at birth, by families, although young spouses may not live together and frequently do not have sexual relations until after they reach puberty. Marriage becomes a major vehicle for establishing and reinforcing social alliances, between kinship groups, villages, even regions.

Marriage also regulates the social group membership, social identity, and social status of children born to women. Family and kinship relationships are the core of most human societies and include many relatives beyond the U.S. *nuclear family* (mother-father-offspring). Children are essential for the continuation of this extended family, the lineage, and the social group.

Children, in human cultures, do not necessarily *belong* to their birth mothers, in a social or legal sense, even though it is rather clear, biologically speaking, whose body produced the child. The husband of the woman and his family may claim the child, arguing he has contributed the "seed" or sperm, or paid the *bride-wealth* (gifts to the bride's family at marriage). Alternatively, the child may "belong" to the mother's family or descent line, because of common ancestry with the child (the mother is my daughter). This latter situation (called "matrilineal descent") is relatively infrequent. More often, the child belongs to the father's kin group (patrilineal descent). Sometimes, as in most U.S. families, children belong to both maternal and paternal sides. Regardless, the assignment of children's social status and family membership is a cultural process, following culturally established practices, with cultural consequences.[1] The European and U.S. concept of an "illegitimate" child reflects a distinction between biological parentage and social rights gained through socially "legitimate" relationships, that is, marriage.

Societies with arranged marriages are not necessarily restrictive when it comes to sex outside of marriage. In some small-scale societies, a girl waits until puberty to have sex with her husband—but may have sexual relations with other younger males. Or a young married woman may take a male lover, especially if her husband is much older and marries her primarily to give him additional offspring. Should she get pregnant by her lover, the child still "belongs" to her husband (and his family).

Individual desire, attraction, mating, and biological reproduction is, then, in most cultures, controlled by an array of institutions, social practices, and laws. Families, kinship groups, local communities, religion, and the legal system all work together to regulate social interaction, to ensure that mating and marriage and the production of offspring follow culturally prescribed and socially legitimate lines. From a societal perspective, the reproductive and social consequences are too great to leave to the whims of young people!

Control over sexuality and mating is particularly intense in stratified societies with significant social inequality. Upper-status groups tend to be most restrictive, since they have the most to lose, both economically (through inheritance) and in terms of status. Societal barriers are erected to prevent marriage between ranked social groups, whether between "castes," "classes," or other groups, like "commoners" and "royalty." For example, those British of "royal" birth are supposed to marry other royalty, ensuring that family wealth, titles, and other rights and privileges remain sole prerogatives of this elite strata. This is facilitated partially through creating social institutions restricted to high-status groups, whether social clubs, private educational institutions, or more informal social networks and activities.

Sexual segregation and the regulation of sexuality, especially of upper-status females, is one mechanism for reinforcing social stratification. Sexual segregation not only reduces opportunities for male-female sexual relations but for voluntary sexual relations between different social strata. Restrictions, especially on women of reproductive age, range from limiting movements outside the home, establishing all-female spaces (for worship, schools, travel), the use of body-hiding clothing in public, and, of course, arranged marriages. Family concerns for the "purity" of the upper-status family tree and lineage can lead to "chastity belts," virginity tests at marriage, or honor killings.

On the other hand, upper-status males have traditionally been able to coerce or in other ways gain access to lower-status females. The "right" of the male dominant landowner to have sexual relations with lower-status female serfs or peasants did not begin on 19th-century U.S. plantations. What occurred during slavery has been replicated throughout the world for thousands of years, whether in India, Latin America, or Europe. But the offspring of such matings normally did not share in the social status or acquire the social rights of their fathers. They were not, as noted above, the offspring of socially "legitimate" marriages.

In short, while intergroup mating may be biologically advantageous, adding to genetic variability, marrying within one's own high-status group helps preserve economic, political, and other social assets. For dominant status groups, then, restricting marriage is a way to maintain one's position from generation to generation and to reproduce the prevailing system of inequality.

Maintaining Racial Boundaries in the United States

> And for prevention of that abominable mixture and spurious issue which hereafter may increase . . . whatsoever English or other white man or woman being free shall intermarry with a negroe, mulatto, or Indian . . . shall . . . be banished and removed from this dominion forever. (The Laws of Virginia, April 1691)[2]

Within the United States, social control of sexuality, mating, and marriage have been crucial for maintaining a system of stratification based on race. Culture was used to shape biology in ways that served the cultural goals of high-status groups. Kinship definitions; *antimiscegenation laws* (for an example, see above quote); segregated schools, neighborhoods, churches, and recreational facilities; occupational discrimination; and distorted mass-media representations are all cultural processes for maintaining racial boundaries, preventing new hybrid races from emerging and old ones from disappearing, and keeping the stratified racial hierarchy fixed and permanent.

Cultural and legal barriers to interracial mating and marriage did not always exist in the United States. During the early colonial period, European–African and European–American Indian unions were common. Europeans and Africans lived and worked in the same households and were initially treated as similar, legally and socially.

Some historians put the number of biracial individuals in the colonies around the time of the American Revolution at between 60,000 and 120,000 (Cruz & Berson, 2001). The famous "Pocahontas exception," the marriage of Pocahontas and John Rolfe in 1614 in Jamestown, was apparently not a complete anomaly. Consistent with English kinship traditions, the children of Pocahontas belonged to their father—that is, they acquired the legal status and primary social group identity of their father, not their mother.

Other interracial marriages occurred. Patrick Henry once suggested using tax incentives and cash stipends to encourage intermarriage between Whites and Indians. The shortage of Anglo women and the importance of families, especially offspring, to Anglo farmers may have prompted his proposal.

With the emergence of race-based slavery and racial stratification, the legal system was employed to prevent interracial mating, marriage, and the growth of a racially ambiguous and, therefore, problematic population. The U.S. racial system and racial worldview required a set of visible markers of racial identity. During slavery, there were pragmatic considerations. Multiracial slaves could more easily escape and melt into the White or Indian population.

Multiracial individuals also challenged the ideology of racial science, with its notion of discrete, distinct, and ranked subspecies. They were constant, visible manifestations of the "continuous distribution" of human traits and lack of clear boundaries between groups (see chapter 1). Multiracial offspring also challenged the racial "purity" argument that race mixing would produce inferior "mongrels." Most important, interracial mating and multiracial offspring threatened a system of social, economic, and legal discrimination based on visible markers. What if these markers disappeared? How could dominant groups identify subordinate racial groups? The failure to control interracial mating and the gradual expansion of an interracial population could, within a few generations, destroy visible racial divisions, leaving only a continuum. "Nature" had to be controlled. Racial endogamy—intragroup mating and marriage—especially among Whites, was essential to preserving racial hierarchy.

Antimiscegenation Laws: Preserving the White Race

The word *miscegenation*, from Latin *miscere* "to mix"+ *genus* "kind" (Merriam-Webster, 2003), did not appear until the 1864 presidential campaign. It apparently was invented by Democrats to smear Lincoln by saying (falsely) that he advocated interracial sex and marriage. Yet state laws forbidding interracial marriage and sexual relations appeared in 17th-century colonial America. In 1691, Virginia passed antimiscegenation legislation and then added laws prohibiting ministers from marrying interracial couples. The fine was apparently 10,000 pounds of tobacco (Cruz & Berson, 2001, p. 2). These laws applied to all non-Whites (e.g., Native Americans), not just European and African Americans.

The most extreme sanctions were directed toward liaisons between Euro-American women and African American males. Initially the major concern was how to maintain the slave status of the offspring of women. Male slave owners, in their status as males and slave owners, engaged in sexual relationships, usually illicit and often forced, with African American women, generally bonded women. Under traditional British law, "legitimate" children acquired the family and legal status of their father. If this precedent were to be applied, children of Euro-American fathers and African American slave women would have been both "free" and White. But since these were not "legitimate" children, that is, the result of legally sanctioned marriages, this "problem" could be circumvented.

Legislatures adopted the principle of "*partus sequitur ventrem*—the child inherits the condition of the mother" (Stampp, 1961, p. 193). This was advantageous for the dominant male planter class. Children born of slave women were slaves and, conveniently, legally considered the property of their mother's owner. Slave women's offspring, then, increased the slave population of the slave owner.[3]

Once the principle that children inherit the status of their mother was established, it made European female–African male sexual relationships particularly problematic. Because virtually all European women were "free," their children would also be free. Should she have a child with an African slave, that child would be free, providing an avenue out of slavery for the offspring of slaves. Such children would also expand the free African American population, threatening the race-based system of social stratification. If the father was already biracial, the children might easily pass for White, destabilizing the boundaries between Whiteness and Blackness on which race-based stratification depended.

Despite sanctions, some Euro-American women apparently had relationships with African American men (see Moran, 2001). Social and legal weapons were used against these women. They were stereotyped as depraved, lustful, prostitutes, and outcasts, especially if they were poor. In 1691 Virginia required that any White woman who gave birth to a mulatto child must pay a fine or face indentured servitude for five years for herself and thirty years for her child. In Maryland, a White woman who married a Black slave had to serve her husband's owner for the remainder of her married life (Cruz & Berson, 2001, p. 2). Some planter-class women apparently had relationships with slave men, but their elite status partially shielded them from public criticism.

The spread of antimiscegenation and related laws ensured that interracial relationships would not be legally sanctioned and offspring would be denied rights of "legitimate" children. In 1715 and 1717, Maryland's legislature made cohabitation between a person of African descent and a "White" person illegal. By the time of the American Civil War, at least five states had enacted antimiscegenation laws (Cruz & Berson, 2001).

Interracial mating (with multiracial offspring) continued, initiated primarily by slave owners. The "mulatto" slave population increased by 67 percent between 1850 and 1860; the African American slave population by only 20 percent (Cruz & Berson, 2001). Stampp reports that according to the census of 1860, more than one-half million (about 12 percent) of the "colored" people in the slave states were "mulattoes." But he considers this an underestimate because census takers classified people by appearance, and many people with Black ancestors looked White.

The end of slavery disrupted more than the plantation system. It threatened the system of racial stratification and race-based structural subordination. White identity was no longer linked to one's free status. The color line, to be maintained, required more rigid social separation of European and

African Americans, enforced through increasingly harsh laws and other, less formal methods of coercion.

Alabama's antimiscegenation laws were designed to achieve that end. Originally instituted in the early 1800s, the laws prohibited weddings between members of different races and punished transgressions with $1,000 fines, an exorbitant amount of money at that time. Interracial sex was not prohibited, perhaps because it would have impacted the sexual activities of elite Euro-American men! But if an African American man, free or slave, raped or attempted to rape a Euro-American woman, he was legally subject to the death penalty. After the end of the Civil War, Alabama law was quickly revised to recriminalize miscegenation, but in a gender-neutral way. Similar laws appeared in other states. California outlawed interracial marriages between Whites and *any* non-White in 1905—and these laws persisted until 1948. Interracial marriages during this time frame, especially for Euro-Americans, were rare.

In the 1920s, at the height of racism and ethnocentrism, a new Virginia law, the Racial Integrity Act[4] (Goodman, Moses, & Jones, 2012, p. 453), prohibited "Whites" from marrying anyone with a single drop of African blood. Earlier laws had struggled with definitions of Whiteness and took into account proportions of African ancestry. But this new law excluded any person with any African "blood," regardless of how much or how far back in time.[5] By 1924, marriage between Whites and Blacks was illegal in thirty-eight states. This coincided with a series of strict anti-immigration laws, part of the attempt to preserve the dominance and purity of the Nordic race (see chapters 6 and 7).

As late as the 1950s, nearly half of all states had antimiscegenation laws. And the legislation had been extended beyond Whites and Blacks to include Mongolians, Malayans, Mulattoes, Native Americans, Mexicans, East Indians, and other non-Europeans who were deemed to be "not White."

The One-Drop Rule

Contradictions have always existed between elite Anglo rhetoric of preserving its "racial purity" and powerful Anglo male involvement in sexual relationships, often long-lived, with African American women. The case of Thomas Jefferson has received much attention, especially with new DNA testing (see chapter 4). But more recent 20th-century examples are easy to find. U.S. Senator Strom Thurmond (1902–2003), a staunch South Carolina segregationist who filibustered for over twenty-four hours to block the Civil Rights Act of 1957, had a child from an illicit (and probably coercive) relationship with a sixteen-year-old African American woman servant employed in his family's household.[6]

Such relationships, and more importantly, the children they produced, challenged the system of racial stratification. During the slave period, all children of slave women were legally slaves, so their proportion of African ancestry became irrelevant. Yet, according to historian Kenneth Stampp[7] and more recent scholarship, the legal basis for deciding an individual's *racial status* was never uniform across states.

The 1849 Virginia code states, "Every person who has one-fourth part or more of negro blood shall be deemed a mulatto, and the word 'negro' . . . shall be construed to mean mulatto as well as negro" (Stampp, 1961, p. 195). Other states specified different proportions, such as African ancestry to the third generation, or having one grandparent (*quadroon*) or one great-grand-parent (*octoroon*). In South Carolina, the Court of Appeals rejected the notion that all persons "of any mixture of negro blood" were legally Black. Instead it ruled that there must be a "visible mixture" and referred to the person's "reputation" among his neighbors for evidence on the visibility part (p. 195).

According to Stampp, in some states during slavery, anyone with African ancestors too remote to be classified as a mulatto was legally White, even though that person could still be held as a slave (1961, p. 196). There also was practical incentive to reject a **one-drop** approach especially for individuals who appeared to be White. If these persons blended into the White population, their small amount of African ancestry would have had little impact on the European population. But as part of the African slave population, they would have had a "whitening" effect.

Gradually, more states moved toward **hypodescent**, rules of ancestry where the child's racial status comes from the racially lower-status parent (see chapter 8.) What this essentially does is preserve the "purity," and the small size, of the upper-status group—since anyone with even a single drop of "inferior" blood is automatically excluded from the dominant racial or caste group. It acts as an additional barrier to interracial marriage by stigmatizing, inevitably, the children of such liaisons, regardless of the high status of the other parent. And it creates a cultural system that actually ignores biology, a rigid, bipolar, bounded racial system where one is either White or Black. There is no continuum. Biology is manipulated by culture to maintain a racial hierarchy–based system of inequality.

These culturally and socially created restrictions on mating and marriage over the past 300-plus years preserved, then, among North Americans of African and European ancestry, many of the most visible physical markers of their geographically diverse ancestral roots. However, recent DNA and other studies of Euro-American and African American U.S. populations (see part I) reinforce historical evidence that legal and social restrictions against interracial marriage did not totally prevent mating, both coercive and voluntary.

Overall estimates for the percentage of European ancestry in contemporary U.S. African American populations are around 20 to 25 percent, based on data from self-identified African Americans (cf. Jurmain et al., 2014, p. 97). Jackson and Borgelin (2010, p. 94) suggest the frequencies of European Y chromosomes are closer to 26.4 percent +/- 8.9 percent, in different geographical locations. But there is also variability in the U.S. populations sampled, from an atypical low of 4 percent among the relatively isolated Gullah of South Carolina, to 23 percent in New Orleans (Relethford, 2013, p. 361). Interestingly, at least one major study by Parra et al. (1998, 2001) found European ancestry generally higher in northern city populations, like Pittsburgh, Detroit, or New York than in southern cities like Charleston. On the other hand, as Relethford points out, these are only population *averages*, and individuals within each population can vary significantly. For Columbia, South Carolina, the average European ancestry found among African Americans was 18 percent; but individuals ranged from less than 10 percent to more than 50 percent (Relethford, 2013, p. 361)!

Not surprisingly, there are significant gender differences in the sources of European versus African ancestry in contemporary African American populations. European DNA is far more likely to come from paternal lineages; African from maternal lineages. This is consistent with other historical data indicating that interracial matings were most likely to occur between Euro-American males and African American females, especially in coercive plantation situations.

According to Jackson,

> The genetics of the African Diaspora show evidence of strong asymmetric, sex-biased genetic blending in the founding and ongoing history of the New World African population, with the African and Amerindian contribution being highest from maternal lineages (as measured by mitochondrial DNA) and the European contribution foremost from paternal lineages (estimated from Y chromosome haplogroups). This phenomenon has been observed in Brazil and in several other Latin American countries, suggesting that it might constitute a universal characteristic of both the Iberian and English (and probably French) colonizations of the Americas. (Jackson & Borgelin, 2010, p. 94).

Mating and Marriage Restrictions for Other Non-Whites

Attempts to "preserve the White race" through restrictions on mating and marriage affected other populations in the United States, especially immigrant populations. U.S. naturalization laws, as we saw earlier, allowed only White immigrants to become citizens. Non-White immigrant males could not bring spouses or sponsor female relatives, exacerbating an already skewed U.S. sex ratio.

Predictably, as in the slave states of the Southern United States, Anglo males used social and legal mechanisms to discourage Euro-American women from even considering non-Euro-American males as potential mates. Immigrant males were portrayed negatively, described as "sexually avaricious," and in other ways morally and intellectually unappealing. Many states extended antimiscegenation laws to Mexicans, then various Asian groups. For example, California in 1880 passed a law prohibiting the marriage of a White person to a "negro, mulatto, or Mongolian." By 1945, this was extended to "Malays."[8]

Barriers also were erected to prevent White women, citizens or not, from marrying non-Whites. Until 1931, a woman married to a non-White foreigner was automatically ineligible for citizenship, even if she was personally eligible (e.g., was White). Moreover, female Euro-American U.S. citizens who married racially barred "aliens" could be stripped of their citizenship (Haney-Lopez, 1996, p. 15; Koshy, 2005). Both laws reflect the intersection of gender and racial bias. Under traditional English and U.S. laws, married women's legal status was dependent on their husband's status, including his citizenship status. But these laws were also deliberate efforts to curb the growth of the non-White population through penalizing Euro-American women for marrying non-White foreigners.

These kinds of laws shaped the reproductive choices and histories of a large segment of the U.S. population. Ironically, the shortage of women of their own ethnic group prompted at least some male non-White immigrants to cross cultural and ethnic boundaries and pursue mates, and sometimes spouses, from other ethnic groups. Early California reports, for example, report competition for women among Anglos and Mexican Americans, Chinese, Filipinos, East Indians, and perhaps other ethnic groups.

One result was low birth rates among some immigrant populations, such as the Chinese. Entire age cohorts of Chinese males remained bachelors throughout their lives. Some had sexual encounters with prostitutes, Chinese and non-Chinese. And many offspring were multiracial.[9]

These restrictions produced some new and interesting alliances. Chapter 7 described the controversy over whether East Indians were White. Once the courts declared them Caucasian but not White, they were ineligible for naturalization. If they married Indian wives they could not bring them to the United States. And the Asiatic Barred Zone, created by Congress in 1917, applied to India. But as non-Whites, antimiscegenation laws in many states prevented them from marrying Euro-Americans.

South Asians who immigrated to the agricultural areas of the Central Valley of California and Arizona in the early 20th century ("the tide of turbans") often ended up marrying Mexican American women, mainly long-term inhabitants of the U.S. Southwest. Sometimes called "Mexican Hindus," even though most were of the Sikh religion, this long-standing community has developed a distinct cultural identity and place in California history (Bigler, 2003).

More recent research has identified at least three other groups of South Asian men, mainly Bengali Muslims, who came to the United States around the same time, often "under the radar" of U.S. immigration laws (Bald, 2013, p. 6). One group of silk peddlers, mentioned in chapter 7, started coming in the 1880s to sell their "exotic Oriental" goods at newly emerging tourist destinations in New Jersey, the South, and the Caribbean. Some eventually stayed, settling and marrying into a predominantly African American and "Creole of Color" neighborhood of New Orleans called Tremé. Around the time of World War I, another group, seamen working on British steamships, began jumping ship in New York. While most eventually returned to India, a small group remained, marrying women from African American, Puerto Rican, and other Caribbean communities in Harlem. Others traveled to the Midwest, pursuing employment opportunities in the newly emerging factories of Detroit and elsewhere, again integrating into local communities, often by marrying African American women.

U.S racial policies, while treating South Asians as somewhat different from African Americans, nevertheless placed them on the "non-White" side of the White–not-White divide. Race, class, and their small numbers prompted these South Asian male migrants to forge networks with African American and Caribbean local communities. Marriage was a crucial element, helping them adapt economically, socially, and emotionally, producing hybrid communities which are just now being discovered. Once established, these networks also provided assistance to other South Asians, including temporary sojourners who eventually returned to India.

THE BARRIERS ARE FALLING

World War II, the horrors of Nazism with its ideology of racial superiority, and the civil rights movement all accelerated the crossing of racial boundaries. Antimiscegenation laws were initially challenged in several states, and California declared such laws illegal in 1948. Other states followed suit, albeit slowly, and often against enormous resistance.

The Virginia antimiscegenation law was challenged in 1967 and initially upheld by the lower court. The Virginia judge, quoted below, explicitly articulated the long-standing theme of "preserving the White race" (see chapter 7) through controlling mating and marriage.

> Almighty God created the races, white, black, yellow, malay and red, and he placed them on separate continents. . . . The fact that he separated the races shows that he did not intend for the races to mix. —1967, statement of the

Virginia judge who upheld his state's anti-miscegenation law. (Cited in Cruz
& Berson, 2001, p. 4)

Eventually, the Supreme Court, in the now famous *Loving v. Virginia* case,
found all laws against interracial marriage unconstitutional. This ruling in-
validated the remaining state laws. At the time of the ruling, sixteen Southern
states had such laws. [10]

Simultaneously, other segregation laws were ruled unconstitutional. Beginning with *Brown v. Board of Education* (1954), racially segregated
schools were challenged. Many people today have no memory of a time
when African American children walked past closer White schools to attend
more distant Black schools. Without school segregation, many Southern
"neighborhood schools" would have been multiracial. But then . . . that was
at least partially the goal, to keep the races, especially young people, socially
separated.

Non-Southern states didn't need formal school segregation. They simply
used residential discrimination to accomplish the same ends, including inserting "restrictive covenants" into real estate contracts, which not only covered racial minorities but often Jews. It was not until 1963 that the Rumford
Fair Housing Bill outlawed housing discrimination in California.

Racial segregation in housing is a complex subject, as seen in the film
Race: The Power of an Illusion. But wealth accumulation in the United
States often occurs through home ownership. And access to quality housing
helps to ensure access to quality schools, libraries, recreational facilities, and
long-term property appreciation. Federal, state, and local government and
banks, by allowing, and sometimes actively promoting, racial discrimination
in access to residential housing and loans, especially in post–World War II
suburbs, not only reinforced but accelerated a race-based wealth gap that
continues today. [11]

Another rarely discussed but significant impact of residential segregation—or desegregation—is on interracial mating. Schools, especially in the
United States, as we well know, are a potent site of cross-gender interaction,
with a myriad of opportunities for racial (and other) boundary crossing (see
part III, especially chapter 13). And as children get older, dating and mating
across racial and ethnic boundaries become more likely and, to many families, at least in the past, more problematic.

As we've seen earlier, all human communities try to control gender and
sexual interaction. Virtually all major religious groups traditionally discou-
raged, and sometimes explicitly forbid, marriage with members of other
religions, whether of the same or different race. Even one Native American
group, the Cherokee, at one point opposed and eventually outlawed interracial marriage with African Americans, partially as part of a strategy to assim-

ilate into the dominant Euro-American U.S. society (Davidson et al., 2005, p. 342–3).[12]

This historical tendency toward marriage endogamy, especially in stratified, inegalitarian societies, continues today, to varying degrees. Many racial, ethnic, and religious groups tend to have strong preferences (and prohibitions) when it comes to marriage, sometimes as part of a strategy for preserving their own culture or religion, especially if they are small in size; sometimes to maintain their social and economic status.

Pressure against racial intermarriage has probably been most intense among Euro-Americans, at least by older family members. This is consistent with the traditional behavior of high-status groups. Even self-identified progressive Euro-American families have often balked at free mate choice when it comes to race. But other groups, such as African Americans, Filipino Americans, Vietnamese Americans, South Asian Americans, and Mexican Americans, are also traditionally race and ethnic (and religion) conscious when it comes to mating and marriage.[13]

Whether articulated or not, interracial mating and marriage continue to threaten racial boundaries and a system of stratification and group identity based in part on race. Perhaps it is not so surprising that, as recently as 2000, a Christian university in South Carolina had a ban on interracial dating, which it has since lifted (see chapter 13).

Interracial Marriage Trends

Although people still, by and large, tend to initiate and maintain relationships with people of similar characteristics (Lee & Bean, 2004), demographic studies point to an increasing trend toward interracial marriage as well as cohabitation. In fact, interracial cohabitation rates are higher than marriage rates (Ford, Sohn, & Lepkowski, 2003).

Current trends suggest that the old color barriers may be lessening and that sometime in the future, we could have a society in which race no longer matters in love and marriage. But statistics that lump everyone together should be interpreted with caution because they do not explain *why* these trends are occurring, nor do they specify variations within the general trend.

Discussions about interracial relationships tend to be framed as a matter of Black and White, ignoring other racialized groups such as Latino, Asian, and Native Americans. This may reflect the persistence of the historic racial binary as well as Black-White marriages historically being the most heavily sanctioned and stigmatized. Only since the 1970s and 1980s have other interracial relationships received scholarly attention (Moran, 2001; Koshy, 2005).

This more comprehensive research indicates that not all groups, at least at the macroracial group level, are crossing the "color line" with the same frequency. Lee and Bean report, in 2004, that European Americans and

African Americans are the most likely to marry within their racial group, with about 93 percent of marriages being endogamous. In contrast Asians and Latinos marry within their racial group about 70 percent of the time and American Indians do so only 33 percent of the time (Lee & Bean, 2004). Furthermore, when Asians and Latinos marry outside their group, they usually do so with Euro-Americans. Omi reports that more than one-quarter of all married Asians (27.2 percent) have a spouse of a different racial background and 87 percent of the non-Asian partners are Euro-American (Omi, 2012, p. 184).

More recent data suggest that intermarriage rates may be increasing among younger Asians and Latinos, especially with Euro-Americans. Racial boundaries, partially for historical reasons, seem less permeable among Blacks and Whites, at least in the 2000 census data, and in the analysis by Lee and Bean (Lee & Bean, 2004, Bean & Lee, 2009). The reasons have yet to be fully explored, such as the role of proximity (e.g., living in the same neighborhoods), socioeconomic class, racial prejudice. Ethnic pride, including among some African Americans, may also create internal community pressures to marry within one's own group (cf. Shankar, 2008; Twine, 1997). In some immigrant groups, like Indian Americans, parents and other family members may play significant, even central roles, in marriage decisions. Other communities, such as Latinos, may view intermarriage flexibly and fluidly, not having fully bought into the U.S. racial paradigm (Arriaza, 2004).

Lee and Bean (2004) offer two alternative interpretations of these trends. In the first scenario, they suggest that if Asians and Hispanics, traditionally racialized, ascribed status groups, are now crossing racial marriage boundaries, then eventually the historically stronger proscriptions against Black-White marriages will also disappear.

The alternative scenario is that Asian Americans and Hispanics are becoming less racialized, becoming incorporated, as did earlier "marginal" European American ethnic groups, into the "White" category. And this process is being reflected in increasing patterns of intermarriage, especially as these groups advance socially and economically. In contrast, this is not happening with African Americans. According to Lee and Bean, this could lead to a new color line. Instead of the old Black-White line (actually, the White–not-White line), we could end up with a Black–non-Black divide, which "would be a disastrous outcome for many African Americans" (Lee & Bean, 2004, p. 239).

One problem with these studies is that they utilize aggregate data on large macroracial categories, such as Asian, White, or Hispanic, that ignore the complexity and diverse histories of the component ethnic groups. Even among African Americans, more likely to share a common history, language, and religion, there are still significant differences, especially as the African and Caribbean immigrant populations expand. Differences in language, religion, national cultures, and histories, as well as current class status, are far greater in other macroracial groups, especially Asian Americans. And these kinds of differences have traditionally been major considerations in marriage choices. But the use of macroracial group data can also mask significant cultural boundary crossing that may be occurring *within* each of these categories, such as intermarriage between Chinese and Japanese Americans, Cuban and Mexican Americans, Indian Hindus and Muslims, or African Americans and Puerto Rican or Jamaican Americans. And the children of these marriages may not be included in the "multiracial" statistics normally cited.

THE END OF RACE-BASED IMMIGRATION
AND NATURALIZATION POLICIES

As the U.S. becomes a postcolonial global village, long-standing racial barriers are dissolving. By 2002, immigrants and their children constituted about 23 percent of the U.S. population, nearly sixty-six million people (Lee & Bean, 2004, p. 221). The 2010 Census included fourteen different races (besides "other") and divided the "White" race into two "ethnicities," non-Hispanic and Hispanic Whites. The current three Hispanic subgroups will likely expand in the future to reflect growing diversity within this category. According to the 2010 census, the Hispanic population increased by 33 percent between 2000 and 2008, from 35.3 to 46.9 million (Kottak & Kozaitis, 2012, p. 70). And there will have to be recognition of other Latinos, such as Portuguese-speaking U.S. Americans from Brazil, Portugal, or Cape Verde Islands.

Relatively recent immigrants, like Tongans, Hmong, and Sri Lankans, also want their distinct identities publicly acknowledged. But so do Hawaiians, Filipinos, Puerto Ricans, and other long-marginalized members of the U.S. American "family" who wish to reclaim their heritage and ancestry.

The 2000 U.S. Census, for the first time, formally acknowledged multiple racial backgrounds and identities. Earlier "mixed" options, like "mulatto" (e.g., 1890) were never intended to legitimize the idea of interracial mating or of multiple, distinct, and equally valued racial identities. And even this "mongrel" category disappeared by 1930. In contrast, the 2000 (and 2010) census allowed individuals to have more than one racial designation, to recognize all their ancestral strains, to have multiple identities, to embrace their multiracialism in contrast to the connotation of the term *mixed*, which originally contrasted with "pure" and undiluted.

Perhaps most crucial of all, the census, beginning in 1970, uses self-identification, rather than the estimate of the census enumerator, as the basis for racial classification. This represents a significant shift away from the concept of race as a fixed, objective, and externally imposed, ascribed, naturalistic category. Instead, race is now recognized as more of a social identity, something one can choose, alter, use strategically, and that can change over time and place. And one can have multiple racial identities, along with a myriad of other identities and community "belongings" (e.g., gender, age, nationality, etc.).

The 2000 and 2010 censuses, with their multitude of racial categories and multiple racial identities, also reflect the end of former racially discriminatory immigration and naturalization laws. In 1952, the McCarran-Walter Immigration and Nationality Act stated that a person's right to become a naturalized citizen could not be "denied or abridged because of race." This allowed many longtime residents to become citizens; once naturalized, they could now sponsor other family members.

Civil rights–era legislation fully dismantled the old immigration system designed to preserve a White Nordic (Christian) nation. By abolishing the old national quotas system, based on the racial and ethnic balance of the United States at the time of the 1890 census, immigration from non-European regions dramatically increased.

The new legislation also removed prior immigration barriers on non-White spouses married to U.S. American citizens, even if their spouses were White. This affected U.S. servicemen who had married women in Japan, Korea, the Philippines, and other places with large U.S. bases during World War II and the Korean War. By the time the Vietnam War ended, these laws had been dismantled.

As culturally erected barriers to interracial social interaction fall and new and more diverse populations enter the U.S. population "mix," these groups challenge simple White–non-White dichotomies, the fixity and ascribed nature of racial and ethnic identities. They also challenge narrow national identities, as more and more U.S. Americans participate in a global culture that crosses national boundaries.

According to the 2009 census data, 12.5 percent of U.S. Americans are foreign born, with the numbers much higher in states like California (24.9 percent), New York (21.4 percent), and New Jersey (20.2 percent). In the largest cities, the percentage foreign born reaches nearly 40 in Los Angeles, 38 in San José, 35.6 in New York City, 34.1 in San Francisco, and at least 25 in a number of other cities, like Houston, Dallas, Boston, and San Diego (U.S. Census Bureau, Statistical Abstract of the United States, 2012, table 38–39). Over sixty-seven million Americans (4.2 percent) speak a language other than English at home (ibid., table 53)[14] ; a much larger percentage of Americans speak both English and another non-English language. Again, these figures vary dramatically across the United States and even within states like California or New York.

Millions of U.S. Americans have relatives in other countries, with whom they are in regular contact, through phones, e-mail, Twitter, Skype, as well as ordinary travel.[15] More and more people have friends (or in-laws) with these types of backgrounds and may travel abroad not simply as tourists, but to participate in social events, like weddings. In short, a growing number of U.S. Americans have, and embrace, multiple, cross-national, cross-ethnic, cross-"racial," cross-national, global identities.

THE URGE TO MERGE

We have seen earlier that human nature, the urge to merge, is again taking its course. If current U.S. racial and ethnic intermarriage rates continue, "multi-racial" or at least "multiethnic" may soon become the largest U.S. racial group. The number of people who listed two or more races on the 2010 census increased to 2.9 percent of the total population from 2.4 percent in 2000.[16] This represents an increase from 6.8 million to 9 million people (U.S. Census Bureau, 2012). Four multiple-race groups exceeded more than one million people in 2010. People who reported both White and Black number 1.8 million; White and some other race, 1.7 million; White and Asian, 1.6 million; and White and American Indian and Alaska Native, 1.4 million (U.S. Census Bureau, 2012, p. 5).[17] One in seven new marriages in 2008 was between spouses of different races or ethnicities. By the year 2050, given these trends, as many as 20 percent (or one of every five) U.S. Americans will have a multiracial background (Lee & Bean, 2004, p. 222).

For the West Coast, and perhaps all major urban centers, the figures are much higher. Hawaii has, by far, the highest percentage of multiracials, 23.6 percent in the 2010 census. But California has the highest multiracial population, numerically, with over 1.6 million in 2000, increasing to over 1.8 million in 2010 (U.S. Census Bureau, 2012, p. 11). In the 2000 census, 4.7 percent identified as multiracial; in 2010, it had increased to 4.9 percent. But these figures ignore generational changes. In 2000, over 7.3 percent of Californians under the age of eighteen (one out of every fourteen) reported a multiracial identification. The numbers are surely higher in 2010 and are likely to increase in the future (Lee & Bean, 2004, p. 236; see also chapter 13).[18]

The trend towards "multis," boundary crossing, boundary merging, and multiple racial/ethnic identities continues on many levels in the United States. On college and university campuses there's an increase in the number of student clubs and organizations with a multiracial or multiethnic theme. These clubs and organizations provide an opportunity for people to claim and celebrate their multiple heritages. This was not the case fifteen years ago. For example, in 1998 when one of the author's daughters, of African American and Euro-American ancestry, attended a meeting of the Black Students Union at Tufts University, she was asked why she was there, as she was not really Black. She ended up creating an ad hoc network of students who felt, like her, that there was no place for them on campus.

However, things have changed. In 2002, the Multiracial and Biracial Association was founded at the University of Maryland, College Park. Since then the organization's activities have included sponsoring an annual week-long program to raise awareness of multiracial identities, proposing new classes and hosting movie nights, dinners, parties, and social media broadcasts. The group also sees their mission as helping educate students about what it means to have all facets of your identity accepted. One member described their experience as "finding a group of people who can accept you for who you are and being able to accept yourself, to just be able to look in the mirror and say 'I am o.k. just the way I am!—honestly, I feel that's a blessing" (Saulny, 2011).

The current group of students going through U.S. high schools and colleges is the largest group of multiracial students in the history of the country. With increasing numbers of interracial and interethnic marriages, they represent the wave of the future. And they are asserting their multiple identities in creative ways.

An example is "the original Seoul brother," a self-description of a young man born in South Korea, of a Korean mother and an African American father, who has lived in the United States since he was six years old. A U.S. American citizen, he embraces his multiple ancestries, noting, "Everyone sees me as black. But I'm more than that; my nature is mixed, and my culture is rich" (Kottak & Kozaitkis, 2012, p. 127). His self-description expresses pride in his Korean ancestry, by referring to Seoul, and his identification with African Americans, by his reference to "brother." His body language, gestures, facial expressions, and speech patterns convey both the complexity of and his comfort with multiple identities. Indeed, he has traveled to India, contemplates settling in Brazil, and considers himself to have a cosmopolitan orientation (ibid.).

If California leads the nation on interracial marriage and cultural boundary crossing, as it has on many other trends, race-based stratification may become a remnant of the past. Of course, as we have pointed out in chapter 7, this will not mean the end of class-based stratification, of economic and political inequality. But our culture will have to abandon race as a basis for legitimizing, rationalizing, and masking a system of privilege and inequality.

KEY CONCEPTUAL POINTS

- Race is culturally invented, but there are superficial, visible, biological markers of U.S. racial groups. This is the biological component of race.

- Biological markers reflect diverse geographic origins and historical and cultural processes (slavery, colonialism, antimiscegenation laws, and other institutional practices created to prevent race "mixing" and to preserve the markers of racial hierarchy and racial privilege).
- All cultures regulate marriage and mating and can use marriage to either extend the group's alliances (marrying out) or to restrict access by marrying within (endogamy).
- Endogamy is a common way upper-status social groups (including racial elites) preserve their wealth, status, and other privileges.
- The U.S. system of racial stratification developed cultural and legal mechanisms to prevent interracial dating, mating, and marriage and preserve the visual markers of race.
- The civil rights era dismantled much of this, including antimiscegenation laws, school segregation laws, and racially discriminatory immigration and naturalization laws.
- More U.S. Americans are crossing racial barriers and challenging old racial categories as reflected in the 2000 and 2010 U.S. Census and in the growing population of multiracials and "others."

KEY TERMS (ITALICIZED AND BOLDED IN TEXT)

markers
antimiscegenation laws
hypodescent
endogamy
miscegenation
exogamy
one-drop rule
gene flow

ACTIVITIES (ALSO APPROPRIATE FOR CHAPTER 13)

Activity Plan 1: Mating Activity

Objectives:

- Understand the role social factors (vs. individual desires) play in mate choices, especially in family preferences, cultural norms, and societal laws.
- Be able to provide examples of social criteria (group traits) versus individual criteria (attributes of the person).
- Understand the continuing role of racial endogamy in mate/date choice.

Time: Thirty to sixty minutes, depending on how much time is spent analyzing participant responses.

Materials Needed: Sheets of paper for participants to write individual responses and to summarize group responses.

Procedures:

Step 1. My Ideal Mate. Participants list characteristics of their "ideal mate" on a piece of paper. Tell them to imagine writing an ad for a long-term mate. What characteristics or attributes would they be looking for? Give them five to ten minutes. They should do this individually.

Step 2. My Parent's Ideal Mate for Me. OR My Ideal Mate for My Children. Participants make a separate list of the kind of characteristics or traits parents or other adult family members would look for if they were choosing a long-term mate for their offspring. Again, have them do this individually.

Step 3. Participants analyze results (in small groups or the class as a whole), beginning with their ideal mate. Ask participants to look for patterns in the type of traits they listed. Do some types appear more often than others? See what participants come up with. Then analyze their lists using the following framework. Usually, participant trait lists can be classified into three main categories—physical traits, personality or character traits, and common activities-interests-goals. For example, ask how many participants listed physical features and if so, what kinds? You could make a list on the board, under Physical Traits. You might discuss if some physical features have cultural elements (e.g., does the concept of "physically fit" have a cultural dimension? Is "a nice smile" really an indicator of culturally valued personality traits?). Or try to get them to be specific about what traits make someone "attractive" or what is meant by "good features" and whether these are culturally shaped notions. Point out that many seemingly "physical traits," like "being fit" or having a "good body," have additional culturally shared meanings.

Ask what other types of traits besides physical traits are listed. Participant lists tend to emphasize personality or character traits. So you might create another list on the board, Personality/Character Traits, and have participants add items that fit. You may need a third list, Common Activities or Interests, for additional traits not covered by the first two categories.

Next, introduce the notion of individual traits versus social characteristics of persons (see chapter 7 for a discussion of *social status* and related terms). Point out that their ideal mate traits usually refer to the individual person, with respect to physical, personality, or interest considerations. Virtually all fall into a more comprehensive category called Individual Traits. Contrast this with the concept of Social Traits—that is, traits having to do with one's social status or group membership, whether achieved or ascribed (see chapter 7). These would include things like religion, race, ethnicity, gender, occupation, nationality, social class, sexual orientation, age, or family background. Ask for any ideal mate traits on their lists that would fall in this category (sexual orientation is often one, although unspoken; race or religion may be others).

Step 4. Participants compare their own list to the list their parents/family elders would create (in groups or as a class). Notice similarities and differences. This time, ask them to use the different categories (especially the notion of social vs. individual traits) when comparing lists. Generally, they will find that families are much more interested in social status characteristics than in individual traits, like looks or personality.

Step 5. Discuss the most common type of social status characteristics. Even in culturally diverse settings, we have found that race, ethnicity, gender, and religion are the most frequently mentioned. This provides an opportunity to discuss these "hot-button" issues (see also chapter 13). What is often less vocalized but also present are economic and social status considerations, such as money, job, educational level, family background, and family status.

Step 6. Link results to earlier chapters on class and racial stratification. If relevant, link to school hot-button issues, like conflict and mating/dating issues (see part III).

Follow-Up: To add a cross-cultural comparative aspect and to provoke discussion and reflection on U.S. culture, introduce participants to a culture with a different system of mating, marriage, and perhaps family arrangements. See modules on kinship, sex, and marriage in the Cultural Anthropology section of the Palomar College website, at http://anthro.palomar.edu/ tutorials/cultural.htm, or see films like *Maasaii Women, Dadi's Family,* or other films at Documentary Educational Resources. For arranged marriages, see popular films by Mira Nair or an accessible article by Serena Nanda on arranged marriages in India (2000).

ADDITIONAL ACTIVITY IDEAS

Activity Idea 1: Film and Discussion: *The Loving Story*

View and discuss *The Loving Story*, which describes the *Loving v. Virginia Supreme Court* case which declared laws against interracial marriage and mating as unconstitutional. See film with a downloadable teacher's guide at http://www.icarusfilms.com/new2012/ls.html.

Activity Idea 2: Comparison of Interracial and Same-Sex Marriage Laws

Review arguments in *Loving v. Virginia* and other cases on interracial marriage. Compare recent arguments made in the Supreme Court decisions on DOMA and on other same-sex marriage cases. Review arguments for and against California's Proposition 8, the ban on same-sex marriage.

Activity Idea 3: Race, Gender, and Class in Popular Culture

Explore some of the videos on popular culture and the images of gender and race they convey, at the Media Education Foundation. Explore such films as *Tough Guise*, *Hip-Hop Culture*, and *Dreamworlds III*. Discuss in what ways models of masculinity or femininity are racial, class-based, or ethnic-based. See http://www.mediaed.org/. This is particularly relevant to part III.

Activity Idea 4: *Guess Who's Coming to Dinner?*

Show film (entire or parts) as an entry into a frank discussion of parental/family concerns over who their children date/marry.

1. Separate family issues from participant concerns for discussion purposes.
2. Identify the range of factors such as cultural identity, racism/ethnocentrism, external pressure, other issues of cultural "endogamy," such as religion, social class, nationality, or language.
3. Discuss other pressures (other than individual preference) that affect participants' current dating and marriage decisions (see also chapter 13).

Activity Idea 5: The Ethnic Me (or Who *Did* My Ancestors Marry?)

This explores another facet of the "Exploring My Ancestry" project mentioned earlier in this book. Here, participants trace the ethnic and religious aspects of family marriage patterns, currently and in the past. This could include participants interviewing family members (one to three generations removed) about attitudes toward interracial, interethnic, and interreligious dating and marriage.

Activity Idea 6: Explore Antimiscegenation Laws

Explore, using Web sources, specific antimiscegenation laws, their wording, historical context, justification used, popular coverage, and challenges to the laws, if any, in court. Participants could compare the debates over these laws to those over gay marriage today. Materials to do this are available through several websites (see part IV). The Cruz and Berson article, cited earlier, includes excellent teaching ideas as well as other links.

Activity 7: Being "Multi"

Explore what it means to be multiethnic/multiracial in today's world. Draw on participants' own experiences, talk with other people, view the DVD on the Cafeteria Conversation in the RACE project. Discuss the multiple "identities" and "racial groups" one could have as a multi. Use President Barack Obama as an example of a multi, in multiple ways, who could identify with a myriad of communities, if he chose to and if it were simply his own choice. Explore the complexities.

NOTES

1. Kinship and marriage, cross-culturally, is a major research area within anthropology. See any standard cultural anthropology textbook for a glimpse into this fascinating, diverse realm. Or look at the online tutorials on kinship and family at the Palomar College website (see above).

2. From the RACE project timeline, *Inventing Whiteness, 1650–2000: A Time Line*. See part IV, RACE website links.

3. According to Stampp, "The offspring of a Negro slave father and a free white mother was free. The offspring of a free white father and a Negro, mulatto, quadroon, or octoroon slave mother was a slave" (1961, p. 194). Stampp notes that not all slaves were Black and not all slave owners were White.

4. For more information see Virginia's Racial Integrity Act of 1924 (http://www.understandingrace.org/history/gov/eastern_southern_immigration.html).

5. The law allowed "persons who have one-sixteenth or less of the blood of the American Indian and have no other non-caucasian blood" to be "deemed to be white persons."

6. For two somewhat different descriptions see http://www.washingtonpost.com/blogs/she-the-people/wp/2013/02/05/strom-thurmonds-black-daughter-a-flesh-and-blood-symbol-of-americas-complicated-racial-history/, http://en.wikipedia.org/wiki/Essie_Mae_Washington-Williams.

7. The work of Kenneth Stampp, a prominent University of California, Berkeley, Civil War historian in the 1960s, remains significant even today.

8. A 1909 statute added persons of Japanese descent to the list of "undesirable" marriage partners of "White Californians." Pressure by the Japanese government, however, resulted in the Gentleman's Agreement of 1907, where the United States agreed to allow the entry of Japanese women married to Japanese men in the United States (in return for Japan stopping the emigration of Japanese laborers). As a result, Japanese Americans were one of the few Asian immigrant groups with a relatively balanced sex ratio (Koshy, 2005).

9. See also the website of the National Women's History Museum: http://www.nwhm.org/online-exhibits/chinese/15.html.

10. For an excellent documentary film about this case, see *The Loving Story*, with a downloadable teacher's guide (http://www.icarusfilms.com/new2012/ls.html).

11. See Wealth and Disparities segments in *RACE: The Power of an Illusion*. See part IV, "Websites," for links.

12. They and mulattoes were also excluded from voting or holding office (Davidson, et al., 2005).

13. Religion, gender orientation, socioeconomic class, and for many immigrants, language compatibility are often additional family criteria for their children's mates.

14. The most frequently spoken language, by far, is Spanish, followed by Chinese, Tagalog, French, Vietnamese, German, and Korean, all with over one million people citing this as a language spoken at home. At least thirty other languages were mentioned by at least 90,000 people, usually by several hundred thousand.

15. On recent trips to India, when arriving at the airport, the "foreigners" line (that is, the line for non-Indian citizens) is overwhelmingly people of Indian origins who are now settled abroad.

16. About 92 percent of people reporting multiple races reported exactly two races (U.S. Census Bureau, 2012, p. 4).

17. Interestingly, the largest numbers of multiracial individuals were "White-Black" combinations, 20.4 percent of all individuals reporting two or more races (U.S. Census Bureau, 2012, p. 7). White and Some Other Race was 19.3 percent and White and Asian was 18.0 percent. This seems inconsistent with the trends Lee and Bean report, at least for 2000 census data. Moreover, among the multiple-minority combinations, (i.e., no Whites), the largest growth was in Black and Asian multis, which grew by 74 percent from 2000 (p. 9).

18. For online access, go to http://www.census.gov/prod/cen2010/briefs/c2010br-13.pdf.

III

Race and Hot-Button Issues in Educational Settings

Rosemary Henze

How do the concepts presented in parts I and II play out in the real world of U.S. education? In part III, our aim is to connect these concepts with race-related hot-button issues that are part of the everyday experiences and realities of students, teachers, principals, parents, and other people involved with education—especially in K-12 schools, teacher education programs, and colleges. While we focus on the United States in this section, we make connections where relevant with cross-cultural studies.

In chapter 10, we consider the multiple definitions of the terms "racism" and "racist," as well as the relatively newer term "cultural racism." Why is it that we sometimes don't agree on what constitutes racism? Are these different definitions just a matter of semantics, or is there more to it? What is the relationship between our notions of race and our notions of culture? What causes some tensions to erupt into conflicts that are considered "racial"? How can educators challenge conventional notions of race and racism to help students understand the complex and underlying causes of racial/ethnic conflict? What can educators do to take a proactive rather than a reactive stance against racism?

In chapter 11 we address the highly charged issue of educational inequality known as the "achievement gap." Data from decades of study show that despite sixty-plus years since *Brown v. Board of Education*, the United States continues to show a persistent disparity in academic achievement in which Whites and Asians outperform Latinos and Blacks on standardized measures.

What explanations have been offered to explain the achievement gap? Is it really an achievement gap, or is it more of an opportunity gap? How is discipline meted out, and is this also unequal across racial groups? What efforts to reduce the achievement gap have been successful in various settings?

In chapter 12, we examine how schools and colleges, as microcultures, impose classification schemes on the diverse realities of student identities. For example, what role does race/ethnicity play in the organization of school assemblies and clubs? What racial identity labels come and go as students as well as adults grapple with an increasingly fluid and complex landscape of identities? What are we to make of the changing meanings of the "N-word" and other words that used to (almost) always be slurs? These contemporary issues provide readers with an anthropological view of school cultures as dynamic and changing systems, both reinforcing and challenging existing categories, and sometimes offering potential for change.

In the final chapter of this section, we look at cross-group dating in schools, which some refer to as "interracial" dating. We examine the pressures on young people to date only within their own ethnicity or "race," even as these boundaries are said to be rapidly falling away. What roles do educational institutions, parents, and peers play in maintaining or dissolving ingroup dating patterns? Does the ubiquitous use of social networking sites among students change these patterns? Do those seeking same-sex relationships experience the same pressures to stay with their own "race" as those identifying as straight?

Each chapter in part III includes reflective questions intended to stimulate discussions in classes or workshops. In addition, each chapter includes at least one teaching activity that challenges taken-for-granted categories and ideas about race in schools or colleges, and helps students and teachers "see" how our racialized system has been constructed to maintain certain classification systems. These chapters also encourage readers to engage in a cycle of inquiry and reflection; many activities ask readers to do inquiry-based projects in which they explore their own questions and gather data to answer those questions. Then, given the results, we ask them to consider how they would change their own behavior as well as structures or procedures in their schools or colleges.

Chapter Ten

When Is It Racism? Who Is a Racist?

In this chapter, we begin by addressing the often contentious issue of how the very words that are used to point out mistreatment on the basis of race (e.g., calling someone a racist, accusing someone of racism, or pointing out that a particular activity or institutional practice is racist) can in themselves become trouble spots in our efforts to communicate about race. Where one person might point to an incident and call it "racism," another might resolutely claim it has nothing to with race. What happens then? Is one person right and the other wrong? Do they actually see the incident differently, or do they just have different understandings of racism that they are applying to the same situation? Our aim in this chapter is to provide educators and their students with tools to develop working understandings of these concepts and their inherent complexity, to understand why others might see things differently, and to analyze the genesis of tensions that have a racial component to them. Life in schools, colleges, teacher preparation programs, and organizations provides ample opportunities to use real incidents, questions, and issues as "teachable moments." While it is useful to have time in the planned curriculum devoted to the study of race, educators can also increase learning by using participants' interest and questions to create more student-centered, inquiry-based lessons.

CONCEPTUAL BACKGROUND

We have seen in parts I and II that the "race" concept is very complex because it has had a biological meaning that is refuted by current anthropologists and most other scholars, and it simultaneously has a cultural meaning which is very much alive and operational. Part of that meaning, as we have explained in part II, is that race is a way of socially dividing up humans into a stratified system. For the purposes of this chapter, we focus on the cultural meanings—that is, the way in which race has been constructed and used to socially rank humans for the purpose of maintaining power.

The words derived from "race"—racism, racist, and *racialization*—are equally complex because the concept of "race" is socially constructed and constantly shifting, and therefore, its derivative words are also fluid and complex in their meanings and associations to differently positioned people. However, we believe it is important to delve into their use here because they are so often at the heart of debates and tensions in education.

WHEN IS IT RACISM?

Many people have been taught that racism is a belief or attitude or discriminatory behavior on the basis of visible racial features, often encapsulated and included in the term "skin color." It is often pointed out that racism can reside in individuals or in groups of people. These defining characteristics might be called the *simple racism view*. They only focus on skin color or obvious physical features, and they do not include any mention of power dynamics, nor of institutional racism. In the simple view of racism, anyone can perpetrate racism regardless of his or her position in society.

The more *complex view of racism* adds further elements that help to clarify how racism operates in society in often invisible ways. These additional elements include the idea that racism occurs not only in individuals and groups but also in institutions. Thus, an entire institution can operate in ways that result in racially discriminatory outcomes, as we have seen in cases where an entire police department is found to regularly and systematically use racial profiling. Furthermore, in the more complex view, racism is constituted by the power to oppress or subjugate others, often in invisible ways (Della-Dora, 1972; Lee, 1998; Harrison, 2012).

More complex views often distinguish racism from individual prejudice and discrimination, noting that people may be prejudiced or act in discriminatory ways against those of another group, but if the perpetrators have no power to keep that other group down, then their individual beliefs are racially prejudiced but not powerful enough to be considered racism (Harrison, 2012). Della-Dora (1972) is credited with developing a short formula for racism: racism = racial prejudice + power. This formula is used in many diversity training and antiracism seminars and workshops.

In addition to the power to oppress other people, racism, according to the more complex views, includes a system of advantages for those in power. This system of racialized advantages is often invisible to those who benefit from it (i.e., Euro-Americans in general, and particularly Euro-American males from middle- and upper-class backgrounds). This system of advantages has been called ***white privilege***—"A consequence of racism in the United States that has systematically, persistently, and extensively given advantages to so-called white populations, principally of European origin, at the expense of other populations" (http://understandingrace.org/resources/glossary.html).

Lastly, more complex views consider racism to be ***systematic*** (meaning that it occurs across institutions such as employment, legal system, health care, and education) and ***intersectional*** (meaning that it is connected with other forms of oppression such as sexism, classism, and religious intolerance). Taking these complexities into account, the AAA *Race: Are We So Different?* project defines ***racism*** as follows: "The use of race to establish and justify a social hierarchy and system of power that privileges, preferences or advances certain individuals or groups of people usually at the expense of others. Racism is perpetuated through both interpersonal and institutional practices" (http://understandingrace.org/resources/glossary.html).

Ordinarily, such differentiations of meaning wouldn't be a big deal. But because race and racism are so profoundly inscribed in U.S. culture, our differing views of what these concepts mean can have serious consequences. We will explain further. But first, we take a look at the similarly complex views of the concept "racist."

WHO IS A RACIST? WHAT IS A RACIST INSTITUTION?

Given the many views of what constitutes racism, it stands to reason that there are also differing views of who—or what—is racist. Note that this word can be both a noun denoting an individual and an adjective describing an individual, a behavior, an institution, or a pattern of institutional outcomes. ***Simple views of "racist"*** follow closely with the simple view of racism. That is, a racist is any person or a group, regardless of their positioning in society, who is prejudiced against or discriminates against others on the basis of skin color or other visible physical features associated with "race."

The more ***complex views of "racist,"*** like the more complex views of racism, include specific attention to power and who holds the ultimate power in a place like the United States. One popular definition in 1973 stated that in the United States asserts only whites can be considered racists because they control the powerful institutions in the United States. Those without such power cannot be considered racists, although they certainly have prejudices against other groups (National Education Association, 1973). While this definition ignores, at minimum, intersecting identities and positionalities of gender, class, religion, and sexual preference, it does call attention to the importance of power. A racist institution or person reinforces an oppressive structure of uneven power relations that is oppressive (Harrison, 2012). Such reinforcement may be racist even when there is no intention to cause harm. In fact, well-intended, antiracist interventions in education can sometimes have racist consequences, as for example when a school principal reorganized a middle school into four communities based on "learning styles," with the hope that this would engage students and teachers by using their preferred learning and teaching styles. Unfortunately, this led ultimately to a racialized system in which the four learning communities were to a large degree segregated by race/ethnicity (Henze, 2008).

It is almost a truism in anthropology and linguistics to say that meanings are not fixed and immutable, but rather take on different shades and connotations depending on the perspective of speakers and the context. This is certainly true for the concepts of racism and racist. And herein lies the potential for conflict: Multiple meanings coexist and sometimes compete. We are interested in probing questions such as when does a comment become racist, in a subtle way; and what are the subtle processes through which comments and events become viewed through a racial lens; and should the same standards be applied toward all racial, ethnic, and religious and gendered groups? Is it racist (and sexist) for a student to call another student or teacher a "white bitch"?

The advantage of the more complex concepts is that they provide a clear framework for dismantling the institutionalized practices that have for centuries led to racist outcomes favoring Euro-American (preferably Christian) men. The problem we see in the simple racism definitions is that they focus only on color and only on individual or group attitudes and beliefs. This then leads to the conclusion that if our laws and educational practices only remove the reference to color or physical features, then they are no longer involved with the practice of racism.

As Lopez (2012) points out, this assumption underlies the *"color-blind" rhetoric* that has guided many recent court decisions that abolish any kind of affirmative action. The simple views of racism, like the argument that our laws and institutional practices must be "color-blind," ignore the depth of history. "Under this vision, racial groups exist only as individuals irrationally lumped together on the basis of arbitrary differences in physical appearance" (p. 85). Rather, Lopez argues, non–European American groups are "constructed through a history of subordination and exploitation," and as a result they are situated differently than European Americans today (p. 85).

Let's say we were to remove all racial descriptors from our laws and institutionalized practices in an effort to be "color-blind." Let's say that in schools, we abolished the laws that currently require educators to monitor and assess student outcomes by race, gender, class, and so on. This does nothing to address the fact that the playing field today remains far from level due to that history. In fact, such "color-blind" laws and policies actually allow the more hidden forms of racism to continue unabated and unchecked.

Similarly, some would argue that the election in 2008 and reelection in 2012 of the United States' first Black president, Barack Obama, signifies that we live in a postracial society where racism no longer exists. While it is certainly an important achievement that a man who identifies, at least partially, as African American, can now be president of the United States, it would be naïve to think that with this election, racism in the United States or any other country would be wiped away. The achievement of one individual does not mean that the multiple and systematic barriers facing African Americans and other minorities in this country have suddenly disappeared (Donner & Dixson, 2013).

Earlier, in part II, we noted that some scholars identify a form of racism they call *cultural racism*. This notion pertains to yet another way in which the concept of racism is shifting in its usage, especially in the wake of restrictive immigration policies and the Al Qaeda attack on the United States on September 11, 2001.

> Cultural racism is a form of racism that does not even mention the word "race." It is focused on the cultural inferiority of a group of people. Usually it is framed in terms of the inferior habits, beliefs, behaviors, or values of a group of people. It is close to biological racism in the sense that cultural racism naturalizes/essentializes the culture of the racialized/inferiorized people. The latter are often represented as fixed in a timeless space. (Grosfoguel & Mielants, 2006, p. 4)

The authors go on to explain how in the late 15th century, "people with the wrong god" in the Christian imaginary were mapped onto the emerging racial worldview in which humans were placed in a hierarchy from savages to civilized. Rather than only casting non-Christian religions (primarily Islam and Judaism were known in Europe) as inferior, European clerics made a "crucial transformation" to inferiorizing the non-European people who practiced the "other" religions. In this process, "the distinction between practicing a non-Christian religion and being racialized as an inferior human became increasingly erased" (p. 4).

This means that cultural traits that are not "racial"—in other words, not visible physical characteristics—can become racialized. "Racialization is a process through which individuals and groups of people are viewed through a racial lens, through a culturally invented racial framework" (http://understandingrace.org/resources/glossary.html). Cultural habits, beliefs, behaviors, or values, including religion, may be placed into a hierarchy which closely maps onto the earlier physical hierarchy based on skin color and facial features.

For example, the categories Irish, Jewish, and Italian were at one time racialized in the United States (in other words, they were used to rank people in a falsely biological hierarchy of inferiority to Anglo Saxon Protestants). Now, however, they have been assimilated into "whiteness" (Urcioli, 2012, p. 151) to the point where many European American students whose ancestors immigrated three or more generations ago cannot identify what part(s) of Europe their family came from. In fact, many European American high school and college students, when asked about their culture, say they don't have any culture; rather, they say they are "simply white" (Henze et al., 2002).

Muslims, on the other hand, despite the fact that they have ancestries that literally span the globe (including Europe) are now, especially since September 11, 2001, racialized and essentialized in the mainstream media as inferior human beings, terrorists, Arabs, and dark skinned. According to a report by the Commission on British Muslims and Islamophobia, public organizations that seek to address racism should "actively encourage all public bodies to incorporate a commitment to avoiding religious discrimination in their race equality schemes and policies" (Muir et al., 2004, p. 80). The video *Just a Piece of Cloth* (2013), in which four San Francisco Bay Area Muslim women of diverse backgrounds share their stories about wearing (and not wearing) *hijab* (the Muslim headscarf), provides a counterpoint to mainstream media portrayals of Muslim women as submissive, oppressed, and uneducated.

EDUCATIONAL APPLICATIONS

For educators, it is important first of all to understand that all of these words (race, racism, racist) can and will have different meanings depending on whether the people using these terms are relying on a simple view of racism or a more complex one. When educators are committed to countering and ending racism, our commitment entails that we must step into this arena and provide guidance. We need to be able to guide students toward an analysis of situations that have been labeled as "racially charged," as well as situations where race may be a hidden or underlying factor.

Let's take for example a situation in which someone uses a racial slur by talking about "those beaners"[1] in a hostile way, or a young man refuses to date a young woman because he says he doesn't like Asians. In these cases, it may seem pretty obvious that racial or ethnic prejudice is involved. But are these all examples of racism? The more complex views of racism lead us to find out more. Who are the perpetrators, and do they have the power to systematically keep the victims in an inferior position? What if the man who refuses to date Asian women is European American? What if he is Filipino? Does it make a difference? If the person making slurs about "those beaners" is a European American male and the principal of the school, then clearly this person has the power to inflict harm on the Latino students and it can legitimately be argued that this is a case of racism. If on the other hand the person using this slur is a Filipino student, the complex view of racism would tell us that he exhibits racial prejudice. He may be individually prejudiced against Latinos, but he and other Filipinos do not have the power in U.S. society to keep Latinos as a group in an inferior position. His racially prejudiced behavior lacks the broader implications of the principal, who is in a position of power.

Whether or not people invoke the term "racism" to define a particular situation, an educator who provides guidance in the above situations can ask questions in a way that clarifies and educates, rather than in a way that traps people into defensive, either/or positions (Chang & Conrad, 2008). Rather than immediately putting a student on the defensive by characterizing the "beaner" comment as racism, an educator can ask, "What would make you call X a beaner?" or "What does 'beaner' mean to you?" In the case of the boy who doesn't want to date "Asians" an educator might ask, "Is anyone pressuring you to date? What have you been told about who you should or should not date?" Chang and Conrad point out that adults in an educative role need to try to listen to children and young people's questions and comments about race, and then ask questions to try to understand and make visible the assumptions underlying these questions and comments. When working directly with young people, Blum (2008) suggests that the educator should encourage students to articulate precisely and deeply what is wrong with a particular scenario, rather than to seek a judgment that a person is or is not a racist. People in nondominant positions who make harmful, racially tinged comments, while they may not have institutional or societal power, do have agency. And it is this agency that we need to tap into as educators. How can change begin at the level of individuals and collections of individuals? And how can these individuals, both together and individually, become part of the larger effort to rid U.S. society of racism?

A European American high school principal of a large, ethnically diverse campus in the San Francisco Bay Area was asked what he does when a parent, for example, accuses him of racism. He replied that while he still feels a knee-jerk defensiveness when he hears such accusations, he has, through participation in several professional development sessions that focused on antiracism, learned to take a more inquiry-based stance. Rather than immediately trying to defend himself, he instead asks the other person, "Can you tell me what I did that made you think I was racist?" In this way, the focus shifts from "you are a racist"/"no I'm not"—a bind that is ultimately not helpful—to his specific behavior. It allows him to listen and try to understand the other person's perspective. In some cases, it leads to his being able to apologize for something that unintentionally gave the other person the impression that he is racist. In other cases, it allows him to explain himself and establish a deeper dialogue. He also said that he has learned to never assume he really knows what it feels like to be in the shoes of a person who has experienced a lifetime of racial discrimination and stereotypes. Instead of saying "I know how you feel" he now says, "I haven't experienced life in your shoes, but I'm willing to listen and learn so that I can understand better" (Henze et al., 2002).

Because race is still such a pervasive way through which many see the world in the United States, we often find that conflicts that had nothing to do with race originally quickly become racialized. For example, if two people get involved in an argument because one stepped on the backpack belonging to the other, the initial argument is not racial. Race becomes involved, however, when those two people (or onlookers) make it racial, calling attention to the fact that the two people are of different "races." The conflict then becomes not only about a person stepping on a backpack but also about the underlying tensions between their two "races."

Do ethnic or racial differences necessarily lead to conflict? Educators can ask students this question to open up a discussion. Anthropology's cross-cultural perspective is useful for exploring this question because it shows us clearly that in some cultures, physically different–looking people are not normally expected to have conflict with each other. For example, in Brazil until recently, race was considered relatively unimportant in whether people were successful. The more salient issue was class. Similarly, many Caribbean Island cultures such as Cuba and the Dominican Republic do not recognize racial or ethnic differences in the way U.S. Americans are conditioned to see race (see chapter 8). Despite diverse and often mixed ancestries (indigenous American, African, Asian, European), they tend to identify as Cubans or as Dominicans first, and not primarily as members of discrete racialized groups within their country. When people realize that ethnic and racial differences do not *have* to lead to conflict, that there is nothing inherent about ethnic or racialized differences that requires people to be in conflict, this frees them from feeling trapped in assumptions of inevitable, predestined conflict just because we are classified as "different."

What makes U.S. society more prone to ethnic and racialized conflict? As explained in chapter 8, first race has to become associated with stratification, which then leads to inequalities in resource distribution, economic or political competition, and prejudice or discrimination based on race. One way to create or maintain inequality is for governments to enact laws and policies that create or enforce segregation by race, such as Jim Crow laws, which made racial segregation legal in the United States. Also, when segregation of racial groups is the norm, people lack meaningful contact and knowledge of individuals of another race or ethnicity, and they tend to develop stereotypes about the other group. Stereotypes may also be used discursively to cast people as "other" and inferior from ourselves, to put distance between "us" and "them." Through the regular and systematic use of stereotypes and other-ing strategies, lines of difference become hardened; in this environment, conflicts develop easily because there is little personal basis for communica-tion, friendships, and understanding (Carter, 2013; Briscoe et al., 2009).

The model of conflict presented in the following pages can be employed in classes as a way to analyze the genesis of conflicts and to learn how people in the same institution—for example, students, teachers, and administra-tors—can work together to counter the underlying roots of conflict.

THE "ICEBERG" MODEL OF CONFLICT

The same principles that operate in society as a whole also operate in schools, colleges, and other organizations. If we look at schools as *microcul-tures*, we can see the same dynamics. When teaching people about how and why racial conflicts arise, it's important to convey the idea that conflicts have histories, just like medical symptoms have etiologies. One has to understand the roots of conflict, not just the triggers that set it off at a given point in time. The *iceberg model of conflict* (see figure 10.1) can help us to conceptualize the development of conflict. Educational institutions that do a good job at addressing the root causes of conflicts and paying attention to the subtle tensions that precede an overt conflict tend to have fewer overt, violent kinds of conflict. Conversely, schools or colleges that are constantly "putting out fires" may never address the underlying causes of those fires.

Each school, college, or organization has a somewhat unique microcul-ture. Why is it that some multiethnic institutions are relatively free of ethnic and racial conflicts, while others are deeply troubled by racial and ethnic hatred and violence?

Research points to two explanations. One is that the knowledge, skills, actions, and attitudes of those in leadership roles make a big difference. In other words, even when the surrounding community is ridden with ethnic or racial conflict, the school can be an oasis of safety and hope. Henze et al. (1999, 2002) portrayed in detail what proactive school leaders, including teachers, principals, and other leaders, do to create these schools. Especially critical is the notion that *proactive leaders* create positive conditions for interaction and understanding among diverse groups. They try to address underlying issues such as segregated and unequal programs or classes, and they try to ensure that students are educated about racial and other kinds of diversity, not only through extracurricular activities such as multicultural assemblies but also in the required curriculum, so that these issues become central to the school's mission and educational goals.

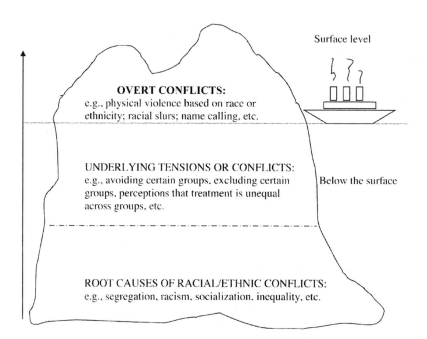

Overt conflicts: Physical fighting or the use of racial slurs. This stage of conflict is exposed and easy for others to detect because you can see it, hear it, or read it.

Underlying, latent, or potential conflicts or tensions: The people affected by these conflicts and tensions may or may not be aware of them; for example, when people are excluded from participation in a group because of culture, ethnicity, language etc., they may feel uncomfortable and hurt, but may not recognize it as a form of racial tension. Such conflicts or tensions may remain hidden indefinitely or surface later as overt conflicts.

Root causes of racial/ethnic conflict:
- segregation, which allows for the development and maintenance of stereotypes about other groups with whom one has little actual contact;
- institutionalized racism and individual racial prejudice;
- socialization in which parents and other adults consciously or unconsciously transmit to children negative information about other groups; and
- inequality, in which power, status, or access to desired goods and services are unequally distributed among groups.

Figure 10.1.   The Iceberg Model of Racial/Ethnic Conflict
Adapted from Henze, R., Katz, A., Norte, E., Sather, S., Walker, E. (2002). *Leading for Diversity: How School Leaders Promote Positive Interethnic Relations*. Thousand Oaks, CA: Corwin Press, p. 45.

Another explanation is that in some institutions there is less inequality among the different groups to begin with. For example, if students of different ethnic groups are mostly from middle-class households, chances of conflict will be less than if some students are from poor and working-class homes while others are from middle- and upper-income homes. As noted in chapters 7 and 11, income and resource disparities among students are easily observed and so set the stage for conflict. Scarcity—of resources or goods, of partners that are seen as desirable—will often lead to more competition. When conflict does arise in an environment of ethnic or racial differences, it is usually triggered by real or perceived inequalities in material or social resource distribution, or because one group's values, beliefs, and cultural expressions offend or stigmatize another group (Kreisberg, 1998).

In societies where segregation occurs in a context of great inequality, as in the United States, people at the lower rungs of society tend to have conflict with each other rather than between the lower and upper classes. In large cities in the United States, for example, there is a higher incidence of "Black on Black" and "Brown on Black" violence than there is between White and Black, White and Latino, and so forth. Why?

Simply put, under conditions of poverty and frustration at shrinking resources, it is easier to strike out at whoever is nearby, in the same neighborhood, than to look for the underlying structural and often invisible sources of your problems. During the Los Angeles riots in the aftermath of the Rodney King assault, it was African Americans and Korean immigrants who fought each other. The Korean immigrants had established themselves as owners of "mom-and-pop" stores and other small businesses in South Central Los Angeles, primarily in African American neighborhoods. As in many urban areas, there was existing tension because immigrants had moved in and taken over businesses that were frequented by primarily African American customers. The immigrants were also, as a group, slightly better off economically.

But the immediate cause of the problem wasn't between African Americans and Koreans, but rather the behavior of the four Euro-American policemen who brutally beat Rodney King, an African American man, after a car chase. Their subsequent acquittal further outraged African American residents. The root of the problem was in the institution of law enforcement in Los Angeles that dated back at least to the Los Angeles riots of 1965 and in the U.S. justice system. Because of the history of racial stratification in this country, the penalty for violence against poor African Americans and Latinos is often less than it would be if the same violence were perpetrated on middle-class European Americans. Although this disparity in treatment is no longer legally sanctioned, it remains in practice, as we have witnessed in the recent trial and acquittal of George Zimmerman for the death of Trayvon Martin (Mullings, 2013).

This pattern of people lashing out not at the source of their oppression but at whoever is within striking distance is also played out in schools. Segregated schooling in which poor and minority students are isolated from the mainstream and provided with substandard schools creates conditions that make violence possible.[2] Students in crowded, badly maintained schools with high teacher turnover rates and poorly prepared teachers are more likely to turn their frustration and anger toward each other, not toward the less visible policies and policymakers that allow such conditions to exist. (See also activity in chapter 11.)

In Los Angeles in the spring of 2005, riots between students broke out at Jefferson High School, a large, urban, predominantly Latino high school that had been a predominantly African American, poor, and working-class community only a few decades ago. African American students (roughly 10 percent of the student body) interviewed for National Public Radio said they felt that they were being ignored by both teachers and administrators. They complained that because they were not bilingual, most resources were used up by immigrant students who were not necessarily even American citizens. (See activity for more information.)

Segregation, as we noted earlier, can also lead to superficial or stereotypical understandings of those perceived as "different." Because many schools are large and depersonalized, and because teachers often don't live in the neighborhood where the school is located, teachers often are unfamiliar with the students' parents and communities. In one large high school, writes Pollock (2004a), new staff members were actually given a "bus ride through the ghetto" so they would see the impoverished neighborhoods some students came from. While this might have been well intentioned, it "framed 'blacks' as the school's most needy population" (p. 196) and ignored other neighborhoods and students. A different and more effective approach is described by González, Moll, and Amanti (2005), who show us how teachers who know their students' communities well come to view parents and community members as potential sources of local knowledge who can be invited in to build bridges with school knowledge. This approach to community involvement, called *funds of knowledge*, is more effective at engaging students and getting them to see the relevance of school to their own lives. Furthermore, teacher education programs become more relevant when they connect meaningfully with the social justice work that is taking place in community organizations and beyond (Zeichner & Payne, 2013).

At the college level, racial conflicts have sometimes centered on fraternities and sororities. These organizations have long served as ways for male and female students to organize themselves into communities within their educational settings, especially given that many are living away from home for the first time. One does not volunteer to join, but must be invited through a process called pledging. As late as the 1960s, fraternities and sororities were for the most part segregated by race as well as by religion (that is, mainly Christian—with Jewish sororities and fraternities forming in reaction). African American sororities and fraternities also existed, perhaps partially because of segregation but perhaps also voluntarily. A study on fraternity bias in 1963 reported that although bias had lessened since the end of World War II, the resistance to admitting Jewish students into fraternities was not so much between the students and the administrators, but between the organization and the alumni or the "old guard" who did not want the change (Jewish Telegraphic Agency, 1963). Some European American fraternities and sororities continue to engage in stereotypic and insulting behavior toward other racial/ethnic groups. These activities usually include using parties and pledge activities to get members to dress up as members of other groups. When called on this behavior by authorities and the media, the response is usually that "it was a joke." Or "we did not mean to offend anyone, we were just having fun." For example, at the University of Wisconsin in 1988 the Zeta Beta Tau fraternity had a talent show with skits portraying the Jackson 5 and Oprah Winfrey in blackface. They apologized for the incident (Worthington, 1988). In 2001 the University of Alabama moved to try to end the segregation that still existed between black and white fraternities (*New York Times*, 2001). At Johns Hopkins University just a few years ago, the administration suspended a fraternity for holding a "Halloween in the Hood" party that included a mock lynching (Reddi, 2006).

Lest we think that all of this is in the past, the next examples are from 2010 to 2013. The first is from the University of Chicago, one of the nation's most prestigious universities. What was ironic is that the incident involved two members of what had become more of a multicultural fraternity having a wide range of racial and ethnic members. The incident involved two students dressing up as gardeners wearing large sombreros mowing the grass on campus with Latin music blasting in the background. Again the leadership of the organization apologized (Fitzpatrick, 2012). The next two come from the University of California. The first is from the University of California San Diego. In 2010, a fraternity on campus instituted a series of incidents to mock African Americans. It began with a barbecue called the "Compton Cookout." Partygoers were urged to sport gold chains, flashy clothes, and gang tattoos. The invitation told girls to dress like ghetto chicks with gold teeth and suggested guys come dressed in hip-hop wear. The next incident involved a racially charged show on a student-run TV station on which participants defended the cookout concept. The third incident involved a student who left a noose hanging in the university library. Needless to say, the students eventually apologized for their behavior, but to this day these incidents haunt the campus and the San Diego community (Wayland, 2010). The final example is from the University of California Irvine, and it involves Lambda Theta Delta, the largest Asian interest fraternity at UC Irvine. This fraternity made up of Asian Americans is accused of dressing up in blackface on videos on several occasions in April of 2013. When confronted with their behavior, they apologized (Ebright, 2013). So, even in situations where there is a majority minority population, there can be racial misunderstandings and insensitivities that education can begin to correct.

TRIGGER ISSUES

Table 10.1, based on a study of twenty-one schools across the United States, identifies issues that triggered racial or ethnic conflicts in those schools. By examining the table, one can get a sense of the range of issues that were presented by school personnel and students as triggers of tensions or conflicts with a racial edge. Of course, the table only presents *trigger issues* based on a limited number of schools. Other triggers may certainly arise in other schools. But the table can serve as a useful stimulus for discussion with students. Do you see similar triggers in your school or college? Are there other triggers that you do not see on this table?

To illustrate, consider the trigger issue in section A of the table, "distribution of disciplinary referrals or consequences." As we will see in chapter 11, there is a wide *discipline gap* in the United States that is racial as well as gendered. African American and Latino boys tend to end up being suspended or expelled at a much higher rate than other racial groups (Noguera, 2008; U.S. Commission on Civil Rights, 2011). One of the reasons this happens is that there is wide variation in teachers' and administrators' decisions about what kinds of behaviors they consider "disciplinable." Culturally preconditioned ways of seeing and understanding student behavior play a key role in the interpretation of what is disciplinable and what is not. Most schools have "menus" of choices that teachers and administrators can use to refer a student to the principal's office for disciplinary action. A common category is "defiance of authority." However, different individuals will have quite different perceptions of what counts as defiance of authority. For some, it may be merely talking loudly in the classroom. For others, it may be restricted to directly insulting the teacher. Because many categories of referrals are quite open to interpretation, teachers' immediate judgments come into play—judgments that are partially based on the teachers' own cultural norms and racial biases. In the end, students may be referred to the principal's office not so much because of what they say but because of the way they speak and the fact that their communicative norms differ from those of the dominant culture of the school and the classroom, in which sitting still, being quiet, and working independently are valued (see chapter 6 for a discussion of *cultural discontinuities* between home and school).

In the following excerpt, Mr. Aguirre, an assistant principal in a large high school, discusses these cultural differences in the interpretation of behavior:

> There are also a lot of stereotypical things. And the best example I could say is today, the African American students tend to speak loudly and in high tones and maybe sometimes animated. And staff here takes that oftentimes literally as a threat. And so, as soon as they see it they write down in a report, "I was

Table 10.1.   Issues That Can Trigger Racial/Ethnic Conflicts in Schools

A. Distribution of material or social resources

Distribution of **academic expectations** through tracking and other means of demonstrating what is expected of different groups

Distribution of **staff positions** based on race/ethnicity

Distribution of **disciplinary referrals or consequences**; e.g., high referral rate for African American and Latino males

Control of **territory** on or off campus; may be gang related

Distribution of **power** (decision-making, voice, etc.) based on ethnicity or race

Distribution of **assemblies** and other celebratory events

Inclusion or exclusion of multicultural perspectives in **curriculum**

Distribution of **time and schedules**

Distribution of **financial resources**

Distribution of **respect**

Distribution of **sports opportunities**

B. Values, beliefs, and cultural expressions

Talking about race/ethnicity versus belief that we should all be color-blind

Appropriate or best instructional methods

Staying within group versus mixing with others (includes dating issues)

Use of racial slurs within or between groups (e.g., "nigga" or "nigger")

Culturally appropriate ways to discipline students

Use of languages (English and others)

Expression of religion in schools

Assuming preferences or dispositions based on race/ethnicity

Cultural differences in clothing

Adapted from Henze, R., Katz, A., Norte, E., Sather, S., & Walker, E. (2002). *Leading for diversity: How school leaders promote positive interethnic relations.* Thousand Oaks, CA: Corwin Press, p. 50.

threatened by this person." But when I talk to them—look, it's just manner-isms and things like that. And without that understanding—yeah, on paper you can write anything and make it sound like something is a real serious threat, but it just turns out to be a real verbal back and forth and nothing serious. But, it's gotten to the point where I know students have gotten into real serious trouble because a teacher insists on calling it a threat. . . . So, there's a lot of the institutionalized way of thinking in terms of discrimination and race that's still going on here. (Henze et al., 1999)

Another category of referrals is "fighting." But what constitutes a fight? This, too, is open to culturally shaped interpretations. A security officer in a

Seattle school reported that African American boys are more likely to engage in "play fighting" than non–African Americans. School officials who don't understand this will tend to overreport fighting.

Sometimes students engage in what looks to the outside eye like conflict, but is in fact staged as a way to gain respect or admiration from peers. The people involved actually have no intention of really fighting. Arriaza (2003) documented this *symbolic fighting* at a middle school that went from having many physical conflicts to one in which students, both males and females, often postured but avoided actual physical fights: "Symbolic fighting becomes, therefore, a metaphorical strategy that students use to negotiate their personal space within their friendship groups, gain respect from the larger group, and go through the rituals of growing up in school" (p. 11).

Open-ended categories such as "defiance of authority," "disruptive," and "fighting" create an opportunity for culturally biased assumptions to influence authorities in making disciplinary decisions. One way to interrupt this tendency is to better prepare teachers to be aware of their own cultural biases and to be more cautious about jumping to the conclusion that a student is being "defiant" or "disruptive" just because the teacher finds the behavior irritating. Another way to intervene is to make the categories themselves less "squishy"—that is, more grounded in observable behavior and less open to interpretation (Denn, 2002b).

A third and much more comprehensive way to address the discipline gap is to focus on engaging students in real learning, as suggested by Noguera (2008) and the U.S. Commission on Civil Rights (2011). In most cases, according to Noguera,

> what separates teachers who experience frequent behavior problems from those who do not is their ability to keep their students focused on learning. . . . Schools that suspend large numbers of students, or suspend small numbers of students frequently, typically become so preoccupied with discipline and control that they have little time to address the conditions that influence teaching and learning. (p. 136)

Educators who wish to engage students in learning activities to seek a deeper understanding of conflict (and how it can become racialized) have many resources available to them. The iceberg model and the trigger issues can be used to lead in to an activity (described at the end of this chapter) that helps students analyze incidents they have witnessed or been involved with at their own school or college.

Many other activities are available in the websites listed at the end of this book, as well as in Mica Pollock's book *Everyday Antiracism* (2008). Of particular interest is the use of conflict resolution programs and curricula in elementary, middle, and high schools. A key element in most conflict resolution programs is that young people are prepared to be the facilitators and leaders to help other students resolve conflicts. In Henze et al.'s study of intergroup relations in twenty-one schools, the researchers found that while many schools had conflict resolution programs in place, some of those programs did not address race specifically. These programs took a more "colorblind" approach, addressing all conflicts as basic human problems constituted as individual problems with other individuals.

Others took a more proactive and explicit approach, naming race as one among many intersecting identities (e.g., gender, sexual orientation, immigration status, class, etc.) that might be a factor in conflict. The list provided in their 2002 book indicates which programs addressed race specifically (pp. 184–87). Of course, programs are regularly updated and changed, so programs that include race as a topic in conflict resolution may be more numerous today than when the study was completed. Two examples of curricula/ programs that do appear to address race as part of their model can be found through Educators for Social Responsibility or the National Conference for Community and Justice.

CONCLUSION

While many of us have been raised with an idealized notion that all social conflict should be eradicated, in fact social conflict is a normal part of human existence in communities; however, it doesn't have to be destructive, and it doesn't have to be racial. When people are educated to express their frustration, anger, or hurt with words rather than with physical attacks, and when schools and colleges provide support systems to help people understand and resolve conflicts, there is tremendous learning potential. People can, when guided by knowledgeable and skilled teachers, develop a better understanding of each other and the issues that made them behave as they did. In essence, people who learn to talk about their conflicts develop empathy and understanding for the other perspective, even if they ultimately "agree to disagree." This is particularly true in the case of tensions between people across racial/ethnic lines, as well as gender, class, sexual orientation, religious, and other kinds of differences. Social conflict, if handled well, helps us all to learn.

Applying anthropological perspectives to conflict in schools and colleges can help students and teachers view conflict in a comparative way, recognizing that not all societies that are racially diverse have racial conflict. The particular way that racial conflict has evolved in the United States grows out of our history and is socially constructed, not natural or universal. Recognizing this point can be very empowering to both students and teachers because it allows us to consider how we might change the underlying structures of racial inequality in order to construct our society differently—and thus make racial conflict not inevitable but more the exception rather than the rule.

REFLECTIVE QUESTIONS

- Think of an incident that you believe illustrates "racism." What, in your opinion, makes this incident count as an example of racism? Did other people have a different opinion? How do you think their views differed from yours?
- Think of an educator you have known whom you see as a proactive leader on matters of racial and/or social justice. What did this person do that helped to advance his or her community to be antiracist and/or socially just?

KEY CONCEPTUAL POINTS

- The terms "racism" and "racist" can range in their meanings, from simple to more complex. The more complex definitions include an analysis of power relations and recognize institutional, systemic racism as well as individual racism.
- "Cultural racism" is a form of racism that does not use racial terms at all. Instead it focuses on cultural attributes such as religion, language, or practices.
- Ethnic and racial differences do not inevitably produce conflict; peaceful multiethnic societies exist in other parts of the world.
- Racial and ethnic conflicts are often triggered by real or perceived inequalities or stigmatized cultural patterns.
- Segregation leads to superficial or stereotypical understanding of "other" groups, which in turn can result in conflicts based on miscommunication.
- Conflicts tend to have a history, and learning that history helps educators and students address the roots of ethnic/racial conflict instead of just reacting to the most immediate or overt conflicts.
- When oppressed or targeted by discrimination, people tend to strike out at those within range, and not necessarily at the sources of the problem.
- The interpretation of conflict (and hence, disciplinary consequences for engaging in conflict) is susceptible to wide cultural variation.

KEY TERMS (ITALICIZED AND BOLDED IN TEXT)

racism—simple definitions and complex definitions
racist—simple definitions and complex definitions
White privilege

systematic
intersectional
cultural racism
racialization
color-blind rhetoric
iceberg model of conflict
trigger issues
microcultures
proactive leaders
funds of knowledge
discipline gap
cultural discontinuities
symbolic fighting

ACTIVITIES

Activity Plan 1: Understanding Racial Conflict

Objectives: Participants will be able to

- explain how nonracial conflicts can become racialized,
- identify trigger issues that are often the justification for racial or ethnic conflict,
- distinguish overt conflict from underlying tensions and root causes that might lead to overt conflict, and
- develop recommendations for healing racial/ethnic violence in their school or community.

Other Information: This activity is appropriate for secondary students or adults. It requires approximately two to two and a half sessions of about fifty minutes each. Materials needed include overhead transparencies or Power-Point and poster-making supplies for participants.

Procedure:

Step 1. Session prior to activity: Participants do a journal entry on the following prompt:

> Write a one- to two-page journal entry about a time when you were involved in, witnessed, or knew about a conflict that was related to the people's race or ethnicity. Change names to protect people's identity (so you don't spread gossip). Be prepared to share your story with other participants.

Facilitator collects and reads journals before next class, making notes on how many participants wrote about overt (vs. underlying) conflict, name calling as the beginning of the incident, or incidents that didn't start out as racial but ended up that way. Also note which "trigger issues" (see table 10.1) appear to be involved most often and which groups appear in conflicts most often.

Step 2. Next class: Tell participants you read their journals and comment on what patterns you noticed. Introduce the activity. Say they are going to learn about what causes racial conflicts and come up with some ways to use this knowledge to help prevent these conflicts.

Step 3. Return journals. Using the iceberg model of conflict (figure 10.1) as an overhead projection, ask participants what the expression "that's just the tip of the iceberg" means. Explain if necessary. Then, explain the iceberg model of racial/ethnic conflict, giving examples of each "layer," as indicated in figure 10.1. Emphasize that racial conflict is not inevitable or universal. By changing the underlying conditions that allow racial conflict to arise, we can make racial conflict less likely.

Step 4. Recognize those who wrote about overt conflicts versus underlying tensions or root causes, and if there are more overt ones, ask participants why (because it's more obvious, easier to detect, can be reported to an authority figure, etc.). But just because we can see or hear or read it (graffiti may be overtly racist!), does that mean there are no deeper issues?

Step 5. Place participants in diverse pairs (based on ethnicity, gender, religion—depending on the mix in the group). Tell them to read each other's journals and then ask each other the questions below. Remind them of the need to respect each other while doing this exercise, since some people may have very personal and important things to share. The reader asks the writer:

- How did you feel when you were writing about this conflict? (This question is important because some students may write about painful experiences, and they need to have an opportunity to have someone listen to how they felt or feel.)
- Where would you place this conflict in the "iceberg model"? Why?
- What do you think is the root cause of this conflict?

If there's time, ask at least one participant to volunteer to read his or her piece.

Step 6. Make an overhead transparency or PowerPoint slide of the "trigger issues" presented in table 10.1. Use this to elicit the following information: Can you find a trigger issue on this list that is similar to the one you wrote about? Are there any other trigger issues you can think of that are not on this list?

Step 7. Ask if anybody write about a conflict that didn't start out racial, but ended up that way? If so, ask the person to read his or her entry. If no one has an entry on this point, read the one from chapter 10. Ask the group to come up with reasons why a nonracial conflict becomes racial. What happens to make it racial? List stages or steps on the board. For example:

- Two people of different racial or ethnic groups have an argument or misunderstanding.
- Other people see or hear this.
- Friends of each person come to give support.
- If each person mainly has friends who are of the same race or ethnicity, it can quickly begin to appear as if the conflict is racial (in other words, people will assume that the conflict started because someone expressed racial prejudice or slurs).

Step 8. Did anybody write about a conflict over dating? Ask for volunteers to read their journals, if they are not too private. Ask whether problems with gender sometimes overlap with racial or ethnic conflicts. For example, at the high school level, what happens if a woman or girl refuses a date with someone of a different race or ethnicity? Does that mean she is racist? Or does it mean that she just doesn't want to date that individual? Can a male pressure a female to date him by saying she's a racist if she refuses? Do people ever pressure each other not to date someone of a different race?

Step 9. Note any journal patterns regarding which groups are in conflicts and discuss reasons and root causes with participants.

Step 10. Ask participants to read the mini-case below; have them (in pairs or groups) draw the conflict in an "iceberg model" and answer the discussion questions.

At Jefferson High School in Los Angeles, conflict and violence between Latino and African American students has been increasing in the early 21st century. While the students may see these confrontations as primarily based on a racial or ethnic dislike for each other, the conflicts are really about a lot of things, including the following:

- Twenty-five years ago Jefferson High School was predominantly Black and today it is predominantly Latino.
- Both groups tend to be poor and live in poor neighborhoods with high unemployment rates; their parents compete with each other for low-paying jobs.
- Jefferson High School was built for 1,500 students; in 2004, it had over 4,000, so there is a lot of overcrowding and the sharing of old equipment.
- The majority of students do not speak English as their first language, so a lot of resources go toward ESL courses, leading African Americans to believe they are not getting equal resources or attention.
- The high school has been grossly underfunded for decades.

- The tensions from the local neighborhoods are brought to the high school campus and are often played out in the lives of the students.
- School officials have been complaining that this situation was going to blow up for years.

Discussion Questions

1. Draw an "iceberg model" of the conflicts at Jefferson High, identifying root causes, subtle or underlying tensions, and overt conflict. Then compare your iceberg with that of your partner. How are your icebergs different or the same?
2. Discuss who is responsible for these conflicts. What can be done to address the underlying or root causes of these conflicts?

Step 11. Assessment: Participants do a group change-oriented project (in class or as homework). They should now be able to identify strategies to address root causes of racial conflict. They will now show the results of their learning by making "Recommendations for healing racial/ethnic violence." Organize participants into groups and ask them to create posters of their group's recommendations for healing racial violence. The recommendations can be specific to the school or the community they live in, or more generalized. They can also be targeted to a certain issue in their school or community. The assessment should be based on how well they incorporate key concepts, such as the trigger issues, and the distinctions between overt conflicts, underlying tensions, and root causes. If possible, posters should be displayed in a public area so that others will be able to see and discuss them.

ADDITIONAL ACTIVITY IDEAS

Activity Idea 1: Understanding the Conflict over the Rodney King Beating

The following website is a resource that students can use to develop a critical understanding of the 1991 conflict in Los Angeles over the Rodney King beating.
  http://www.usccr.gov/pubs/larpt/main.htm

NOTES

1. A racial slur used in the United States to refer to Latinos.
2. Even though racially segregated schooling was declared illegal in 1954, de facto segregation still exists. Most schools draw students from the immediate neighborhood, and most communities are residentially segregated. "White flight" from inner cities also leaves behind

mostly Blacks, Latinos, and other people with no choice but to send their children to inner-city schools.

Chapter Eleven

The Academic Achievement Gap and Equity

The notion of an "academic achievement gap" and what to do about it has been a focal point for much discussion in U.S. education in the past decades. In this chapter we examine this issue by (1) presenting a short history of different explanations offered by social scientists, including anthropologists of education; (2) highlighting what some schools are doing to raise the achievement levels of racial minority and low-income students; and (3) suggesting activities for those who are learning about the so-called achievement gap. The primary focus of this chapter is to provide conceptual background for educators. However, we also think there is value in having learners (including young people and adults) participate in studying sources of inequality in their own educational communities.

What do people mean when they talk about an *achievement gap*? In the United States, the term usually refers to a difference in academic achievement by race-based populations, using standardized test scores as the main indicator. The term "achievement gap" could be used to talk about many kinds of populations, including those differentiated by gender, class, language background, and so on. For example, one could talk about an achievement gap in math between boys and girls. But the most pervasive use of this term refers to a so-called racial achievement gap—in other words, an achievement gap that is predictable on the basis of race:

> The achievement gap shows up in grades, standardized-test scores, course selection, dropout rates, and college-completion rates, among other success measures. It is most often used to describe the troubling performance gaps between African-American and Hispanic students, at the lower end of the performance scale, and their non-Hispanic white peers, and the similar aca-

229

demic disparity between students from low-income families and those who are
better off. In the past decade, though, scholars and policymakers have begun to
focus increasing attention on other achievement gaps, such as those based on
sex, English-language proficiency and learning disabilities. (*Education Week,*
July 7, 2011, paragraph 1)

Educators and policy makers have been trying to narrow the race-based
achievement gap for many decades, with limited success. While some
schools have shown bright spots and success stories, the gap persists overall,
as an analysis of data from the National Assessment of Educational Progress
(NAEP) shows. Data for 2003 were compared with data for 2011:

> While concerted efforts over the past several years have resulted in progress at
> the low end, moving students out of below basic and inching up the level of
> the 10th-percentile student, our work is not done here. Nor are we paying
> nearly enough attention to those students caught in the middle of the spectrum
> who are out of the academic red zone, but still far from advanced performance.
> And, although we have made progress at the high end for all students, a lot
> more, and faster, progress is needed, particularly with our students of color and
> low-income students so they are equally represented at the advanced level of
> performance. (Education Trust, May 2013)[1]

The present chapter approaches the achievement gap as a manifestation of
the historical inequality in U.S. schools and society. This chapter is closely
linked to chapter 7, which provided historical background on how U.S. racial
categories evolved to justify economic and social inequality. Nonetheless,
the social construction we know as race has become so powerful, and the
historical processes that led up to it so deeply entrenched, that we end up
with the outcomes we see today: Racialized identities do make a difference,
and statistically speaking, students categorized as European American and
Asian American do continue to outperform African American, Native
American, and Latino students on standardized tests and other indicators of
academic achievement at the K-12 and college/university levels. Of course,
by this point in the book readers are already aware that these racial groups
falsely homogenize an enormous range of human diversity. Yet, analyses of
educational progress such as NAEP do continue to disaggregate achievement
by racial groups, socioeconomic status, gender, and other indicators in an
effort to track progress in undoing the legacies of racism, poverty, and sexism and other forms of inequality.

But how do we explain this gap? Even the language we use to talk about
this issue is loaded with assumptions. The term "achievement gap" focuses
our attention on the students who fail to achieve, meanwhile obscuring or
drawing attention *away from* the real problem—which lies in our social and
institutional structures, historically designed to use race as a sorting mechanism (see chapter 7). An alternative term, suggested by Cammarota (2005)

and others, is ***opportunity gap***. This phrase locates the problem with the institutions and environmental conditions that provide opportunities for certain students and not others—opportunities that are predictable on the basis of race.

Ultimately, this chapter shows readers that the racial achievement gap, and the opportunity gap that underlies it, is the logical outcome of hundreds of years of a racialized hierarchy in Europe and the United States. We are reaping what was sown for us. It shows us how powerfully cultural constructions of inequality based on race have worked—to the point that even now, when most people want to undo the legacy of racism, that legacy persists.

CONCEPTUAL BACKGROUND

Scholars in a wide variety of disciplines, including biology, sociology, psychology, anthropology, and economics, have advanced many different explanations for the achievement gap. Here, we provide a brief overview of some of the major ones.

The Biological Explanation

As we have seen in part I, there are no biological races. However, the idea persists to this day that the racial achievement gap can be explained by positing biological (inherited) differences that make some groups more "intelligent" or more capable of abstract thinking. One resurgence of this idea came in 1994, with the publication of *The Bell Curve,* by Herrnstein and Murray. The authors argue that IQ tests measure general intelligence, that these tests show that an individual's IQ is largely inherited, "that the human 'races' were differentially gifted with IQ, and that IQ is a cause, rather than an effect, of economic success or poverty" (cited in Cohen, 1997, p. 253).

A more recent example of the same biological explanation is Jason Richwine's 2009 Harvard dissertation, titled *IQ and Immigration*, in which he claims that the average IQ of "Hispanic immigrants" in the United States is lower than that of the "white native" population in the United States and will remain so for at least three generations.

Both of these publications make a number of scientific errors and need to be seen as bogus applications of science. Chin (2013), writing a reply to Richwine's dissertation, states,

> As an anthropologist I cannot sign off without seriously challenging the implicit ideas about race upon which your entire thesis is built. Throughout the work, you strive to link IQ to genetics and heritability. You further assert that inheritance of IQ is empirically reflected in the data you present, and that the patterns reflect accurately in racial and ethnic groups. The massive underlying

problem is that this model assumes that the ethnic and racial groups you discuss possess relatively homogeneous gene pools, and, moreover, that the gene variance and distribution of one group are substantially distinguishable from those of another: "Hispanics," in your formulation, are genetically different from "whites" and this is seen in their differential IQ scores. First of all, "Hispanics" have only existed for a little less than 400 years, not nearly enough time evolutionarily to produce significant genetic distinctiveness. Second, those in the contemporary "Hispanic" population include descendants of indigenous peoples, enslaved Africans, and European immigrants. These are groups that you treat separately in your U.S. data. On what scientific basis can populations be treated as genetically separate groups in one geographic location (the United States), then be grouped together genetically in another (Latin America)? (paragraphs 11–12)

Publications such as Herrnstein and Murray's *Bell Curve* and Richwine's *IQ and Immigration* feed into existing American prejudices against minority groups, upholding "cherished beliefs such as the idea that access to success was based purely on merit and open to anyone with sufficient intelligence" (Cohen, 1997, p. 253). Yet these recent biological explanations are as flawed as earlier attempts to link intelligence with race. We have seen in part I that "races" are not scientifically different biological categories. The individual traits that make up typical racial stereotypes (skin pigmentation, eye shape, hair texture, etc.) do not covary. Even if a trait such as intelligence were measurable by a single, culture-free test, there is no reason to expect that it would covary with "racial" traits.

Furthermore, despite attempts to make IQ testing unbiased, it is virtually impossible to create a test that is not rooted in culture. It is not merely a matter of removing obviously culture-specific words such as "escalator" or drawings that might be culturally ambiguous. The IQ tests, and all tests, are cultural in much deeper ways, including their structure and logic. For example, analogies that ask students to complete a comparison (e.g., acorn is to seed as oak is to _____) are entirely based on categorizing, and as we have seen in chapter 6, categorization is a fundamental way in which culture is expressed (see chapters 6 and 7).

In addition to the above problems with IQ tests, scientists have also challenged the notion of intelligence as a general capacity. Howard Gardner, well known among educators for his work on *multiple intelligences*, provides convincing evidence that there are many different types of intelligence. While he fully acknowledges that the creation of separate types is his own construct—"nature brooks no sharp discontinuities" (1983, p. 70), he nonetheless suggests that it could be useful for educators to think in terms of intelligence types such as linguistic, spatial, musical, bodily-kinesthetic, and so on. Others, including Rogoff (1990) and Lave, Murtuagh, and de la Rocha (1984), draw on Vygotsky's *sociocognitive theory* to show that all cognitive activity is deeply social and situational. There is no such thing as learning that is not embedded in a social and cultural context.

In summary, then, to argue that there is an inherited, biological thing called intelligence that is devoid of cultural influence and that correlates with "racial" traits flies in the face of all scientific research in the latter part of the 20th century and the early part of the 21st century.

The Cultural Deficit Explanation

When race-based biological explanations for the achievement gap began to be discredited in the mid-1900s, a new explanation emerged that focused on culture. It began to take shape in Oscar Lewis's book on the "culture of poverty" (1966), in which he argued that poverty and unemployment among Puerto Ricans was partially the result of habits and beliefs that differed from those of mainstream U.S. culture. This "culture of poverty," however, was itself an adaptation to and emerged in the context of poverty and inequality (Mukhopadhyay & Chua, 2008). While there are many different versions of cultural explanations, one that was prominent in the 1960s and still exists today is the *cultural deficit* explanation. From this perspective, certain racial groups, especially African Americans, Latinos, Native Americans, and some Asians, lack cultural predispositions and experiences that would help them succeed in school and college. This ethnocentric position places cultures in a hierarchy, with Western, middle-class, and usually European American people at the pinnacle of cultural development, while other groups fail in school because of "cultural deficits" (Barker, 1981).

One can easily come across such comments among educators. Rosemary Henze, while conducting research in various school districts around the United States in the late 1990s, heard the following comments: A health educator in Alaska, upon realizing that Henze was about to travel for the first time to several Yup'ik villages, tried to be helpful by sharing his knowledge with her. He stated, "They don't have concepts in the Yup'ik language." Although both people in this conversation were European American and neither had any proficiency in the Yup'ik language, the health educator nonetheless felt a need to pass along "information" that he had probably heard from other non-Yupik speakers. In another example, the assistant principal of a school in Georgia which had recently seen a large increase in the number of Mexican children explained to Henze some of the challenges the school faces: "Children from rural Mexico are coming to school with a lot of cultural deficits; for example, they don't know what an escalator is because they've never been on one." Yolanda Moses, who often serves as a consultant on diversity issues in colleges and universities, hears similar remarks about minority students at the college level. A dean of students at a small liberal arts college in the Midwest explained to Moses the lack of success of students from an urban area as follows: "These students are uncomfortable out of their urban environment; being at a small liberal arts college in a rural area is not an environment for them."

The problem with comments such as these is that they rigidly fix certain cultural groups as deficient in some fundamental way and therefore incapable of achieving success academically. Rather than saying that the students need to acculturate to some of the new cultural practices and forms they will encounter in school or college, and build bridges between home culture and school culture, they paint the students' home culture as a negative, something that stands in the way of academic success.

Anthropologists point out that the term "culture" has many meanings (see chapter 5). But one thing they agree on is that everyone has culture. A useful distinction can be made between Culture with capital C and culture with a small c. The capital C denotes what is often called "high Culture"—that is, the practices and values of the elite or dominant group in any culture. In the United States, high Culture would include learning to play the piano, taking art classes, traveling widely, speaking French, and so on. When we hear phrases such as "He's such a cultured person," the speaker is usually referring to this notion of "high culture." Culture with a small c, on the other hand, is the everyday practices, knowledge, attitudes, and values of any group of people who share a common heritage (Kramsch, 1998). We all acquire culture as a normal part of growing up in communities, and we participate in and enact it all the time, no matter what we do. In other words, everyone has culture.

Thus, from an anthropological perspective, saying that a particular language has no concepts, or that children from an immigrant culture have "cultural deficits" makes no sense at all —except in terms of a hierarchy of cultures that places the dominant group's culture at the peak of the pyramid. Everyone acquires the culture of the communities they have participated in— especially the culture of origin plus any additional cultures (such as the culture of the wider society, the culture of school, or the culture of a foreign country). We acquire as much culture as we need to behave appropriately in our communities of origin and other social networks. When people need to participate in wider social networks (such as attending higher education) or function in a foreign country, they usually are able, over time, to acquire enough of the new culture to be able to function, assuming that they can access the proper opportunities to acquire the needed tools and understandings.

Of course, this is not to say that children do not experience real cultural differences when they attend school, as Heath (1983) described in her ethnographic study of working-class African American and middle-class Euro-American communities. All children experience some degree of culture shock when they first attend school. But those whose home lives are the most different from the mainstream, middle-class, European American cultures on which the U.S. educational system was based tend to experience greater disparity between the cultural practices of the home and the cultural practices of the school. It remains important for educators to have a strong understanding of culture (see chapters 5 and 6) if they wish to understand young people's diverse backgrounds and experiences in order to support their achievement in school.

Acknowledging real cultural differences is not the same as ranking cultures into a hierarchy of superior to inferior cultures. When someone says that an individual or a group has cultural deficits, this can only be understood to mean "deficits" in relation to some other culture that the speaker implicitly assumes to be superior. The cultural deficit explanation for the academic achievement gap fails to recognize the implicit power dynamics hidden behind the term "cultural deficit." For this reason, some have called it *cultural racism*—a thinly veiled substitute for the old biological racism (Barker, 1981; Grosfoguel & Mielants, 2006).

Poverty as an Explanation

Some have argued that the achievement gap is not so much a function of racial identity but rather of poverty. Because African Americans, Latinos, and some recent immigrants to the United States are disproportionately poor, it is often difficult to untangle the effects of racialization and the effects of poverty. And if we add gender and parenting status into the analysis, an even more complex picture emerges. African American boys are often the focus of interventions to improve educational success, but other groups, such as low-income women, women of color, and student parents, continue to experience lower rates of college completion compared to men overall (Park et al., 2013). Despite the interweaving and overlapping of class, gender, race, and other factors, researchers who have studied the relationship between poverty and race in school and college achievement find that race consistently emerges as a major contributor to the achievement gap, even when poverty is factored out.

For example, Myers (2000) conducted a statistical study to determine whether poverty was a primary cause of the poor performance of Black students on the Minnesota Basic Standards Test. Seventy-five percent of African American students failed the math test, and 79 percent failed in reading, compared to 26 percent and 42 percent respectively for Euro-Americans. The findings show that being poor in and of itself is not necessarily linked to low school achievement. But being poor *and* being African American or Latino does have an impact (cited in Skiba & Rausch, 2004).

In the Education Trust's study of K-12 achievement between 2003 and 2011, the race gap is shown to persist. "Overall, the results suggest that a portion of the gap between white students and students of color [in this study, Hispanic and African American] might be related to low family income, yet large gaps exist even after splitting students into low-income and higher income groups" (Education Trust, 2013, p. 8). The same study notes that while racial gaps at the "below basic level" have mostly narrowed over time, racial gaps at the advanced level have actually widened, especially when comparing higher-income groups by race.

The question of whether income disparities explain differential achievement across racial groups pervades the policy and legal debates that surround affirmative action in higher education admissions. The most recent example is the 2013 *Fisher v. University of Texas Austin* case, in which the Supreme Court was asked to rule on whether to continue to allow race-based preferences in college admissions at the University of Texas. Fisher, a European American woman, sued the university because she wasn't offered admission to the university despite the fact that, as required by the university's policy, she was in the top 10 percent of her high school graduating class and was therefore eligible to be admitted. She claimed she was denied admission because of the university's race-conscious admissions program. Although the Supreme Court did not make a ruling and referred the case to a lower court, the case caused many people to debate again whether poverty alone explains racial disparities. In other words, if colleges use poverty as proxy for admissions that give preference to underrepresented racial groups, will colleges be able to achieve the same desired result (a diverse student body) without using race as a consideration? Columbia Law Professor Patricia Williams commented as follows:

> The latest attestation to [the] miraculous salutary power [of wealth] is the assertion that African-Americans who would but barricade themselves within a wall of middle-classness will be structurally exempted from racial resentments. According to this logic, when comfortably situated black people move into all-white areas, the neighbors will be delighted; property values will rise; police will not stop and frisk their children on their way to school; the neighborhood watch will not follow them about and demand to know their business. (Williams, 2013, paragraph 2)

Patricia Hill Collins (2009) has long reminded us that in seeking explanations for the achievement gap, we cannot lull ourselves into simple, "one-factor" explanations. Race, socioeconomics, religion, sexuality, and gender intersect and overlap profoundly in the ways they affect our lives. She calls for more *intersectional analyses* that account for this complexity. Educators, too, need to acknowledge this complexity by avoiding oversimplified explanations of different student achievement levels. Yet within this complexity, the research continues to show us that race matters profoundly in educational outcomes.

Tracking and Other Forms of Inequality as an Explanation

There is convincing evidence that being on the "down side" in various forms of inequality is associated with poor academic outcomes. In other words, it is not poverty in itself that causes low academic achievement, but the juxtaposition of unequal opportunities both in school and in life outside of school. In Myers's study in Minnesota, success on the tests was related to how an individual had been tracked, regardless of racial group. Only 6.9 percent of students of color[2] compared to 23 percent of Euro-American students had access to "gifted and talented" programs. According to the evidence in this study, tracking and other unequal opportunities in school influence not only how well a student does on the standardized test but also academic performance generally (Myers, 2000). A large study of eighty-one Los Angeles County school districts in 2013 found that African Americans are less likely than other racial groups to take college preparatory courses, and that African American males are "more likely to go to prison than to college" (Education Trust West, 2013).

The practice of ***ability tracking***, defined as the sorting and grouping of students by perceived ability, can take place at various levels of organization, from whole schools being designated as "college prep" versus "regular," to within-school tracking by classes (such as honors, regular, "consumer math," etc.). Tracking can also occur within classes, for example, through assignment of students to different reading groups.

When considering the effects of tracking, it is important to distinguish between tracking that is temporary—designed to help students improve their achievement and "catch up"—versus tracking that is permanent. A well-implemented summer bridge program between middle and high school that is designed to give low-achieving students the extra boost they need to do well in ninth grade may help reduce the achievement gap. However, a tracking system that assigns low-achieving students to classes where they never receive the enrichment-type curriculum and instruction that college prep classes receive tends to relegate low-achieving students to a permanent underclass. It also has implications for whether or not students are counseled, encouraged, or advised about pathways into postsecondary education.

While school policy may claim that it is possible to "jump tracks" and go into a higher-level class the next semester or year, in practice this is often impossible because lower-track classes typically do not prepare students for the work expected in higher-level classes, which usually involves more problem solving and critical thinking. "In this way . . . tracking is one of the means by which the race- and class-linked inequalities notable in our schools and in society at large are reproduced" (Rubin, 2003, p. 541).

In an ethnographic study of a detracked ninth-grade program in an urban, diverse high school, Rubin (2003) found that even in classrooms and schools where teachers tried to faithfully carry out the best practices of detracking, "inequalities were often reinforced rather than challenged" (p. 566). She explains that this is, in part, a result of a system that attempts to isolate school practices as if they were separate from the surrounding society. She points out "the educational reforms that created the need for detracking are rooted in systemic inequalities along race and class lines, which detracking reform alone cannot fully address" (p. 567).

Tracking is not limited only to K-12 schools. It occurs as well in colleges and universities, particularly through the segregation of "less prepared," "developmental," or "remedial" students into non-credit-bearing courses designed to improve reading, writing, and math skills. At San José State University, where part of Rosemary Henze's work entails observing academic English classes, these courses are predominantly populated by racial minority students and immigrant students whose academic English skills are not yet fully developed. While many students do receive excellent instruction and ultimately benefit from such courses and move on to regular, credit-bearing courses, there is no doubt that a stigma surrounds these students (as well as their instructors) and that the courses themselves continue to bear informal labels such as "bonehead English" (Rose, 1998).

Ability tracking in schools appears to reflect larger U.S. economic inequalities. "U.S. income distribution appears to be among the most unequal of all major industrialized countries" (Levine, 2012, p. 1). In comparing household income from 1968 to 2011, Levine reports that "inequality has increased in the United States as a result of high-income households pulling further away from those lower in the distribution" (p. 1). This wealth gap is linked not only to educational achievement but also to health. Contrary to popular opinion, it is not the poorest societies that have the worst health, but rather the societies that have the biggest income disparities between poor and rich (Wilkinson, 1997). There appears to be a racial factor in wealth management as well. People of different racial groups starting off with similar wealth tend to diverge after only a few years. Conley (2001) explains that "financial education processes, or how one acquires, manages, and develops their financial resources" differ across racial groups in the United States (cited in Lucey, 2004, p. 27).

Residential segregation by class and also by race/ethnicity and immigration status, coupled with the fact that schools in the United States provide vastly different educational quality, results in appalling statistics such as the following recent findings in Los Angeles County, California: African American students are six times more likely than white students to attend schools ranked among the bottom third in the state, while Latino and poor students are nearly four times as likely as white students to attend schools in this lowest-ranked third (Education Trust West, 2010).

Social reproduction theory links inequalities in schooling with inequalities in the larger society, viewing unequal schooling as one of the primary ways in which existing relations of power and dominance (related to the labor market and economic gain) are maintained and reproduced. In other words, tracking and other inequalities in education help to continually reproduce different classes for the labor force (Bowles & Gintis, 1976; Collins, 2009), making schools not the engines of equality but rather engines of perpetuating inequality.

Students' Expectations of Academic Success as an Explanation

The inequality explanation above locates the problem of the achievement gap in our institutions, which differentially place students in challenging or "dumbed down" educational experiences. It paints a picture of students as passive victims whose academic outcomes are already determined by their location as poor, racialized people in a greatly unequal society. But this explanation fails to address *how* tracking and segregated schooling, especially at the K-12 level, actually result in low academic achievement by so many racialized minority students—especially African American and Latino. What goes on in the students' perceptions?

According to anthropologist Fordham (1996), the "hidden" and explicit curriculum shapes student aspirations and achievements. Confronted by a stigmatized racial identity in school and an awareness that the playing field is far from even, African American adolescents express profound ambivalence about the value and possibility of school success. An African American student in Fordham's study expressed this as follows:

> "Well, we supposed to be stupid . . . we perform poorly in school 'cause we all have it thought up in our heads we're supposed to be dumb so we might as well go ahead and be dumb," he said. "And we think that most of the things we learn [at school] won't help us in life anyway . . . What good is a quadratic equation gonna do me if I'm picking up garbage cans?" (cited in Berlak, 2001, p. 21)

The anthropologist John Ogbu brought a cross-cultural perspective to the issue of how students respond to different environments of inequality and equality. He looked at a similar ethnic population in two distinct social environments. Ogbu (1978) examined the Burakumin (leather workers) in Japan (see chapter 8) and in U.S. schools. In Japan, where the Burakumin are stigmatized because of their lower-class status and occupations (e.g., touching dead bodies, excrement), children of Burakumin families do poorly in school. Yet when Burakumin families migrate to the United States, their children tend to do well in school. This suggests that doing poorly in school is not an inherent trait of Burakumin but a function of the social environment, namely their stigmatized location in Japanese social structure. In the United States, in contrast, Burakumin children are not singled out from other Asian American children, who on the whole are stereotyped as "good students." Student interviews and focus groups show that students who are aware of the poor resources they receive in school compared to students in middle-class and elite schools exhibit anger, frustration, shame, and a sense that they will not be able to compete in "serious" institutions (Fine & Weis, 2003).

Anthropological studies of the achievement gap tend to be critical of the use of macroracial categories, pointing out that large-scale studies often mask important diversity within racialized groups. Take the racial category "Asians" for example: Asians of all backgrounds are often lumped into one racial group in statistical measures of achievement. Sometimes they are also included in the even broader category "students of color." On the one hand, there is a powerful stereotype in the United States of high Asian educational achievement, sometimes referred to as the "model minority myth." Yet this is not true for all "Asians" such as the Hmong, Mien, and some Vietnamese (Lee, 1996). For the same reason, the even larger macro term "people of color" is also problematic. This term usually encompasses all people who have common experiences of oppression due to racism. However, when used uncritically, it also tends to ignore the experiences of groups who have very different experiences as immigrants, such as Chinese, Japanese, Filipinos, and South Asians—in other words, people who are not European American, but who do not necessarily share the educational experiences of many African American and Latino students.

The Stereotype Effect Explanation

A somewhat similar explanation is that of Claude Steele, an American psychologist. Steele and his colleagues conducted experiments in which Stanford students (all presumably preselected as being successful students) were given challenging items from the GRE. Some were told that it was a test of how people solve verbal problems, and others were told that it was a true test of their abilities.

African American students who were told that the test was a true measure of ability scored significantly lower than the White students, while African American students who were not given any prior commentary scored the same as Euro-American students. For Euro-Americans, it made no difference what they were told. Steele explains that African American students know they are likely to be seen as having limited ability and that this knowledge produces extra intimidation (Steele, 2010).

Steele called this effect "stereotype vulnerability." It suggests that, some-how, low expectations and racist attitudes and behaviors are internalized by the person who is the recipient of these expectations, attitudes, and behaviors. In a follow-up study, Steele found that the students most likely to do poorly on the experimental test were also the ones most likely to be highly motivated and academically focused. This suggests that if these students had not internalized negative attitudes based on racial stereotypes, they might have done well on the test.

Educator Expectations and Teacher Quality as an Explanation

The beliefs and expectations of educators, which are materialized through words and actions, can have a powerful impact on young people. The stereotype effect described above is an example of how young people internalize the expectations of respected elders and the larger society. We have a lot of work to do to make sure that the messages young people hear and see from media, educators, and parents are positive and do not reinforce old racial ideologies. Even small actions can have great import; a principal might wonder, for example, whether a tutoring program targeting "Black students" will assist those students or stigmatize them (Pollock, 2008). Teachers and other school officials make innumerable small decisions daily with racially relevant impacts.

The distribution of high-quality, well-prepared teachers is currently heavily weighted toward schools in higher-income areas. A study of forty-six industrialized countries found that "the United States ranked 42nd in providing equitable distribution of teachers to different groups of students: for example, while 68 percent of upper-income eighth-graders in the U.S. study sample had math teachers deemed to be of high-quality, that was true for only 53 percent of low-income students" (Braeden, 2008, cited in *Education Week* 2011, paragraph 9).

Silence plays a role in reinforcing the achievement gap. Many educators and parents would prefer not to talk about the "achievement gap" at all. As Pollock (2004a) points out, there is a dual standard. Race and the achievement gap are talked about openly in policy meetings, research reports, and other "high-level" discourse. But in schools and colleges themselves, among educators and students, the gap is rarely discussed explicitly or publicly.

One result of this silence is that it allows people adhere to a "color-blind" ideology (see chapter 10). The color-blind ideology is no doubt well intended, or at least not intended to do harm. It is a way for educators to publicly assert that the "color of one's skin" isn't supposed to matter. However, it can have an injurious effect on students because it sends the message that (a) racialized differences are "something we don't talk about here"; they are secret or dirty, something to be ashamed about; and (b) students' experiences as a result of these racialized identities are not important or worth talking about. In the extreme, students who feel harassed or targeted for race-based hate crimes have no place to go and talk about their experience and get help. In reality, "race matters"—still.

Another prevalent myth among the public and some educators is the idea that those who get ahead in the United States do so because of merit. They have "pulled themselves up by their bootstraps" and become successful because they worked hard and saved without seeking outside assistance from government programs such as welfare. This has been called the ***myth of meritocracy*** (Villegas & Lucas, 2002; see also chapter 7). Many still believe this myth of meritocracy—that anyone who is motivated and tries hard can get ahead despite racial and other barriers. This same notion of meritocracy has been extended to the area of school achievement and is equally mythical. It blames the victim, compounding the "stereotype" effect.

POLICIES CAN INCREASE—OR NARROW—THE GAP IN COMPLEX WAYS

The achievement gap is a policy problem in the sense that a nation that prides itself on being democratic cannot simply ignore data that show that certain groups, based on race, class, and other dimensions, consistently do less well in schools and colleges. The achievement gap was the central tenet of the Bush administration's No Child Left Behind Act of 2002. This law attempted, through the institutionalization of accountability practices in schools, to set high standards of achievement for all children, and to hold schools accountable if they did not produce adequate progress from year to year. To receive federal funding, schools were required show that all subgroups, including historically underachieving racial groups, were progressing toward higher achievement, and if they did not, those schools were designated "low performing" and had to redress their weaknesses through approved professional development and curricular interventions. Unfortunately, the achievement gap did not change substantially (Education Trust, 2013). Textbook companies and test makers were the largest beneficiaries of the NCLB Act, as they were the ones receiving large contracts to monitor the results in each school district (Arce, Luna, Borjian, & Conrad, 2005). The Obama administration in 2009 passed its own version, called Race to the Top (RTTT). While similar in its goals to NCLB, RTTT differs in its approach. It provides financial incentives for schools to improve student achievement and narrow gaps through a competitive grant program, whereas NCLB mandated changes as a condition of receiving Title 1 funding. While it is too early to say whether RTTT is helping to narrow the achievement gap, it is safe to say that any policy designed to end or narrow the achievement gap must be looked at critically in terms of who stands to gain the most economically.

Policies and practices that purport to lessen the achievement gap usually rely on one of two notions of fairness. The notion of *equality* presumes that the solution to the academic achievement gap is to treat everyone equally, providing the same books, teachers, schools, and curriculum to all students. The notion of *equity*, on the other hand, assumes that the "playing field" is not level, and therefore giving all students the same things will not close the achievement gap. All students do not start out with the same advantages:

> Even before starting kindergarten, [African American students] are often disadvantaged by poverty, access to quality preschool, and a host of other factors. When they do enter the education system, they too frequently face school segregation, low academic expectations, insufficient resources, minimal educational and socio-emotional supports that fail to leverage the assets they bring, and—dare we say it—racism that manifests itself in the form of overidentification for special education and more frequent suspension and expulsion, particularly among African-American male students. It's no wonder that many African-American students disengage from school, both academically and emotionally, and that their educational outcomes lag behind their more advantaged peers. (Education Trust, 2013, p. 13)

In an equity-based approach, institutional actions are designed to redress these social differences. These actions might include, for example, special summer programs to help students "catch up" before they enter ninth grade or ESL and bilingual programs that help immigrants simultaneously develop academic literacy in English and in their native language. Equity is not a concept restricted to race; it can be applied to a gender gap, an economic gap, or any other group disparity in educational outcomes. In the next section, we relate some positive practices to these notions of equality and equity.

WHAT MODELS SEEM TO WORK? CAN WE STILL FIND HOPE?

Many scholars who study inequality now acknowledge that one cannot isolate the systemic effects of schooling from the effects of the larger society (e.g., residence patterns, wealth distribution, health care, employment, credit, and justice). Therefore, the achievement gap cannot be addressed by *only* changing schools and higher education institutions. Those who seek to address student underachievement need to look for solutions outside as well as inside educational institutions (Reskin, 2012).

One state-led policy effort that seems to have wide support is the new Common Core Standards. These standards attempt to address the wide variation in standards across different states by providing a "rigorous and uniform set of standards for learning." So far, forty-five states and the District of Columbia have adopted the Common Core Standards (Education Trust, 2013, p. 3). We have created a weblink that shows how the material in this book aligns with the Common Core as well as subject specific standards (http://understandingrace.org/resources/for_teachers.html). Having rigorous and uniform standards for all students across all states is one example of an equality-based policy. All students regardless of background should meet these standards. The policy is the same for every school, every learner, and every teacher.

However, in implementing these or other standards, schools need to take an equity-based approach, providing specific supports to help students who are less advantaged to meet the standards. For example, Unity High School in Oakland (http://www.unityhigh.org/) is a small public charter school in operation since 2003. The school serves approximately 250 students from anywhere in Oakland but primarily serves students in the immediate neighborhood, which is mostly low income and Latino. In 2011–2012, the school population was 90 percent Latino, 5.5 percent African American, and the remaining students were either Asian or "multiracial." Eight-nine percent of the students were considered socioeconomically disadvantaged. The curriculum is focused on preparing all students to be eligible for the University of California A-G requirements. In 2012, 82 percent of the students graduated and 90 percent of the graduates met the UC requirements. To achieve this outcome, the school offers small classes (average of twenty-five students per class); a curriculum that embodies high expectations; teachers who are highly qualified and likewise demonstrate high expectations of students; a comprehensive support system that connects school, parents, and community; mentors assigned to students to assist them throughout their high school life, with the goal of students being accepted to four-year colleges or universities; and learning experiences that foster student leadership and effective participation in a multicultural democratic society (paraphrased from School Accountability Report Card—http://www.unityhigh.org/SARC1112UnityEnglish.htm).

Other schools that have been widely reported as overcoming the odds and producing high levels of achievement are schools in Milwaukee that are dubbed 90/90/90 schools (Reeves, 2003). Ninety percent or more of the students qualify for free or reduced lunch; 90 percent or more are from ethnic minority groups; and 90 percent or more meet the state and district standards in reading or another area. It is worth noting, especially in this era of privatization of education, that none of the schools in this study relied on privatized models of education. In other words, these are public schools, using "consistent practices in instruction and assessment, with support from local teachers. For those who believe that education remains an interactive process that cannot and should not be 'teacher-proofed,' these research findings are encouraging" (p. 7).

CONCLUSION

The achievement gap is really an opportunity gap that must be addressed in a comprehensive rather than a piecemeal way. Institutionalized and systemic inequalities have produced the disparities in achievement among different groups that we see in schools and colleges today. Anthropologists are clear that these disparities are not rooted in the biology or DNA of racialized groups, nor in their culture. Rather, these disparities are the result of long-standing discrepancies in residence patterns, wealth distribution, health care, employment, credit, and the criminal justice system, as well as institutionalized inequalities in the opportunities students are afforded in schools. The fact that public schools do exist where racialized minority and low-income students do reach high academic standards demonstrates that we *can* overcome the achievement gap. We have the tools and the knowledge to do so. Summoning the political will to do so is another matter, and one that we hope will engage educators and anthropologists in making sure that these few "exceptional" schools become the expected norm in the coming decades.

REFLECTIVE QUESTIONS

- Which of the explanations for the achievement gap have you heard before? Do people at your school or college talk openly about the achievement gap? What do they say about it? Which explanations do you think seem most plausible, and why?
- What have you and others in your school, college, or community already done to try to reduce the achievement gap? What more could you do?

KEY CONCEPTUAL POINTS

- The term "achievement gap" constructs students as failures, rather than acknowledging the institutional structures that make the gap real. A more appropriate term is "opportunity gap."
- The racial achievement gap, while real, is not based on biological capacities but on a system of social inequality and institutional racism that perpetuates unequal opportunities.
- Cultural deficit explanations for the achievement gap replace biological explanations of achievement with cultural ones.
- Both poverty and race play a role in the racial achievement gap.
- Inequality has a psychological component. Students internalize others' perceptions of their competence, and this affects their academic behavior. Negative racial stereotypes, especially linked to educational or intellectual capacity, can have negative educational impacts.

- Some schools have demonstrated that it is possible to achieve high academic performance with majority populations of low-income, racial minority students. These schools serve as models and beacons of hope, demonstrating that we do have the capability to overcome the racial achievement gap.

KEY TERMS (ITALICIZED AND BOLDED IN TEXT)

achievement gap
opportunity gap
ability tracking
social reproduction theory
cultural deficit
cultural racism
intersectional analyses
myth of meritocracy
equality
equity

ACTIVITIES

Activity Plan 1: Unequal Resources

This plan is adapted from Youth Together's unpublished curriculum. Another activity that can accomplish similar objectives is "Starpower"; a brief description is in chapter 7 with a weblink to a detailed plan.

Objectives: Participants will be able to

- understand what people do to protect what's theirs and what happens when people work together,
- identify what inequalities of resources exist in their school/community, and
- identify what they can do about negative conditions in their school/community.

Other Information:

- This activity, appropriate for high school and college courses, requires three or more class sessions. Materials needed include the following: 4 envelopes, 4 instruction sheets, 1 pen, 1 pair of scissors, 1 glue stick, 1 ruler, 1 pencil, and a package of multicolored construction paper (see below).

Procedure:

Step 1. Prior to class, prepare the contents for the four envelopes. Each envelope should contain the instruction sheet plus the following: Envelope 1: one pen, two sheets of gold paper; Envelope 2: one pair of scissors, one glue stick, two sheets of white paper; Envelope 3: one ruler, one pencil, two sheets of black paper; Envelope 4: two sheets of blue, two sheets of red, and two sheets of green paper. The instruction sheet should say:

Please create each of the following items:

- a three-colored flag
- a four-ring chain
- a 3" X 3" gold square
- a 2" X 4" rectangle
- a T-shape that is 3" high and 3" across

Step 2. Divide the participants into four groups and place them at different tables or in different corners of the room, well-spaced. Have participants leave their belongings aside. You will provide them with all they need for the activity. Tell the groups you are giving each of them a packet that includes instructions inside. When all groups are ready, ask them to open their packets and begin.

Step 3. The groups will need to work together to complete the instructions, but they have to discover that. Do not give clues if you can avoid it. Do not allow groups to use their packet envelope or instruction sheet as supplies (they can be reused). Do not allow them to get supplies from backpacks, closets, purses, and so on. If you stay in the room, you may want to take notes on what you observe. For example, how long does it take for groups to start working together? Who starts the sharing? What are the conditions placed on sharing? What do you hear people saying?

Step 4. When all groups are finished, ask them to show their finished products and explain how they made them.

Step 5. Ask the participants the following questions:

a. What happened in this activity? How did you make it work?
b. Did you have any problems or frustrations? Explain.
c. Although you had the same instructions, did different groups solve problems differently? Is that okay? (make note of the diversity of group responses).
d. The name of this activity is "Unequal Resources." Does this relate to your life? In what ways do groups have unequal resources? How are they shared or protected? How does it make you feel when you have

less than others? How does it make you feel when you have more than others?

Step 6. Assessment activity: Have participants write in their journals about what happened in the activity and how it felt for them to have less or more than others.

Step 7. Preparation for next class: Ask participants to think about an example of unequal resources in their own school or college. Be prepared to discuss the situation in class.

Step 8. Extension: Read the information on the following website about global inequality. Discuss in class why the United States is the most unequal of all the industrialized nations (see http://www.pbs.org/now/politics/income.html).

ADDITIONAL ACTIVITY IDEAS

Activity Idea 1: Chairs

This activity, appropriate for secondary students and adults, is highly interactive. Through the unequal allotment of chairs per people, it is designed to simulate the unequal and crowded conditions of inner-city poverty versus the spacious, luxurious living of the wealthy. By the end of the activity, students will be able to articulate that crowded and segregated environments tend to make people lash out at those closest to them, rather than at the sources of the problem. The activity can be done in one class period, with optional (but strongly recommended) follow-up assignments. For complete activity, see the website for this book, http://understandingrace.org/resources/for_teachers.html.

Activity Idea 2: The Growth of the Suburbs and the Racial Wealth Gap

Video segment and teaching activity based on the film *Race: The Power of an Illusion*. The website provides a detailed lesson plan that explores how the opportunity to accumulate wealth has been racialized: http://www.pbs.org/race/000_About/002_04-teachers-07.htm.

Activities and Resources for Educators

The following resources and activities are focused on equity and addressing the achievement gap.

- http://www.eraseracismny.org/. This is the New York website of ERASE, which stands for "Expose Racism and Advance School Excellence." This website has a number of materials that will be useful to educators. Of particular interest is the report "Facing the Consequences" by Gordon, Della, and Kelleher, who offer recommendations for school districts to address both the racial achievement gap and the discipline gap.
- http://www.justicematters.org/. The Justice Matters website provides publications related to how schools can turn around the achievement gap and the discipline gap. Of particular interest is the publication by Susan Sandler and the Justice Matters Discipline Task Force, "Turning to Each Other Not on Each Other: How School Communities Prevent Racial Bias in School Discipline." This report profiles schools across the country that are models of strong communities with caring discipline approaches and that get excellent results.
- http://www.usccr.gov/pubs/School_Disciplineand_Disparate_Impact.pdf. The "School Discipline and Disparate Impact" Report examines the effect of the U.S. Department of Education's disparate impact initiative announced in the fall of 2010 for schools and school districts across the country. The commission asked teachers and administrators from racially diverse public school districts how they have responded to the new initiative; specifically, whether their teachers and administrators have changed their policies and practices as a result, and what those changes were.
- http://sciencenetlinks.com/science-news/science-updates/race-and-achievement/. This article discusses the data showing that African American students lag far behind whites in academic performance, and few measures have helped. Yet remarkably, a recent experiment closed that gap by 40 percent over just one semester—with a single, fifteen-minute writing exercise. University of Colorado psychologist Geoffrey Cohen says they had seventh-graders start the year by writing about their values.
- http://mediamatters.org/issues/race-ethnicity. In addition to reviewing print and online media, Media Matters monitors at least 150 hours of television and radio each week. This section features highlights (or lowlights) from our monitoring efforts, other noteworthy clips, as well as original videos
- http://www.aecf.org/KnowledgeCenter/PublicationsSeries/RaceMatters .aspx. This toolkit from the Annie E. Casey Foundation is designed to help decision makers, advocates, and elected officials get better results in their work by providing equitable opportunities for all. The toolkit presents a specific point of view on addressing unequal opportunities by race and offers simple, results-oriented steps to help you achieve your goals
- Page, Clarence. (2001). *Closing the Achievement Gap.* This video looks at Amistad Academy, a public charter school for mostly poor fifth- through eighth-graders who often enter performing at lower-than-average levels

but leave performing on par with students from wealthier areas. Available from the PBS website: http://www.pbs.org/closingtheachievementgap.

NOTES

1. The authors examine national, public school trends from 2003–2011 in fourth and eighth grades in reading and math. Twelfth-grade results run on a different assessment cycle and were presented separately. They analyze achievement patterns for low-income and higher-income students, using free and reduced-price lunch as a proxy for family income, as well as for students of color and white students. They spotlight achievement gaps in (1) the percent of students in the below basic and advanced performance categories; and (2) the achievement of the top and bottom 10 percent of students in each racial/ethnic and income group. They also examine trends separately for low-income black, Hispanic, and white students versus higher-income black, Hispanic, and white students. They describe results that are statistically significant.

2. The category "students of color" in this study included African American, American Indian, Asian, and Latino students.

Chapter Twelve

Assemblies, Clubs, and Racial Labels

Both educators and students are often perplexed by the tension between *pluralism* (recognizing, valuing, and incorporating differences) and *assimilation* (the idea that everyone can and should "melt" into the dominant culture). Nowhere is this tension more evident than in discussions and arguments on campuses about whether and how to recognize racial or ethnic groups through special events, whether schools should have clubs and after-school programs for particular racial, ethnic, or religious groups, and when and how racial labels take on positive or negative meanings.

This chapter supports educators and students in applying their knowledge of culture as classification, presented in chapters 5 and 6, to their own institution's events and clubs and too-often-unintended consequences of using racial labels. Specifically, this chapter will assist educators in developing students' abilities to perceive and critique the cultural assumptions that underlie existing racial divisions of clubs and special events, as well as to question the use of racial labels (including slurs) and the potential for altering their use among peers. By studying their own school's or college's classification systems, students can learn not only how deeply embedded our assumptions about race are, but also how the socially constructed categories of difference and diversity in their own environment came to be the way they are. The chapter will also show how students and educational authorities are complicit in both making and unmaking racial categories and will engage them in inquiry about how to change those categories to fit the more complex identities of real people in classrooms and on campuses today.

CONCEPTUAL BACKGROUND

Assemblies and Clubs Organized by Race/Ethnicity

Ethnic assemblies and clubs have not always been present in U.S. educational institutions. They arose in the decades following the Civil Rights Act in 1964 and in keeping with the movement in the United States to "celebrate diversity" and become a more openly pluralistic society. Instead of privileging only European American accomplishments and holidays, as they had done in the past, schools and colleges began to have special events for Martin Luther King Day, Cinco de Mayo, Vietnamese Tet Festival, and so on. At the same time, in order to provide an opportunity for students who shared similar cultural backgrounds to affirm their own identities and have a "safe space" beyond the regular school day and curriculum, many institutions began to see a flourishing of "ethnic clubs" that paralleled the "ethnic events." At large high schools and colleges, there may be literally hundreds of such clubs, some organized by ethnicity, others organized by sports interest or other hobbies.[1]

To illustrate how assemblies and clubs can be a hot-button issue, we provide the following discussion among students at Ohlone High School in California, which for many years has held a series of noontime assemblies sponsored by different ethnic clubs on campus.[2] The school is large and ethnically diverse, with over 4,100 students who speak over seventy different home languages. The discussion below was part of a facilitated process in which students gave input on the design of a series of unifying events called "Days of Respect" that would serve as a catalyst to help racialized groups see each other as allies. In the excerpt, students are expressing what they feel and think about ethnic assemblies, which are typically brief noontime events designed to educate students about diversity and unity.

> Jerri, an African American senior who is about to graduate with high honors, says to the group, "Assemblies are not the solution" [to the problem of racial stereotyping and racial conflict].
>
> Karina, another African American girl, agrees: "Nothing happens afterwards. Students sit there and say 'ugh.'"
>
> A boy comments that freshmen and sophomores have more negative attitudes. "The effort has to start with younger kids." He goes on to explain that the middle schools that feed into Ohlone High School don't have such a diverse population, so kids are not used to it.
>
> Fatima, a Mexican American girl, adds, "People say assemblies are boring . . . We're here because we care, but what about all those other students who express intolerance in assemblies?"
>
> A ninth-grade African American boy, James, talks about his own experience in going from middle to high school: "I used to hang out with a more diverse group, but at Ohlone, it's back to the same old factions, we hang out

with all the Blacks. Me and my El Salvadoran friend, we made a pact that we would not let culture divide us."

Sheila from Nicaragua says, "Assemblies are tedious; it's a waste to think you can educate people in 45 minutes."

Jerri adds, "There's too much factionalizing. It's beautiful to have so many clubs, but nobody is communicating with anybody else. Clubs tend to cater only to their own group. The educational message is lost. The same is true for assemblies."

As the dialogue shows, school assemblies and clubs organized by race or ethnicity do not always produce the desired results of affirming students' cultures and educating students about each other's history and culture. In fact, classifying special events and clubs by race or ethnicity and using the time to showcase a "race" or ethnic group can lead to students having a competitive or simply jaded view of diversity. Students and faculty members who are dissatisfied with these divisions create "contested terrain" in which the categories themselves are opened up for questioning.

An anthropological view of culture is useful in analyzing how schools and colleges divide people into races, ethnicities, or cultures. In many ways, schools are small cultures, or *microcultures* (see chapter 5). Even though they are part of the larger regional and national culture, they develop their own particular ways of doing things, as do organizations of any kind. That's why we so often hear phrases like "That's not the way we do it here." As with any culture, much of what goes on is implicit, taken for granted by people who are insiders of that culture. Anthropologist Clyde Kluckhohn once said, "The fish would be the last creature to discover water" (1949, p. 16). The same is true, metaphorically, for educational institutions. We get so used to "the way things are done here" that we think those ways are immutable, somehow part of the landscape, like water to the fish. It seems natural, therefore, to have assemblies and clubs organized by racial/ethnic groups. Yet these groupings, like the concept of race itself, are not natural in any biological sense. Rather, they are socially and culturally constructed for certain purposes that are rooted in the history of the school or college and the community.

For example, when Ohlone High School was first established, the surrounding community was primarily Euro-American, Latino, and African American. The early assemblies and clubs in the 1960s focused on Latinos and African Americans because they were the largest and most visible minorities. As more diverse ethnic groups moved into the community in the 1970s–1980s, the school administration tried to "keep up" with the demographic changes by gradually adding other assemblies so that no one would feel "left out." Eventually the school ran out of available calendar days, and smaller groups (such as immigrant students from Pakistan and India) were told they had to be consolidated into the "Asian" assembly, along with Pacific Islanders, Japanese Americans, and others. Students who identified as European American or white did not have a spot on the assembly calendar.

Each institution, given its particular demographics and culture, molds taken-for-granted societal categories into a local shape and design. In order to understand that design, we have to know something about the history of the local community. Assemblies and clubs are not the only extracurricular activities that raise issues of racial/ethnic classification and identities. Other extracurricular areas, such as the ethnic makeup of sports teams, after-school and summer programs, and "color-blind" casting in theater productions, may also reveal these tensions.

Although the dialogue among students was an attempt to engage students in questioning the way separate ethnic assemblies and clubs affect the school climate, there are times when more dramatic conflicts arise over ethnic/racial events and clubs.

> In the same high school, a conflict emerged during the final preparation for a big Cinco de Mayo assembly, organized by the Mexican American students' club, MECHA. Just days before, an African American young man had been killed in a car chase. He had fathered a child with one of the African American students and thus was considered "family" by many students. The African American students were offended that the celebratory Cinco de Mayo event, which traditionally involved music and dancing, was going to take place when they were grieving the loss of a member of their community. So several African American students confronted the Latino organizers in a courtyard, and a physical fight was barely averted by several teachers.
>
> Eventually, they persuaded the leaders of the two groups to talk—first separately, with a facilitator, and then together. They reached an agreement in which the Latino students agreed to change the way their event was organized. Instead of beginning with music and dance, they would begin with a solemn address in which the speaker would acknowledge the sadness of the loss of the young man's life, and ask everyone to share a moment of silence. The initial speech would continue in a serious tone, and only later would the music and dancing take place.

This conflict, which simmered very close to the boiling point, might be classified as "racial." The underlying issues, though, were really about showing respect for those mourning the loss of a friend, and communicating plans to those who might be affected. The fact that African American and Latino students each had their separate clubs and assemblies, however, heightened the tendency of the groups involved in the conflict to perceive a racial difference as the problem. As we saw in chapter 10, conflicts about ordinary things like respect or lack of clear communication—both of which can also easily happen among people of the same racial group—can quickly become ***racialized***; that is, they *become* conflicts involving race even though they didn't start out that way.

Since assemblies and other special events are key moments when racial or ethnic identity is highlighted, conflicts over assemblies can involve complex, seldom-discussed feelings about which group is given more "air time" or status at the school. If students are given only a limited number of "slots" for their particular group to take center stage, the situation is ripe for conflict if any of the groups perceive an imbalance. Lustig (1997) described a similar conflict in a high school involving immigrant students (mainly Latino) and African American students. The African American students felt that the Latinos were more favored by the school faculty because they spoke a different language and had special dances from their regions. The "multicultural" events that were supposed to bring greater appreciation of diversity actually backfired, leaving the African American students feeling as if they didn't have "culture."

Clubs and after-school programs with a focus on students of a certain ethnic/racial background can provide a safe place where this particular aspect of identity can be explored and strengthened. By affirming students' ethnic/racial identity, these groups help students to find their own place within the larger social structures of school. Educators often point out that "you have to know who you are" in order to make healthy choices both educationally and personally. However, this question of "who you are" is more complex that just ethnic/racial identity. While ethnic identity might be supported in one type of club, the same club might not be so supportive of a student's gender identity or immigration status. Yasmin, a Muslim student, described being hurt when a student on a school bus called her a "f-ing Afghan"; yet when she joined an after-school program focused on Muslim students, she was insulted when the organizer told her to move to the back of the lecture hall to maintain segregation between male and female participants. In the first context, she was identified as a "foreigner" due to her ethnic (and probably religious) identity, but when she participated in an after-school program that affirmed her ethnic identity, she felt placed in a subordinate position to the males (Khan, 2009, p. 179).

A high school counselor described how student clubs sometimes "police" student identities. Ana, a Filipina American, was told by members of the Filipino Club at her school, "You're not a real Filipina." Club members, who were mainly first-generation immigrants, made Ana feel unwelcome. She didn't protest, but she stopped coming to the club meetings. She told the counselor, "They don't understand. . . . I'm just as much Filipina as they are. Even though I was born in the U.S., I'm still Filipina." The club that she thought was there to provide a safe affiliation with her ethnic heritage actually turned out to be exclusionary—because the club leader had decided that U.S.-born Filipinos were not authentic Filipinos, and the club was only for "real" Filipinos (Henze et al., 1999).

Rather than serving as a positive place for students to explore commonalities and differences among first- and second-generation Filipinos, the student leader created a rigid—and arbitrary—border that included some and
excluded others. The student leader, however, is not an independent agent.
She is part of a network of other students and adults at the school. This
incident raises the question of who is responsible for the divisions among
identities that student clubs represent? Do adults play a role, or is it entirely
up to students to establish open, partly open, or closed borders for their
clubs? Technically, such clubs do not have the legal right to restrict membership. However, subtle and not so subtle push and pull factors can make these
clubs welcoming to those who are culturally and ethnically similar, and
unwelcoming to others.

Like the high schools in the previous examples, colleges and universities
until recently have been predominantly Euro-American institutions where
racial/ethnic minority students were in the minority. To make these students
feel at home, ethnic clubs and organizations were often started to provide
"safe havens" for students who had very few people who looked like them in
their classes or in their residence halls (Moses, in press). More recently, the
focus on ethnic clubs and holidays for only ethnic minority groups (and not
European American students) has given way to colleges and universities
promoting the importance of the clubs, organizations, and activities for all
students, not just ethnic minority students.

The examples we have shared show how the microculture of a school or
college shapes the way events and clubs are organized and which particular
ethnic or racial borders will become salient and meaningful in a given school
at a given time. Such shaping may be based on administrators' or students'
assumptions about racial differences and is not always done with full awareness of the nuances and implications. However, they also illustrate how
complex and overlapping the concept of identity is. As educators, if we really
want to support students to develop strong and healthy identities, we need to
not only support their ethnic/racial identity but also the many other aspects
that form identity, including gender, sexuality, immigration status, religion,
and others.

While it might seem as if the organization of assemblies and clubs
presents a rather static picture of structures already in place in a particular
school (almost like a map), in some cases, changes in these structures occur
through *resistance and advocacy* in which students or faculty members exert
their *agency* to question, challenge, or transform existing categories of people.

One such instance occurred at Ohlone High School in the late 1990s when
a group of European American students requested an assembly for "White
culture." For many years, the assembly calendar did not include them as a
specially featured group. Administrators told them it was because white peo-

ple are the dominant culture in the United States, so it isn't necessary to have special assemblies for them. But student leaders eventually prevailed on the administrators several years later, pointing out that Euro-American students were actually a numerical minority at the school.

The administrators granted the request, although the students were told that they had to call it a "European American" assembly rather than a "White" assembly, so as not to arouse suspicions of organizing by the Aryan Nation, KKK, or some other hate-based group. Many people were convinced that even with the name change, this was not a wise idea. After all, they argued, the whole reason for ethnic assemblies was to highlight groups who are underrepresented in the curriculum. Given all the "dead white men" who dominate the history and language arts curricula, European American students could hardly claim lack of representation. But the students' point that in this school they were small in number did give their request more credibility. Also, the administration saw educational value in students exploring their diverse European ancestries so that the category of White would be shown to be more complex and less monolithic.

The first European American assembly at Ohlone turned out to be primarily a celebration of English and Celtic heritage, with little mention of Italian, Portuguese, Slavic, or other European heritages. In subsequent years, having received criticism of the narrow scope, the organizers incorporated more of the true diversity of the European American students' backgrounds. Focusing on Euro-American students' history and cultures shows that pluralism is about everybody learning about themselves and everybody else, in all their complexity; it is not only for "people of color" or historically marginalized cultures. It takes a step toward recognizing and deconstructing the invisibility of "whiteness" as the unspoken norm. In Richard Dyer's 1997 book, he states that in the idealized, homogeneous notion of whiteness, "Whites are not of a certain race . . . they just are the human race, a colour against which other ethnicities are always examined. . . . As long as race is only applied to non-white peoples, as long as white people are not seen and named, they/we function as the human norm. Other people are raced; we [Euro-Americans] are just people" (p. 1).

Yolanda Moses shared another instance in which educators and college students consciously moved beyond the stereotyped notions of separate celebrations for separate cultures. She organized a Seder dinner at City College of New York in which African American Christian and Jewish students shared the ceremony, and for the first time students saw the similarities between African Americans' history of slavery in the United States and the Jews' history with slavery in Egypt. This example shows how celebrations can be an opportunity to explore commonalities that students themselves do not initially see—probably because U.S. society has overemphasized differences rather than what we share.

The examples we have shared here all take place in high schools and colleges, where adolescents and young adults are actively constructing their social identities. The adults in schools and colleges play a role in shaping the possibilities that are available for identity construction; they have a responsibility to help students recognize that identity is not an either/or choice. It is not about choosing to be one kind of person and not another. Everyone has multiple and cross-cutting social identities—for example, the same person can feel fulfilled as a female, Latina, Irish, volleyball player, good student, member of the drama club, daughter, older sister, and so forth. Schools and colleges have the obligation to demonstrate to students, through special events, clubs, the core curriculum, instructional practices, and so on, that identities are complex. When educational organizations and practices reduce such complexity to simple, racialized groups, we severely limit the potential of younger generations to achieve the goals they choose to pursue in life and to view themselves and other people as equally complex.

THE "N-WORD" AND OTHER RACIAL LABELS

Both students and adults often raise serious questions about the "N-word" and other racial labels, pointing out that more and more young people are using slurs such as "nigger" or "nigga" either as in-group terms or even across groups. Shifts in usage are occurring in labels that used to only be insults. They are occurring in labels for recent immigrants (such as "fresh off the boat" or "FOBs"), labels for people of multiple ethnicities (such as "mongrel" or "mutt"), labels for women and girls (such as "bitch" and "slut"), and labels for gay people (e.g., "queer," "queen," "faggot," etc.). For many people, especially older generations, such words immediately call forth their usage as hate language, used to demean or trivialize those so labeled. And yet, some younger people claim they are now used as affectionate terms, terms that show one is part of an in-group—or that they have simply lost their negative connotations.

In the following excerpt, an African American high school senior in Henze et al.'s study (unpublished) discusses these tensions in the use of the word "nigga":

> Just yesterday, I was appalled because I was walking along, and there was this Filipino girl and Filipino guy, and they're just, talking and she's saying, Yeah, you know my nigga's coming down, and . . . And I was like, am I hearing things? You know, she wasn't saying it in a derogatory way, but I'm like, that's not a word you throw around . . . but the only thing I can say is, they get it from us. They hear us calling each other nigga this and nigga that like it's just a pastime, and they think, "Oh, new word, new slang word" rather than knowing the history and understanding. That's why I think education is impor-

tant; people really don't understand. Even people within the African American culture don't fully understand, or if they do understand, they brush it to the side, like that was then and this is now. And it's not . . . It's ignorant. We've had that discussion in our group, where people say, "Well, it means something different now." Well, just because you say it means something different still doesn't take away the original definition of the word. If I say the F word doesn't mean F you anymore, it doesn't make it any better. Just like people calling each other, you know, bitches . . . that doesn't make it any better . . . I don't understand it personally. But that's just me, and there are a lot of people who'll disagree with me.

Most educational institutions have policies and consequences about the use of racial slurs and insults. This is understandable and necessary in a school context where both young people and adults need to know what the limits are, and in particular students need to know what behaviors incur disciplinary consequences and what behaviors do not. Racial labeling and slurs hurt people, as does physical violence, and therefore schools and colleges must have policies about their use; educators should also be prepared to address such behavior when it occurs (see, e.g., Thompson, 2004; Luttrell, 2008).

However, educators can also engage students in inquiry projects to learn how language involving racial labels is used in different contexts. Such projects do not condone the hurtful use of racial slurs, but rather seek to educate students about language, social variation, and power (Gillespie, 2010). Similarly, while we teach children not to throw rocks at other people or property, we still teach them geology!

The process of changing a term's social meaning from negative to positive can be carried out by those originally the object of the slur or insult. This process is called ***appropriation***. Writing about the term "nigga," Moses and Mukhopadhyay say "by taking a negatively charged word and appropriating it for themselves and for their *own* use, it is first neutralized and eventually comes to be used in a positive way as a 'core blackness' or authenticity that African Americans reaffirm among themselves. It is taboo for a non-African American person to use it" (1997, p. 95).

Other words that used to be and still are slurs have been similarly appropriated. Nam describes this process in relation to the word "yellow" as a slur against Asian people:

> It is the radical act of reclaiming and redefining the word yellow that thrills me. . . . "Yellow" takes on a new meaning. Old newspapers, magazines, and travelogues reveal phrases like "yellow peril," "yellow-face," and "yellow-skins," which remind us of the ways in which "yellow" has historically been linked to negative stereotypes of Asians. Society has reinforced these images, pushing Asian Americans to the periphery in all areas of our culture. "Yellow" has been used to define skin color (even though Asian skin comes in a wide variety of colors and hues), and carries with it other racist assumptions. On our

terms, however, the hyphenated "yell-oh" does not define or create barriers between Asian Americans. Simply put, the term "YELL-Oh" is a call to action. (Nam, 2001, p. xxviii)

This excerpt illustrates not only that insulting terms can be redefined and reclaimed by the group that was originally the object of the insult, but also that the meaning attributed to words is always context dependent. The context, or larger social situation, determines how a particular utterance functions. Thus, the same label might at one time be a slur that demeans a person as a member of a separate, racialized group (e.g., "you ——s are all alike."); at other times, the same label might be used in a "scientific" way to examine data related to different groups ("——s are not performing as well in school as ——s"); at other times, the same label might be used to affirm a positive sense of within-group identity ("Let's affirm the contributions of ——s to U.S. society"). And finally, the same label can be used to talk about the label itself (e.g., "The term —— seems to be shifting."). The only way to know what a racial label really means to speakers and listeners is to study the context in which it is used and observe how people react to it.

In addition to terms changing their meaning depending on who says them and in what context, other labels may be discarded and replaced with new terms to reflect a new social consciousness or "political correctness." Consider the changes in the past fifty years or so in the use of terms like "Negro," "Black," "African American," and "Caucasian," or the shifting usage of "illegal aliens," "illegal immigrants," and "undocumented workers." Teacher-supervised inquiry projects about how labels and slurs are used in everyday life can reveal a great deal about the society we live in and the ever-changing cultures we construct. Labeling behavior and slurs are like a lens that helps us "see" social relations among different groups and how people use language to reinforce, contest, and change existing relations. Language-in-use is like a two-way mirror—it reflects back to us what is, the existing status quo of social relations and power dynamics.

But it also constructs those very relations as we speak. When we say that somebody is Latino, or African American, or White, or Caucasian, we construct for those who listen to us a social world in which these words stand for meaningful categories and contrasts. By using the words, we affirm the reality of the categories they stand for. Some social scientists say that if we want to change the way people think about the social world around them, one thing we can do is to change the words we use to categorize and describe people. Even if that doesn't completely change the way they think, it at least raises questions, disturbs conventional ways of thinking and perceiving, and presents an alternative way to think about and use language (Briscoe, Arriaza, & Henze, 2009). According to linguist George Lakoff, "Because language activates [conceptual] frames, new language is required for new frames. Thinking differently requires speaking differently" (2004, p. xv).

Take, for example, the changes in the last several decades in gendered language. "Chairman" with its male bias was changed to "chairperson" or just "chair." "Stewardess" with its female bias became "flight attendant." Likewise, labels for U.S. racial and ethnic groups have also changed over time, as we saw in part II. Terms like "Mongoloid," "mulatto," "octaroon," "half-breed," "Negroid," "Hindoo," and "Oriental" were once common labels, often used in census categories. Terms for African Americans have included "colored," "Negro," "Black," "Afro-American," and recently "African American." Surprisingly, the term "Caucasian" is still in use as a word meaning White or European American, but as Mukhopadhyay (2012) points out, it is a relic of the old pseudoscientific racial categories invented in the 19th century.

CONCLUSION

As people become more aware of the negative connotations of such terms, or of their outmoded and inaccurate representation of reality, they can make a conscious effort to change their language. Gradually, changes take hold and become encoded in the policies of publishing companies, airlines, newspapers, schools, and so forth. Now, when we think about a person who chairs a meeting, most of us don't automatically think of a man. And we're surprised if someone uses the term "Negro." Language reflects culture, but people also change language as a way to actively construct and change culture and shift the power relations represented in our language.

Similarly, the organizations on campuses that reflect categories of identity—such as the Filipino/a Club, the Black Students organization, the Muslim Students Association—all can become the focus of inquiry. The landscape of campus identities is a constructed landscape, not a natural one. As students embrace multiple ethnic and racial and other identities, so the organizations on campuses need to change to reflect identities that are meaningful today.

REFLECTIVE QUESTIONS

• What is the history behind the categories of assemblies and clubs at your school or college? What groups are included? Who is excluded? What assumptions are evident in the way your school/college organizes these events and clubs? What do you think people learn from these classifications? Is this learning explicitly taught or implicitly acquired? (In other words, do people just pick it up from the environment?)

- Has your school or college experienced conflicts over special events dedicated to particular racial or ethnic groups? If so, what were the underlying issues? Did conflicts that didn't start out being about race end up becoming racialized? Why do you think this happened?
- If your school or campus has ethnic clubs, how are the borders of those clubs managed? Is everyone welcome, or are some people less welcome?
- Can you imagine a different way to organize assemblies and clubs at your school or college? What message would this reclassification send to people at your school, and how would it differ from the message they currently receive?
- How do you respond when you hear young people using the "N-word"? Is it ever okay for them to use this word? Why or why not?
- Can changing labels change the way we think about people? Is changing language enough to change social relations? Or must these language changes be tied to broader changes in policies, laws, or economic conditions?

KEY CONCEPTUAL POINTS

- The organization of events and clubs by race or ethnicity seems natural, but isn't. The categories reflect the institution's implicit microculture and local community history.
- Racial classification systems reflected in assemblies, clubs, and racial labels teach us to "see" race in a certain way and affirm it as important. They also teach us which groups are invisible or unraced.
- Racial classification systems can be changed to reflect more complex identities—that is, if people want to change them and can exert enough power and influence to do so.
- Conflicts involving racial or ethnic events and clubs can reflect resistance to categories but may also reinforce group boundaries.
- Nonracial conflicts associated with special events and clubs can quickly become racialized.
- Language both reflects and constructs the world, and can be a tool for changing social relations.
- Appropriation of negative labels can be a tool for self- and group empowerment.
- The meaning of words and utterances (including racial labels) is always dependent on the context.

KEY TERMS (ITALICIZED AND BOLDED IN TEXT)

assimilation

pluralism
appropriation
microculture
racialized conflict
resistance and advocacy
agency

ACTIVITIES

Activity Plan 1: Investigating Events and Clubs

Objectives:

- Identify campus events and clubs that have a racial or ethnic basis.
- Identify and explain problems with these events or clubs in terms of who is included or excluded, and how well or poorly they reflect the actual student population.
- Explain that the categories of events and clubs are not natural, and that they are created by people for certain purposes, such as compensating for past "invisibility" of minority groups.
- Explain that because they are created by people, they can also be changed by people.
- Articulate what they would change about these events/clubs, and create a prioritized list of those changes.

Other Information: This activity requires two class sessions, about forty-five minutes each, with possibility of an extension project (student survey) that continues for several weeks. Materials needed include whiteboard, markers, chart paper, an official list of yearly special events at the school, and a list of student clubs, if they exist.

Procedure:

Step 1. Ask participants to create a list of on-campus assemblies and clubs. Facilitator or teacher creates two *unlabeled* columns on the board: (1) clubs and events not ethnically or racially specific and (2) those that *are* ethnically or racially specific. Facilitator fills them in from participants' list but does not reveal the title of either column.

Step 2. Participants guess the difference between the two columns.

Step 3. Ask participants to get into groups of three or four, and tell them they should choose people who have the same or similar race/ethnicity as themselves. Ask each group to discuss the following questions (each group should have a facilitator, note taker, presenter, and time keeper). Allow fifteen minutes:

   a. Is there an annual event and/or club at this school or college that is specifically for your ethnic or racial group? What is it?
   b. Do you belong to this group or participate in this event? Why or why not?
   c. Do you know of other people who would like to be part of this group, but don't feel comfortable? If so, why do you think they are uncomfortable?
   d. Who are these events or clubs for (in other words, who benefits)? The insiders? The outsiders? Anybody else?
   e. Do you think the events/clubs that are *for* this group actually do a good job representing the diversity of this group of people? Why or why not?

Step 4. Reconvene class; groups present findings.

Step 5. Ask participants if they noticed any patterns in different presentations. (For example, groups have problems distinguishing who "fits" and who doesn't, or some groups aren't represented in events or clubs, while others are.)

Step 6. Ask participants: How did these come to be? Who created them? Why? Some suggestions might be "They're just natural, they represent the groups that are here," and so on. Facilitator can point out that "We heard that the groups don't fit all the people who are here, and that sometimes people feel excluded . . . so that means they are not simply 'natural.'" Eventually, facilitator should state explicitly the main point of the lesson: that social divisions (clubs) are cultural and historical inventions, organized the way some people think human beings in this school should be classified. We could in theory have clubs for tall people, short people, people with long hair, and so forth. But we don't organize ourselves that way. Why not? And who decides? Are these events organized top down by administrators, or do students decide?

Step 7. Ask participants, if we wanted to change something about these events or clubs, could we do it? What would we have to do to change it? (You may want to discuss issues of power involved in change.)

Step 8. Organize participants into groups of three or four, making sure groups are as diverse as possible, racially and ethnically. Give each group a set of questions (allow twenty minutes).

   a. What do you like about the way the school organizes events and clubs by racial or ethnic group?

b. What do you *not* like about the way the school/college organizes events and clubs by racial or ethnic group?
c. What do you think should be changed? Why? Make a list of the things your group thinks should be changed.
d. Now, prioritize your list (first priority, second, etc.).

Step 9. Group presenters post their priority lists on the board. Participants compare responses. Note similarities and differences, and discuss reasons for differences.

Step 10. Facilitator asks, do you think it is possible for us to come up with one priority list that the whole class can agree on? If participants feel they can, they should go ahead and make the priority list. If they don't think they can (because of deep divisions on some issue), then make sure each group understands why other groups feel the way they do. This becomes an activity to either build consensus, and/or to develop understanding of other perspectives.

Assessment Activities

Choose one or a combination:

1. Write a reflection (one to two pages) about your thoughts and feelings about the past two class sessions.
2. Conversation with a nonclass member: Tell a friend, acquaintance, or parent what was discussed in the two class sessions and get their reaction. Write down what the person said and share this with the class. This serves two purposes—it helps participants recall the main points of the class sessions and helps disseminate key concepts beyond this classroom.

Extension Activity

Participants develop a short questionnaire to find out how other students feel about campus events or clubs. Design survey questions and pilot questions; decide who will answer the questionnaire (sampling). Administer questionnaire; analyze results; discuss results in class; share results with student leadership, faculty, and administrators. Develop recommendations for change.

ADDITIONAL ACTIVITY IDEAS

Activity Idea 1: Collecting and Analyzing Data on Racial Slurs and Racial Labels

This inquiry-based activity involves students in studying the use of racial slurs and racial labels at their own school or college. By doing collaborative research, they will discover patterns in the way slurs and labels are used and why people use them (for example, to signal group identity, to delineate power relations, to draw a line between insiders and outsiders, etc.). They will see that racial labels and slurs reflect their school's own social structure. Finally, they will begin to articulate their position on slurs and labels and see how they can interrupt current labeling practices and propose alternatives. Requires about three class sessions of fifty minutes each, with two or three days in between to collect data. For a detailed plan, see the book's website, http://understandingrace.org/resources/for_teachers.html.

Activity Idea 2: Explore the Teaching Tolerance Website

This website http://www.tolerance.org contains many classroom activities focused on addressing racism, sexism, and other "isms" in the classroom. One can also order teaching kits and handbooks. One classroom activity is called "Facing the N Word" by Kathryn Knecht. The author explains how she handles the use of slurs in literature at http://www.tolerance.org/teach/.

NOTES

1. It's interesting to note that the rise of ethnic clubs and assemblies in the 1960s followed the disputes that took place in the 1950s over the expression of religion in public schools (mainly characterized by Jewish groups protesting the many expressions of Christianity in both curriculum and extracurricular activities).

2. All school-based examples in this chapter are drawn from original data collected by Henze, Katz, Norte, Sather, & Walker (1999). Pseudonyms are used for both individuals and schools.

Chapter Thirteen

"Interracial" Dating

How is the social construction of race manifested in the kinds of choices and pressures young people experience when they consider who is an attractive partner? A partner for a long-term relationship? A partner for marriage? Building on the content of chapter 9, this chapter takes up these questions in the context of contemporary schools and colleges, with a focus on the United States

In chapter 9, we showed how cultures regulate mating and marriage either by discouraging marriage outside their group or by encouraging it—or some combination along this continuum. In the United States, the prevention of interracial dating, mating, and marriage was one way that the visible differences we call "race" were preserved, both by legal measures and by social pressures. By marrying and having children with someone of your own ethnic or racial group (*endogamy*), it is likely that your children will look somewhat like you and your spouse, and you and your family will thereby fit the physical features that make people of your ethnic or racial group look similar. In this respect, we can say that culture has an influence on the biological traits your children inherit. In other words, the specific culture of mating and marriage, by imposing restrictions on whom you can mate with or marry, shapes the way people look across generations. In a group that restricts marriage to endogamous couples, the population's visible markers of racial identity are reinforced and people of a different ethnicity or "race" whose genes would introduce some minor and superficial physical differences are screened out. As we saw in chapters 8 and 9, endogamy was used in U.S. history as a way to maintain a system of racial stratification in which Euro-Americans were the dominant group.

This chapter focuses on the contemporary educational settings in which young people navigate "fluid, intermingled, and often conflicting" cross-currents of peer group, familial, and institutional pressures regarding what type of person to date, or whether to date at all (Hemmings, 2004, p. 5). Dating, as we noted in chapter 10, is one of the "trigger issues" that can lead to racial conflicts in educational settings. The goal of this chapter is to articulate how the social construction of race in the United States influences the decisions and dilemmas which young people experience about flirting, dating, and mating. We focus on how cultural and institutional norms influence young people's choices and pressures to date (or not date) certain people. But we also highlight resistance and agency, showing how young people are currently changing or "bending" the status quo of race relations (Pollock, 2004b; Roberts et al., 2008) because they do not always fit, or want to fit, into static categories of identity. Ultimately, this chapter should help readers see how particular struggles around dating people who are of a different "race" are a part of the larger—and continually changing—social construction of race.

CONCEPTUAL BACKGROUND

The Language of Interracial Dating

Before we delve into current trends in dating across racial or ethnic groups, we need to raise critical questions about the very terms used to describe relationships across different population groups—terms like "interracial" and "mixed." Unfortunately, the English language has not yet developed widely accepted terms that can easily and quickly convey the complexity of our incredibly commingled genetic and cultural human history. Both terms assume that races are real biological entities with clear boundaries, and that people must be one or the other, or some type of "mongrelized" version (mixed). Terms like "interracial" and "mixed" assume that there are people who are not "mixed" and who must therefore be "pure." But pure what? Given the intermating among populations that has occurred since human history began, the idea of such purity is absurd!

Young people are challenging these terms more and more, even as they continue to struggle with the outmoded systems of classification that they encounter, both formally and informally. A common question heard on middle, high school, and college campuses today is "What are you mixed with?" (Pollock, 2004b). While this question still uses the term "mixed," it also succeeds in normalizing mixture as the default condition; that is, it assumes that the addressee *is* mixed with at least two or more entities. This stands in stark opposition to earlier uses of the term "mixed" which implied impurity or deficiency—a status to be ashamed of, akin to the term "mongrelized."

What do people mean when they say they are in an "interracial relationship"? Usually, what they mean is that the partners look physically different in terms of skin color and other superficial markers of race, and that they have different cultural or possibly religious backgrounds. But these definitions of "mixed" have changed and are continuing to evolve. For instance, a marriage between a Jewish person and a Protestant, both of them Euro-American and light-skinned, probably would not be called "interracial" these days, although it would involve some discussion, at least, about who performs the ritual and where it takes place. However, a marriage of two people of the same religion, but different visible markers of racial identity, would probably be called "interracial." It is clear that the old biological boxes based on superficial physical features like skin color and hair texture, as well as ancestry and culture, are still being used today to delineate and police the boundaries of marriage and dating, but they are no longer taken for granted. Young people challenge the old categorizations every day through the use of terms like "Latinegra" and "Japapino" (Pollock, 2004a) and through questions that assume that everyone is mixed. They use language to not only reflect social reality but also to register a challenge to the old system and begin to construct a new social categorization system. This back and forth, strategic use of old as well as new ways of categorizing groups of people is what Pollock calls *race bending*. It is a great example of the culturally constructed and evolving nature of classification systems, and how people can exert their *sense of agency* to change them to suit various purposes (see chapter 6). However, we have to remember that the young people who are practicing race bending do not (yet) have the institutional power to completely do away with the old classifications. We live with multiple systems that operate simultaneously at different levels—from informal systems that seem to fit the here and now, to very formalized systems such as the ones used by the U.S. Census, or by school districts when they track data on how various racialized groups are doing academically, or by colleges and universities as they keep track of who their students are and whether their campus is as welcoming to a diverse clientele as it claims to be.

ARE MARRIAGE TRENDS THE SAME AS DATING TRENDS?

As discussed in chapter 9, we know from U.S. Census data that the general trend toward intermarriage is increasing (Lee & Bean, 2004). However, we also know that the rates of increase are different across so-called racial groups, with marriages between European American and African American showing the smallest increases. It is unclear whether the same "raced" patterns apply as well to dating. Some studies show that interracial cohabitation rates are higher than those for marriage (Ford, Sohn, & Lepkowski, 2003; Lichter et al., 2011). This might suggest that dating across racial lines is even more common, as people see dating as a time of experimentation.

A very interesting trend which shows up in the Latino population is that while intergroup marriage rates between Latino and other groups were on an upward trend prior to the 1990s, the rate of intermarriage declined in the 1990s. While one might assume that this is due to the large increases in the Latino population and hence a larger pool of "coethnic partners," Lichter, Carmalt, and Zhenchao et al.'s multivariate analysis from 1995–2008 discovered that another explanation fits the data much better. They looked at first-, second-, and third-generation immigrants to see if they could find differences among the marriage patterns of these three generations. The drop in intermarriage, they find, is due to "abrupt increases in intermarriage between the second and third generations of Hispanics" (Lichter et al., 2011, p. 258). In other words, second-generation Latinos are marrying immigrant Latinos rather than third-generation Latinos or "whites." Meanwhile, third-generation Latinos continue to marry other third-generation Latinos or whites. "[E]vidence of declining Hispanic-white intermarriage is perhaps suggestive of a newly emerging social and cultural isolation of the foreign-born Hispanic stock[1] in the United States. At a minimum, recent patterns of intermarriage imply an unprecedented 'demographic pause' in the incorporation of America's new second generation of Hispanics" (Lichter et al., 2011, p. 260).

Keeping in mind that trends in intergroup marriage probably imply even stronger trends in intergroup dating, we turn now to the role played by educational institutions in fostering or restricting dating across "racial" lines.

INSTITUTIONAL PRESSURES AND OPPORTUNITIES

As McPherson et al. (2001) point out, "Relationship formation is strongly rooted in space" (p. 5), and thus the typical coeducational school or college in the United States provides an important source of potential mates. Schools and colleges are physical places where friendships are formed. More intimate relationships are also formed, developed, and perhaps consummated through sex, commitments to date only one person, engagements, births, and so forth. Relationship formation is also rooted in time. The amount of time students spend on campus each week, as well as the fact that they usually attend for at least four years with a cohort of same-age peers, makes it very likely that many young people find both friendship and intimate relationship material in school or college.[2]

SCHOOL INTEGRATION AND INTERRACIAL DATING

Schools in the United States used to be racially segregated. This meant that the potential mates a student might meet in school were going to be of the same "race" and usually the same socioeconomic class and religion, because schools, especially in the North, where Jim Crow laws were not operative, were neighborhood based. Residential segregation based on economic status and race was and remains the norm. So schools didn't become sites where interracial mating and dating was even an issue until intentional school integration took place.

With the end of legalized school segregation (*Brown v. Board of Education*, 1954), schools had to accommodate an influx of racially diverse and economically diverse students—primarily African American and European American, since this was prior to large-scale non-European immigration. To accomplish integration, students in large-city school districts were bussed from distant neighborhoods. But little else was done to ensure that students of different "races" (as well as other lines of difference) got to know each other. It was assumed that simply placing them in the same schools would suffice to develop positive interracial friendships. In fact, this assumption turned out to be false, since schools that had been integrated continued practices such as tracking, which segregated diverse students within the school. Thus, actual opportunities for diverse students to get to know one another on a personal level were—and continue to be—less available than is commonly assumed (Fine, Weis, & Powell, 1997; Carter 2013).

A similar assumption is that an integrated environment will lead to students dating more across racial groups. But does an integrated environment necessarily lead to more interracial dating? Some support for this thesis is found in a national study by Ford et al. (2003), which looked at the effects of residential community on partner choice, including the likelihood of choosing partners of a different ethnic or racial group. The authors note that partner choice seems to be affected by whether that community is residentially segregated, as well as how accepting the community is of interethnic or interracial dating. They suggest that the immediately local community may constrain adolescent partner choices even more than adult partner choices because adolescents often are less mobile than adults. A more recent study of 347 ninth- and twelfth-grade students in U.S. high schools in the Mid-Atlantic region found that students with high intergroup contact tended to have more cross-race friendships as well as experiences with cross-race dating. According to the authors, these associations were not due to students' perceptions of parental attitudes for or against intergroup friendships and dating. Rather, the data show that "intergroup contact rather than perceptions of parents' attitudes were likely to have facilitated the development of these relationships" (Edmonds & Killen, 2009, p. 16).

However, institutional restrictions may dampen or limit the positive effects of a superficially integrated environment. In the next section we turn to specific examples of recent school policies regarding proms.

DATING POLICIES AND PROMS—FACILITATING OR
RESTRICTING RACIAL INTEGRATION?

While the *Loving v. Virginia* case finally lifted the last legal national restriction on interracial marriage in 1967, this legal decision did not mean that social and cultural change immediately took hold across the country. In some cases, educational institutions held on to explicit restrictions against interracial dating until very recently. For example, one conservative Christian college in South Carolina, Bob Jones University, made headlines in 2000 when its president finally decided to lift the institution's five-decades-long ban on interracial dating (CNN, 2000).

High school proms are one of the most institutionalized and public ways in which society's attitudes about interracial relationships are played out. Though many people believe that ethnic/racial identity doesn't or shouldn't make any difference in matters of love, in some parts of the country, stark racial lines have remained until quite recently. In February 1994, the Euro-American principal at Randolph County High School in Alabama called an assembly of seniors and juniors.

> The school's student body was 62% white and 38% black. Holand Humphries, who had been principal for 25 years, asked if anyone was planning on attending the prom "with someone who was not of the same race." When several students indicated that they were planning to do just that, the principal threatened to cancel the event. The junior class president, ReVonda Bowen, whose father is white and mother is black, asked the principal what his order meant for her. The principal allegedly replied that Bowen's parents had made a "mistake" and that he hoped to prevent others from doing the same.
>
> Community condemnation was swift. Parents organized demonstrations and called for a boycott of classes. In response, about one fifth of the high school students did not attend classes for several days. Although the principal withdrew his threat of canceling the prom, he was suspended with pay by a four-to-two vote from the local school board. Bowen's parents filed a civil rights lawsuit for the degrading comments their daughter endured. Even still, there were some white parents who applauded the principal's strict approach, and Humphries was reinstated two weeks later. (Cruz & Berson, 2001, pp. 4–5)

What is particularly interesting in this example is the pushback from not only students but also parents and community. We can see the tension between the old racial order, represented by the principal, and the generational changes that are taking place. Several students in interracial relationships were planning to go, and some, like ReVonda Bowen, were from interracial families. The fact that there was enough outcry to suspend the principal shows the power of people's collective agency to demand change. The fact that the principal was reinstated two weeks later, under pressure from a group of

European American parents, shows the continuing manipulation and use of power by those who continue to wield it.

In Georgia in 2002, Taylor County High School held the school's first-ever integrated prom. But in 2003, African American students learned that a group of Euro-American students were planning a "Whites only" prom at a private club (Williams, 2003). The White students went ahead and held the separate prom, although later, a more inclusive event was held, which some of the same students also attended (Hightower, 2003).

In 2013, at Wilcox County High School, Georgia students were raising money to hold the school's first integrated prom. Despite the fact that the school was integrated thirty years ago, proms have been separate (African American and European American) until 2013. Again, it is worth noting that the movement to make the prom integrated came from students (Gumbrecht, 2013).

Perhaps these instances seem extreme to people in some other parts of the country. The South, after all, is the region with the deepest legacy of slavery. But the South is also a part of "us," and the history of race relations in the South is part of our collective history as Americans. Most proms across the country became integrated many years ago, and it seems that in the examples cited above, it is parents, not students, who have held out for segregated proms.

Proms, according to Best (2000), "are a central part of the larger process of schooling, in which kids make sense of who they are and where they are" (p. 137). Because they are the culminating social event for many high school students, they take on many layers of significance. Through the negotiations over music and other decisions that must take place as proms are organized, racial, class, and other identities are reinforced and sometimes challenged. Proms are fraught with inequality, with some paid for by the school; others paid for by students themselves. Some students cannot afford to attend; others simply refuse to go because they do not see a place for themselves in the prom, which is often cast as a reflection of White privilege. In some high schools, faculty have raised funds to buy prom outfits for students who cannot otherwise afford to attend prom. Others have organized donations of used prom clothing and then taken low-income students "shopping" to get an outfit. All of these efforts show how important proms are as a symbolic ritual that reflects social classifications, both past and future.

FAMILIAL AND PEER GROUP ATTITUDES

Another factor that may influence young people's dating choices is of course parental or familial attitudes and restrictions. In some cases, such restrictions are the province of an entire extended family, not only the nuclear parental unit. Thus, in studying the pressures young people face regarding dating, it is important to look beyond the nuclear parents to understand where pressures originate. Many psychological studies make the mistake of assuming that a nuclear parental unit of mother and father is the only important source of attitudes and restrictions regarding dating. This ignores the fact that young people from diverse cultural backgrounds might have many other kin who are involved in shaping the partner choices of the family's next generation. Furthermore, some families might for religious or other reasons insist on a "no dating" policy for their children. For example, some Hindu, conservative Christian, Muslim, and orthodox Jewish families try to avoid unnecessary intermingling of adolescent females with males (Khan, 2009). Thus, educators need to bear in mind that not all adolescents are going to date, whether due to family or religious restrictions or the individual's own preference.

A misplaced focus on the traditional nuclear family also ignores the growing number of "nontraditional" families consisting, for example, of a single parent; a blended family in which the children of former marriages now live with a parent plus stepmother or stepfather; or two same-sex parents. In some parts of the country, the term "nontraditional" is almost meaningless, since the majority of families do not consist of the biological mother, father, and their children.

In their survey of high school students (mentioned earlier), Edmonds and Killen reported that parents tended to be more direct with their adolescent children on questions of cross-race dating compared to cross-race friendships:

> [P]arents might be uncomfortable discouraging a cross-race friendship, which is essentially harmless, for fear that it would make them appear racist. Rather than focus on race as a reason, they turn to concerns with safety or make negative comments or jokes as an indirect means of discouragement. This is a safe and indirect route to take without being overtly opposed to the relationship. Dating, on the other hand, might be too salient a relationship to ignore and to push to a subconscious level. (Edmonds & Killen, 2009, p. 17)

However, most students in the study reported that they made their own decisions. Some of them said they chose not to bring cross-race dates home, "but they insisted that they did what they wanted despite their parents' disapproval" (Edmonds & Killen, 2009, p. 18). The students who experienced the most vulnerability to parents' disapproving messages were those who did not have a high level of intergroup contact (e.g., friendships, social activities, and other casual contact across groups). Thus, Edmonds and Killen suggest that high levels of intergroup contact act as a kind of buffer that allows young people to see that there is a normalized, everyday reality of intergroup relationships; they hypothesize that this reality outside the home allows them to be less influenced by parental opposition, compared to students who do not have a lot of intergroup contact.

In another study, interracial couples on a college campus were asked to share other people's perceptions about their relationship. Ten college couples were interviewed, all of them consisting of a "White" partner and an "African American" partner (however, one male was actually from Kenya). This college campus was 90 percent "Caucasian" and was located in a rural area in the midwestern United States. The authors found that the only negative perceptions these couples experienced came from older people (their grandparents' generation), young African American women, and family members who grew up in the South. One member of a couple stated the following: "I'd say with an elderly crowd it's a lot more awkward because they're not used to it as much" (Rose & Firmin, 2013, p. 78). In explaining these perceptions, the authors note that the "older people" referred to in the study grew up prior to the civil rights era and may hold on to old racist attitudes.

African American women sometimes provided negative feedback about white women dating African American men, as this African American male comments:

> We've [he and his "Caucasian" girlfriend] been to some places, a mall where some African-American girls looked at her really funny. African-American women tend to be a little more vicious toward that kind of circumstance. They'd feel that a Caucasian woman, if she's dating a black guy, that she's taking a black guy, a good black guy from an African-American woman. So I'm kind of taken off the market by somebody I shouldn't be taken off the market by. (Rose & Firmin, 2013, p. 79)

This point may be related to high rates of death and imprisonment among Black males in this country, which makes it difficult for African American women to find eligible African American men as partners. Also, because African American women have higher educational levels than African American men, choosing a same-race partner may mean choosing someone with a lower educational level or job status (Moran, 2001).

Finally, several couples noted that family members who were from the South tended to exhibit more negative feedback toward the interracial couple, and that the couple would not consider living in the South because of its history of racial tensions.

One of the main recommendations coming from this study is that if administrators of college campuses wish to normalize interracial dating, they need to show the campus community evidence that this is the case. For example, they can enhance opportunities for interethnic mingling, invite a panel of speakers who are in interracial relationships, show posters of interracial couples, and so on (Rose & Firman, 2013).

GENDER-RACE DYNAMICS IN DATING

A number of gendered racial stereotypes operate in the sphere of dating and intimate relationships. When we think about the general trend toward more "interracial dating," it doesn't mean that males and females are dating randomly across racial lines. In Yon's study (2000), female African Americans claimed that African American boys went out with White girls because they perceived them as "easier" than Black girls. Espiritu (2001) found that Filipino families counsel their daughters not to be like White girls who "sleep around." The myth of Black male hypersexuality is well known, and also cultivated by some of the rappers. Asian women are said to be "hyperfeminine" (Moran, 2001). These sexual stereotypes exert a powerful influence on people's choices in both dating and marriage. For example, the rate of marriage between European American men and "Asian" women in the United States far exceeds that of "Asian" men and European American women. If this lopsided pattern is at least partially related to male partners' attraction to a "hyperfeminine" and "submissive" woman, then one wonders whether progress in breaking racial barriers in marriage is nonetheless tied to another form of unequal power relations.

SAME-SEX RELATIONSHIPS AND RACE

So far, we have been discussing heterosexual relationships. What about same-sex relationships that cross ethnic or racialized boundaries? Do gay and lesbian partners experience the same racialized dynamics as straight partners?

In Morrison's 2013 study of gay and lesbian relationships on college campuses, 44 percent of the respondents reported that they had dated or been in an intimate relationship with someone of a different race/ethnicity. Morrison points out that being in an interracial relationship may add a layer of complexity, and that gay and lesbian college students may avoid such relationships because they do not feel ready to deal with negotiating potential differences based on cultural values, expectations, and so on.

According to one young man who identifies as Cuban and Black, tensions related to race and ethnicity are just as common in gay relationships as in straight ones. This may surprise some people because they expect people in the gay community to be very accepting of others given that they have had to struggle to be accepted themselves.

> The first time I ever was excluded from someone's list of dating possibilities based upon my cultural backgrounds was about a year ago. I had just recently come out, and to celebrate my newfound pride in being gay, I wanted to share it with someone special—a boyfriend! Being that I was only 17, I didn't have

access to many gay people besides those who worked with me at the mall. There was no place that I could meet guys like myself, so I started to meet them online (as do many gay teenagers). I talked to one guy for three days. We had a lot in common, but once we exchanged pictures he had an immediate problem. He said that he only dated other white guys. That hurt a lot and it was the first time that I ever felt like I wasn't good enough for someone to be with because of the color of my skin. —"Nickolas," 2005

Nickolas attributes the prejudice he experienced to two things—people's tendency to want to be with others who have similar background and experiences because it makes them feel more comfortable, and secondly, to the degree of openness to other cultures and ethnicities in your family of origin.

Although it may be true that same-sex partners encounter the same pressures and conflicts regarding interracial relationships as straight people do, communities and families differ greatly in their acceptance of openly gay children. Marlon Riggs's video, *Black Is . . . Black Ain't* (1994), describes his own journey of gaining acceptance as a gay man in an African American community ridden with homophobia. In communities that are less accepting of homosexuality, gay people tend to stay "in the closet" more and are therefore not available as potential partners in interracial relationships. This is confirmed by Morrison's study, which found that European American students "were significantly more 'out' to immediate family, extended family, and close straight friends at the time they completed the survey than were respondents of other racial/ethnic self-identifications" (2013, p. 105). Thus, when we interpret statistical analyses of the rates of interracial relationships among same-sex partners, we need to recognize that societal prejudice and homophobia have already skewed the data.

THE INTERNET AND CELL PHONE TECHNOLOGIES

Given the ubiquity of the Internet, social networking, and cell phone use, we wondered whether any studies have been done to investigate how these technologies are affecting intergroup dating. Does the use of these technologies open up more possibilities for intergroup dating among young people? The dominant view promoted by the technology industry is that the Internet promotes diversity because it increases the opportunities for contact with people from different backgrounds and, with regard to dating sites, it reduces the influence of third parties such as parents or other family members (Schwartz, 2013, p. 8). However, Schwartz observes that in the literature on Internet dating, people's stated preferences for mates are very similar to the actual matches that occur in the general population. This suggests that Internet dating may not change people's preferences for within-group or intergroup dating. However, a third possibility is that the new technologies may actually *increase* the tendency to date within one's group. Cell phones and social networking sites such as Facebook enhance the ability of individuals to stay in touch with old friends, and as a result "may have lengthened the reach of schools as marriage markets further into adulthood" (Ellison et al., cited in Schwartz, 2013, p. 8). The jury is still out, but clearly more studies need to be done to delve into the relationship between these new technologies and intergroup dating.

THE STRATEGIC NATURE OF RACE TALK

Not surprisingly, the topic of interracial dating is highly sensitive to context. The responses one gets depend on how the questions are asked and in what circumstances. Asking students about the relevance of race to their dating preferences often results in students denying that race is important at all. Interviewers may think they are getting accurate information about what students really believe, but such talk is often constructed for strategic purposes—that is, to create a certain impression with the interviewer or the others who may be listening in (Pollock, 2004a).

People will usually say what they think is socially desirable at the moment, in that context. Given the ideology that in the United States race shouldn't matter, it is not surprising that students will often produce the socially desirable answer. In addition, public statements about interracial dating may differ from private beliefs (Yon, 2000). Nonetheless, ideology is important, and the present ideology that race shouldn't matter in one's dating and marriage choices represents a huge shift from the past, as seen in chapter 9.

One way to mitigate the problem of the ***socially desirable answer*** is through ethnographic studies of young people in their schools and communities. ***Ethnography***, a cultural anthropological approach to doing research involving fieldwork, immersion in a culture, participant-observation, and an emphasis on "native" perspective, is a particularly rich vehicle for understanding how students are "navigating the cross-currents" of interracial relationships. Several ethnographic studies have included a focus on interracial dating (Best, 2000; Hemmings, 2004; Yon, 2000).

"CROSS-CURRENTS" THAT YOUNG PEOPLE MIGHT NEED TO "NAVIGATE"

Young people who are trying to sort out the multiplicity of opinions and pressures that surround interracial dating might hear the following messages from parents, other family members, or peers:

- *Sticking to Your "Own Kind" Is Better Because Greater Understanding Is Possible.* Crossing boundaries by engaging in interracial relationships invites trouble and misunderstanding because cultures are different. In statements of this kind, "culture is imagined as acting upon people and setting the terms for who can belong and who cannot" (Yon, 2000, p. 109). By saying that it's preferable to date someone of your own culture, avoiding people of other races becomes an "innocent by product, a kind of racial coincidence. Cultural compatibility regularly leads to the selection of a spouse who happens to be of the same race" (Moran, 2001, p. 125).
- *Dating Someone of Another Race Will Create Conflict in the Family.* Students may be told that if they marry across racial lines, their children and grandchildren will suffer society's lingering prejudice. While students may or may not directly worry about their future children's experience of prejudice, they are often pressured by adult family members' concerns. According to Root (2002), European American family members often fear the loss of privileged status, while other ethnic groups' families may fear loss of cultural identity through assimilation.
- *Love Knows No Color.* In other words, love will overcome any racial or cultural differences (Yon, 2000). This statement, while representing an ideal of a "color-blind" society, is also very real to many people. Young people in particular often fervently advocate this position. However, as noted earlier, public statements of this kind may not reveal private feelings about particular relationships.
- *Interracial Relationships Can Start Out Being about Love, but Can Quickly Become Racialized.* A young African American woman in Yon's study (2000) gave a particularly telling example of this, pointing out that if she were in a relationship with an African American man, "Your man might slap you around the ears; that happens. But you know if a white guy raises his hand to me, well, it's like slavery all over again" (p. 110). The same behavior, which in the first instance is abusive and degrading, takes on additional meaning in the second situation, becoming a racialized (as well as gendered) act of abuse.
- *Try to Find Someone of Our Own Race but with a Lighter Skin Tone.* The preference to date people of lighter skin tone within one's own racial group, reminiscent of the **pigmentocracy** in the Caribbean, is called **shadeism** among some young people today (Yon, 2000). These preferences are heard in phrases like "nice skin" and "nice hair." In a high school class on Filipino American Heritage, Filipinas were discussing the pressures they felt from their older female relatives to maintain the lightest complexion possible so that they would be more "attractive" to potential husbands. Efforts to maintain a light skin tone even included bleaching the skin in some cases (Henze, 2001; David, 2013).

- *Girls of the Other Group Are "Easier"; Boys of the Other Group Have Bigger Penises or Are More Sexually Aggressive.* Sexual stereotypes in our society have become attached to certain racial groups and genders. As we noted earlier in this chapter, these stereotypes play a powerful role in shaping young people's ideas about who is "datable." Thus, European American males may be drawn to the stereotypical "hyperfemininity" or "submissiveness" of Asian females. Young African American men may believe in the stereotype that European American women are "easier" than African American women (Yon, 2000; Espiritu, 2001; Moran, 2001).
- *If You Date Someone of Another Race, You Are Betraying Your Race.* This is heard particularly among African American women, some of whom argue that when African American men date White women, they devalue Black womanhood (Edwards, 2002; Rose & Firmin, 2013). As we noted earlier in this chapter, high rates of death and imprisonment among African American males in this country are a possible explanation leading to a scarcity of eligible males (Moran, 2001).
- *Stay with Someone of Your Own Religion—or Class.* While these messages are not explicitly about race, they often end up being racial messages due to the racial stratification of class in the United States, and due to the tendency of religious congregations to be organized along racial and ethnic lines. However, there are also strong religious prohibitions against marrying someone of another religion, totally independent of race. These prohibitions occur within Christianity as well as among Muslims, Jews, Sikhs, Hindus, and so on.

With such a multiplicity of messages coming at young people, from all kinds of sources—parents, peers, the media—it is no wonder that young people struggle to sort out their own beliefs and actions with regard to dating across racial lines. A good example is found in the "Cafeteria Video" (see http://www.understandingrace.org/home.html). Given this broad range of messages, it would be normal to feel conflicted or ambivalent. But young people are not merely acted-upon, passive recipients of these conflicting messages. They are also active agents who daily transform these messages into new meanings that better fit—at least for the moment—their reality.

CONCLUSION

As young people continue to meet, flirt, date, have sex, and marry (not necessarily in that order), will the old racial lines fade, as some suggest? The research points toward two different conclusions. We saw in chapter 9 that interracial marriage is becoming more commonplace among all ethnic and racial groups, but it is increasing at a slower rate among African Americans and European Americans. Segregation by both class and race in educational institutions still limits to some extent our opportunity and willingness to meet, date, and marry someone of another racial group, and young people are still faced with conflicting messages from family and the media about what type of person is acceptable as a mate. Because of these conflicting messages, and the importance of sexuality and sexual identity in adolescence and young adulthood, intergroup dating is clearly a hot-button issue that is worth examining as part of the formal or informal curriculum in schools and colleges. As the next generation comes of age, they have the potential to make race less or more meaningful in partner selection, and in doing so, they act as cultural agents shaping the future of "race." Clearly, many if not most of the younger generation is already acting upon that potential. And a new generation of "multiracials" embodies through their very existence the challenge to outmoded racial classifications.

REFLECTIVE QUESTIONS

- If proms could still racially separate in Georgia in 2012, what does that mean for people in other parts of the United States? Would you attend a prom that was racially segregated? Why or why not?
- What terms do you hear in your community or school that describe people with mixed ancestry? Who uses these terms? Are they institutional terms that appear on official forms, or informal terms that are used to challenge traditional race categories? What does the term "interracial relationship" mean to you?
- In your school or college, are some types of interracial relationships more stigmatized or encouraged than others? In what ways does your school or college limit (subtly or explicitly) access to potential partners? What other peer pressures are there? Do students in your school or college date anyone regardless of race? How could you conduct research on this issue to get at people's real beliefs and behaviors rather than "socially desirable" answers?
- Which of the "cross-currents" messages (see last section before conclusion) do you hear in your community, school, or college? Who is sending these messages? Are the messages consistent, or conflicting? How do you respond?
- What patterns do you notice in terms of men of a certain racial identity dating certain racial groups more than others? For example, do you find it to be true that European American men tend to date Asian women, but Asian men are less likely to date European American women?

KEY CONCEPTUAL POINTS

- Mating and marriage are culturally regulated, explicitly and subtly, to preserve and strengthen the group (see also chapter 9).
- Terms such as "interracial" and "mixed" are themselves misnomers, implying there are "pure" races that then are "mixed." This is biological fiction.
- Young people frequently engage in "race bending"—both the strategic deployment of traditional race labels and creative use of new words and phrases to challenge old models.
- Interracial marriage (and presumably, dating) in the United States is increasing, but not all racial groups intermarry at the same rates. Black-White boundaries remain partially due to the legacy of history and class-based racial stratification. Furthermore, intermarriage and dating show gendered patterns in terms of preferences.
- Despite school integration, there is still considerable within-school segregation.
- Interracial homosexual relationships involve similar racial dynamics as in heterosexual relationships.

KEY TERMS (ITALICIZED AND BOLDED IN TEXT)

endogamy
race bending
sense of agency
ethnography
shadeism
pigmentocracy
socially desirable answer

ACTIVITIES

Activity Plan 1: Enforcing *Within* Group Dating versus Encouraging Intergroup Dating

Objectives: Participants will be able to

- explain that culture creates norms of what is an ideal mate, and that these norms are reinforced through parents, peers, laws, and religious texts; and
- explain some of the methods that cultural agents use to enforce traditional cultural mating and marriage patterns.

- explain some of the methods that cultural agents use to encourage inter-group dating.

Other Information: This activity is appropriate for high school or older. It requires about two class session of about fifty minutes, plus homework. Materials needed include construction paper cutouts of squares and triangles that can be stuck onto each student's forehead. Six or seven signs to represent the following groups: the media, Benjamin's family, Lisa's family, Lisa's friends, Benjamin's friends, Benjamin's religious group, Lisa's religious group (the last two can be combined if you only have six groups).

Procedure:

Step 1. Explain the following:
The Square Heads and Triangle Heads are two groups of people. The Square Heads have more money, power, and status than the Triangle Heads. Benjamin, a 17-year-old Square Head boy, has been flirting with Lisa, a 16-year-old Triangle Head girl.

Step 2. Ask participants to form six or seven groups (random or purpose-fully diverse by gender, ethnicity). The groups are to represent:

- The media (TV, radio, the Web, newspapers, etc.)
- Benjamin's parents and other family members who are both Square Heads
- Lisa's parents, and other family members, who are Triangle Heads
- Lisa's friends
- Benjamin's friends
- Their religious institutions (they both belong to the same religion, but attend different services).

In your groups, your task is to figure out what you or your organization can do to "police the border"—that is, to prevent people like Benjamin and Lisa from getting together as mates. Remember, intershape relationships were declared legal in 1967, so you cannot actually throw Benjamin and Lisa in jail. (20 minutes)

Step 3. Ask groups to present their strategies. (15 minutes)

Step 4. Ask participants, "How did you feel while you were doing this activity?"(15 minutes)

Step 5. Ask, "What did you learn by doing this activity?"(10 minutes)

Step 6. Now, repeat steps 2 through 5 but this time, the task is to open up the border and encourage Benjamin and Lisa to get together.

Step 7. Summarize the key concepts: that culture creates norms of what is an ideal mate. How is this reinforced? Through parents, peers, laws, religious texts, and other cultural practices, people and institutions "guard the borders" of each "race" or ethnic group—or encourage or at least remain open to young people dating across racial lines. What are those methods? Ask participants to be specific. For example, a cultural agent might use misinformation to restrict intergroup relationships (the other is physically deficient, the other is less intelligent, the other has a bad character—mean, abusive, loose, etc.); or they might use a value statement to open up the possibility of intergroup dating (e.g., we will welcome whoever you choose as long as we know that you are happy).

Step 8. Assessment: Participants write a learning reflection about this activity: What did you feel? What did you learn? How would you apply what you learned in your own life?

ADDITIONAL ACTIVITY IDEAS

Activity Idea 1: Change Agents in Interracial Relationships

This activity engages participants in a classroom inquiry project that allows students to uncover their own attitudes and beliefs about interracial dating, and to identify specific comments and misinformation they would like to change. A detailed plan is available from the book's website, http://understandingrace.org/resources/for_teachers.html

Activity Idea 2: Film and Discussion: *Black Is . . . Black Ain't*

Marlon Riggs's film, discussed in this chapter, provides a moving portrait of the complexity of Black identity in the United States, including the filmmaker's challenges in being accepted as a gay Black man. A detailed discussion guide for use with students is available for free at http://www.newsreel.org/guides/blackgui.htm.

Activity Idea 3: Film and Discussion: *The Loving Story*

This documentary film tells the story of Mildred Jeter (African American) and Richard Loving (European American) and their quest to be able to marry legally in the State of Virginia.

See weblink for lesson plan: http://edsitement.neh.gov/websites/loving-story.

NOTES

1. The word "stock" in this quotation is reminiscent of old biological race concepts. We are also struck by how the same word is used to discuss animals.
2. The *New York Times Sunday Magazine* (July 14, 2013) recently reported on the "hook-up" practices of women college students at the University of Pennsylvania. The article indicat-

ed that many young women who are career driven and pressured to focus on their education before finding a mate, choose to engage in casual sex without any pretense of a deep and committed relationship. The article has been criticized for its focus on elite universities and ignoring the practices of women at less elite universities.

IV

Resources

Yolanda T. Moses

Comprehensive List of Activities

Activity Plans (AP) include fairly detailed, step-by-step procedures; *Activity Ideas* (AI) are short descriptions, sometimes referencing a website for more detailed plans; *Websites* (WE) are sites linked to Activity Plans or Activity Ideas. See also Major Website Resources for additional useful websites.

Part I: The Fallacy of Race As Biology

Chapter 1: Why Contemporary Races Are Not Scientifically Valid	AP	AI	WE
Human variability: faces		X	X
How many ways are there to create "races"?	X		
Where is the racial dividing line? continuous vs. discrete traits	X		
Racial traits do not covary	X		
What racial traits shall we choose?	X		X
Take the Human Variation Quiz		X	X
How can you tell someone's race?		X	X
The human spectrum of height		X	X
Explore human diversity further		X	X
Chapter 2: Human Biological Variation: What We Don't See			
Sorting by blood type and race	X		
Lactose intolerance and race	X		
Rh factor	X		
Explore human blood		X	X
Play the Blood Typing Game		X	x
Explore the human genome project research further		X	X

Explore genetics and human heredity		X	X
Exploring my ancestry		X	X
Who should be tested for sickle cell in the United States?		X	X

Chapter 3: If Not Race, How Do We Explain Biological Similarities?

Body type, climate, and ancestry	X		X
Facial size, shape, and geographic ancestral location	X		X
Ancestry and skin color		X	
Milk lactose intolerance and lactase persistence		X	X
Gluten intolerance		X	X
Gene flow illustration		X	X
Sickle cell anemia		X	X
Environmental adaptations		X	X
Modern evolutionary theory		X	

Chapter 4: More Alike Than Different, More Different Than Alike

Human biological variation: More alike than different?	X		X
Exploring one's own ancestry		X	X
Sorting people into races using online modules		X	X
The story of Desiree's baby		X	X
Exploring our African ancestor—Eve		X	X
Exploring my ancestry		X	X
Endless human variability		X	X
Explore the 1000 Genomes project		X	X
Explore the HapMap project		X	X

Part II: Culture Creates Race

Chapter 5: Culture Shapes How We Experience Reality	*AP*	*AI*	*WE*
The Hug: Transforming nature to culture	X		
The Albatross: Culture as a symbolic system that shapes how we see the world	X		X
The pervasiveness of culture		X	
Exploring the concept of culture using school culture		X	X
Teaching about race—additional activities		X	X
Chapter 6: Culture and Classification: Race Is Culturally Real			
Color terms	X		

Classifying relatives	X	X
Classifying in other cultures: A cultural IQ test	X	X
Examine old and nonmainstream U.S. IQ tests	X	X
Classifying people on social media sites	X	X
Create an IQ test for peer group	X	
Analyze a current IQ test for cultural bias	X	X

Chapter 7: Race and Inequality: Race as a Social Invention to Achieve Certain Goals

Census activity	X	X
Starpower: Experiencing a stratified society	X	X
Ethnic diversity in the United States	X	
Relevant social categories on public documents	X	
Exploring my ancestry: The ethnic me	X	X
Mating choice activity	X	
Race, class, gender intersections	X	X
Explore educator resources at *RACE: Are We So Different?* project website	X	X
Explore activities developed for *Race: Power of an Illusion* video series.	X	X
Jamestown: Planting the seeds of tobacco and the ideology of race		X
Just an environment or a just environment? Racial segregation and its impacts		X
The growth of the suburbs and the racial wealth gap		X
Racial inequality and human biology	X	X

Chapter 8: Cross-Cultural Overview of Race

Census categories in other nations	X	X
Fitting the world into the U.S. white–non-white binary model of race	X	X
How immigrants experience the U.S. racial system	X	
How history and local circumstances shape racial classification	X	

Chapter 9: If Race Doesn't Exist, What Are We Seeing? Sex, Mating, and Race

Mating activity	X	X
Film and discussion: *The Loving Story*	X	X
Comparison of Interracial and Same-Sex Marriage Laws	X	
Race, gender, and class in popular culture	X	X
Film and discussion: Guess *Who's Coming to Dinner?*	X	
The ethnic me (or who did my ancestors marry?)	X	

Explore antimiscegenation laws	X	X
Being "multi"	X	

Part III: Race and Hot-Button Issues in Educational Settings

Chapter 10: When Is It Racism? Who Is a Racist?	AP	AI	WE
Understanding racial conflict	X		
Understanding the conflict over the Rodney King beating		X	X
Chapter 11: The Academic Achievement Gap and Equity			
Unequal resources	X		
Chairs		X	X
The growth of the suburbs and the racial wealth gap			X
Resources for educators to foster equity and address the achievement gap			X
Chapter 12: Assemblies, Clubs, and Racial Labels			
Investigating events and clubs	X		
Collecting and analyzing data on racial slurs and racial llabels		X	X
Explore the Teaching Tolerance website			X
Chapter 13: "Interracial" Dating			
Enforcing within group dating vs. encouraging intergroup dating	X		
Change agents in interracial relationships		X	X
Film and discussion: *Black Is Black Ain't*		X	X
Film and discussion: *The Loving Story*		X	X

Major Website Resources

The following list includes websites cited in the text as well as additional web resources. For some websites, we have indicated (in parentheses) the most relevant book chapters or book sections. The website for this book, *How Real Is Race?*, is also listed, both separately and under the AAA RACE Exhibit entries. Mukhopadhyay's website is also listed separately.

African American Lives 2

- A variety of online and hands-on human classification exercises that provide opportunities for participants to see how difficult it is to classify people into distinct races. This lesson is from a PBS show hosted by Henry Louis Gates Jr.
    http://www.pbs.org/wnet/aalives/teachers/rationalizing_race.html

The African Burial Ground Project (most useful for parts I and II)

- These two websites tell the story of how the site was discovered, what it revealed, and how it became a national monument.

    - **New York Public Library, Schomburg Research Library**
        http://www.nypl.org/research/sc/afb/shell.html
    - **The U.S. National Park Service**
        http://www.nps.gov/afbg/index.htm

American Anthropology Association Websites Related to *RACE: Are We So Different?* Project

- The following four major websites and their related links represent the compendium of websites of the American Anthropological Association that contain material and resources important to this book and for the users of materials about race in classrooms, in workplaces, and in communities.

    1. The Official American Anthropology Association Website—Resources—*Race: A Public Education Project*
       This site describes the overall project with its mission to "help promote a broad understanding of race and human variation." The project includes a traveling museum exhibit, an interactive website (which is explored in detail below), and educational materials including the second edition of this book. The project looks at race in the United States through the lenses of biology, history, and lived experience (racism). The project was funded by the Ford Foundation and the National Science Foundation in 2003 and launched in 2007. Over two million people have visited the website and the exhibits to date. On this official site for the project, readers can take a virtual tour of the exhibit, see the introductory video to the project, and purchase project merchandise such as CDs and DVDs from the exhibit that have been grouped together for classroom and professional learning. The CD/DVD contains powerful vignettes from the "Living with Race" section of the exhibit that focuses on such issues as transracial adoption, multicultural identity, and coping with racism in the United States.

       - Virtual Tour of the Exhibit
         http://www.understandingrace.org/about/virtour.html
       - Introductory Video
         http://www.youtube.com/v/8aaTAUAEyho
       - Race Project Merchandise (CD/DVD)
         http://www.aaanet.org/resources/RACE-Educational-Sets-and-T-shirts-Now-Available.cfm

    2. AAA RACE Project Official Interactive Website (useful for all chapters)
       The official website of the *RACE: Are We So Different?* project is designed to provide information about what race is, and what race isn't. The site is organized around and explores the three major themes of the exhibit: biology and human variation, history, and how race is experienced in the lives of people in the United States

today. This book, *How Real Is Race? A Sourcebook on Race, Culture, and Biology,* is one of two books expressly written to complement and enhance the materials on the website and in the exhibit of the RACE project. The other book written to complement the materials in the exhibit and website is *RACE: Are We So Different?* (see reference list in this section for complete citation). The weblinks below are listed under the broad headings mentioned above—human variation, history, and lived experience. The numbers in parentheses refer to chapters in our book, *How Real Is Race?*

- *RACE: Are We So Different?* website (Main website page) http://www.understandingrace.org
- General Information from the Website

  - Glossary   http://www.understandingrace.org/resources/glossary.html
  - *RACE: Are We So Different?* Introductory Video to the Project http://www.youtube.com/v/8aaTAUAEyho
  - RACE Project Bibliography http://www.understandingrace.org/resources/pdf/annotated_bibliography.pdf

- History

  - Defining   Whiteness   http://www.understandingrace.org/history/gov/eastern_southern_immigration.html
  - Race   History   Timeline   (Movie)   http://www.understandingrace.org/history/timeline_movie.html

- Human Variation

  - Basic   Genetics   (2)   http://www.understandingrace.org/humvar/molecular_01.html
  - Human   Spectrum   (1)   http://www.understandingrace.org/humvar/spectrum.html
  - Human   Variation   (3)   http://www.understandingrace.org/humvar/race_humvar.html
  - Macroevolution   (3, 4)   http://www.understandingrace.org/humvar/sickle_01.html
  - Our   Molecular   Selves   (Video)   (1)   http://www.understandingrace.org/humvar/molecular/index.html
  - Out of Africa Theory (3, 4) http://www.understandingrace.org/humvar/africa.html

- Sickle Cell Trait (2, 3) http://www.understandingrace.org/humvar/sickle_01.html
- Skin Color—Nina Jablonski (3) http://www.understandingrace.org/humvar/skin; http://www.understandingrace.org/humvar/skin_01.html

- Lived Experience

  - *A Girl Like Me* (Video) http://www.understandingrace.org/lived/video/index.html
  - Global Census http://www.understandingrace.org/lived/global_census.html
  - Who Is White? http://www.understandingrace.org/lived/who_is/index.html

3. RACE: A Teacher's Guide (on project website) (useful for all chapters)

   - This guide serves as a teaching tool to assist educators in addressing race and human variation in the classroom. The guide meets national and select state standards for science and social studies, and teachers may use the various lesson plans to develop a module on race and human variation for biology, social studies, or social science classes. We encourage educators to present the topic of race and human variation in an integrated fashion as we have done in the guide. All material is downloadable. There are two guides: one for middle school and one for high school (description taken from website).

     http://www.understandingrace.org/resources/for_teachers.html

4. *How Real Is Race? A Sourcebook on Race, Culture, and Biology*: Official AAA Website for the 2nd Edition of the Book

   - This website is designed to complement and enhance the 2nd edition of a companion book to the AAA Race project, *How Real Is Race? A Sourcebook on Race, Culture, and Biology* by Carol C. Mukhopadhyay, Rosemary Henze, and Yolanda T. Moses (AltaMira Press, 2014). This website, designed by the authors, three nationally noted anthropologists, provides materials and resources to widen and deepen the understanding of topics covered in the book. In addition, the website explores areas not covered in the RACE exhibit, such as cross-cultural issues of race, multiancestral identities, and race and immigration in the

21st century. The website is designed for educators, students, and professionals in many fields. It includes linkages to the new Common Core Standards, useful for pre-college educators. It will be periodically updated with new materials and resources.
http://www.understandingrace.org/resources/

Anthro Notes—Department of Anthropology, Smithsonian National History Museum

- This newsletter provides information to teachers all over the United States on topics related to the four subfields of anthropology. It explores such issues as human evolution, human variation, and language and culture. The overall mission of the newsletter is to disseminate information about anthropology to other anthropologists, archeologists, professionals, and teachers, especially in schools. But the material is useful in college settings in introductory classes as well.
http://anthropology.si.edu/outreach/anthnote/anthronotes.html

Black Is . . . Black Ain't (Film) (13)

- This 1995 award-winning film focuses on the diversity of what it means to be Black in the United States.
http://www.newsreel.org/nav/title.asp?tc=CN0011

  - **Facilitator's Guide for Film**
http://www.newsreel.org/guides/blackgui.htm

California Newsreel Website (Films)

- California Newsreel is a leading resource center for the advancement of racial justice and diversity, and the study of African American life and history as well as African culture and politics. It provides films on a wide variety of social justice and health issues as well.
http://newsreel.org/about-California-Newsreel

Census and Related Websites (useful for all chapters)

- This series of websites gives an overview of the range of census data that is collected and kept by the U.S. Census Bureau. In addition to reporting on the data from the 2010 census in this website, it also provides a link to historical censuses, to data on specific ethnic groups, and to Internet sites for those interested in genealogy.

- **Main Access Page**
  http://www.census.gov/main/www/access.html
- **Reports from the 2010 Census**
  http://www.census.gov/prod/cen2010/briefs/c2010br-02.pdf
- **Measuring America: The Decanal Census: From 1790 to 2000**
  http://www.census.gov/prod/2002pubs/pol02marv.pdf
- **Census Finder—A Directory of Free Census Records**
  http://www.censusfinder.com
- **Southeast Asian Categories**
  http://www.census.gov/prod/cen2010/briefs/c2010br-11.pdf
- **2010 Demographics on Dominicans**
  http://www.law.cornell.edu/supct/html/02-241.ZO.html
- **Internet Sites for Genealogists**
  http://www.azlibrary.gov/is/genealogy/handouts/documents/
  InternetSitesforGenealogists.pdf
- **Historical Census Browser, University of Virginia Library**
  http://fisher.lib.virginia.edu/collections/stats/histcensus/

Closing the Achievement Gap Video (11)

- This video looks at Amistad Academy, a public charter school for mostly poor fifth- through eighth-graders who often enter performing at lower-than-average levels but leave performing on par with students from wealthier areas. Available from the PBS website.
  http://www.pbs.org/closingtheachievementgap

Conflict Resolution Programs

- The two websites listed here provide information on conflict resolution programs endorsed by Educators for Social Responsibility and National Conference on Community and Justice.
  http://esrnational.org/professional-services/high-school/prevention/
  conflict-resolution-violence-prevention-lessons-high-school/
  http://www.nccjctwma.org/whatwedo/anytown.html

Dadi's Family (Film) (9)

- *Dadi's Family*, a documentary film, provides an intimate portrayal of a patrilineal, patrilocal joint family household in Northern India, with a particular focus on women of different generations, particularly mothers and daughters and daughters-in-law. It describes both stability and changes in Indian joint family life in the 1980s.
  http://www.der.org/films/dadis-family.html

Documentary Educational Resources (Films) (8, 9)

- Documentary films that explore the culture and lives of people around the world. There is an extensive collection of films about race relations cross-culturally.
  http://www.der.org/
  http://www.der.org/films/index-by-subject.html#race

The Dolan DNA Learning Center (2, 4)

- Cold Spring Harbor Laboratory, Cold Spring Harbor, NY. A rich DNA Learning Center for students. Opportunities for engagement include a range of programs and educational resources that can be downloaded.
  http://www.dnalc.org
  http://www.dnalc.org/programs/
  http://www.dnalc.org/resources/

EDChange Website (10–13)

- Established by educators and dedicated to equity, diversity, multiculturalism, and social justice. They have developed resources, workshops, and projects that contribute to progressive change in individuals, schools, and American culture.
  http://edchange.org

EDSITEment: The Official Humanities Website for Educators (parts II and III)

- EDSITEment is a partnership among the National Endowment for the Humanities, Verizon Foundation, and the National Trust Foundation. As a member of the Thinkfinity consortia of websites for educators, EDSITEment particularly focuses on literature, language arts, history, foreign languages, art and culture, and even social studies.
  http://edsitement.neh.gov (general)

Educators for Social Responsibility (10)

- This website provides valuable information to students and teachers on conflict resolution and violence prevention strategies for high school.
  http://esrnational.org/professional-services/high-school/prevention/conflict-resolution-violence-prevention-lessons-high-school/

ERASE Project (Expose Racism and Advance School Excellence) (11)

• The ERASE Project contains materials useful to teachers to help them to understand and develop strategies and actions to shift thinking about the achievement gap to thinking about the issue as an "achievement opportunity."

  http://www.eraseracismny.org/

  At the http://www.arc.org website please see two other documents of interest:

  • **The Racial Equity Impact Assessment Toolkit**
    http://www.arc.org/content/view/744/167/
  • **The Race and Public Policy Video**
    http://www.arc.org/content/view/742/167/

For Colored Girls Who Have Considered Suicide When the Rainbow Is Enuf **(Film)**

• This 2010 film produced by Tyler Perry is based on a 1975 best-selling book of the same name by Ntozoke Shange. The book was turned into an award-winning Broadway play in addition to the TV movie. It is the story of a group of African American women of all ages as they face the tragedies and joys of their lives.

  • **Wikipedia Site**
    http://en.wikipedia.org/wiki/For_Colored_Girls_Who_Have_
    Considered_Suicide_When_the_Rainbow_is_Enuf
  • **Amazon**
    http://www.amazon.com/colored-girls-considered-suicide-rainbow/
    dp/B0057D901U

Genomics Science Program

• This website is hosted by the U.S. Department of Energy, Office of Science. The goal is to provide suitable material for educators searching for information on genomics, systems biology, and microbes. The materials are designed to enhance existing curricula. Supplements include modules on Genomics for Energy and Environmental Placement, the Biofuels Primer, the Image Gallery, and a virtual genomics library among other supplements.

  http://www.genomicscience.energy.gov/education/index.shtml

Genetics and Social Science: Expanding Transdisciplinary Research

• This website has useful materials, especially for social scientists, biology-social links.
  http://www.nchpeg.org/bssr/

Gluten Intolerance (2, 3)

• This website looks at the archeological research around the history of the domestication of grains in Europe. It looks at this phenomenon at the macroevolutionary and genetic levels.
  http://www.mcdonald.cam.ac.uk/projects/genetics/projects/cereals/index.html
  http://www.shef.ac.uk/archaeology/research/domestication

Guess Who's Coming to Dinner? (Film) (9)

• This film is set in 1967 San Francisco and tells the story of issues surrounding an interracial marriage between a Euro-American woman and an African American man. In the same year that the film was released, the Supreme Court struck down antimiscegenation laws in seventeen states in the *Loving vs. Virginia* case (see entry in this website). YouTube has a free copy of the movie available. See link below.
  http://en.wikipedia.org/wiki/Guess_Who's_Coming_to_Dinner
  http://www.youtube.com/watch?v=xCAaEbCDovQ

Hawks, John Web blog—Paleoanthropology, Genetics, and Evolution (1)

• This website by John Hawks focuses on paleoanthropology, genetics, and evolution. It provides a wealth of information on topics covered in part I of this book. The website includes photos of "shovel-shaped incisors."
  http://johnhawks.net/weblog/hawks/about.html

How Real Is Race? A Sourcebook on Race, Culture, and Biology

• This website link, part of the official RACE project website, contains additional materials and resources related to this book. See also American Anthropology Association websites related to the RACE: Are We So Different? Project, for a fuller description of this website.

Human Genome Project (1, 2, 3)

• Completed in 2003, the Human Genome Project (HGP) was a thirteen-year project coordinated by the U.S. Department of Energy (DOE) and the National Institutes of Health. The following are weblinks that provide useful information related to part I of this book.

  • **Information Archive**
    http://www.ornl.gov/sci/techresources/Human_Genome/home.shtml
  • **Human Genome Project Education Resources**
    http://web.ornl.gov/sci/techresources/Human_Genome/education/index.shtml
  • **Exploring Genes and Genetic Disorders**
    http://web.ornl.gov/sci/techresources/Human_Genome/publicat/genegateway/GeneGatewayHandout.pdf

Intelligence Tests, Wikipedia (useful in parts II and III)

• This website discusses the intelligence quotient or IQ. It discusses the history of IQ tests; the variety of modern tests; their uses and reliability; genetics and environment; heritability; age and IQ; and music and IQ among other topics.
  https://en.wikipedia.org/wiki/Intelligence_quotient

Jim Crow Laws in California—A Timeline (9)

• This website lists the Jim Crow or segregation laws in the state of California from 1866 to 1952. In California, concern about Asian immigration produced a series of segregation laws in the areas of miscegenation, education, employment and housing, right to vote, sale of alcohol, and others. Some of these laws also pertained to Native Americans and African Americans.
  https://sites.google.com/a/aveson.org/www-salimcrowe-com/jim-crow-laws-california-a-timeline

Just a piece of cloth **(video) (13)**

• In this 34-minute documentary, four San Francisco Bay Area Muslim women share their stories about wearing and not wearing the Muslim headscarf (hijab). The website includes a discussion guide. Although the film was completed in 2013, it has not yet been released; the website will provide updated information on the release date and how to order it.
  http://www.justapieceofcloth.com

Justice Matters (10, 11)

- This site provides a variety of professional development activities for teachers and other personnel to build their skills to impact policies on behalf of justice for students in schools.
  http://www.justicematters.org/

Lactose Intolerance (2, 3)

- These two websites provide basic information on what lactose intolerance is and how it works, and its geographic distribution among the world's population.

  - **Ohio State University Medical Center**
    http://medicalcenter.osu.edu/patientcare/healthcare_services/
    digestive_disorders/lactoseintolerance/Pages/index.aspx
  - *Geocurrents* **News Site**
    http://geocurrents.info/cultural-geography/culinary-geography/
    global-geography-of-milk-consumption-and-lactose-intolerance

Lip Shapes (1, 2)

- This article, "Top 10 Lip Shapes That Guys Love the Most," provides photos which illustrate the variability of lip types found among European women.
  http://www.mmmglawblog.com/top-10-lip-shapes-that-guys-love-the-most/

***The Loving Story* (Video) (9, 13)**

- *The Loving Story*, a documentary film, tells the story of Richard and Mildred Loving to examine the drama, the history, and the current state of interracial marriage and tolerance in the United States. (Description is taken from the website.)
  http://edsitement.neh.gov/websites/loving-story

  - **Downloadable Teacher's Guide**
    http://www.icarusfilms.com/new2012/ls.html

***Maasai Women* (Film) (9)**

- This 1980 documentary film explores the lives of women in a patrilineal, patrilocal, pastoralist (cattle-herding) society in East Africa. Interviews

with Maasai women provide interesting cultural perspectives on topics such as polygamy, marriage, sexuality, and concepts of wealth.
http://www.der.org/films/maasai-women.html

Maryland, State of: Relevant Websites and Teaching Materials (most useful in part II)

- **Maryland State Archives: Documents for the Classroom**
  http://msa.maryland.gov/
- **The Maryland Toleration Act of 1649**
  http://www.let.rug.nl/usa/D/1601-1650/maryland/mta.htm   (accessed July 21, 2013)

Matters of Race (Website) (10–13)

- ROJA Productions created four documentaries that address questions of race. Each program focuses on one or more communities in which racial attitudes and beliefs are being challenged. Teacher's guides are included.
  http://www.pbs.org/mattersofrace/

Media Education Foundation (most useful in part III)

- The Media Education Foundation has produced such films as *Tough Guise 2*, *Hip-Hop Culture*, *Dreamworlds III*, and most recently, *Joystick Warriros: Video Games, Violence & the Culture of Militarism*. These films do an excellent job of exploring the intersections of race with issues of masculinity, femininity, class, and ethnicity. In addition the website contains a catalog of dozens of films, discussion guides, handouts, and full transcripts of their films.
  http://www.mediaed.org

Monsoon Wedding (Film) (9)

- This popular commercial film made in 2001 and directed by Mira Nair, a world-renowned filmmaker and native of India, portrays the stresses of a modern, upper-middle-class Indian family as they prepare for the marriage of their thoroughly modern daughter. It looks at how traditions of arranged marriages often clash with the realities of modernity and individual choice.
  http://www.imdb.com/title/tt0265343/

Mukhopadhyay, Carol C., Professional Website. See especially link to "Teaching about Race."

- http://www.sjsu.edu/people/carol.mukhopadhyay

Myths of Human Genetics: An Introduction (2, 3, 4)

- This website by John H. McDonald at the University of Delaware explores the myths of human genetics by having students collect data on themselves and perform a variety of in-class experiments.
  http://udel.edu/~mcdonald/mythintro.html

National Center for Biotechnology Information (1–4)

- This website of the National Center for Biotechnology Information (NCBI) is a division of the National Library of Medicine (NLM) at the National Institutes of Health (NIH). Below are two links that give an overview of the site and a look at the HapMap project mentioned in part I.

  - **Genomics Primer and Other Materials**
    http://www.ncbi.nlm.nih.gov/About/primer/genetics_genome.html
    http://www.ncbi.nlm.nih.gov/genome
  - **HapMap Project**
    http://hapmap.ncbi.nlm.nih.gov/

The National Conference for Community and Justice (10)

- "The National Conference for Community and Justice was founded in 1927 as the National Conference for Christians and Jews. It is a human relations organization promoting understanding and respect among all races, religions, and cultures; providing education and advocacy; and building communities that are inclusive and just for all." Activities and curricula for students, teachers, and community groups, including the well known "Anytown" program for youth leadership development in social justice.
  http://www.nccj.org/

NPR (National Public Radio) Books (8–13)

- Author of book *Americanah* explains how it was that she learned to be black in America. Novelist Chimamda Ngozi Adichie grew up in Nigeria before immigrating to the United States. This is an online interview.

http://www.npr.org/2013/06/27/195598496/americanah-author-explains-learning-to-be-black-in-the-u-s

National Women's History Museum Online (most useful in part II)

• The National Women's History Museum (NWHM) website hosts online exhibits with rich materials on subjects that affect women in U.S. history as well as today.
   http://www.nwhm.org/online-exhibits/

  • **Chinese American Women: A History of Resilience and Resistance**
    http://www.nwhm.org/online-exhibits/chinese/1.html

OAH Magazine of History—Family History (9)

• This Organization of American History special online issue on family history, published in 2001, offers an array of articles, lesson plans, educational resources on teaching, and classroom media. An extra bonus is that it also includes primary source documents as well as an annotated bibliography on teaching family history.
   http://magazine.oah.org/issues/154/

Oakland Unity High School (11)

• It is the mission of Oakland Unity High School (Unity) to prepare its students for admission to and success in college. This school shows how against the odds, they are able to graduate a high number of low-income students who go on to college. To see the School Accountability Report Card, click on the SARC link at the school's website below.
   http://www.unityhigh.org/

OMIM—Online Mendelian Inheritance in Man Website (2, 3)

• The Online Mendelian Inheritance in Man website and catalog is a comprehensive authoritative compendium of human genes and genetic phenotypes that is freely available and updated daily. OMIM is authored and edited at the McKusick-Nathans Institute of Genetic Medicine, Johns Hopkins University School of Medicine.
   Online Catalog of Mendelian Inheritance in Man
   http://www.omim.org/

1000 Genomes Project (4)

- A worldwide collaboration among over 400 genetic scientists to continue to unlock the secrets of the genome on a global level. Provides articles and background reading as well as charts and graphs.
  http://www.1000genomes.org/

Palomar College, Tutorials in Biological Anthropology and Cultural Anthropology, Organized by Dr. Dennis O'Neil (see parts I and II, especially maps in part I)

- The Palomar College website, Department of Behavioral Sciences, provides a wealth of information for both students and educators through their online tutorials on a wide variety of anthropology topics developed by Dr. Dennis O'Neil. Below are listed topics in both biological and cultural anthropology that help to illustrate concepts discussed in the chapters of this book.

  ### Biological (General) (1–4)
  http://anthro.palomar.edu/tutorials/biological.htm

  - **ABO Blood Groups (2)**
    http://anthro.palomar.edu/blood/default.htm
  - **Bergman and Allen Rule (1–4)**
    http://www.pbs.org/wgbh/nova/neanderthals/mtdna.html
  - **Environmental Adaptations (3)**
    http://anthro.palomar.edu/adapt/- general
  - **Exploring Our African Ancestry (4)**
    http://anthro.palomar.edu/hom02/mod_homo_4.htm
  - **Human Geographic Distribution (3)**
    http://anthro.palomar.edu/adapt/adapt_4.htm
    http://anthro.palomar.edu/vary/vary_3.htm
    http://anthro.palomar.edu/adapt/adapt_3.htm
  - **Modern Evolutionary Theory (3)**
    http://anthro.palomar.edu/synthetic/default.htm
  - **Skin Color (1–4)**
    http://anthro.palomar.edu/adapt/adapt_4.htm

  ### Cultural Anthropology (5–13)
  http://anthro.palomar.edu/tutorials/cultural.htm (general)

  - **Characteristics of Culture (5)**
    http://anthro.palomar.edu/culture/culture_2.htm
  - **Kinship (6, 9)**

http://anthro.palomar.edu/kinship/default.htm
- **Language and Culture (6)**
  http://anthro.palomar.edu/language/default.htm
- **Methods for Learning about Culture (5, 6)**
  http://anthro.palomar.edu/culture/culture_3.htm
- **Related Internet Sites (5–9)**
  http://anthro.palomar.edu/culture/links.htm
- **Sex and Marriage (9)**
  http://anthro.palomar.edu/marriage/default.htm

Pink Sari (Film)

- This recent award-winning film by Kim Longinoto explores the lives of women who have formed an activist organization to fight for the rights of women in unhappy domestic situations in India. They wear pink saris to show their solidarity.
  http://www.wmm.com/filmcatalog/pages/c789.shtml

Policy Mic Website: "Wilcox County High School Students Organize School's First Racially Integrated Prom" (13)

- This 2012 online article tells the story of Wilcox County High School, located in rural Rochelle, Georgia, and how it has never had an integrated prom. It also describes how four friends—two Euro-Americans and two African Americans—began to change the tradition.
  http://www.policymic.com/articles/33073/wilcox Mic

The Power of Two (Film) (part I)

- The film *The Power of Two* is the story of twin sisters, Anabel Stenzel (recently deceased) and Isabel Stenzel-Byrnes, whose mother was Japanese and father was Euro-American, and their fight to overcome cystic fibrosis. The film is based on their 2007 book, *The Power of Two*. The film documents not only their struggle to survive, including double lung transplants, but their efforts to inform the Japanese about the disease, long thought to be associated only with Europeans. The site also contains a discussion and action guide and extensive interviews with the two sisters.
  http://www.thepoweroftwomovie.com/the-film/
  http://www.thepoweroftwomovie.com/home/

Race: The Power of an Illusion **Companion Website (useful for all chapters)**

- This comprehensive website is a companion to the California Newsreel film *Race: The Power of an Illusion*. It has a comprehensive teacher's guide as well as a discussion guide for the three films in the series.
  http://www.pbs.org/race (general site)

  - **ABO Blood groups (2, 3)**
  - *Desiree's Baby* **(4)**
    http://www.pbs.org/race/000_About/002_04-teachers-06.htm
  - **Human Diversity (1, 2, 3)**
    http://www.pbs.org/race/004_HumanDiversity/004_01-explore.htm
  - **Race and Wealth Disparities (11)**
    http://www.pbs.org/race/000_About/002_04-teachers-07.htm
  - **Sorting People Interactivity Module (1–4)**
    http://www.pbs.org/race/002_SortingPeople/002_01-sort.htm

Race Matters Toolkit—Annie E. Casey Foundation (11)

- This toolkit is designed to help decision makers, advocates, and elected officials get better results in their work by providing equitable opportunities for all. The toolkit presents a specific point of view on addressing unequal opportunities by race and offers simple, results-oriented steps to help you achieve your goals (description taken from website).
  http://www.aecf.org/KnowledgeCenter/PublicationsSeries/RaceMatters.aspx

Science NetLinks Website (2, 3, 11)

- Science NetLinks is a project of the Directorate for Education and Human Resources Programs of the American Association for the Advancement of Science. This website gathers lesson plans, teaching tools, and resources about science writ large for teachers and other educators.

  - **General**
    http://www.sciencenetlinks.com
  - **Protein Synthesis Tool (2, 3)**
    http://sciencenetlinks.com/tools/protein-synthesis/
  - **Race and the Achievement Gap (11)**
    http://sciencenetlinks.com/science-news/science-updates/race-and-achievement/

Sickle Cell and Sports (2, 3)

- These two websites provide information about how college and professional sports teams are looking at the pros and cons of sickle cell anemia testing for all athletes.
  http://www.npr.org/blogs/health/2012/01/26/145923225/blood-doctors-call-foul-on-ncaas-screening-for-sickle-cell
  http://www.cbssports.com/collegefootball/story/11903550

Sickle Cell Websites—Additional (2, 3)

- **Sickle Cell Information.Net**
  Website dedicated to educating the public about the structure of sickle cell hemoglobin and the mechanism of sickle cell disease. This also contains a link to the Mukherji Lab website (go into "links" after reaching the website).
  http://www.sicklecellinfo.net/index.htm
- **Centers for Disease Control and Prevention**
  CDC is one of the major operating components of the Department of Health and Human Services. This website focuses on explaining the disease, providing healthy tips for living with the disease and trait, and free materials to download.
  http://www.cdc.gov/ncbddd/sicklecell/index.html

Sita Sings the Blues **(Film)**

- This beautifully illustrated animated film takes a critical, modern, bordering-on-feminist look at the classic Hindu epic *The Ramayana* and the tale of Sita, who was captured by the demon Ravana, and then, after her return, had her "loyalty" (and sexual fidelity) challenged by her husband, Rama. The film weaves together multiple Indian interpretations of this classic along with stories of modern life, contemporary characters, and the music of blues singer Annette Hanshaw (as Sita). Available for downloading at:
  http://www.sitasingstheblues.com/

Strom Thurmond's Black Daughter: The Complicated Story of Race in the United States

- These two websites explore the complexity of race in the United States by looking at the lives of Senator Strom Thurmond, a onetime segregationist senator from the state of South Carolina, and the African American daughter that he fathered as a young twenty-two-year-old with the sixteen-year-old African American maid in his parents' household. The Thurmond

family and the daughter, Essie Mae Washington-Williams, kept the family secret until 2003.
http://www.washingtonpost.com/blogs/she-the-people/wp/2013/02/05/strom-thurmonds-black-daughter-a-flesh-and-blood-symbol-of-americas-complicated-racial-history/
http://en.wikipedia.org/wiki/Essie_Mae_Washington-Williams

Teaching Tolerance Website (12)

- Classroom activities focused on addressing racism, sexism, and other "isms" in the classroom, described in part III:
http://www.tolerance.org/

Thinkfinity Website

- "Thinkfinity is the Verizon Foundation's free online professional learning community. They provide access to over 60,000 experts in curriculum enhancement, along with thousands of award-winning digital resources for K-12 that are aligned to state standards and the common core."
http://www.thinkfinity.org/community/about-us

Tracing Ancestry with mtDNA **(Video Online) (2, 3, 4)**

- *Tracing Ancestry with mtDNA* from *NOVA* is a film about the "Eve" who, on the basis of analysis of mitochondrial DNA (mtDNA) in modern humans, was hypothesized to be the common ancestor of all living humans, whose origins are in Africa. Although a bit dated, the website provides useful information on mtDNA in tracing ancestral history.
http://www.pbs.org/wgbh/nova/neanderthals/mtdna.html.

Two American Families **—Documentary (Online) (parts II and III)**

- Since 1992, Bill Moyer, noted American journalist and commentator on the television show *Frontline*, has been following the lives of two ordinary American families, one black and one white, in Milwaukee, Wisconsin. They are called the Stanleys and the Neumanns. He is particularly interested in how the economic downturn of 2008 has impacted their families' economics and their places in society.
http://billmoyers.com/2013/07/10/two-american-families/

Understanding Prejudice—Website (10, 11, 12, 13)

- This website, which includes a "teacher's corner," has over 2,000 links to help students understand prejudice and stereotyping. It also has a searchable database.

  http://understandingprejudice.org

U.S. Commission on Civil Rights (11)

- The U.S. Commission on Civil Rights website provides information and reports on various topics related to discrimination and prejudice in the United States. The Disparate Impact Report shows how race intersects with the treatment of minority students in schools in the United States.

  - **General Site**

    http://www.usccr.gov/pubs/larpt/main.htm
  - **Disparate Impact Report**

    http://www.usccr.gov/pubs/School_Disciplineand_Disparate_Impact.pdf

Women Make Movies Website

- This website provides over 550 award-winning films by women independent filmmakers. The movies are about the lives and issues of women all over the world.

  http://www.wmm.com

References Cited

Adams, M., Bell, L. A., & Griffin, P. (Eds.) (1997). *Teaching for diversity and social justice: A sourcebook.* New York: Routledge.

Allende, Isabel. (1999). *Daughter of fortune.* New York: Harper Perennial Modern Classics.

Arce, J., Luna, D., Borjian, A., & Conrad, M. (2005). No child left behind: Who wins? Who loses? *Social Justice: A Journal of Crime, Conflict, and World Order, 32*(3), 56–71.

Arriaza, G. (2003). The schoolyard as a stage: Missing cultural clues in symbolic fighting. *Multicultural Education, 10*(3), 7–13.

Arriaza, G. (2004). Welcome to the front seat: Racial identity and Mesoamerican immigrants. *Latinos and Education Journal, 3*(4), 251–65.

Bald, Vivek. (2013). *Bengali Harlem and the lost histories of South Asian America.* Cambridge, MA: Harvard University Press.

Ball, A., & Tyson, C. (Eds.). (2011). *Studying diversity in teacher education.* Lanham, MD: Rowman & Littlefield.

Bamshad, M. J., &. Olson, S. E. (2003). Does race exist? *Scientific American, 289*(6), 78–85.

Banks, J., & Banks, C. M. (Eds.). (2012). *Multicultural education: Issues and perspectives* (8th ed.). New York: Wiley.

Barker, M. (1981). *The new racism.* London: Junction Books.

Bartlett, L., & Ghaffar-Kuchler, A. (Eds.). (2013). *Refugees, immigrants, and education in global South: Lives in motion.* New York: Routledge.

Bean, F., & Lee, J. (2009). Plus ça change . . . ? Multiraciality and the dynamics of race relations in the United States. *Journal of Social Issues, 65*(1), 205–19.

Benson, J. (2003). Asian Americans. In R. Scupin (Ed.), *Race and ethnicity: An anthropological focus on the United States and the world* (pp. 242–66). Upper Saddle River, NJ: Prentice Hall.

Berlak, H. (2001). Race and the achievement gap. *Rethinking Schools Online, 15*(4). Retrieved March 20, 2006, from http://www.rethinkingschools.org/archive/15_04/Race154.shtml.

Berlin, B., & Kay, P. (1969). *Basic color terms: Their universality and evolution.* Berkeley: University of California Press.

Best, A. (2000). *Prom night: Youth, schools, and popular culture.* New York: Routledge.

Bigler, E. (2003). Hispanic Americans/Latinos. In R. Scupin (Ed.), *Race and ethnicity: An anthropological focus on the United States and the world* (pp. 208–41). Upper Saddle River, NJ: Prentice Hall.

Blum, L. (2008). Racial incidents as teachable moments. In M. Pollock (Ed.), *Everyday antiracism: Getting real about race in school* (pp. 236–41). New York & London: New Press.

Bohannon, L. (2000). Shakespeare in the bush. Reprinted in J. Spradley & D. McCurdy (Eds.), *Conformity and conflict* (10th ed., pp. 23–32). Boston: Allyn & Bacon.

313

Bowles, S., & Gintis, H. (1976). *Schooling in capitalist America.* New York: Basic Books.

Briscoe, F., Arriaza, G., & Henze, R. (2009). *The power of talk: How words change the world.* Thousand Oaks, CA: Corwin Press.

Brison, K. (2003). The Pacific Islands. In R. Scupin (Ed.), *Race and ethnicity: An anthropological focus on the United States and the world* (pp. 373–401). Upper Saddle River, NJ: Prentice Hall.

Brodkin, K. (1998). *When Jews became White folks and what that says about race in America.* New Brunswick, NJ: Rutgers University Press.

Cammarota, J. (2005, December 2). *Youth participatory action research: Praxis of transformative education.* Paper presented at the American Anthropological Association, Washington, DC.

Carter, P. (2013). *Stubborn roots: Race, culture, and inequality in US and South African schools.* Oxford: Oxford University Press.

Chang, K., & Conrad, R. (2008). Following children's leads in conversations about race. In M. Pollock (Ed.), *Everyday anitracism: Getting real about race in school* (pp. 34–38). New York & London: New Press.

Chin, E. (2013, May 29). What Jason Richwine should have heard from his dissertation committee. *Anthropology Now.* Retrieved June 4, 2013, from http://anthronow.com/articles/what-jason-richwine-should-have-heard-from-his-phd-committee.

CNN. (2000, March 4). Bob Jones University ends ban on interracial dating. CNN Online. Retrieved from http://archives.cnn.com/2000/US/03/04/bob.jones/.

Cobern, W. W. (1995). Science education as an exercise in foreign affairs. *Science and Education, 4*(3), 287–302.

Cohen, M. (1997). Culture, rank, and IQ: The bell curve phenomenon. In J. Spradley and D. McCurdy (Eds.), *Conformity and conflict* (9th ed., pp. 252–58). New York: Longman.

Collins, P. H. (2009). *Another kind of public education: Race, schools, the media, and democratic possibilities.* Boston: Beacon Press.

Cruz, B. C., & Berson, M. J. (2001). The American melting pot? Miscegenation laws in the United States. *Organization of American Historians Magazine, 15*(4). Retrieved July 23, 2012, from http://magazine.oah.org/issues/154/.

David, E. J. R. (2013). *Brown skin, white minds: Filipino-American post-colonial psychology.* Charlotte, NC: Information Age Publishing.

Davidson, J. W., Gienapp, W. E., Heyrman, C. L., Lytle, M. H., & Stoff, M. B. (2005). *Nation of nations: A narrative history of the American republic* (5th ed.). Boston: McGraw Hill.

Davis, A. (1981). *Women, race and class.* New York: Random House.

Della-Dora, D. (1972). The schools can overcome racism. *Educational Leadership, 29*(5), 443–49.

Denn, R. (2002a, March 15). How one school almost succeeded. *Seattle Post-Intelligencer.* Retrieved July 24, 2006, from http://seattlepi.nwsource.com/disciplinegap/61966_jameslick13.shtml.

Denn, R. (2002b, March 15). Blacks are disciplined at far higher rates than other students. *Seattle Post-Intelligencer.* Retrieved July 24, 2006, from http://seattlepi.nwsource.com/disciplinegap/61940_newdiscipline12.shtml.

Dewan, S. (2013). Has "Caucasian" lost its meaning? *New York Times Sunday Review.* Retrieved July 16, 2013, from http://www.nytimes.com/2013/07/07/sunday-review/has-caucasian-lost-its-meaning.html?_r=0.

Donner, J. K., & Dixson, A. (2013). *The resegregation of schools.* New York & London: Routledge.

Dyer, R. (1997). *White: Essays on race and culture.* London and New York: Routledge.

Ebright, Olsen. (2013, April 26). 2nd blackface video linked to UC Irvine fraternity. NBC Los Angeles Channel 4 news story. Retrieved October 28, 2013, from http://www.nbclosangeles.com/news/local/UC-Irvine-Fraternity-Lambda-Theta-Delta-Blackface-204882971.html.

Edmonds, C., & Killen, M. (2009). Do adolescents' perceptions of parental racial attitudes relate to their intergroup contact and cross-race relationships? *Group Processes and Intergroup Relations, 12*(1), 5–21.

Education Trust. (2013, May). Breaking the glass ceiling of achievement for low income students and students of color. Retrieved July 17, 2013, from http://www.eric.ed.gov/PDFS/ED543218.pdf.

Education Trust West. (2013). *At a crossroads: A comprehensive picture of how African American youth fare in LA County schools.* Oakland, CA.

Education Week. (2011, July 7). Achievement gap. Retrieved July 17, 2013, from http://www.edweek.org/ew/issues/achievement-gap/.

Edwards, A. (2002, November). Bring me home a Black girl. *Essence,* 176–77.

Espiritu, Y. L. (2001). We don't sleep around like White girls do. *Signs, 26*(2), 415–40.

Estroff, S. E. (1997, March). Recognizing race: Whose categories are these, anyway? *Ethos, 25*(1), 113–16.

Fine, M., & Weis, L. (2003). *Silenced voices and extraordinary conversations.* New York: Teachers College Press.

Fine, M., Weis, L., & Powell, L. (1997). Communities of difference: A critical look at desegregated spaces created for and by youth. *Harvard Educational Review, 67*(2), 247–84.

Fish, J. M. (2003). Mixed blood. In J. P. Spradley & D. W. McCurdy (Eds.), *Conformity and conflict* (11th ed., pp. 270–80). Boston: Allyn & Bacon.

Fitzpatrick, L. (2012, June 2). University of Chicago fraternity apologizing for racial insensitivity. *Chicago Sun-Times.* Retrieved October 28, 2013, from http://www.suntimes.com/news/education/12932080-418/story.html.

Ford, K., Sohn, W., & Lepkowski, J. (2003, May). Ethnicity or race, area characteristics, and sexual partner choice among American adolescents. *Journal of Sex Research.* Retrieved July 30, 2013, from http://www.findarticles.com/p/articles/mi_m2372/is_2_40/ai_105518223.

Fordham, S. (1996). *Blacked out: Dilemmas of race, identity, and success at Capital High School.* Chicago: University of Chicago Press.

Fuentes, A. (2012). *Biological anthropology: Concepts and connections* (2nd ed.). New York: McGraw Hill.

Gardner, H. (1983). *Frames of mind: The theory of multiple intelligences.* New York: Basic Books.

Gledhill, J., & Wade, P. (2012). North and Latin American National Societies from a Continental Perspective. In R. Fardon, O. Harris, T. H. J. Marchand, M. Nuttall, C. Shore, V. Strang, & R. A. Wilson (Eds.), *The SAGE Handbook of Social Anthropology* (vol. 1, pp. 487–510). Thousand Oaks, CA: Sage.

Gillespie, C. (2010). The N-word, the F-word, and all that jazz: Race, sex, and transgressive language in contemporary American literature and popular culture. In S. J. Behrens & J. A. Parker (Eds.), *Language in the real world: An introduction to linguistics* (pp. 123–36). New York & London: Routledge.

Gochenour, T. (1977). The albatross. In D. Batchelder & E. G. Warner (Eds.), *Beyond experience: The experiential approach to cross-cultural education* (pp. 131–36). Brattleboro, VT: Experiment Press.

González, N., Moll, L., & Amanti, C. (Eds). (2005). *Funds of knowledge: Theorizing practices in households, communities, and classrooms.* Mahwah, NJ: Lawrence Erlbaum.

Goodman, A., Moses, Y., & Jones, J. (2012). *Race: Are we so different?* West Sussex, UK: Wiley-Blackwell.

Gould, S. J. (1981). *The mismeasure of man.* New York: W. W. Norton.

Grant, C., & Sleeter, S. (2011). *Doing multicultural education for achievement and equity.* New York: Routledge, Taylor and Francis Group.

Gravlee, C. C. (2009). How race becomes biology: Embodiment of social inequality. *American Journal of Physical Anthropology, 139*(1), 47–57.

Grosfoguel, R., & Mielants, E. (2006). The long-durée entanglement between Islamophobia and racism in the modern/colonial capitalist/patriarchal world-system: An introduction. *Human Architecture: Journal of the Sociology of Self-Knowledge, 5,* 1–12.

Gumbrecht, J. (2013, April 13). Segregated prom tradition yields to unity. CNN Living. Retrieved October 27, 2013, from http://www.cnn.com/2013/04/30/living/wilcox-integrated-prom/.

Haney-Lopez, I. F. (1996). *White by law: The legal construction of race.* New York: New York University Press.

Harrison, F. (2012). Race, racism, and antiracism: Implications for human rights. In A. Goodman, Y. Moses, & J. Jones, *Race: Are we so different?* (pp. 237–42). West Sussex, UK: Wiley Blackwell.

Haviland, W., Prins, H. L., Walrath, D., & McBride, B. (2005). *Cultural anthropology: The human challenge* (11th ed.). Belmont, NY: Wadsworth.

Heath, S. B. (1983). *Ways with words: Language, life, and work in communities and classrooms.* Cambridge: Cambridge University Press.

Hemmings, A. (2004). *Coming of age in U.S. high schools: Economic, kinship, religious, and political crosscurrents.* Mahwah, NJ: Lawrence Erlbaum.

Henze, R. (2001). Curricular approaches to developing positive interethnic relations. *Journal of Negro Education, 68*(4), 529–49.

Henze, R. (2008). Naming the racial hierarchies that arise during school reforms. In M. Pollock (Ed.), *Everyday antiracism: Getting real about race in school* (pp. 262–66). New York & London: New Press.

Henze, R., Katz, A., Norte, E., Sather, S., & Walker, E. (1999). *Leading for diversity: Final cross-case report.* Oakland, CA: ARC Associates.

Henze, R., Katz, A., Norte, E., Sather, S., & Walker, E. (2002). *Leading for diversity: How school leaders promote positive interethnic relations.* Thousand Oaks, CA: Corwin Press.

Hernández, H. (2001). *Multicultural education: A teacher's guide to linking context, process, and content* (2nd ed.). Columbus, OH: Merrill Prentice-Hall.

Herrnstein, R., & Murray, C. (1994). *The bell curve: Intelligence and class structure in American life.* New York: Free Press.

Hightower, N. (2003). Memories of a prom—in color. *Teaching tolerance: Mix it up stories.* Retrieved January 17, 2006, from http://www.tolerance.org/teens/stories/index.jsp.

Hirschfeld, L. (1997, March). The conceptual politics of race: Lessons for our children. *Ethos, 25*(1), 63–92.

Hyde, J., & DeLamater, J. D. (2014). *Understanding human sexuality* (12th ed.). New York: McGraw-Hill.

Jablonski, N. G., & Chaplin, G. (2005). Skin deep. In E. Angeloni (Ed.), *Annual editions, Physical anthropology, 2005–2006* (14th ed., pp. 169–72). Dubuque, IA: McGraw-Hill/Dushkin.

Jablonski, N. G. (2012). *Living color: The biological and social meaning of skin color.* Berkeley: University of California Press.

Jackson, F. L. C., & Borgelin, L. F. J. (2010). How genetics can provide detail to the transatlantic African Diaspora. In T. Olaniyan & J. Sweet (Eds.), *The African Diaspora and the Disciplines* (pp. 75–100). Bloomington: Indiana University Press.

Jewish Telegraphic Agency (1963). Anti-Jewish bias in college fraternities still alive, study shows. Retrieved October 28, 2013, from http://www.jta.org/1963/01/31/archive/anti-jewish-bias-in-college-fraternities-still-alive-study-shows.

Jurmain, R., Kilgore, L., Trevathan, W., & Ciochon, R. L. (2014). *Introduction to Physical Anthropology* (2013–2014 ed.). Belmont, CA: Wadsworth, Cengage Learning.

Kaba, A. J. (2011). Inter-ethnic/interracial romantic relationships in the United States: Factors responsible for the low rates of marriages between Blacks and Whites. *Sociology Mind, 1*(3), 121–29. Retrieved from http://works.bepress.com/cgi/viewcontent.cgi?article=1073&context=amadu_kaba.

Kephart, R. (2003). Latin America and the Caribbean. In R. Scupin (Ed.), *Race and ethnicity: An anthropological focus on the United States and the world* (pp. 288–308). Upper Saddle River, NJ: Prentice Hall.

Khan, S. (2009). *De-MIST-ifying the adolescent development of Muslim American high school students: A qualitative study of schooling and program experiences of participants in the Muslim Interscholastic Tournament.* PhD dissertation, Warner Graduate School of Education and Human Development. University of Rochester.

Kidd, K. (2012). In A. Goodman, Y. Moses, & J. Jones, *Race: Are we so different?* (pp. 134–39).

Kittle, R. A., & K. M. Weiss, (2003). Race, ancestry and genes: Implications for defining disease risk. *Annual Review of Genomics and Human Genetics, 4*, 33–67.

Kluckhohn, C. (1949). *Mirror for man: The relation of anthropology to modern life.* New York: McGraw-Hill.

Koshy, S. (2005). *Sexual Naturalization: Asian Americans and miscegenation.* Redwood City, CA: Stanford University Press.

Kottak, C. P. (2013). *Cultural anthropology: Appreciating cultural diversity* (15th ed.). Boston: McGraw-Hill.

Kottak, C. P., & Kozaitis, K. A. (2012). *On being different: Diversity and multiculturalism in the North American mainstream* (4th ed.). New York: McGraw-Hill.

Kramsch, C. (1998). *Language and culture.* Oxford: Oxford University Press.

Kreisberg, L. (1998). *Constructive conflicts: From escalation to resolution.* Lanham, MD: Rowman & Littlefield.

Kronenfeld, D. B. (2008). *Culture, society, and cognition: Collective goals, values, action, and knowledge.* Berlin, NY: Mouton de Gruyter.

Kronenfeld, D. B., Bennardo, G., de Munck, V. C., & Fischer, M. D. (Eds.) (2011). *A companion to cognitive anthropology.* New York: Wiley-Blackwell.

Lakoff, G. (2004). *Don't think of an elephant: Know your values and frame the debate.* White River Junction, VT: Chelsea Green.

Lave, J., Murtuagh, M., & de la Rocha, O. (1984). The dialectic of arithmetic in grocery shopping. In B. Rogoff & J. Lave (Eds.), *Everyday cognition: Its development in social context* (pp. 67–94). Cambridge, MA: Harvard University Press.

Lee, D. (1974). Lineal and non-lineal codifications of reality. In J. Spradley & D. McCurdy (Eds.), *Conformity and conflict* (2nd ed., pp. 111–17). Boston: Little, Brown.

Lee, E. (1998). *Beyond heroes and holidays: A practical guide to K–12 anti-racist, multicultural education and staff development.* Washington, DC: NECA/Teaching for Change.

Lee, E., Menkart, D., & Okazawa-Rey, M. (Eds.). (1998). *Beyond heroes and holidays: A practical guide to K-12 anti-racist, multicultural education and staff development.* Milwaukee, WI: Teaching for Change.

Lee, J., & Bean, F. D. (2004). America's changing color lines: Immigration, race/ethnicity, and multiracial identification. *Annual Review of Sociology, 30,* 221–42.

Lee, S. (1996). *Unraveling the "model minority" stereotype: Listening to Asian American youth.* New York: Teachers College Press.

Lee, S. J. (2007). *Up against Whiteness: Race, school, and immigrant youth.* New York: Teachers College Press.

Lee, S. Y. (2011). Changing faces: Colonial rule in Korea and ethnic characterizations. In Y. Takezawa (Ed.), *Racial representations in Asia* (pp. 53–74). Kyoto: Kyoto University Press.

Levin, S., Taylor, P., & Caudle, E. (2007). Interethnic and interracial dating in college: A longitudinal study. *Journal of Social and Personal Relationships, 24,* 323.

Levine, L. (2012). *The U.S. income distribution and mobility: Trends and international comparisons.* Washington, DC: Congressional Research Service.

Lewis, O. (1966). *La vida: A Puerto Rican family in the culture of poverty in San Juan and New York.* New York: Random House.

Lewontin, R. C. (1972). The apportionment of human diversity. In T. Dobzhansky et al. (Eds.), *Evolutionary Biology* (vol. 6, pp. 381–98). New York: Plenum.

Lewton, K. L. (2012) Complexity in biological anthropology in 2011: Species, reproduction, and sociality. *American Anthropologist, 114*(2), 196–202.

Lichter, D. T., Carmalt, J., & Zhenchao, Q. (2011). Immigration and intermarriage among Hispanics: Crossing racial and generational boundaries. *Sociological Forum, 26*(2), 241–64.

Lieberman, L. (2003). A history of scientific racialism. In R. Scupin (Ed.), *Race and ethnicity: An anthropological focus on the United States and the world* (pp. 36–66). Upper Saddle River, NJ: Prentice Hall.

Lieberman, L., Kirk, R. C., & Corcoran, M. (2003). The decline of race in American physical anthropology. *Anthropological Review, 66,* 3–21.

Long, J. C. (2004). *Human genetic variation: The mechanisms and results of micro-evolution.* Based on a presentation at the 2003 annual meeting of the American Anthropological

Association. For an online PDF version of this paper, see Scholar's Website at AAA RACE Project Website http://www.understandingrace.org/resources/papers_author.html.

Lopez, I. A. H. (2012). Colorblindness. In A. Goodman, Y. Moses, & J. Jones, *Race: Are we so different?* (pp. 82–89). Malden, MA, & Oxford, UK: Wiley Blackwell.

Loving, C. (1997). From the summit of truth to its slippery slopes: Science education's journey through positivist-postmodern territory. *American Educational Research Journal, 34*(3), 421–52.

Lucey, T. (2004). Commencing an educational dialogue about the economic disparities among racial groups in the United States populations. *Multicultural Education, Summer,* 27–34.

Lustig, D. (1997). Of Kwaanza, Cinco de Mayo, and whispering. *Anthropology and Education Quarterly, 28*(4), 574–92.

Luttrell, W. (2003). *Pregnant bodies, fertile minds: gender, race and the schooling of pregnant teens.* New York: Routledge.

Luttrell, W. (2008). Responding to the "N-word." In M. Pollock (Ed.), *Everyday antiracism: Getting real about race in school* (pp. 274–78). New York & London: New Press.

Merriam-Webster's Collegiate Dictionary (11th ed.). (2003). Springfield, MA: Merriam-Webster.

Miller, B. D. (2002). *Cultural anthropology* (2nd ed.). Boston: Allyn & Bacon.

Montagu, A. (1997). *Man's most dangerous myth: The fallacy of race* (6th ed.). Walnut Creek, CA: Altamira Press. (Originally published in 1942)

Moran, R. F. (2001). *Interracial intimacy: The regulation of race and romance.* Chicago: University of Chicago Press.

Morgan, J. P., Jr., & Beeler, K. (1981). The albatross. In L. Thayer (Ed.), *Strategies for experiential learning, book two.* San Diego, CA: University Associates.

Morgan, L. H. (1877). *Ancient society.* Chicago: C. H. Kerr.

Morrison, A. (2013). *Dating and relationship experiences of gay and lesbian college students.* Dissertation, Psychology Department, Wright State University, Dayton, OH.

Moses, Y. T. (in press). Diversity, excellence and inclusion: Leadership for change in the 21st century. In D. G. Smith (Ed.), *Diversity in higher education: Emerging cross-national perspectives on institutional transformation.* London: Taylor and Francis.

Moses, Y. T., & Mukhopadhyay, C. C. (1997). Using anthropology to understand and overcome cultural bias. In C. P. Kottak, J. White, R. Furlow, & P. Rice (Eds.), *The teaching of anthropology: Problems, issues, and decisions* (pp. 89–102). Mountain View, CA: Mayfield.

Muir, H., Smith, L., & Richardson, R. (2004). *Islamphobia issues, challenges and actions: A report by the Commission on British Muslims and Islamophobia.* Stoke on Trent, UK: Trentham Books.

Mukhopadhyay, C. C. (2004a). Culture as knowledge: Do we see reality or reality filtered through culture? In P. Rice & D. McCurdy (Eds.), *Strategies in teaching anthropology* (3rd ed., pp. 160–66). Upper Saddle River, NJ: Pearson/Prentice Hall. Also available through RACE project teacher's guide.

Mukhopadhyay, C. C. (2004b). A feminist cognitive anthropology: The case of women and mathematics. *Ethos, 32*(4), 458–92.

Mukhopadhyay, C. C. (2006). The hug. In P. Rice & D. McCurdy (Eds.), *Strategies in teaching anthropology* (4th ed., pp. 162–65). Upper Saddle River, NJ: Pearson/Prentice Hall.

Mukhopadhyay, C. C. (2008). Getting rid of the word "Caucasian." In M. Pollock (Ed.), *Everyday antiracism: Getting real about race in school* (pp. 12–16). New York: New Press.

Mukhopadhyay, C. C. (2012). Caucasian. In A. Goodman, Y. Moses, & J. Jones, *Race: Are we so different?* (pp. 59–63). West Sussex, UK: Wiley-Blackwell.

Mukhopadhyay, C. C., & Chua, P. (2008). Cultural racism. In J. H. Moore (Ed.), *Encyclopedia of Race and Racism* (vol. 1, pp. 377–83) . Detroit, MI: Macmillan Reference USA .

Mukhopadhyay, C. C., & Moses, Y. T. (1997). Re-establishing "race" in anthropological discourse. *American Anthropologist, 99*(3), 517–33.

Mullings, L. (2013). Trayvon Martin, race, and anthropology. *Anthropology News* (online). http://www.anthropology-news.org/index.php/2013/07/19/trayvon-martin-race-and-anthropology/.

Myers, S. (2000). *Racial disparities in the Minnesota Basic Standards Test scores, 1996–2000: Key findings.* Minneapolis, MN: Roy Wilkins Center for Human Relations and Social Justice.

Nam, V. (Ed). (2001). *YELL-Oh girls: Emerging voices explore culture, identity, and growing up Asian American.* New York: Quill/Harper Collins.

Nanda, S. (2000). Arranging a marriage in India. In P. R. deVita (Ed.), *Stumbling toward truth: Anthropologists at work* (pp. 196–204). Long Grove, IL: Waveland Press.

National Educational Association. (1973). *Education and racism: An action manual.* Washington, DC: Author.

Nickolas. (2005). Interracial dating in the GLBTG world. Retrieved July 5, 2005, from Youth Resource: A project of Advocates for Youth, at http://www.youthresource.com/index.htm.

Nieto, S. (2011). *Affirming diversity. The sociopolitical context of multicultural education* (6th ed.). New York: Longman.

Noguera, P. (1995). Preventing and producing school violence: A critical analysis of responses to school violence. *Harvard Educational Review, 65*(2), 189–212.

Noguera, P. (2008). What discipline is for: Connecting students to the benefits of learning. In M. Pollock (Ed.), *Everyday antiracism: Getting real about race in school* (pp. 132–37). New York & London: New Press.

NOW. (May 17, 2002). Losing ground: Global inequality. *PBS/NOW.* Retrieved July 19, 2006, from http://www.pbs.org/now/politics/income.html.

Ogbu, J. U. (1978). *Minority education and caste: The American system in cross-cultural perspective.* New York: Academic Press.

Omi, M. (2008). Asian Americans: The unbelievable whiteness of being. *Chronicle of Higher Education, 55*(5), B56–58.

Omi, M. (2012). Asian Americans: The unbearable whiteness of being? In A. Goodman, Y. Moses, & J. Jones, *Race: Are we so different?* (pp. 183–85). West Sussex, UK: Wiley-Blackwell.

Omi, M. A., & Winant, H. (1994). *Racial formation in the United States* (2nd ed.). New York: Routledge.

Park, V., Cerren, C., Nations, J., & Nielson, K. (2013, February). What matters for community college success? Assumptions and realities concerning student supports for low-income women. , *UC Accord.* Retrieved June 20, 2013, from http://pathways.gseis.ucla.edu/publications/201302_WhatMattersPR.pdf.

Pollock, M. (Ed.) (2008). *Everyday antiracism: Getting real about race in school.* New York & London: New Press.

Pollock, M. (2004a). *Colormute: Race talk dilemmas in an American high school.* Princeton, NJ: Princeton University Press.

Pollock, M. (2004b). Race bending: "Mixed" youth practicing strategic racialization in California. *Anthropology & Education Quarterly, 35*(1), 30–52.

Reddi, S. (2006, October 31). Hopkins fraternity accused of racism: Black students protest mock lynching, language on Halloween party invitation. *Baltimore Sun.* Retrieved October 28, 2013, http://www.phigam.org/NetCommunity/Document.Doc?id=354.

Reeves, D. (2003). High performance in high poverty schools: 90/90/90 and beyond. Milwaukee, WI: Center for Performance Assessment. Retrieved July 19, 2013, from http://www.lmsvsd.net/cms/lib2/CA01001633/Centricity/Domain/566/90%20Schools.pdf.

Reiss, M. J. (1992). How should science teachers teach the relationship between science and religion? *School Science Review, 74*(267), 126–30.

Relethford, J. H. (2013). *The human species: An introduction to biological anthropology* (9th ed.). Boston: McGraw-Hill.

Reskin, B. (2012). The race discrimination system. *Annual Review of Sociology, 38*, 17–35.

Riggs, M. (1995). *Black is . . . Black ain't.* San Francisco: California Newsreel. Video.

Roach, R. (2013). *Study calls attention to NYC effort on Black and Latino male college readiness.* Retrieved July 17, 2013, from http://diverseeducation.com/article/54675/#.

Roberts, R., Bell, L., & Murphy, B. (2008). Flipping the script: Analyzing youth talk about race and racism. *Anthropology and Education Quarterly, 39*(3), 334–53.

Rogoff, B. (1990). *Apprenticeship in thinking: Cognitive development in social context.* New York: Oxford University Press.

Root, P. P. (2002). The color of love. *American Prospect, 13*(7), 54–55.

Rose, M. (1998). The language of exclusion. In V. Zamel & R. Spack (Eds.), *Negotiating academic literacies* (pp. 9–30). Mahwah, NJ: Lawrence Erlbaum.

Rose, S., & Firmin, M. (2013). A qualitative study of interracial dating among college students. *International Journal of the Sociology of Education 2*(1), 67–92. Retrieved June 20, 2013, from http://www.hipatiapress.info/hpjournals/index.php/rise/article/view/460.

Rubin, B. C. (2003). Unpacking de tracking: When progressive pedagogy meets students' social worlds. *American Educational Research Journal, 40*(2), 539–73.

Ruiz-Linares, A. (2012). Reconstructing Native American population history. *Nature, 488,* 370–74.

Saulny, S. (2011, March 14). The new face of America: The number of young Americans who are multiracial is soaring. How will this shape the country's identity? *Upfront, 43.* (Retrieved from website on July 30, 2013)

Schmidt, C. (2013). Uncertain inheritance: Transgenerational effects of environmental exposures. *Environmental Health Perspectives, 121*(10), A298–A303. Retrieved October 29, 2013, from http://ehp.niehs.nih.gov/121-a298/.

Schwartz, C. (2013). Trends and variation in assortative mating: Causes and consequences. *Annual Review of Sociology, 39*(23), 1–23. Retrieved June 22, 2013, from http://www.annualreviews.org.

Scupin, R. (Ed.). (2003). *Race and ethnicity: An anthropological focus on the United States and the world.* Upper Saddle River, NJ: Prentice Hall.

Shankar, S. (2008). Speaking like a model minority: "FOB" styles, gender, and racial meanings among Desi teens in Silicon Valley. *Journal of Linguistic Anthropology, 18*(2), 268–89.

Sharma, N. T. (2010). *Hip-hop Desis: South Asian Americans, Blackness, and global race consciousness.* Durham, NC: Duke University Press.

Sipress, J. M. (1997). Relearning race: Teaching race as a cultural construction. *The History Teacher, 30*(2), 175–85.

Skiba, R., & Rausch, M. K. (2004). *The relationship between achievement, discipline, and race: An analysis of factors predicting ISTEP scores.* Bloomington: Indiana University, Center for Evaluation and Educational Policy.

Smedley, A., & Smedley, B. D. (2012). *Race in North America: Origin and evolution of a worldview* (4th ed.). Boulder, CO: Westview Press.

Spradley, J., & McCurdy, D. W. (Eds.). (2000). *Conformity and conflict: Readings in cultural anthropology* (10th ed.). Boston: Allyn & Bacon.

Stampp, K. (1961). *The peculiar institution: Slavery in the ante-bellum south.* New York: Alfred A. Knopf.

Steele, C. (2010). *Whistling Vivaldi: How stereotypes affect us and what we can do.* New York: W. W. Norton.

Stokes, C., & Meléndez, T. (2001). Race in 21st century America: An overview. In C. Stokes, T. Meléndez, & G. Rhodes-Reed (Eds.), *Race in 21st century America* (pp. xix–xxiv). Lansing: Michigan State University Press.

Stoler, A. (1997). On political and psychological essentialisms. *Ethos, 25*(1), 101–6.

Strauss, C., & Quinn, N. (1997). *A cognitive theory of cultural meaning.* Cambridge: Cambridge University Press.

Takezawa, Y. (Ed.). (2011). *Racial representations in Asia.* Kyoto: Kyoto University Press.

Tatum, B. D. (1997). *Why are all the Black kids sitting together in the cafeteria? And other conversations about race.* New York: Basic Books.

Thompson, G. L. (2004). *Through ebony eyes: What teachers need to know and are afraid to ask about African American students.* San Francisco, CA: Jossey-Bass.

Tilove, J. (2003). Affirmative action finds its defenders in establishment's highest ranks. Retrieved September 13, 2006, from http://www.newhousenews.com/archive/tilove061903.html.

Twin Triumph Productions. (2011). *The power of two.* M. Smolowitz and A. Byrnes (Producers). English and Japanese with English subtitles. See film synopsis at http://www.thepoweroftwomovie.com/the-film/.

Twine, F. W. (1997). Brown-skinned white girls: Class, culture and the construction of white identity in suburban communities. In R. Frankenberg (Ed.), *Displacing whiteness: Essays in social and cultural criticism* (pp. 214–43). Durham, NC: Duke University Press.

Urcioli, B. (2012). Language and race. In A. Goodman, Y. Moses, & J. Jones, *Race: Are we so different?* (pp. 150–53). Malden, MA, & Oxford, UK: Wiley Blackwell.

U.S. Census Bureau. (2002). Measuring America: The decennial census from 1790 to 2000. Retrieved from http://www.census.gov/.../measuringamerica.pdf.

U.S. Census Bureau. (2012). The two or more races population 2010. 2010 Census Briefs. PDF file.

U.S. Census Bureau. (2012). Statistical Abstract of the United States. Downloadable PDF files.

U.S. Commission on Civil Rights. (1970). *Racism in America and how to combat it.* Clearinghouse Publications, Urban Series 1.

U.S. Commission on Civil Rights. (2011). *School discipline and disparate impact: Briefing report.* Washington, DC.

Villegas, A. M., & Lucas, T. (2002). *Educating culturally responsive teachers: A coherent approach.* Albany, New York: SUNY Press.

Wade, P. (2010). *Race and ethnicity in Latin America* (2nd ed). London: Pluto Press.

Waters, M. C. (2000). Multiple ethnicities and identity in the United States. In P. Spikard & W. J. Burroughs (Eds.), *We are a people* (pp. 23–43). Philadelphia, PA: Temple University Press.

Wayland, M. (2010). Racial tensions boil at UCSD. Reported on NBC 7 television Station. Retrieved October 28, 2013, from http://www.nbcsandiego.com/news/local/UCSD-Students-Enraged-Over-N-Word-Broadcast---84791727.html.

White, J. H. (2008). *The everyday language of White racism.* New York: Wiley-Blackwell.

Wikipedia. (2006). Miscegenation. Retrieved July 18, 2006, from http://en.wikipedia.org/wiki/Miscegenation.

Wilkinson, R. (1997). *Unhealthy societies: The afflictions of inequality.* New York: Routledge.

Williams, D. (2003). Georgia prom: Dancing against history. *Teaching tolerance: Mix it up stories.* Retrieved January 17, 2006, from http://www.tolerance.org/teens/stories/index.jsp.

Williams, P. (2013, May 13). Racism remains alive and well: Room for debate. *New York Times* online.

Yon, D. (2000). *Elusive culture: Schooling, race, and identity in global times.* New York: SUNY Press.

Youth Together. (2002). Unpublished curriculum.

Zeichner, K., & Payne, K. (2013). Democratizing knowledge in urban teacher education. In J. Noel (Ed.), *Moving teacher education into urban schools and communities: Prioritizing community strengths* (pp. 3–19). New York: Routledge.

Zisman, P., & Wilson, V. (1992). Table hopping in the cafeteria: An exploration of "racial" integration in early adolescent social groups. *Anthropology and Education Quarterly, 23*(2), 199–20.

Index

ability tracking, 237

ABO blood system and types, 36, 44n22; activities, 41; population level variations, 38, 45n23

academic achievement gap, 229. *See also* achievement gap

achievement gap, 203–204; activities, 246–250; anthropologists on, 239–240; conceptual background, 231–242; key conceptual points, 245–246; key terms, 246; models for addressing, 243–244; as opportunity gap, 231, 245; overview, 229–231, 245, 250n1; reflective questions, 245. *See also* educational inequality

achievement gap, explanations: biological, 231–233; cultural deficit, 233–235; educator expectations and teacher quality, 241–242; overview, 231; poverty, 233, 235–236; stereotype effect, 240–241; students' expectations of academic success, 239–240; tracking and other inequalities, 237–239, 250n2

achievement gap policy: equality in, 243; equity in, 243; impact of, 242–243; working models, 243–244

adaptation, 50; high altitudes in environmental, 58–59

African ancestry: of Black race, 75; DNA research on, 79, 80–81, 87n3–87n4; models, 3, 80, 86, 87n2; racial

similarities from, 80–83

African populations, genetic diversity, 78–79

African replacement model. *See* Out of Africa model

agency, 256; sense of, 268

AIDS, 60

Albatross cultural activity, 109–110, 111n5

allele frequencies, 48

alleles: codominant, 30, 31; dominant, 30; overview, 30; recessive, 30–31

Alu, 77

ancestry: commonalities from, 82; exploring individual, 85, 86, 155; markers, 177, 178; racial differences and, 83; skin color and, 70; in social classifications, 158. *See also* African ancestry

anthropologists, 157; on achievement gap, 239–240; on biological race, 1–2; cultural, 156; on culture, 91, 93, 94–95, 97, 234

anthropology: as comparative discipline, 157; physical, 1

antimiscegenation laws, 48, 181, 182–184; challenges to, 188–189

appropriation, 259

ascribed vs. achieved status, 134–135

Asian race, 74–75

assemblies and clubs: cultural classifications of, 251; racial labels and,

About the Authors

Carol Chapnick Mukhopadhyay began her career as a junior high school teacher in South Central Los Angeles, immersed in the educational "wing" of the civil rights movement, and later returned to graduate school for a Ph.D. in anthropology. She has over forty years of experience teaching, consulting, and doing research on issues of cultural diversity and education related to race, ethnicity, and gender, in the United States and India. Her publications address both scholarly and general audiences. She was a key advisor for the American Anthropological Association's public information project, RACE, and is professor emerita of anthropology at San José State University, San José, California.

Rosemary Henze brings to this project a background in education, anthropology, and linguistics. She began her career as an ESL teacher and later obtained her doctorate in education with a minor in anthropology. She worked with K-12 schools for fourteen years as a consultant, researcher, and curriculum designer in the areas of multilingual, multicultural, and antiracist education, and has done research and educational projects in Greece, Nicaragua, California, Alaska, and Hawai'i. Her coauthored book, *Leading for Diversity,* focused on how school leaders promote positive interethnic relations in twenty-one schools across the United States. She is professor in the Department of Linguistics and Language Development at San José State University and is currently serving as president of the Council on Anthropology and Education for the American Anthropological Association.

Yolanda Moses is an anthropologist and university administrator at University of California, Riverside, who brings over thirty years of research, writing, and teaching on race and ethnicity from fieldwork in the United States, the Caribbean, South Africa, and Brazil. She has held national leadership roles as president of the American Anthropological Association, the City College of New York/CUNY, and the American Association of Higher Education. She has been a driving force behind the American Anthropological Association's recent initiatives on race and chaired the National Advisory Board of the AAA public information project, *RACE: Are We So Different?*

CPSIA information can be obtained at www.ICGtesting.com
Printed in the USA
BVOW08s1446051213

338185BV00002B/4/P